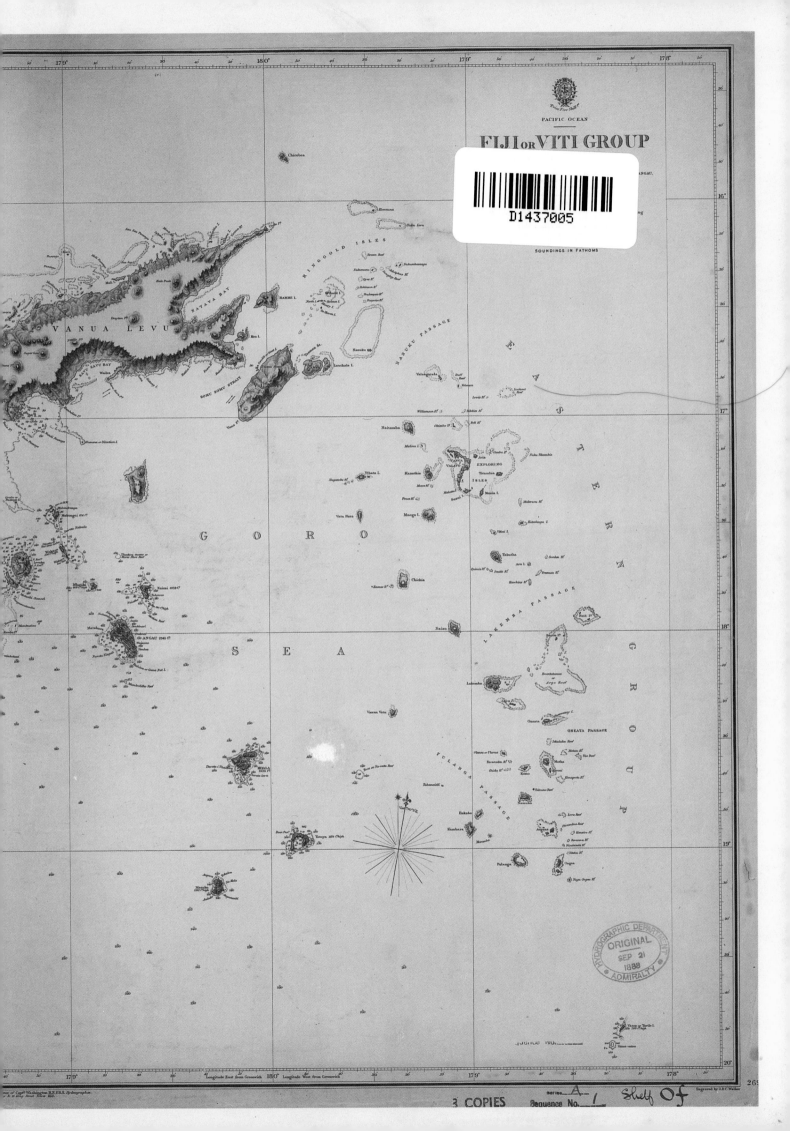

PACIFIC OCEAN

FIJI or VITI GROUP

SOUNDINGS IN FATHOMS

Engraved by J.&C. Walker

THE SUPERYACHTS

VOLUME SIXTEEN ~ 2003

A BOAT INTERNATIONAL PUBLICATION

THE SUPERYACHTS

is published annually by
EDISEA LIMITED
a subsidiary of
Boat International Publications Limited
5-7 Kingston Hill, Kingston upon Thames,
Surrey KT2 7PW, England.
Tel: +44 (0)20 8547 2662
Fax: +44 (0)20 8547 1201

The Superyachts Editorial Office,
Church Lane, Yealmpton, Plymouth, Devon PL8 2HG, England.
Tel: +44 (0)1752 881435
Fax: +44 (0)1752 880429
Email: TheSuperyachts@aol.com

ISBN 1 898524 41 6
British Library Cataloguing-in-Publication Data
A catalogue record for this book is available from the British Library

Publisher	Christian Chalmin
Chief Operating Officer	Ben Hudson
Editor	Roger Lean-Vercoe
Managing Editor	Natalie Doggett
Staff Photographer	Bugsy Gedlek
Editorial Assistants	Jan Davis
	Tineke Endicott
Researcher	Toby Haws
Proof Reader	Kerry Commins
Chief Designer	Susana de Dios
Designer	Nicky Brisker
General Arrangement Drawings	Hugh Welbourn
	David Lewis
Head of Sales	Malcolm Maclean
Group Advertisement Manager	Charles Finney
Advertisement Sales	Andrew Stuart
Advertisement Administration	Caren Lewis
Advertisement Designer	Craig Shuttlewood
Advertisement Coordinator	Heidi Parrott
Advertisement Assistant	Carole Rose
Production Manager	Francis Ransom
Production Assistant	Samantha Collins

Printing and Binding
Lawrence-Allen Limited, England.

RULE THE WAVES

Nigel Burgess – leading specialists in the sale, purchase, charter, management and new construction of the world's largest motor and sailing yachts – over 40 metres – for over 25 years. Our reputation is built on reliability, confidentiality, professionalism and trust.

CONTENTS

N E W   P R O J E C T S

A preview of future superyacht projects

T H E   R E G I S T E R

The world's largest yachts on file

T H E   D I R E C T O R Y

A two-part directory of superyacht companies listed by category and alphabetically

I N D E X   O F   V O L U M E S   1 – 16

A listing of craft featured in this and preceding volumes

M A I N   I N D E X

A C K N O W L E D G E M E N T S

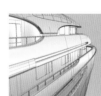

yacht interiors & styling

studio@rwd.co.uk

redman whiteley dixon™

FOREWORD

Over many years I have found *The Superyachts* books very interesting and informative, so I was surprised, flattered and apprehensive in equal measure when asked to write the introduction to this, the sixteenth volume. I must say that if I were to write a book on this subject it would have to be entitled 'From a deck hand's dream to the eventual reality of yachting'. Why? Well, I started my yachting career when I was just 19 years old, hitch-hiking from my home in the UK to Monaco, having just finished my education. On arrival I was fortunate to find a low cost hotel, where I stayed whilst attempting to find a job that would support my holiday.

Each day I would hawk my services around all the yachts in the harbour and, eventually, I was taken on as a jack of all trades – deckhand and assistant steward – on a large motor yacht of some 70m (230ft) in length that was owned by an American film producer. By the standards of the day, this was a truly enormous vessel, but at this hedonistic time there would regularly be two or three of similar size in Monaco, hosting a glamorous mixture of film stars, industrialists and politicians.

It was a fantastic opportunity and one that really excited me. The yacht cruised the Mediterranean for the summer season and, over a period of four months, I was fortunate to visit the Greek islands, Croatia, Venice, Italy and, of course, the South of France. Croatia in particular struck me as being a most beautiful cruising area, just as it is now, although in the months of July and August its light summer winds do not make it the most exciting area for sailing yachts such as the one I now own.

The yacht had 22 crew and I was expected to help out wherever needed. I still clearly remember the task of flaking the chain, down in the rusty depths of the chain locker, as the anchor was raised. With no air-conditioning, Mediterranean summer temperatures and a thumping great chain that had to be laid out by hand, I was certainly relieved when the task was complete. In the evenings, scrubbed, polished, and dressed in a clean white shirt, I was often called upon to assist the yacht's interior staff during cocktails and dinner. If only those glamorous guests to whom I was serving dry Martinis could have seen me a few hours earlier, soaked with perspiration and covered in rust.

That was some 30 years ago. In the intervening times my ability for hard work brought good fortune. I built up a successful company in the manufacturing sector and, during the course of what was a very busy career, I used to charter sailing yachts for Mediterranean or Caribbean holidays, refusing to buy one until I felt that I could do it justice by devoting sufficient time to the enjoyment of ownership.

That moment first came in 1997, when I bought my first yacht, a 37m (121ft) Perini Navi ketch. During my three years of ownership, I spent the equivalent of one year on board, covering a great deal of territory and learning about the responsibility of ownership and the operational demands of the vessel. It was that experience, combined with a long career in design and manufacturing, that made me really want to start a design-and-build project for a new sailing yacht, and this I did in 1999 with the new 53m (174ft) *Salperton*.

For any project to be successful, it is essential that a huge amount of time, effort and energy be applied to the preparation of a comprehensive specification on which the design and construction will be based. I also spent time in visiting and meeting with many designers and the management of several yards. In my meetings with designers, I encountered a man who had built up an extremely successful career, principally designing sailing yachts. His name was Ed Dubois, and I was able to strike up an immediate rapport. Ed had all the technical competence and experience that I expected but also had an appreciation of proportions and styling.

Having sold my telecommunications business to a large international company I had quit work and my new-build project became my job. I am fussy and keen on meticulous attention to detail – and this proved to be a bonus for the finished product. What an excellent way to ease out of an 80-hour working week into an equally busy, but very pleasurable, hobby.

Alloy Yachts was selected to construct the yacht, and whilst New Zealand may not be the most convenient of places to get to, the yard had the benefit of common language and an excellent reputation for construction quality. More important, they also had an attitude not always found today – a pride in its workmanship and an unwillingness to accept anything other than the best solution to any engineering or quality issues. Before the construction process started, a full-sized mock-up of the interior was constructed in one of my old factories in the UK, using plywood and a shopfitting company, and although this was an expensive exercise I found it immensely valuable to ensure that the interior proportions and layout would be as I wanted them. It is an exercise that I would recommend to everyone.

The specification, design and construction took just short of three years, a period made particularly interesting by the fact that the scale and size of the yacht demanded winches, masts, booms, sails – everything – on a scale that had never been produced before. But what a magnificent yacht resulted from this outstanding effort and hard work by everyone involved. The effort that I had spent on the detail of the specification also paid off, as the finished yacht was exactly as I had planned, a luxury, high performance sailing yacht with the ability to sail equally well in light airs as when the wind is up. My dreams had been achieved.

The learning process still continues. *Salperton* was delivered in March 2002, and sailed practically non-stop from Auckland to Antigua for the two weeks of Antigua Race Week and the Mega Yacht Challenge, later crossing the Atlantic to the Mediterranean, where she enjoyed a busy summer season.

I have enjoyed the yacht immensely during my first year of ownership, but I also enjoyed the process of its specification, design and construction so much that when it is fully understood and optimised, I will probably move on to devote my energies to another build. Meanwhile, I commend every prospective yacht owner to pore through these pages, extract every good idea and build it into his own specification – the dream from which yachts are created.

Barry Houghton

Barry Houghton

INTRODUCTION

The last few years have seen the launch of an unusually large number of enormous superyachts: *Carinthia VII* at 97m (318ft), *Tatoosh* at 92m (303ft), *Stargate* at 80m (262ft), *Tueq* at 72m (236ft), *Skat* at 71m (233ft) and Greg Norman's new 70m (230ft) *Aussie Rules*, to name but a few. This year, 2003, will see the 105m (344ft) *Pelorus*, the 88m (289ft) *Asean Lady* and the 85m (279ft) *Annaliesse* added to the fleet. It is clear that large yachts are on the increase but, in reality, these leviathans are just the visible tip of a trend that is affecting all sizes of superyachts. In particular, the numbers of 60m (197ft) and 70m (230ft) launches seem to have risen very significantly, a fact that is reflected within these pages where no fewer than four yachts with a length of 60m (197ft) and above are illustrated. Today, a 50m (164ft) yacht that, not so long ago, would have been considered unusually large, no longer stands out from the crowd.

Given that even 40m (131ft) yachts usually offer five well-sized staterooms, at least two saloons and ample deck space, the question that arises from such statistics is 'What added needs have owners discovered that has caused them to drive the average size upwards so dramatically?' Not just a desire for additional cabins, surely. After all, it must be rare for anyone to wish to host more than a handful of guests for longer than a few days in the close confines of a yacht. Indeed, how many intimate friends can the average person list? Even if you can think of 20, the chance of them all being free at the same time in today's hyperactive world is almost negligible! So in view of the problem of finding a marina berth for a large yacht, the host of practical management and regulatory headaches that increase with size, and the restrictions that size imposes upon the more intimate and beautiful anchorages, just what is the motive for ever larger yachts?

Cynics might suggest that the reason lies in a desire for greater status. In a few cases, this could be so, but it is equally possible that larger yachts may stem from their owners' increasing experience – not only in knowing their own requirements, but also in understanding what the crew needs in order to satisfy them. For instance, take the new 61m (200ft) *Lady Lola*. Armed with the considerable knowledge gained from his earlier 45m (148ft) yacht of the same name, Duane Hagadone and his wife Lola specified the need for an owners' apartment with private deck spaces, a full-sized saloon and a study, in addition to a stateroom with a panoramic view over the yacht's bows. Just four guest cabins were required, one fewer than previously, while deck spaces were enhanced by the incorporation of a tender garage within the hull. In comparison with the previous *Lady Lola*, crew quarters were expanded dramatically, as were her service and storage areas. This new yacht – with owner and guest areas rearranged in their use but not dramatically enhanced in size, and with all the smaller

vessel's compromises eliminated – now perfectly suits the owners' world-encircling cruising ambitions.

Yachts of this size are truly custom products that should fully satisfy the owner's aspirations, but they can only do this if they are truly functional in respect of service areas and the needs of the crew, factors which share equal importance with considerations for the owner and his guests. In the past, a yacht's owner and guest areas were often maximised to the disadvantage of service areas, but it is heartening to note that the undesirability of squeezing a quart into a pint pot is now being increasingly recognised.

This is certainly a dictum of which we have taken note during the preparation of this book. Larger yachts need more pages in which to illustrate them properly and, as a result, this sixteenth volume is the largest ever. As always, The Yachts section contains a carefully balanced selection of vessels, six of which are sailing craft and the remaining 15 are motor yachts. The former encompass a wide range of styles: from the magnificently modern *Salperton*, designed by Ed Dubois and built in New Zealand by Alloy Yachts; through the splendidly minimalist *Alithia*, built in Germany by Abeking & Rasmussen to the designs of Bill Trip and Andrew Winch; to the lovely schooner *Eleonora*, a delightful recreation of the famous NG Herreshoff-designed *Westward*, which was first launched in 1913. At the same time there is a full range of motor yachts from the 81m (266ft) *Bart Roberts*, a dramatically-decorated, converted commercial vessel, to the small but fully-featured 36m (120ft) Heesen-built motor yacht *Duke Town*. Two cruising stories, set in Fiji and Greece, may inspire some readers to visit these delightful, but very different, archipelagos, while the New Projects section, illustrating a large selection of yachts in design or under construction, will surely whet readers' appetites for the future.

Like the owner of *Lady Lola*, we have also made sure that the 'working' areas of this book – the reference sections – also meet the demands placed upon them. The Directory, which lists major companies involved in the superyacht industry, has been thoroughly checked and revised – a painstaking annual process which ensures that no address or other contact detail is published without having been confirmed by the companies themselves. Similarly, The Register, a comprehensive listing of the world's superyachts, has also been enlarged and revised. While we do our utmost to ensure the correctness of both these listings, readers should feel free to contact us if they wish to suggest additional entries or draw our notice to items requiring amendment, such as yacht name changes. Accuracy is our aim.

Finally, I hope that this latest volume will give you reading pleasure and interesting information in equal measure and, at the same time, will provoke thought and inspiration.

Roger Lean-Vercoe
Editor

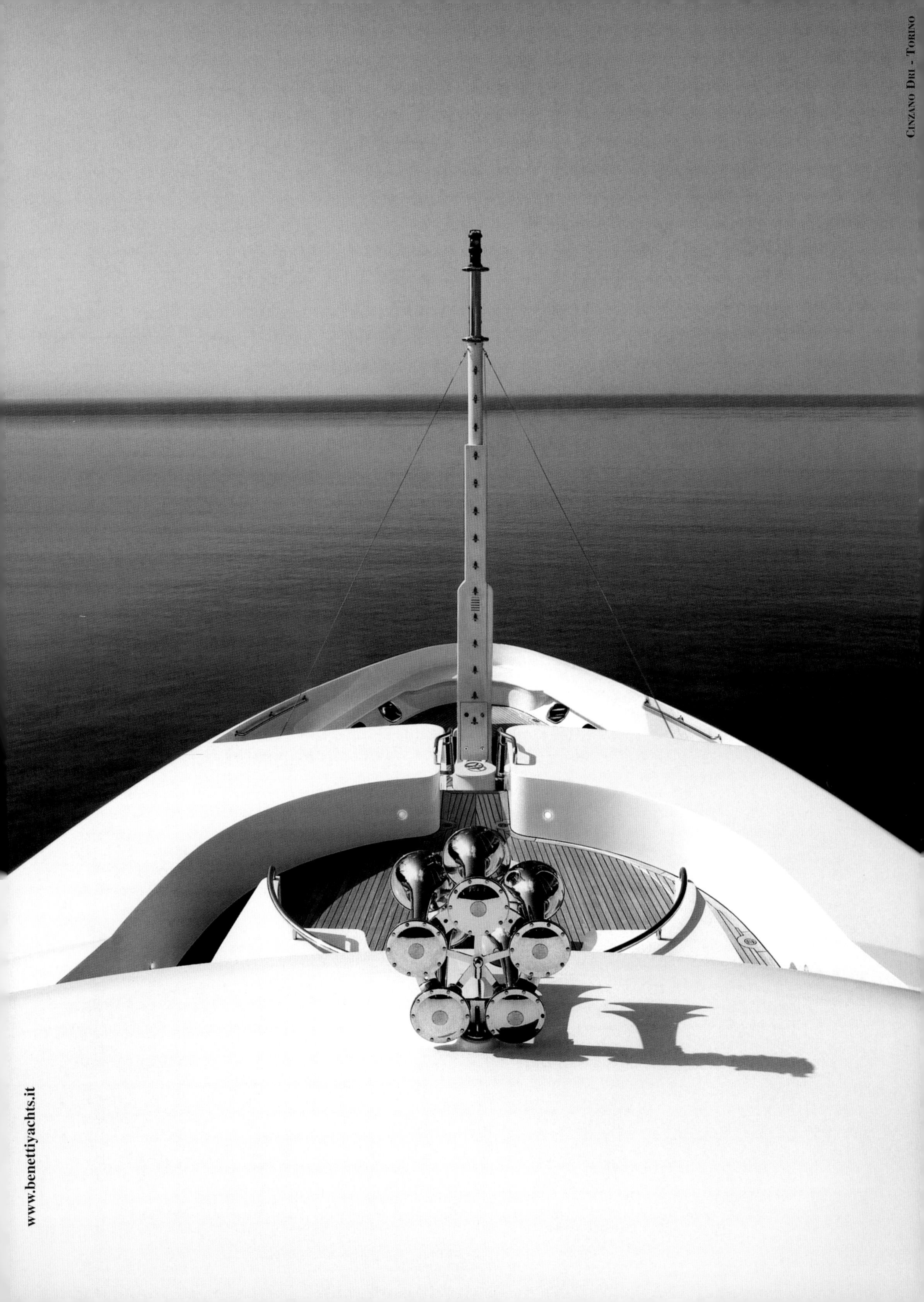
Cinzano Dri - Torino
www.benettiyachts.it

Another point of view. Yours.

Benetti

Italian Excellence since 1873

EDMI

STON

LONDON
TELEPHONE: +44 (0)20 7495 5151
london@edmistoncompany.com

MONACO
TELEPHONE: +377 93 30 54 44
monaco@edmistoncompany.com

LOS ANGELES
TELEPHONE: +1 (310) 777 6535
la@edmistoncompany.com

www.edmistoncompany.com

Official Partner: GBR Challenge
British America's Cup Team

FEADSHIP HOLLAND. Telephone: +31 (0)23-5247000. Fax: +31 (0)23-5248639. www.feadship.nl. info@feadship.nl

BUSINESS OR PLEASURE?

Owning a luxury yacht is one of life's greatest rewards. Or it can be. Cavendish White have the experience to ensure that yachting is a matter of business and pleasure. Our business – your pleasure. We can help you buy, sell or build. We can manage the yacht for charter or just manage it as you would any other business asset. Efficiently and effectively. To find out more telephone for a copy of our brochure – At Your Service.

Cavendish White Limited. 4 Bramber Court, Bramber Road, London W14 9PW
Tel: +44 (0)20 7381 7600, Fax: +44 (0)20 7381 7601, E-mail: yachts@cavendishwhite.com, Website: www.cavendishwhite.com

CAVENDISHWHITE
YACHTING FOR THE CONNOISSEUR

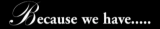

CARINTHIA VI 233'/71m - Offered for sale

CHRISTINA O 325'/100m - Offered for charter

CRETIN

Orfèvre depuis 1850

Sinus by SCANDINAVIAN LIGHT

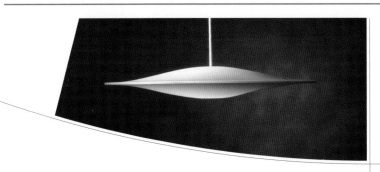

Another approach
to lighting

Sinus

Light as air, completely

devoid of superfluous

details, created with

Piet Hein's usual sense

for geometry and art.

Sinus has been a classic

from the very

beginning.

29 rue des Godrans   21000 DIJON FRANCE

Tel : +33 3 80 30 41 44   Fax: +33 3 80 30 37 36

P E R F E C T I O N

a JONGERT - architect and artisan in perfect harmony

ONE PORT OF CALL

Devonport produces and re-configures some of the world's most admired yachts.
Our blend of traditional craftsmanship and advanced technology provides a unique
combination of exquisite luxury and the finest engineering.
For the yacht of your dreams, there is only one port of call.

DEVONPORT

EXPERTISE...YACHTSPERTISE

Da Vinci's vision...

Leonardo Da Vinci's visionary boat design
The Royal Collection©2002, H.M. Queen Elizabeth II

...our reality

Azimut inherited from Leonardo Da Vinci the quest for

perfection in form, function, beauty and a truly

innovative spirit: the principle that

heightens our aspirations.

Azimut S.p.A.
10051 Avigliana (Torino - Italia), Via M.L. King 9-11,
Tel: (39) 011 93.161, Fax: (39) 011 936.72.70
www.azimutyachts.net

Live the Italian Renaissance

2002 Deliveries   146' M/Y Campbell Bay and 130' S/Y Alithia

· ANDREW · WINCH · DESIGNS ·

The Old Fire Station, 123 Mortlake High Street, London SW14 8SN, Telephone +44 (0) 20 8392 8400, Fax +44 (0) 20 8392 8401, EMail info@ andrew-winch-designs.co.uk

Camper & Nicholsons Yachting

'The first marque... the first choice'

For well over 200 years the name Camper & Nicholsons has been synonymous the world over with superb build quality, performance and style.

The reputation of this famous English yard continues to grow across a spectrum of projects from Classic Restoration, Refit and Repair to New Build.

Make the first marque your first choice.

dixon
yacht design

Antares, currently building at the
Royal Huisman Shipyard is the latest
in a long line of superyachts, sail and
power, to be designed in our studio.

As naval architects, exterior and
interior designers, utilising the latest
technology and our many years of
experience, we aim to achieve the
highest levels of customer satisfaction.

Another star in the making Antares

t: +44 (0)23 8040 5280   e: info@dixonyachtdesign.com   Greydowns, School Road, Old Bursledon, Southampton, Hampshire SO31 8BX

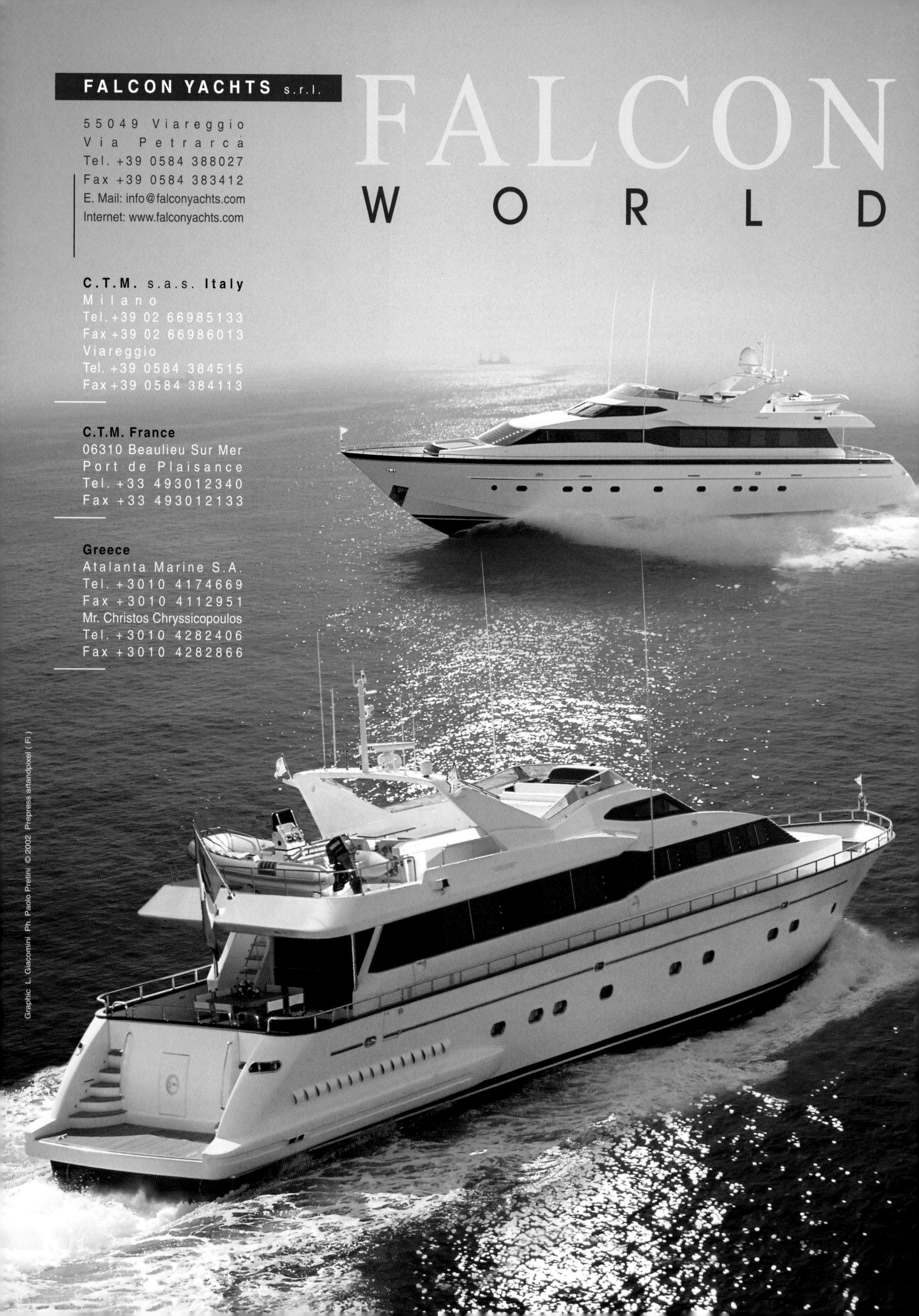

FALCON YACHTS s.r.l.

55049 Viareggio
Via Petrarca
Tel. +39 0584 388027
Fax +39 0584 383412
E. Mail: info@falconyachts.com
Internet: www.falconyachts.com

C.T.M. s.a.s. **Italy**
Milano
Tel. +39 02 66985133
Fax +39 02 66986013
Viareggio
Tel. +39 0584 384515
Fax +39 0584 384113

C.T.M. France
06310 Beaulieu Sur Mer
Port de Plaisance
Tel. +33 493012340
Fax +33 493012133

Greece
Atalanta Marine S.A.
Tel. +3010 4174669
Fax +3010 4112951
Mr. Christos Chryssicopoulos
Tel. +3010 4282406
Fax +3010 4282866

FALCON
W O R L D

Graphic L. Giacomini Ph. Paolo Pretini © 2002 Prepress artandpixel (Fi)

SUPERLATIVE

BERTHS

St Katharine Haven is a tranquil oasis next to the Tower of London and Tower Bridge in the heart of the City of London. We can easily accommodate Superyachts up to 40 metres in length and 12 metres in beam.

Enjoy the convenience of St Katharine's own amenities including the yacht club, shops, restaurants, health club and the famous Dickens Inn.
If you wish to travel further afield there is easy access to the shops, restaurants, galleries and theatres of London's West End.

Whatever you choose to do you will be well looked after by the St Katharine's team.

St Katharine Haven Ltd
50 St Katharine's Way
London E1W 1LA
Tel. 020 7264 5312
Answer Machine. 020 7481 8350
Fax. 020 7702 2252
Website. www.stkaths.co.uk

SUPERB

WELCOME

Perseus model. Image *Giuliano Sargentini*

PERINI NAVI, *Blue-Water Sailing Yachts*

BERNIE COHEN
designs

CREATING SUPERIOR YACHTS & INTERIORS

Supercharter

Fiji

The Cyclades

Fijian Surprise

The 16-seater aircraft droned eastwards along the north shore of Viti Levu, the largest of the 300 islands that make up Fiji. We were heading from Nadi, the main airport where our flight from Australia had landed, to an airstrip at the north of Taveuni Island, some 329nm to the east. Here we would rendezvous with the 35m (114ft 10in) expedition yacht *Surprise* for a week-long cruise. The flight is remarkably scenic. At first the open expanse of Bligh Water, named after the famous captain of *HMS Bounty*, is to port and the lush green valleys that lead upwards to the high volcanic mountains at the heart of Viti Levu to starboard.

Leaving the emerald green behind us, we set out over the 30nm strait towards Vanua Levu, the second largest land mass of the archipelago, flying over meandering coral reefs that lie like carelessly flung ropes of pearls on a silk carpet of the most incredible blue. After a brief stop on the tiny grass airstrip at Savusavu, we headed onwards, again with our eyes glued to the breathtaking scenery, across the narrow Somosomo Strait to Taveuni where, just before touching down, we spied *Surprise* lying quietly at anchor, resplendent in her blue and white livery and proudly flying her Fijian colours.

Met by the captain, Carol Dunlop, we were introduced to *Surprise's* Fijian crew and settled into our very comfortable accommodation. The remainder of the guests would not be arriving until the next day so, after a perfect lunch on the aft deck overlooking the palm-fringed shore of Taveuni, we decided to spend the rest of

Main picture: The Bay of Islands at the north-western tip of Vanua Balavu, seen from Allardyce's grave. The white line of the island's encircling reef can be seen to the left.
Above: A traditional dancer from Rabi Island.
Right: Fijian children always have a ready smile.
Far right: The expedition yacht, Surprise, *built in New Zealand by McMullen & Wing.*

the day exploring the island by car. The island's encircling road is mostly dirt, but the local section had recently been surfaced for the first time. Babu, our delightful driver and font of local knowledge, grinned with pleasure as he wound his speedometer up to 80km per hour, a reckless pace that would have been unthinkable a few weeks beforehand. When asked to show us the local sights, his first thought was that we must see the 180° meridian, which cuts across Taveuni Island near Somosomo, just a few miles away.

The island rejoices in the fact that it is one of the few places in the world where the meridian passes over land. The inconvenient fact that the actual date line is diverted around Fiji to avoid having two parts of the same island in different days had not seemed to worry the locals when planning their millennium party, which drew in revellers

Above: Yellowfin tuna,
freshly caught for dinner.
Left: Dancers from Rambi
Island perform a meke *for
guests aboard* Surprise.
Below: Vanua Balavu has the
most splendid beaches –
all of them deserted.

from around the globe. Like all good parties, the memory is usually better than the aftermath, and today all that remains is a board – buried deep within a field of sugar cane – that proclaims this to be the first place on Earth to see in the 21st-century.

Returning clockwise around the island at a slower pace, as Babu shouted greetings to his huge clan of relatives, we took in the shady palm groves and fields of pineapple and taro, interspersed with glimpses of the blue sea. We passed scatterings of small wooden houses, roofed in thatch or corrugated iron and set among gardens brimming with flowers, mango and papaya. At our next stop, well past the end of the surfaced road, we walked through undergrowth to a splendid waterfall that tumbled down a cliff face into a pool in which a dozen or so of the local children cavorted, together with a handful of backpackers. Its cool waters were a welcome treat.

Next morning our cruise started in earnest, having collected *Surprise's* owners Mark and Sandra Johnson from the airport, together with the other guests, Allan Jouning and his wife Daphne from New Zealand, plantation owner Greg Lawlor and boatbuilder Colin Dunlop, the captain's husband. Concerning our cruising plans, Mark explained that Fiji remains a deeply traditional society and *Surprise*, new to the region where she is to be available for charter, needed to pay her respects to several local chiefs so as to ensure good relations during future cruises. Our route was to be roughly clockwise, with the first stop being Rabi Island 20nm to the north, followed by the Ringgold Islands 15nm to the east, and then on to our

the dancer's sinuous hand movements than we could detect. As we walked back to the tender accompanied by a throng of giggling children, we realised that this was one of those delightful evenings that will remain in our memories forever.

A tropical cyclone, centred some distance away near Papua New Guinea, brought overcast skies with a touch of rain next day. Such conditions made the many uncharted reefs more difficult to identify as we snaked eastwards towards the remote Ringgold Islands, named after the captain of *USN Porpoise*, one of the ships in Captain Wilkes' expedition to the region between 1838 and 1842. (See front endpaper chart.) Today, this collection of sparsely inhabited volcanic islands is best know internationally for its huge colonies of booby and noddy seabirds, but we had come to see its people in their small village on Yanuca Island (pronounced yanutha). It was Sunday, a significant day for the highly religious islanders, so an advance party of Ben and Solo, *Surprise's* steward and second engineer, went ashore to request permission for us to meet the chief and make *sevusevu* – a formal ceremony involving an introduction, the asking of requests, an answer from the chief and the presentation of gifts. Permission was received and we landed to find a pretty, well-kept village backing the sandy beach.

Welcomed by an elder, we were escorted to the chief's traditionally thatched bure house, where we sat cross-legged on the floor facing his inner council. It is not fitting for the chief nor his visitors to converse directly, so Solo spoke for us, requesting in a lowered, almost penitent, voice, that we may float our yacht on the chief's waters,

major engagement at Vanua Balavu in the more remote Northern Lau group of islands – 75nm to the south-east and well off the tourist track.

We were a little unsure as to how warm our reception would be from the people of Rabi (pronounced rambi) who represent a shameful tale of colonial exploitation. Their historic home is far north-west of Fiji on Banaba (Ocean Island) in Kiribati where, in the early 1900s, their ancestors had been misled into signing away their island to a phosphate mining company on a 999-year lease at a rate of £50 per year. Evicted from their homeland by the Japanese during the war, they were prevented from returning by their British colonial masters and rehoused on Rabi while the phosphate company stripped their island bare of soil, making it all but uninhabitable. A long-running court case against the British government has recently provided them with some compensation, and although they are still relatively poor they have been able to keep alive many of their traditions in their new homeland. In this respect, we had been invited to a Banaban-style *meke* – a display of traditional song and dance – in the village of Buakonikai.

As we soon found out, we need not have worried about our welcome. Solemnly introduced by an elder, the evening evolved into a 90-minute performance in full dress by a 40-strong troupe. It was not only ourselves who were enchanted by the melodic rhythm and hip swaying dances – the whole village had turned out to watch and, judging by their frequent bursts of side-splitting laughter, there was much more to be read into

Above: *The idyllic Yanuca village in the Ringgold Islands.*
Right: *Yanuca children dressed in their Sunday best.*
Below: *Clothes-washing and fish-cleaning share the same running water on Taveuni Island.*

Top: Guests hunt for shells on a beach in the south of Vanua Balavu.
Above: Everyone looked forward to the traditional feast in Lomaloma, except the pigs we had brought as a gift.
Above left: The kava ceremony is taken very seriously.
Left: The dancer representing a forest pygmy spirit caused much mirth.

catch his fish and walk on his beaches, asking, additionally, for forgiveness in advance should any of our actions cause offence. The request, relayed to the chief by his spokesman, was well received and smiles broke out all round as a bundle of yaqona root was passed to the chief as a gift. Much valued in the islands, yaqona is pounded to a powder and infused with water to create kava, a popular, mildly narcotic beverage. Perhaps on account that it was a Sunday, we were not offered a bowl of the beverage itself, but instead were shown around the village. There seemed to be three distinct groups: those that were taking their day of rest in houses and beneath palm-thatched shelters; and those who packed the two rival churches — Non-conformist and Mormon, we guessed — where we could hear melodic singing unaccompanied by any instrument.

Returning to *Surprise* we took immediate advantage of our newly granted privileges, taking the tender to the island of Cobia, (pronounced thombia) a few miles to the north. This 500m-diameter (1,640ft 5in) circular island is a classic example of a collapsed volcanic caldera, with a high razor-topped ridge and a central lagoon open to the sea through a small gap on its northern side. Sadly, following a mistaken policy of the Fijian Agriculture Department, the island had goats introduced which were now well into the process of denuding its foliage. Still, the lagoon was an impressive sight, with a large, deep hurricane hole but for its coral-strewn entrance, which only offered around 1.5m (4ft 11in) of water.

Next day we headed to Vanua Balavu (Long Island), passing the southern tip of the Heemskerq Reef, where a long sand spit terminates in the little island of Nanuku

Levu. Examining it through binoculars, we thought we could make out a couple of Europeanised versions of bure houses among the casuarina trees and, as we passed by, someone ran down the beach waving what appeared to be his trousers. Was he indicating that a visit was not welcome, or warning us that we were near the reef? We could not tell. At midday, we landed for a walk around the fabulous pink shell-sand beach of the deserted coral atoll of Weilagi Lala, where Allan Jouning picked up a perfect nautilus shell. Later that day, as *Surprise* passed through the reef that encircles Vanua Balavu, and we gathered on the sun deck for cocktails, we considered another possibility – might he have been summoning help? We sincerely hoped not!

Dusk was falling as Carol Dunlop guided *Surprise* into a sheltered cove on the island's north-west corner, promising us a surprise in the morning. Her pledge was true. We had anchored in an area known as the Bay of Islands where, fringing the bay in which *Surprise* lay, severe erosion had created a maze of interlinked narrow channels dotted with mushroom-shaped pinnacles, all sculpted from razor-sharp grey limestone. Most spectacular of all were the fabulous colours. Illuminated by shafts of brilliant sunlight, these ranged from a pale turquoise to the most vivid sapphire blue to provide a startling contrast with the green foliage and grey rock. Entranced by this miniature wonderland of water and fantastically weathered limestone crags – our imaginations saw a hippo here and a horse and rider there – we could understand why this island group was named the 'Exploring Isles' by its first European visitors. Like them, we had discovered so many visual delights that we had difficulty tearing ourselves away.

Later that morning, *Surprise* rounded the northern tip of this seahorse-shaped island and turned southwards along Vanua Balavu's picturesque eastern shoreline as we took lunch on the bridge deck aft, a position which gave us splendid views towards the dense forest and coconut groves that clad this heavily indented shore. We were bound for the village of Lomaloma on the south-eastern tip of the island, where a meeting had been arranged with

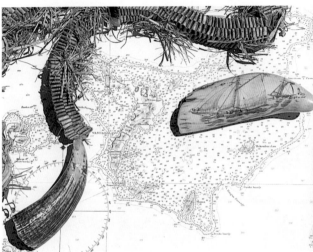

Top: Guests use the tender to explore the creeks of Vanua Balavu Island.
Right: A whale's tooth on a necklace is a very highly prized gift, as is scrimshaw, that on the right made by Surprise's captain, Carol Dunlop.
Below: The solemn sevusevu ceremony in Lomaloma village, during which the chief was asked for his permission to let us visit his waters, walk on his beaches and catch his fish.

the headman, Ratu Poasa. Well sheltered by an offshore islet, we dropped anchor off the village and solemnly made our way ashore to meet Temo, our appointed spokesperson, who had already arranged for the delivery of our gift of two suckling pigs from Greg Lawlor's plantation together with two sacks of flour and sugar.

The *sevusevu*, which was performed with particular *élan*, had the village elders adding choruses of approval to each of Temo's requests, and culminated in the presentation of an additional kilo of yaqona as well as a particularly high status gift among the islands – a whale's tooth on a plaited necklace. To our surprise and delight, the gifts were reciprocated with a smaller bundle of yaqona and a similar tooth – a real honour. One more gift remained. Mark Johnson had bought a fax machine for the local clinic and this was handed over on site in a short ceremony that, followed by home-made tea and cakes, was entirely reminiscent of an English tea party.

Sadly for the pigs, another treat was to follow. That evening we had been invited to a *lovo*, a full-scale feast, and as we walked back to the tender it was clear, from the delicious smell of cooking wafting through the village, that preparations were already in full swing. Dusk was gathering as we returned, at first for a kava ceremony with the senior males of the village, where polished half-coconut shells of the muddy (both in looks and taste) drink were served with due ceremony, while the women

centrepieces and were surrounded by great plates of yam, taro and cassava and such delicacies as stuffed crab, whole fish cooked in the *lovo* and fresh oysters. Delicious as it was, it was difficult to make much of a dent in the feast but our consciences were relieved when we heard that the men would soon finish up what was left.

After supper came the *meke*. The Lomalomans were not so practised as the Banabans and some of their efforts were drowned in hilarity, particularly the comic acts that mimicked the *veli* (pygmy spirits from the forest) and the story dances that, we suspected, had a strong sexual content. Like us, the villagers were having a wonderful time and the party continued at full swing until well after midnight, when we made our thanks to the headman and headed back to *Surprise*.

Next morning we sailed a few miles south, to explore the southern tip of Vanua Balavu with the tender. This is another fabulous area, quite different in character from the north of the island, with larger islands and enchanted inlets dotted with some of the loveliest beaches we had

and girls who were preparing the meal sneaked curious glances at us from behind the huts. By now the smell was so mouth-watering that we just had to get a closer look at the food preparation. One of the pigs was on a spit over a charcoal fire, while the second was underground, accompanied by the vegetables, all wrapped in banana leaves and being cooked on pre-heated stones. Four or five bowls of kava later – it was only polite to keep pace with the locals – our lips, and some said the rest of their bodies too, had a slightly numbed feel as we were ushered to three trestle tables, which were set end-to-end and groaning with food. The two pigs formed the

Above: Surprise *in the Bay of Islands, a maze of enchanting waterways, large and small.*
Above right: *Freshly caught crayfish await the guests for lunch.*
Right: *Greg Lawlor's 'stretched limo' carries guests to his house on the heights of Vanua Balavu Island.*

ever seen. Our swim there was wonderfully refreshing.

Sadly, our time in Vanua Balavu was approaching its end, but there was one last treat in store – a visit to Greg Lawlor's plantation. Nabavatu (meaning 'rock walls' and pronounced nambavatu) is a magnificent, steep-sided inlet with a safe anchorage that gives superlative shelter in the worst of weather. Halfway along its northern shore is a small house that Greg was in the process of converting into a clubhouse to attract more cruising yachtsmen to the island. As the afternoon's watersports session turned into a rather competitive affair, we decided, perhaps optimistically, that this was the first annual regatta of the 'Royal Exploring Isles Yacht Squadron'. If one is starting a new club, it was decided, one might as well choose a grand name.

Later we took the plantation's quad-bike and Greg's 'stretched limo' – a tractor and trailer – up the steep track through the coconut plantation to Allardyce's grave, the last resting place of a former owner of the property, which offered mouth-watering views over the Bay of Islands. The day was rounded off sipping cocktails from the veranda of Greg's house, located high above Nabavatu inlet with a perfect westward view over the wide ocean towards the setting sun and the peacefully anchored *Surprise*.

A few months earlier, Carol Dunlop had heard local rumours of an ancient war canoe hidden in a cave high up on the mountainside of Yacata Island, about 20nm to the west of Vanua Balavu and directly on course for Ovalau Island, our next stopover. Her contact on Yacata said that, for the very first time, it might be possible for *kaivalangis* – foreigners – to see the canoe. After an early morning fishing expedition to nearby Trigger Rock, which

Above: The finish of the canoe race in the inaugural Royal Exploring Isles Yacht Squadron annual regatta held in Nabavatu Inlet. If one is starting a new yacht club, it might as well have a grand name!

Above right: The 'towed toys' race finished in a dead heat!

Below: Surprise *in the spectacular Nabavatu Inlet on the north-east of Vanua Balavu Island.*

brought a pair of yellowfin tuna into the purpose-built tender, *Surprise* nudged out through the pass, trolling a pair of lines from her fishing cockpit so as not to be outdone by her tender.

Halfway to our destination, there was good news and bad news. The good was hauling two tuna into the cockpit and a strong, but ultimately unsuccessful, strike from a swordfish that tail-danced across the surface – while the bad was that disagreement had erupted among the Yacata elders over our proposed visit to the war canoe, and that our contact now advised against proceeding with the visit. Naturally we were disappointed but, as a substitute, a guided visit had been arranged to the island of Vatuvara, nine nautical miles to the east. Vatuvara is imposing, uninhabited and beautiful, but the passage through its reef too shallow for our own tenders so to go ashore we used the long, flat-bottomed scow that Maika, our guide, had driven over from Kaibu. While showing us the island's caves and beaches he explained the controversy over the war canoe. Apparently, long,

long ago, a party of Tongans had visited Yacata in the canoe but, following a disagreement, they had been killed and eaten. Fearful of a reprisal from the notoriously warlike Tongans, they had cut up the canoe and hidden it well out of sight in the cave. Ashamed at their actions, the affair had remained a tribal secret and, even today, the thought of displaying the canoe as a tourist attraction still arouses the strongest feelings.

The early focus of European commerce in the Fijian islands was the town of Levuka on Ovalau Island, some 90nm west of Vatuvara across the Koro Sea, an overnight sail for *Surprise*. Levuka became Fiji's capital and centre of

Above: Surprise *motors southwards along the lush east coast of Vanua Balavu Island.*
Right: *A Fijian policeman, clad in traditional uniform, stands guard in Levuka.*
Below: *The main waterfront street in sleepy Levuka, once the capital of Fiji.*

administration after sovereignty was amicably handed over to Britain in 1874 by the Fijian King Cakobau. In 1881, following the capital being moved to Suva on Viti Levu, it fell into decline. Today, it is a quaint backwater, whose early colonial origins remain clear in the charming frontier town architecture of its main street shops, hotels and churches that line its Beach Street seafront. All colonial outposts had a watering hole and, amazingly, Levuka's remains alive within the Ovalau Club, a wonderfully atmospheric building whose wooden-walled rooms enshrine a fantastic collection of photographs and memorabilia from the colonial period, including a 1917 letter from Count von Lückner, the captain of a German commerce raider, written before his capture on Wakaya island, 11nm to the east.

As was the case for von Lückner, Wakaya Island was also to be our last stop in Fiji as our time aboard *Surprise* came to a reluctant end. Wakaya today is a rarity, being

one of the very few Fijian islands to be entirely privately owned, but its international renown undoubtedly stems from its highly exclusive Wakaya Club hideaway – a complex of nine luxurious bure cottage suites, restaurants and a wide range of sports facilities all set in perfectly groomed and lawned beachside grounds. It certainly tempted us as much as it had Bill and Melinda Gates, who spent their honeymoon there, but ours was just a fleeting visit to make use of the club's private aircraft to fly us back to Nadi and our waiting flight overnight to Los Angeles.

Mark Twain described Fiji as 'the very home of romance and dreams and mystery', but today the availability of *Surprise* has added more than a touch of

Above left: *Maika, our guide to Vatuvara Island, proudly displays a coconut crab.*
Above: *Heading towards Vatuvara in Maika's boat.*
Below: *Taro roots.*

luxury and mobility to this delightful archipelago. Without her and her Fijian flag, many of the remarkable places that we had visited, together with the intimate glimpses of traditional Fijian life that we had experienced, would have been closed to us and her future charter parties. Opening the door to such possibilities is surely the most outstanding aspect of superyacht cruising.

FACT FILE

Geographical: The Fijian archipelago, comprising 300 islands (106 inhabited), is centred on 17°S and 179°E in the south-west Pacific Ocean. Fiji's boundaries enclose an area of 1,300,000km², of which less than 1.5% is dry land. Viti Levu (big Fiji) and Vanua Levu (big land) are the largest islands, and are surrounded by smaller archipelagos. The larger islands have volcanic origins, while many of the off-lying groups also contain relatively low uplifted limestone islands and coral atolls that only rise a few feet above sea level. Suva, the country's capital, is on the south-east shore of Viti Levu.

Historical and political: The Fijian native culture has been shaped by invasion from other island groups, inter-tribal wars and internal rivalries. Following its discovery by Abel Tasman in 1643, European pressures to trade and colonise gradually brought missionaries and the introduction of Indian labourers to work on the plantations. From 1874 until independence in 1970, Fiji was a British Crown Colony, since when modernisation has resulted in several upsurges of ethnic tension between the native Fijians and the steadily growing Indian population. Recent tensions followed the election of an Indian-led government. Strain still exists between ethnic communities, but these do not appear to affect daily life where, to a visitor, all ethnic groups appear to happily co-exist.

Climate: Prevailing winds are the east and south-east trades. The wet season is from November to April, when cyclones are most likely. Temperature averages around 25°C – rising to 30°C in December and January and falling to 18°C in July and August.

Language: English is the official language and is spoken by most locals, although their mother tongue is either Fijian or Fijian Hindi.

THE FIJIAN ARCHIPELAGO

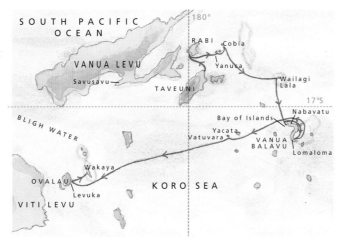

Etiquette: Complex codes of etiquette exist and reference should be made to a suitable guide book. For instance, visits to villages need permission from the local chief and may involve a gift of yaqona root, from which your welcoming kava drink will be made.

Recommended reading: *The Lonely Planet Guide to Fiji* is an excellent reference. For historical interest, try *Narrative of the US Exploring Expedition Volume 3*, reprinted by Fiji Museum, Suva in 1985, if you are able to obtain a copy.

Nautical matters: Inbound clearance is only obtainable in Suva, Savusavu, Levuka, Nandi and Lautoka. Within 24 hours of arrival, yachts should hoist a Q flag and call port control on VHF for instructions. A US$60 charge is made for arrivals on Friday afternoon, Saturday and Sunday. No pets can be taken ashore. All arms must be declared and surrendered to customs for safe keeping by the Fijian police. Passports must be valid for three months after entry. Initial clearance is given for four months, but can be extended to 12 months maximum. A cruising permit is required to visit islands, ports or anchorages outside Suva, Lautoka, Savusavu or Levuka. Yachts are advised to employ an agent, such as Williams & Gosling, Ships Agency Division, Suva. Tel:+697 3312 633.

Nautical reference material: *Pacific Islands Pilot Volume 2*, published by Admiralty Charts & Publications; *A Yachtsman's Fiji, 2nd Edition*, published by The Cruising Classroom, Australia.

Places To visit: Contact: Wakaya Club, PO Box 8009, Aspen, CO, USA E-mail: info@wakaya.com

Yacht charter: Contact Thirty Seven South, 15 Halsey Street, Auckland, New Zealand. Tel:+64 (0)9 303 0178, E-mail: service@37south.co.nz or call your charter broker.

Gitana in the Cyclades

The flight south-eastwards from Athens to the island of Mykonos is as spectacular as it is short. Once clear of the mainland, the sea is dotted with the picturesque islands of the Cyclades, which stretch interminably into the hazy blend of sky and sea that is the horizon. The Ancient Greeks called these waters 'the principal sea' – *Archipelago* – a word that, until recently, referred only to this area. Another word first coined here – but in quite different use today – is 'cruise'. In the Middle Ages this meant an armed ship patrolling with no particular destination, in a 'crusade' against 'infidel' shipping and property but, happily, today's use is more peaceful. Currently one of the world's most popular destinations for yachtsmen, this archipelago cruising

ground is the embodiment of both words, so we looked forward to joining the 36m (118ft) Perini Navi-built sloop *Gitana*, on which we were to spend a few days.

The aircraft's sudden descent brings the cliffs and arid fields of Mykonos into close focus, and one is soon bumping down at its tiny airport. The island is brown and barren, but bursts of scarlet poppies and blue cornflowers add occasional splashes of colour to the fields and roadsides, while pretty sky-blue cupolas adorn the many small chapels that dot the landscape. It is only when one reaches the rocky perimeter of Mykonos that one sees that the true glory of these islands lies in their rugged shoreline of coves, beaches and multi-hued waters. This very same lure that charmed the islands' men towards a life at sea is now a

a complete alfresco living area totally suited to Mediterranean cruising – while below, her two saloons and three snug cabins satisfy every need of her guests. With cocktail in hand and a local chart spread out on the cockpit table, we formulated the plan for the cruise. So that we could tour Mykonos, we would not leave until the next afternoon, and then we would head south, stopping at Paros, Antiparos and Ios, as we sailed towards our final destination of Santorini, a spectacular volcanic island.

Preparing for a tour of Mykonos, we studied the local tourist map. In Greece, maps can be confusing as both modern Greek and old Venetian names are in common use, the latter being a relic of several centuries of Venetian domination. Then there is the fact that the main town on many islands is the same as the name of the island itself, while visitors might also be puzzled by the frequent occurrence of a town called Chora. The main town on Mykonos, for instance, is shown on the map as Mykonos and is subtitled Chora,

magnet for tourists from all over the world. This was May, probably the best month to visit the Cyclades, being neither too hot, nor overcrowded. Even so, our taxi kept well clear of the main town's congestion as it headed for Mykonos Marina, five kilometres to the north-west of the airport, where all visiting yachts must now berth.

Even from a distance, the tall sloop rig and elegant, dark blue hull of *Gitana* made her stand out among the yachts and cruise ships in this, as yet, unfinished facility, and we were soon being welcomed aboard by her owner and his young crew. Like all Perini Navi-built yachts, *Gitana* has a huge, awning-shaded cockpit that contains distinct and hugely comfortable areas for dining and sitting, as well as a bar and barbecue –

a name that actually means a defensible village, a much-needed item in an archipelago that was historically used as a ready source of slaves. To outsiders, the main port was synonymous with the island, while to islanders it was the *chora*, a place of refuge in time of attack. As we toured the old quarter of Mykonos town that evening – a charming maze of narrow, twisting alleys in which two persons can just pass each other – it was clear that in the past an armed

Top: *Mykonos Bay, the town and the old harbour.*
Above: *The windmills of Mykonos are one of the sights of the town.*
Left: *A villa on the herb-scented cliffs of Mykonos.*
Below: *A rare, red-domed chapel.*
Below right: *A Mykonos waterside café.*

raid might be deterred by the losses that attackers would have suffered from a spirited defence. Today, the *chora's* alleys are the main tourist attraction of the island. Every building is a shop, mostly selling tourist junk but, thankfully, interspersed every now and then with an interesting artisan jeweller or antique shop, while the tiny, irregularly shaped open spaces are home to a plethora of restaurants, cafes and bars. In these busy, crowded, cosmopolitan streets behind the waterfront, we heard every language and accent as we strolled in search of the ideal restaurant. Of course, we did not find it but we settled for the most attractive, its small linen-covered tables set in the open air beneath a spreading vine trellis. Here, we spent an enjoyable evening sampling the local delicacies – feta cheese salad, fish, squid, octopus and spicy meatballs, all washed down with local wine and finished with sticky-sweet honey-filled pastries. It was certainly a fun evening but, for gastronomy, we decided it would be better to rely on *Gitana's* own chef.

Next morning we toured the island by car, visiting its highlights such as Mykonos port and its windmills, Fanari lighthouse on the north-west corner of the island and a selection of delightful beaches and bays backed by herb-scented scrubland. However, what we

Above: The 36m Perini Navi-built sloop Gitana, an ideal vessel for cruising in the Greek Islands.
Right: A street trader, Mykonos style.
Below: Fresh fruit and vegetables for sale on the Mykonos quayside.

really looked forward to was the afternoon's sail. Our destination was the island of Paros, about 30nm to the south. The wind was light as we motored out of the bay, passing the little island of Delos to starboard. Although just 3.6km² in size, Delos is one of the prime archaeological sites in Greece, being the legendary birthplace of Apollo and his sister Artemis. Once out of the wind shadow of Mykonos, *Gitana* came alive as the local *Meltemi* wind picked up. It was blowing 23

knots true from east-north-east and we flew across the calm sea under full sail, the log showing a steady 10 knots. *Gitana's* cockpit was made for these conditions: lunch at the dining table in the welcome shade of the awning; coffee, taken aft in the deck lounge, then a spot of sunbathing on the aft deck as the mountainous island of Paros slowly changed from its distant misty blue to sharply focused greys and greens, its golden sandy beaches the last to appear.

We had a few hours to kill before taking our overnight berth in the island's north-eastern port of Naoussa, so on entering the huge Naousis Bay we took a sharp turn right into the shelter of Ormos Ayios

Ionnou (St John's Bay). It was time for water sports, and the tender was soon towing the more athletic guests on their water-skis as others swam in the pleasantly warm, crystal-clear water or walked on the beach. By 6pm the temperature was dropping and we motored towards Naoussa where, too large to enter the harbour itself, we tied stern-to the inner mole. While it is still a holiday centre, Naoussa does not embrace the same 'cruise-ship' style of mass tourism as Mykonos. Thus, while its tiny shops and restaurant-lined lanes are perhaps a little less photogenic than those on Mykonos, their quiet, uncrowded air is considerably more attractive. At sundown, the centre of activity moves to the tiny inner port, its brightly painted collection of small wooden fishing caiques moored gunwale to gunwale along the smooth-worn marble quaysides, all bathed in the warm golden light. The quays themselves, a remnant of Venetian colonisation, were one large and busy restaurant, almost completely paved with tables and chairs and wreathed in the mouth-watering aroma of barbecueing fish, squid and octopus, scented herbs and hot olive oil. But the eyes and nose were not the only senses to be charmed – the idyllic scene was rounded off with the babble of many languages, the clink of glass and intermingling snatches of Greek and Western music.

Above left: Gitana in *Ormos Ayious Ionnu (St John's Bay), Paros Island.*
Above: A cove on Kavouras *Islet, off Antiparos Island.*
Far Left: Gitana's *large and comfortable deck lounge.*
Left: A scuba *diving expedition.*
Middle left: An attractive *doorway in the town of Naousis.*
Below: In the heat of the day, *water sports are the best way to combine exercise with a refreshing swim.*
Left below: Naousis town *on Paros Island.*

In the warm evening, it was one of those settings that is instantly attractive, one that positively shouts for you to grab a table, order a bottle of wine and call for the menu – we did just this, and it was great.

Next morning we decided to take a taxi to Parikia, the capital of this oval 19km by 24km island. It was prettier than Mykonos, we decided, still rather arid and not exactly a garden of Eden, but it was saved by gaudy outbursts of bougainvillea and the heady scent of jasmine. Parikia, it turned out, was not only the local ferry port, but also the regional hub of the system, an importance that was reflected in its busy commercial quays and bustling, smoky lorries. In the high tourist season, the town is reported to be a veritable hell-hole! Its most interesting building was, without doubt, the Ekatontapiliani Cathedral – well worth a visit for its attractive cloisters, icons and adornments. For some unfathomable reason, it is also known as the Church of 100 Doors – but, in a count, it is difficult to get past a dozen. It was built in the 6th-century, largely from the remnants of Ancient Greek temples that remain clearly

of Dhiplo and Kavouras where, later, we would get shelter from the afternoon's *Meltemi*. The day's chosen water activity was diving, and while the gear was being prepared we took the tender to find a suitable place. Kavouras, clad in spiny scrub and sparkling mica-rich shale, is dry, hostile and totally uninhabited apart from a colony of gulls that wheeled nervously over our heads as we crossed the couple of hundred metres to the northern shore. *Eureka!* – we had found what we were seeking – a deep, sheltered cove with a couple of promising rock stacks that appeared to be a reasonable diving site and, but for a brief stop at *Gitana* to pick up the gear, the tender was soon around the island and anchored in the cove's limpid blue water. The dive – well, it was cooling, the water was clear and it was an entry in one's divers logbook, but it is difficult to be truly enthusiastic about Mediterranean diving which, like the island itself, is bare in comparison to the abundant technicolour of the Pacific or Indian Oceans. Nevertheless, filled with the buzz that always follows a dive, we were in good spirits as *Gitana* motored cautiously through the narrow and shallow Stenon Andiparou passage, with our tender sweeping ahead of us, seeking out the deepest part of the channel that our 3.2m (10ft 5in) keel-up draught demanded. A mile or so on, when the soundings grew reassuringly deep, we rounded up, and hoisted sail. Heeling to the increasing breeze, we scuttled out of the channel's shelter, past a cluster of tiny islands – one adorned with an isolated sugar-white chapel – and sailed serenely on towards the blue-grey outline of Ios, some 20 miles distant.

visible in its walls and foundations. Was this plain vandalism or recycling ruins – who can judge?

It had been hot and sticky in Parikia and by common consent we decided that water sports should, once again, be on the menu for the afternoon. Our evening stopover was to be on the island of Ios, not more than 40nm to the south, and as our chosen route passed through the narrows that separate Paros from its smaller sister island of Antiparos (literally, 'against Paros'), it made sense to look for somewhere near that channel. After a lazy sail down the north-west coast of Paros – in reality a drift, during which we ate a splendid lunch – we found an anchorage between the little islets

Above: The old Venetian harbour at Naoussa, Paros Island. At sunset, its marble quays become one large restaurant, filled with the delicious aroma of barbecued fish drizzled with olive oil and aromatic herbs.

Below: A pretty chapel guards the entrance to Ios port.

Gitana is too large for the yacht berths in Port Ios, the island's main harbour, so we had been asked to hold off until the inter-island ferry had vacated its berth at 6pm. Our timing was perfect. We passed the little blue ferry as it bustled out of the steep-sided inlet and snugged into its place at the quayside, just opposite a relatively newly built cluster of shops and restaurants. Ios has the reputation as a party island – the Ibiza of the Cyclades – but this is only during the giddy months of July and August, when a wave of hedonistic, holidaying youth descends on the island, hoping to re-create the truly wild legends of the Swinging Sixties. In the month of May, however, it was more like a vicarage tea party. As dusk fell, the port was quietly well behaved, a mere murmur of conversation and gentle bouzouki music wafting over the quayside, so we decided to head for the *chora*. In the Dark Ages,

Top: Gitana *moored stern-to at Ios port.*
Above: *Splashes of colour from scarlet poppies breathe life on the arid landscape.*
Left: Gitana *heels to the afternoon breeze.*
Right: *Guests taking refreshments in* Gitana's *cockpit dining area.*

the town's main defences had been height and distance – too tiring a climb, without sufficient guarantee of success or rewards for an attacker to bother. Today's deterrent, granted the undesirability of scaling the steep, 4km-long mule stairway as a prelude to dinner, was finding a taxi. An hour after our search had started we found just one cab driver prepared to make the three trips required to ferry our whole crew to the town. So it was rather later than we expected when we eventually sat down at a hastily assembled table in the only restaurant able to take our number. It was a charming place, set in a tiny square that sloped down to a chapel – the angle making it rather reminiscent of dining in the cockpit of a heeled yacht. Eating late in Greece, where restaurant food is often pre-cooked and kept warm for hours on end, is not generally recommended. When our request for a menu was met

with an invitation to view the food in the kitchen, we did so with an impending sense of culinary doom. However, we were pleasantly surprised at how good the simple, unsophisticated meal actually tasted this late at night, especially when washed down with the local wine. As we left, well satisfied, we saw what the town might be like at the height of the season – a film crew were shooting in the main, disco-lined alley that was thronged with extras and throbbing with heavy metal music, simulated violence and alcohol abuse.

Above: The view from Fira across Santorini's sunken caldera towards the active volcanic islands of Nea Kameni and Palia Kameni.
Below: The town of Oia, high on Santorini's cliffs, seems like the icing on a dark cake.

Somehow, the calm of May seemed much more attractive – even to the youngest in our group.

The climax of our cruise was fast approaching. Early next day, having stocked up with a mouth-watering selection of fresh breads and pastries from the bakery in the port, we headed 20 miles southwards for Santorini. Initially it was a motor-sail in an oily-dark, calm sea that was only stirred by the faintest of ripples, but by the time we were clear of Ios we had sufficient sailing breeze to roll out *Gitana's* main and genoa. From a distance, Santorini or Thira, its often-used Venetian name, looks much like any other Cycladean island – blue-grey and steep-sided – but as one approaches, its aspect changes. The fault in the black cliffs became first a cleft, and then a channel that dwarfed *Gitana* as we sailed into the huge lagoon beyond. Santorini had once been a classic volcanic pinnacle, a solidly conical Vesuvius-shaped island that had exploded some three and a half thousand years ago – the death knell of the mighty Minoan civilisation. Today this is increasingly considered to be the origin of the legend of Atlantis – the island that mysteriously disappeared – not in the Atlantic to which it gave its name, but in the Archipelago. Today, the island, or rather, the three islands of Thirasia, Santorini and the smaller Aspronisi, marks the outline of this former giant, at the centre of whose lagoon are the still-active volcanic islands of Nea Kameni and Palia Kameni that have been growing steadily over recent centuries. We were headed for Fira, the island's main port and the island's capital, but as we entered the lagoon we became aware of another

fantastic sight. High on the clifftop on our port side the village of Oia was an icing of brilliant white houses topping the crest of the dark caldera rim, just as if the otherwise black island had been picked up by a giant and dipped into a tin of paint. A few miles on across the caldera, the more extensive town of Fira displayed grander buildings and modern technology in the form of a cable car that climbed the steep cliff beside the ancient zigzag of the 587-step mule stairway.

Mooring stern-to the quay, the strong aroma of mule confirmed that the ancient ways still survived – but just for tourists. Overladen, sad-looking mules staggered up the cobbled track, bearing the contents of a cruise ship. With animal welfare at the forefront of our minds, we took the cable car on our way to tour this charming town – the best we had encountered on our cruise – where clifftop lanes and restaurants offer spectacular views over the crater. We could have spent much longer in Santorini touring its beaches, museums, and archaeological sites from several eras, but our time

Above: Guests relaxing on Gitana's foredeck.
Above left and right: Oia town on Santorini Island.
Below: A pretty chapel in Oia.

had run out and our aircraft waited to carry us back to the real world.

This cradle of European civilisation makes a wonderful cruising ground, offering beautiful anchorages, beaches and water sports, as well as fascinating antiquities and the romance of visiting several different islands. Certainly, one can experience the region using hotels and commercial transport, but the comfort and flexibility offered by a yacht such as *Gitana* makes this the only way to experience this region in style, especially during the high season.

FACT FILE

Political: Modern Greece gained its independence in 1829, following a bitter eight-year long war that led to a monarchy being established in 1833. Turmoil followed WWII, when Greece experienced an unsuccessful communist uprising, a military dictatorship, and the abolition of the monarchy in 1975. Following early political instability, Greece is now a stable unicameral parliamentary democracy and a member of the EU.

Historical: The birthplace of European civilisation, Greece has more recorded history than any other nation. Various races have left their marks on the region since the first recorded Early Cycladic people who lived on the islands between 4,500 and 2,000BC. Following them came the Minoans (2000-1500BC); the Myceneans (1500-776BC); the Archaic Period (776-490BC) and the rise of the City States; the Classical Period (490-180BC); the Romans (180BC-395AD); Byzantines (395-1453); Venetians and Ottomans (1453-1830) and lastly the Modern Era of today.

Getting there: Athens is the main airport for Greece and is easily accessible directly by air from all of Europe and North American countries, Australia and New Zealand. From Athens there is

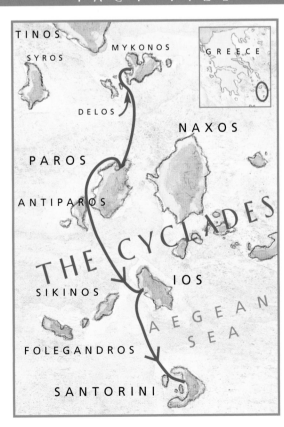

a comprehensive domestic air service to the islands, while the ferry hub for all the Greek islands is from the nearby port of Piraeus. There are international airports on Mykonos and Santorini, but these are mainly served by charter airlines.

Formalities: No visas are required by other EU citizens, nor for citizens of Australia, Canada, New Zealand or the USA for stays of up to three months.

Weather: In general, the Cyclades have hot, dry summers, with average temperatures ranging from 25°C to 28°C, when rain is a rarity, and mild, wet winters. The summer months of June, July and August can be exceedingly hot while the months of April, May, September and October are very pleasant, although at those times there is a risk of some stormy weather. Summer wind is dominated by the *Meltemi* that blows from the north for around 20 days in July and August at strengths of Force 4 and over, reaching Force 6 for an average of 12 days. April, May and June are usually the calmest months.

Money: Greece is in the Euro zone. Cash-dispensing machines are available on most islands in larger towns. Bank opening hours are 08.00 to 13.00, Monday to Friday. Major credit cards are widely accepted at shops and restaurants.

T U R N

O V Ǝ Я .

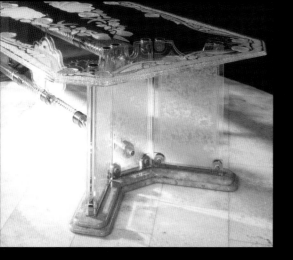

Glass Deco International designs, develops, produces and installs exclusive interior products in among others glass, marble and metal or a combination of these elements. Products like stairs, decorated hard-glass doors, dining tables, dressers, decorated floors, etc.

With use of several techniques as blasting, etching, waterjet cutting, fused application, moulding and blowing, we are able to live up to your expectations, eventually in combination with metal or wood.

Our in-house designers can, in cooperation with external architects, develop a custom-made product for you if desired.

If any information is required, please contact us.

GLASS DECO
INTERNATIONAL

Glass Deco - Mierloseweg 126 - 5707 AR Helmond - The Netherlands
Telefoon 0492 - 524261 - Inteenet: www.glass-deco.com - E-mail: info@glass-deco.com

LUXURY YACHTS

DISCOVER

18 Clarence Beach Road, Henderson 6166 Western Australia. Telephone +61 (0)8 9494 9999 www.oceanfast.com.au

BAGLIETTO

Construction No. 10180 - Launch June 2003
42m (138') full displacement M/Y

There is no limit to the extravagance you can enjoy.

Or the simplicity.

Freedom of choice for the discerning few on the world's finest luxury yachts. For two decades the Crestar approach to private yacht charter has become synonymous with a service that is second to none ~ an exclusive charter formula tailored for those who demand excellence.

CRESTAR
YACHT CHARTERS

COLETTE COURT, 125 SLOANE STREET, LONDON SW1X 9AU, ENGLAND
Tel: +44 (0) 20 7730 2299   Toll Free from USA: 1 800 222 9985   Fax: +44 (0) 20 7824 8691   E-mail: charters@crestaryachts.com

WWW.CRESTARYACHTS.COM

Bart Roberts

80.8m/265' Canadian Vickers, 1968/2002

No more artist's renderings! Here is the real thing! The ultimate exploration vessel, BART ROBERTS is making her debut as the conversion of the century, from Canadian icebreaker/ buoy tender, to mega yacht. All of the attributes of a fine yacht, but oh so much more, BART ROBERTS is Lloyd's Register of Shipping certified and SOLAS (Safety of Life at Sea) approved to carry over 12 passengers for charter.

Other conversions have fallen short, due to excessive draft, or lack of room to carry big toys. BART ROBERTS can carry 3 x 50'/15.5m tenders, 2 x 20' containers, plus a helicopter in a heated/ air conditioned hangar, a 20'/10' (6.1 x 3.1m) swimming pool with jets, a movie theatre, casino, gym, massage/ medical room, elevator, 300 gallon (11, 361) fish tank stocked with piranha, and much, much more!

Seriously for sale. Please call Central Agent Bill Sanderson for details.

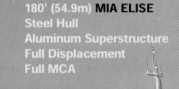

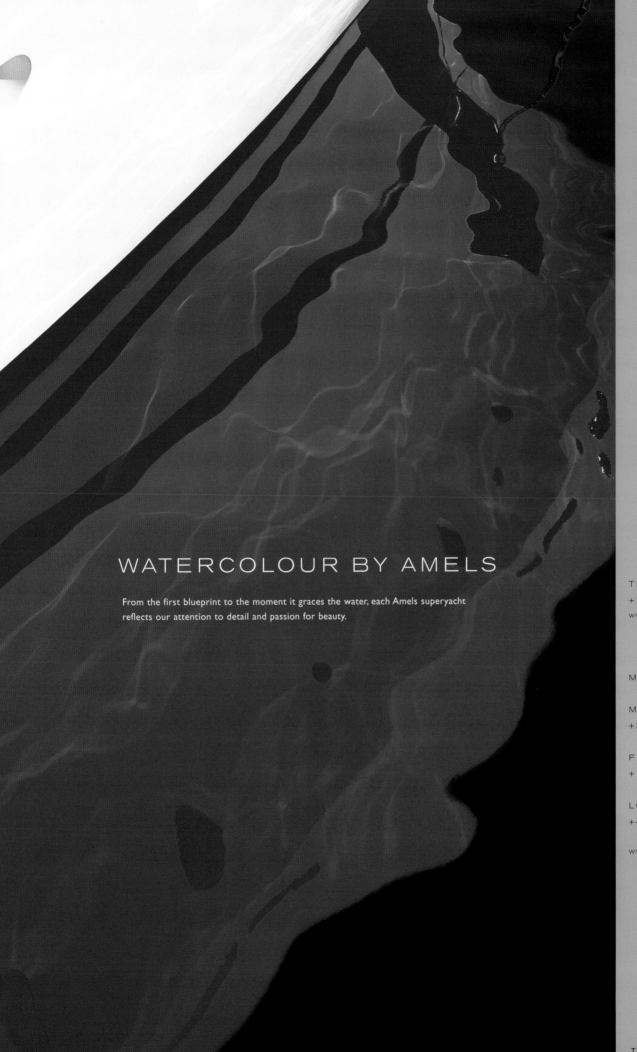

WATERCOLOUR BY AMELS

From the first blueprint to the moment it graces the water, each Amels superyacht
reflects our attention to detail and passion for beauty.

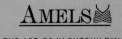

SARNIA YACHTS

~ the solution provider ~

"over thirty years ago we created a small splash in a large ocean, yet the ripples continue to grow"

ANSBACHER

Sarnia Yachts has been providing corporate yacht ownership and registration services for over thirty years.

During this time the business has matured and is one of the oldest established providers in the offshore Marine Financial Services Industry.

Sarnia Yacht's Services encompass:

- Yacht Registration
- Corporate Yacht Ownership
- Yacht Administration & Accounting
- Yacht Finance
- Arranging Marine & Crew Insurance
- Estate Planning
- Other Marine Services

For more information contact us at:
Sarnia Yachts Limited, PO Box 79, La Plaiderie,
St. Peter Port, Guernsey GY1 3DQ, Channel Islands
Tel: +44(0) 1481 709 960 Fax: +44(0) 1481 726 526
Email: info@sarniayachts.co.gg
Web: www.sarniayachts.com

Welcome!
(...to another world)

C.B.I. NAVI
PASSIONS BUILDER

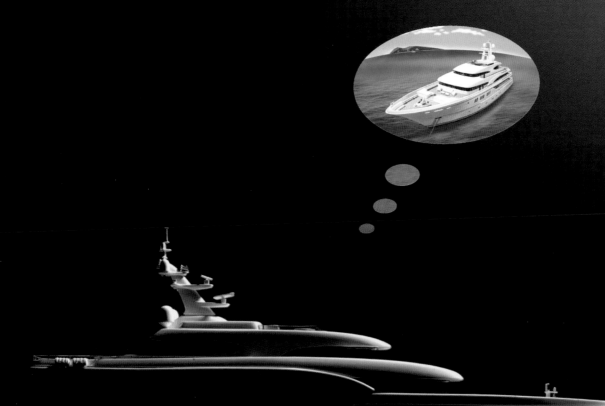

The Yachts

African Queen

African Queen

Below right: African Queen *is the latest evolution in a long series of similarly styled sailing superyachts from the board of Dubois Yacht Design.*

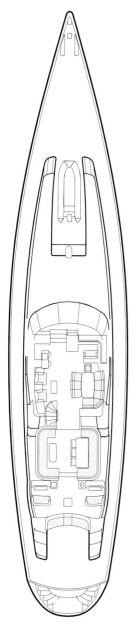

The summer of 2002 saw the Dutch shipyard Vitters deliver the 42.9m (140ft 9in) aluminium sloop *African Queen*, a sailing superyacht that represents the latest evolution in a long series of similar vessels from Ed Dubois' Lymington, England-based studio. This modern yacht, with an attractive flag-blue hull, features a contemporary mahogany interior from designers Redman Whiteley Dixon that is particularly sympathetic to the whole appearance of this vessel.

Outwardly, *African Queen* projects a powerful profile with an attractive hull topped by a low, streamlined deckhouse that offers no obstruction to visibility from her aft steering cockpit. She is driven by a powerful sloop rig with an in-boom furling system from Marten Spars, while her well thought out deck layout matches her racing, cruising and entertainment roles. In this respect her cockpit is divided, with the work areas associated with

sailing the yacht being well separated from guest relaxation zones. The prime deck area for guests is the main cockpit, immediately aft of the deckhouse, which is protected by high coamings and a bimini supported by a chunky stainless steel frame that is kept permanently in position. This area has a large dining table to port and twin tables to starboard to provide flexibility for various sized gatherings. It is also the termination of the central walkway that runs forward from the stern, between the twin steering pedestals and through the guest cockpit to the main companionway, giving easy access to all areas.

Both steering pedestals are backed by helmsman's seats, from which the clear view down either of the wide side decks is helped by the fact that the seats and cockpit bulwarks are actually slightly extended over the deck. In addition, the bimini is of such a height that the helmsman can see directly forward, over the top or

Far left: African Queen's mast incorporates a powered crow's nest, the first to be fitted to a mast from Marten Spars.
Left: The navigation station in the deck saloon has excellent exterior views.

through the slit formed by the top of the deckhouse and the underside of the bimini – a gap that can be closed with a clear screen if weather conditions dictate. The wheel and instrument arrangement at each pod is particularly ergonomic and of satisfyingly high-tech design. Abaft the steering pedestals and separated by the central passageway are two more guest settees, new additions to the Dubois concept, that face aft over the deck to the stern and the yacht's receding wake – delightfully romantic and sheltered places to sit and read. When at anchor, this seating area acts as a centre for water sports in combination with the permanent bathing platform and stairways. Elsewhere the deck is an open expanse of teak, the vast side decks and a huge foredeck not only give ample room for the crew to tend sails, but also provide them with their own deck area, as the companionway from the galley and crew quarters rises to the foredeck at this point.

One of *African Queen's* two tenders, a large 6.25m (20ft 6in) Castoldi Jet, is carried on the foredeck just forward of the mast, sheltered by two 'fingers' that extend forward from the coachroof. This is launched using a 1,600kg-lift (3,527lb) crane concealed within a locker in the superstructure. The second tender, a smaller 3.6m (11ft 10in) Novurania 360 RIB, is stowed in the stern garage, to which access is made through a large hatch on the aft deck. Because the *retroussé* stern has sweeping steps down either side leading to the bathing platform, the stern door is restricted in width, so the tender is also crane-launched – out through the deck hatch and over the guard rails.

The underwater profile of *African Queen* is best described as 'medium-displacement Dubois'. The very fair hull form has an L-shaped bulb keel of 4.1m (13ft 5in)

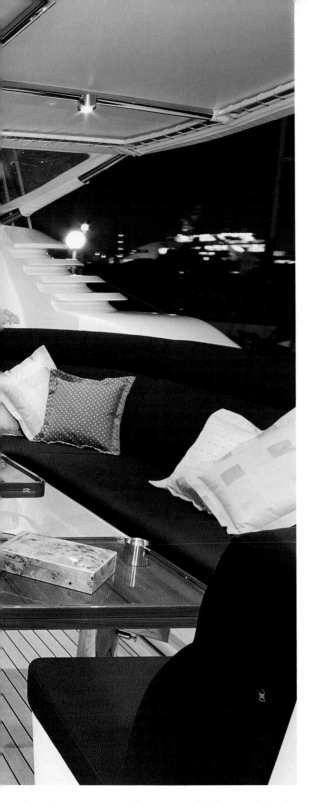

a normal Leisure Furl in-boom furling system, but one cunningly disguised as an elegant Park Avenue-style spar. Interestingly, the mast is also the first from Marten Spars with a powered crow's nest – as entertaining for guests as it is useful for spotting coral reefs, or for maintenance. The sail-handling systems are developed from Dubois' and Vitters' now extensive experience. The mainsheet, which can be loaded up to 17 tonnes, is handled by double captive winches supplied by Rondal. Most of the other custom stainless steel deck hardware and hydraulic systems aboard are the work of Dutch specialists Ascon and Staalart, although a few of the winches are examples of Andersen's new superyacht series.

African Queen is powered by an 820hp MTU 12V 183TE72 diesel driving a variable-pitch Teignbridge propeller. The maximum speed is a little over 14 knots with a typical 13-knot cruising speed. There are 100hp retractable bow and stern thrusters for close quarters manoeuvring, and when not in use these are faired into the hull by hinged doors.

The interior layout for African Queen was developed

draught containing 60 tonnes of ballast, while the semi-balanced rudder is skegless.

She is certainly fast under sail. The high-aspect all-carbon, five-spreader rig from Marten Spars in New Zealand towers 47m (154ft 2in) above her decks and operates with a working compression of up to 190 tonnes. This delivers plenty of power from her 733m² (7,887ft²) total of fore-and-aft sail, beautifully cut by Vela in Palma de Mallorca. Off-wind she adds a 575m² (6,187ft²) gennaker. The 343m² (1,125ft²) blade jib and the reacher are both set on Reckmann R6 roller-furlers, the reacher's incorporating a hydraulic ram on the forestay that allows a 25cm (10in) extension of the sail luff. This adds power to the sail by increasing its fullness. The inner forestay is also on a ram, while the Marten Spars carbon boom is particularly noteworthy in that it is

Above: The guest lobby.
Right: The master cabin.
The en suite bathroom fills the
yacht's beam behind the bed.

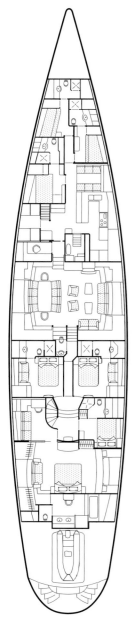

between the owner, Dubois Naval Architects and interior designers Redman Whiteley Dixon, with many areas of the vessel benefiting from the construction of comprehensive mock-ups prior to the finalisation of the design. Naturally, the plan and space arrangement have strong references to previous collaborations by the two design companies, particularly the 40.4m (132ft 7in) sailing yacht, *Kokomo*, but *African Queen's* layout also has many unique features, reflecting the owner's input throughout the project. The design brief for Redman Whiteley Dixon was to create a contemporary mahogany interior, sympathetic to the modern design of the vessel. The result is a sophisticated style that makes use of sapele mahogany joinery finished in satin gloss, the dark veneers being balanced by royal blue leathers and Alcantaras, while brightness is introduced by an array of whites used in the cotton upholstery, panelling, headlinings and carpeting. It is a style that invites touch, especially the faceted

mouldings that are seen on the many curved cabinets throughout the vessel. Such joinery was not only highly challenging for interior contractor Die Oldenburger to construct, but also demanded the best possible quality which, to the company's credit, was achieved with honours. All this is embellished by the owner's collection of African art that reflects his passion for that continent.

The entrance to the deck saloon is made through double glass doors from the guest cockpit that open automatically at the touch of foot switches. Aside from the comprehensive and very functional helm station, the saloon contains a number of distinct areas. To port there is a full bar, alongside which comfortable seating creates a relaxing and informal area, while opposite, there is a raised platform with dining for eight people, who are treated to spectacular external views from the elevated position. Aft, a half-circular stairway descends to a lobby from which the owner's and guest cabins open, while at the forward end of the room a few wide steps flanked by elegant bannisters descend to the main saloon.

Perhaps the most stunning feature of the main saloon is its interlinked relationship with the deck saloon. This provides long sight-lines and abundant daylight, which pours in through the wrap-around windscreen overhead. In addition, the saloon is opened up visually by large hull windows to port and starboard. The dining table, positioned on the starboard side of the room, is of a modern design, with a glass top that enables the whole width of the room to be seen. Opposite, on the port side, are a settee, armchairs and coffee table. Another notable feature of the saloon is that it offers a second direct access

to the guest accommodation by means of a passageway that runs aft, past a day head and between the two largest guest cabins, into the guest lobby. Not only does this allow easy crew servicing of the guest's rooms, eliminating the need to go up and down through the deck saloon, but it is also an added convenience for guests, with only the minimal penalty that the two forward guest cabins, between which the passageway passes, are slightly reduced in size. These two main guest cabins have large en suite shower rooms while, to starboard of the lobby, the third guest cabin is a slightly smaller double with an en suite shower room – ideal for children, a single person or a younger couple.

The large owner's suite is aftmost, its door adjacent to a small cabinet upon which is positioned a bronze sculpture of an African queen. The suite is entered through the owner's study, which is furnished with a large desk, book shelves and a sofa. Beyond is the bedroom which, filling the full beam, is dramatic in its combination of dark wood, bright halogen lighting, and vivid African artwork. It is furnished with a king-sized double bed and a comfortable settee and is provided with extensive drawer and wardrobe space. Behind the bed is a large bathroom extending across much of the beam, offering a bath, shower stall, twin wash-basins, a vanity desk and a separate head compartment.

The crew area fills the yacht forward of the mast, and is entered either from a deck hatch or through a door in the saloon's forward bulkhead. Opening from a short passageway that forms a sound barrier between the saloon and crew area, the yacht's office is unusually large for a vessel of this size, while its positioning allows convenient use by both the owner and the crew. It is fitted with all the usual communications equipment, a computer and various navigation system repeaters. The crew domain proper is finished in the same dark veneers as the rest of the yacht but with greater use of white half-panelling to lighten the environment. Initially, one enters a lobby with the large well-fitted galley to starboard, and the deck stairs and cold stores at one's port hand. From here stairs descend aft, beneath the main saloon to the engine room, a compartment that is particularly worthy of note owing to its exceptional engineering. Beyond the galley is a mess area and crew accommodation for five in three en suite cabins, a double for the captain and the remaining two twin-bunked.

A particularly well-executed development of the Dubois sailing superyacht concept, *African Queen* is a tribute to the detailed input from the owner and his project manager Nigel Ingram of MCM, as well as to interior designers Redman Whiteley Dixon, the highly skilled production team from Vitters Shipyard and her furniture makers Die Oldenburger.

Above: The master cabin is entered through the owner's study.
Far left below: Vibrant African artwork was specially commissioned to highlight the dark mahogany throughout the interior, as exemplified by this double guest cabin.

SPECIFICATIONS

LOA	42.90m (140ft 9in)	Propeller	Teignbridge, CP18HRS
LWL	35.00m (114ft 10in)	Fuel capacity	25,000 litres
Beam (max)	9.00m (29ft 6in)	Generators	2 x 50kW Northern Lights M668D
Draught	4.10m (13ft 5in)	Jib & reacher furling systems	Reckmann, R6
Displacement (light)	215 tonnes	Captive sheet winches	Rondal, RW 600 & RW 800
Ballast	53 tonnes	Radar	Furuno, FR2115
Mast	Marten Spars, carbon-fibre	Autopilot	Segatron
Boom	Marten Spars, Leisure Furl	Paint	Awlgrip
Sails	Vela	Owner & guests	8 in 4 x double cabins
Sail areas (mainsail)	390m²	Crew	6 in 1 x double & 2 x twin bunk cabins
(blade jib)	347m²	Construction	Aluminium hull & deck
(reacher)	510m²	Classification	ABS ✠A1 Yachting Service
(staysail)	123m²	Interior design	Redman Whiteley Dixon
Propulsion	1 x 818hp MTU 12V 183TE72 diesel	Naval architecture & styling	Dubois Naval Architects
Gearbox	ZF, BW211	Builder/Year	Vitters Shipyard/2002

Alexandra

Above: The semi-circular settee allows guests a commanding view forward.
Below: The owner knew his exact requirements following his charter of an earlier yacht in the Golden Bay *series.*

One of the most important projects to be developed by Benetti in recent years has been the *Golden Bay* design for a really modern and glamorous 50m semi-displacement motor yacht. It has been a big success and although the Viareggio yard has since built motor yachts up to 70m in length, the *Golden Bay* series still seems in many ways to be the Benetti flagship. Recently, hull number six in this series, *Alexandra*, was launched for a European owner, with the same exterior lines but a very different interior and some special new features not previously seen.

A special request by the owner was for a dark blue hull, and this makes a surprising difference to *Alexandra's* outward appearance. With a white painted hull and superstructure, the yacht seems to be all one piece but with a dark colour the hull is emphasized and the superstructure looks considerably smaller and better balanced. At the same time, the three large oval windows in the forward part of the main deck are less obvious but in contrast the raised foredeck and pronounced bow overhang look stronger and more purposeful.

In order to refine the concept as exactly as possible, the owner took the very sensible step of chartering *Queen M* which was the third yacht in the series.

This enabled him to decide on details of the layout and also influenced his choice of Terence Disdale as interior designer. In fact *Queen M* was not a typical Disdale design, having quite a bright, colourful look in contrast to the quiet monochromes that are normal from this studio.

If you want an interior that will remain in style there are two possibilities: either a 'classic' design that is deliberately old-fashioned or one with contemporary lines but very understated colours and textures that do not force themselves on your attention. For *Alexandra*, the owner chose the latter course and in addition to Terence Disdale, called in Alan Jones who has designed a number of widely-admired waterside houses in the Mediterranean area and also specializes in a very relaxed but stylish look.

Above: Alexandra's *striking dark blue hull ensures that she stands out from the crowd.*
Far left: The sun deck is *shaded by the radar arch.*
Left: A high degree of privacy *is provided by the tinted glass screens that edge the sun deck.*

Above: The main saloon and dining room are open-plan, thus allowing the furniture arrangement and natural colours to take full effect.
Right: The dining room can be reconfigured as a coffee lounge by lowering the table.
Far right: The open stairways are a feature in themselves.

The whole of the interior is therefore panelled in a light oak of very natural appearance, with a scrubbed, open-grain texture and matt finish. Cabinets and tables are surfaced in burl oak with a lime-scrubbed finish to leave small flecks of white in the grain. Carpets are either beige or off-white and all the bathrooms are decorated with the beige *crema marfil* marble. Against this neutral background, pictures and ornaments take on a new prominence but, above all, views of the seascape seen through the numerous large windows face no competition.

A key decision was to position the owner's cabin in the aft portion of the upper deck, which is clearly the most favoured situation aboard. As the superstructure is full-beam at this upper level, there are no side decks and, as a result, the cabin is extremely spacious and offers splendid exterior views through its floor-to-ceiling windows. With this arrangement, the upper deck can become a private area, but in this owner's case it was not the intention as the main alfresco dining table is placed here.

In addition to this very grand bedroom, the owner enjoys a luxurious bathroom on the starboard side, which is entered via a spacious dressing room, and a separate study across the hallway. On the same level is the bridge, radio room and captain's cabin. Making maximum use of the space available, a Portuguese bridge leads forward to

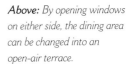

an attractive semi-circular settee that encloses a small table. This gives a perfect forward view and is sure to be a great place to sit when the yacht is under way.

The bridge itself is compact but professional and very smartly fitted out with a dusky blue leather trim. The two radars are from Decca and the principal instruments from B&G. Just behind the bridge on the port side is a fully equipped communications room from where the radio, satcom and satellite television receivers are controlled. The captain has his cabin just across the hallway.

Placing the owner's suite in a prime position at the aft of the upper deck is a good solution for a superyacht that will be based in the pleasantly mild climate of the Mediterranean, where there is little need for the sky lounge that usually fills this position. It also releases the traditional position of the master suite on the forward part of the main deck, which in this case has been filled by a pair of splendid VIP double cabins. Mirror images of each other, these VIP cabins are very pleasant indeed, having large oval windows as well

Above: By opening windows on either side, the dining area can be changed into an open-air terrace.

Right: Having the full-beam owner's cabin aft on the upper deck affords it unrivalled sea views.
Far right above: One of the two twin bedded guest double cabins on the lower deck.
Far right below: The owner's bathroom is entered through a spacious dressing room.
Below: Two splendid mirror-image VIP staterooms are located on the forward part of the main deck.
Below right: A VIP cabin bathroom.

as luxurious bathrooms that incorporate a proper bath.

On the lower deck the four guest cabins are in the conventional arrangement of two doubles and two twins, the double cabins being a little larger and having baths rather than showers. If every cabin aboard is fully occupied, the yacht can accommodate 14 guests, although this number could only be legally taken aboard during private use, as regulations limit the yacht to a maximum of 12 passengers during periods of charter.

The main saloon and dining room are one large space without a divider, and it is here that one of the yacht's most intriguing features is found . In line with the dining table, a pair of large glass doors open onto either deck, where a section of the bulwark folds down to a horizontal position. As a result, the dining room becomes open to the air on either side, and with no obstruction to the view it is transformed into a dining terrace. So as to make up for the loss of an informal place to take coffee – a function

that might have been filled by a sky lounge – the dining table can be lowered to the height of a coffee table.

Huge rectangular windows on either side of the saloon maintain the semi-outdoor impression, especially if the glazed double doors to the aft deck are open. A selection of comfortable suede-upholstered settees and armchairs invite relaxation, while entertainment is offered by a giant television in one corner. This can be concealed behind louvred doors or raised in height when in use.

No modern yacht would be complete without a sun deck, and one of the strong points of this design is that it has a really spacious one. The key to a successful sun deck is that one should be able to relax in the open air with a choice of sunshine or shade, depending on preference and the weather. To meet this requirement a comfortable semi-circular settee and table have been placed directly under the shade of the radar arch, while additional seats and tables can be sheltered by two large

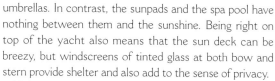

Above: *Alfresco dining, aft of the owner's cabin.*

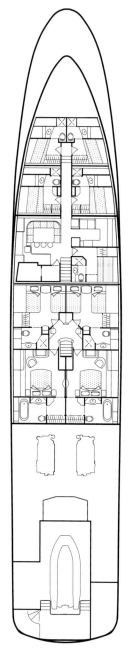

umbrellas. In contrast, the sunpads and the spa pool have nothing between them and the sunshine. Being right on top of the yacht also means that the sun deck can be breezy, but windscreens of tinted glass at both bow and stern provide shelter and also add to the sense of privacy.

If the sun deck is selected as the place for a buffet or barbecue, three special features make this easy to arrange: a sliding hatchway covers a crew stairway that descends through two decks to the galley; beside it a lift speeds supplies from the galley, while to starboard is a bar with a concealed refrigerator and icemaker.

Good working conditions for the crew is very important and this aspect of *Alexandra's* design has been well served, with easy access to each deck without passing through guest areas. The 12 crew have spacious quarters forward on the lower deck in pleasant twin cabins with en suite shower rooms, and there is a comfortable crew mess with

Above: *The communications room is separated from the bridge, allowing clarity of conversation and reception.*
Left: *The compact bridge is delicately trimmed with dusky blue leather.*
Far left below: *The professional galley.*

blue leather seats. The galley is completely professional in character, with all surfaces and equipment in stainless steel. The hobs and ovens, by Zanussi, are all electric and include a steam oven. In addition to the two fridge/freezers in the galley, an additional cold room and dry store are on the lower deck.

Other crucial features include good access to the sea and ample storage for tenders and water sports equipment. A large folding transom door, with direct access from the main deck aft, provides the first and a capacious garage the second. A high capacity overhead hoist, which rolls aft on extending beams, is able to lift a tender of up to two tonnes in weight. Even when a boat of this size is in place, ample room remains for waveriders and other toys.

Alexandra is a semi-displacement motor yacht that has ample power provided by her two MTU main engines of 2,262hp each, giving a top speed of around 18 knots. At maximum power, she uses considerable fuel but when the speed is reduced to 12 knots, the power requirement and fuel consumption drop dramatically, providing a maximum range of around 3,800 nautical miles – easily sufficient to cross the Atlantic. The engine room is placed aft, with a watertight doorway into the garage. Having all the technical equipment concentrated in one area makes life easier for the engineers and quieter for the guests as there are no shafts or propellers below the cabins.

This latest example of the *Golden Bay* series seems to be one of those yachts that excels in every department: she looks good, performs well and has first class technical equipment. Above all she offers luxurious accommodation for her owner and his fortunate guests. It is no surprise that further orders for this design are waiting to be built.

SPECIFICATIONS

LOA	49.95m (163ft 10in)	**Stern gangway**	Opac Mare
LWL	42.00m (137ft 10in)	**Side boarding ladder**	BCS
Beam	9.00m (29ft 6in)	**Fire control system**	Autronica BS60
Draught (full load)	2.56m (8ft 5in)	**Communications**	Nera Satcom B, Sailor Satcom C
Displacement (full load)	425 tonnes	**Radar**	Racal Decca C253/9 (1 x S-Band, 1 x X-Band)
Propulsion	2 x 2,262hp MTU 12V396TE94 diesels	**Autopilot & gyrocompass**	Sperry ADG 3500/G
Gearbox	ZF BW 465	**Magnetic compass**	C. Plath
Propellers	Benetti design, 5 skewed blades, nibral	**Echo sounder**	Raytheon
Speed (max/cruise)	18 knots/17 knots	**Exterior paint**	Awlgrip
Fuel capacity	80,000 litres	**Interior designer**	Terence Disdale Design
Range at 12 knots	3,800nm	**Interior decorator**	Alan Jones
Electricity generation	2 x 125kW Northern Lights	**Stylist**	Terence Disdale Design
Stabilisers	Vosper, 2.0m² fins	**Naval architect**	Stefano Natucci
Bowthruster	Vosper 75kW	**Owner & guests**	14 in 6 double & 2 twin cabins
Watermakers	2 x 12,000 l/d	**Crew**	12 in 6 twin bunk cabins
Water capacity	12,000 litres	**Construction**	Steel hull & aluminium superstructure
Sewage & sanitary system	EVAC vacuum system	**Classification**	ABS ✠A1 Yacht Service, AMS. MCA
Windlass	Nanni	**Builder/Year**	Benetti Shipyard/2002

Alithia

Below: *Designed by Bill Tripp, Alithia's styling offers clean lines and more than a hint of a racing yacht. Her ultra fast performance has already been demonstrated with a 10-day transatlantic passage.*

Alithia is a splendid example of a ground-breaking yacht that was built for the dream of a lifetime. As she entered Antigua's Falmouth harbour, fresh from her very first ocean passage, one look at her incredibly striking sleek profile with flush decks and plumb bow instantly set her aside from any grain of superyacht normality. This was a true 'one of a kind' yacht, and behind her was a quite extraordinary dream.

First and foremost it is a story of an amazingly visionary and close husband and wife team, who have sold their home and broken down all the barriers and expectations of a normal Western family lifestyle, to pursue an inspirational dream for themselves and their family of five young children by sailing around the world. With a real breadth of education as their aim and with the support of a team of teachers, scientists and professional yacht crew, they have set out to visit some of the planet's most remote island communities in order to understand and communicate with the local people, and to experience at first hand the real beauty, diversity, harmony and challenges of nature herself.

In order to make their dream come true, they would need a yacht with real blue water capacity, a yacht that could not only sail anywhere and take good care of its crew but also be as simple as possible, so that it could be maintained by that same crew in remote locations. As this was to be their only home for a lengthy period, they needed large and comfortable living quarters, but the accommodation would have to be large enough to carry teachers for the children, as well as the crew. Above all, safety was of paramount importance – particularly in the need to be medically self-sufficient when in remote places. On-board security would also need to be carefully considered, as they planned to sail through some of the world's less politically stable areas.

Far left: The working cockpit is dominated by twin pedestals, which carry the sailing instrumentation.
Left: The deck saloon. Andrew Winch's brief was to reduce Alithia's *interior to the 'essential', thus eliminating all clutter.*

As the owner's first ever yacht, they were in the unique position of being able to address the whole design phase with a totally unfettered approach that challenged the necessity for any superfluous equipment on board. Simplicity, purity and innovation were the goals, and these were to be achieved by focusing only on the 'essential'. Thus the concept for the design was born – the next challenge was to find a team to make it happen.

The highly experienced project manager, Jens Cornelsen was selected as the owner's representative, while naval architect, Bill Tripp was chosen after the owner had completed a previous transatlantic crossing aboard one of his designs. He was duly given the brief to design a real sailing yacht using all the latest available technology, a yacht that 'one could stand, feel and steer' as opposed to the more usual power cruiser into which some sailing superyacht designs evolve. Andrew Winch was chosen to design the lines of the profile, superstructure and the interior, with a brief to reduce everything to the 'essential'. Finally, Abeking and Rasmussen were contracted for the build, as one of the most respected shipyards in the industry.

Construction for the 39.8m (130ft 7in) sloop got under way in June 2000, with the high grade aluminium, Alustar being used to provide a strong, reliable and lightweight hull form that was just 10 tonnes heavier than a composite equivalent. At her launch in March 2002, the long and exhaustive hours, days and months put in by her dedicated building team finally came to fruition, as the next stage of the dream became reality. Named *Alithia* after the Greek word for truth and truthfulness, she became the very fulfilment of her simple, purist brief. From her sleek dark blue hull, and sweeping metallic silver deckhouse, to her minimalist, totally uncluttered teak decks, she looked every bit the purposeful stylish yacht that her owners had intended.

*Above: An abundance
of natural light emphasises
Andrew Winch's interior.
Right: The aft cabin is
unusually designated as a
schoolroom and dormitory.
Far right: The deck saloon
affords dining for up to 10 with
wide views forward and
through the gull-wing
windows on each side.*

Down below, one is immediately impressed by the beautifully light and voluminous interior which, throughout, has a most homogeneous and cohesive feel. Andrew Winch worked closely with the owners to create an interior using a blend of fabrics, painted Canadian maplewood and an abundance of natural light to achieve the calm spirit that runs freely throughout the yacht.

All the accommodation areas have their own air-conditioning units, satellite telephone and intercom communications, as well as discreet indirect lighting. Furthest forward are two comfortable mirror-image en suite cabins to port and starboard which accommodate four crew members. Aft of these, on the port side, is a crew mess fitted with a video entertainment system, alarm monitoring unit and B&G repeater, while a teak step ladder gives direct deck access through a large hatch just forward of the mast.

The captain and his wife's double cabin is situated to starboard, where one is now already beginning to feel the benefit of increased beam for extra space, good stowage and plenty of natural light. The same eye-catching

shower room design runs throughout the yacht, featuring beautifully simple stand-alone wash basins with mirrored cupboards incorporating attractive backlighting.

Further aft to port, one enters the well thought out galley that offers an abundance of workspace and dedicated stowage for all utensils. It is also comprehensively equipped with a Miele microwave and gimballed oven, rubbish compactor, five-minute dishwasher, two freezers, two refrigerators, while a freezer for longer term stowage is located under the sole boards.

Off to starboard is the multi-function library, which besides offering an extensive choice of books also doubles as extra guest accommodation by expanding the sofa into a double berth. It also has its own washroom and shower, which itself double functions as a superb full-height stowage rack for fresh fruit and vegetables when passage-making. But even more remarkably, the room co-exists as the yacht's medical centre with the provision of a ready stowed, custom-fitting operating table and appropriate equipment to allow for intravenous drips, oxygen supply and a real-time, satellite television monitoring system. This informs the 24-hour standby doctor at an international SOS company in South Africa of the patient's temperature, heartbeat, pulse and blood pressure, while allowing full two-way interaction during any operation.

The main saloon is the yacht's entertainment centre, with Bose surround sound stereo and a JVC video/DVD player, low level coffee tables, informal seating, and plenty of natural light and ventilation from four opening portholes that look out across the water. Five steps lead up into the deck saloon, which offers panoramic views at deck level and incorporates a gull-wing opening glass section to port and starboard, giving a wonderfully natural airflow for tropical climes. The large dining table to port offers ample seating for 10, while to starboard, the system monitoring and alarm displays of the navigation station and communications centre are subtly blended into the interior as a whole. Aft, down seven steps on the starboard side, are two identical cabins for the teachers – light and simple in design and adjoined by a shower room – while the engine room is to port. At the very heart of the yacht, this is a voluminous area, with good headroom and stowage that allows plenty of space for service access to the power systems – a 570hp MTU main engine, two MTU generators, an HEM 12,000 litre per day watermaker, and a Hammann waste treatment plant.

Above: *Pure lines and painted Canadian maplewood reflect the spirit of* Alithia's *interior.*

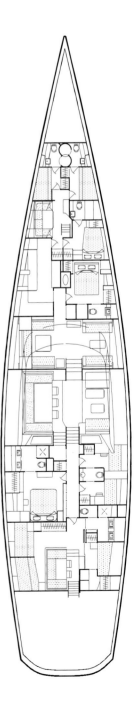

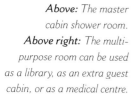

Above: The master cabin shower room.
Above right: *The multi-purpose room can be used as a library, as an extra guest cabin, or as a medical centre.*

Continuing aft down the centreline passageway, on the port side is a most unpretentious yet beautifully light and relaxing owner's cabin, with a double bed appointed with the most delightful cream cotton bedlinen, custom-made by Frette of Italy, while its stylishly simple shower room benefits from double stand-alone glass basin units and backlit mirrors.

Aftermost in the accommodation is one of the yacht's most memorable compartments – a full-beam six-berth children's cabin, adjoined by its own laundry and shower room that is set around a central working table for their schooling. It is here, in the children's cabin, that one can see the whole dream coming together. With the aid of the two specialist teachers on board and the yacht's advanced audio-visual and multi-media infrastructure links via satellite to the French National Centre for Distance Learning, the whole broad educational concept suddenly becomes reality. Indeed there are no less than 14 laptops available, and 24 outlet ports installed throughout the yacht which, together with two wireless LAN networks, give complete roaming access with a laptop from anywhere on board. Furthermore, crew members can communicate with each other through any two of the yacht's on-board servers.

The deck can be accessed by a teak stepladder directly from the children's cabin, where one is immediately struck by the clean look, the flush hatches

Above and left: The portside master cabin is pure and simple with ample light, space and storage.

knots with just one hand on the wheel in 35 knots of wind. Bill Tripp's ultra-fast hull combined the very latest technology with proven hull and foil shapes to create a yacht that sails on the water, not through it. A 10-day transatlantic passage has already set the pace for things to come, with *Alithia* having registered a top speed in excess of 17 knots while in the capable hands of her highly experienced Captain, Graham Pearson, and his wife Olivia. Two of the crew are British ex-military, and will be looking after all aspects of the yacht's security with the help of infra-red passive beams and the yacht's Provilight camera system. They are also advanced paramedics – trained to 'operational standards', so will be well placed to look after their fellow crew members via telemedicine, should the need arise.

In all, one cannot fail to be impressed by the entire concept of *Alithia*, starting from the owners' own personal dedication in sourcing the right team to build their perfect custom yacht, and then organising a first-class professional crew, not only to sail the yacht out over the horizon but also to look after them at all times. And lastly, by providing teachers with the latest electronic means to give their children the opportunity to search for truth in life and learning, aboard the well-named *Alithia*.

and the huge amount of deck space available because the hull design carries the full beam all the way aft. The working cockpit has two steering pedestals, B&G Hydra 2000 displays and four screens upon which the Transas navigation, radar, and systems monitoring alarms can be displayed. All the hydraulic sail handling hardware is by Rondal, while the impressive 49.1m (161ft) carbon mast and internal furling boom from Marten Marine houses a fully-battened North mainsail.

In the cockpit, two large tables fold out to meet each other on the centreline, forming a superbly large dining area where the ample seating receives shade from a cockpit bimini, while a refrigerator ensures a constant supply of cool drinks.

At the stern, a large full-beam transom door lowers to the waterline to launch anything from a pool of exciting watersports equipment that includes two Laser one-design sailing dinghies.

Under way, *Alithia* has proved herself beyond doubt, as the owner himself has proved by sailing her upwind at 12

SPECIFICATIONS

LOA	39.80m (130ft 7in)		**Waste treatment system**	Hamann
LWL	35.20m (115ft 6in)		**Air-conditioning**	Heinen & Hopmann,
Beam (max)	8.38m (27ft 6in)			Marine Air Systems
Draught (centreboard up)	4.00m (13ft 1in)		**Communications**	SSB, 2 x Satcom-B,
Draught (centreboard down)	6.35m (20ft 10in)			Satcom-C, Satcom-Mini M
Displacement	130 tonnes		**Sailing systems**	B&G, Hydra 2000
Spars	Marten Marine		**Electronic charting**	Transas Navisailor3000
Sailmaker	North Sails		**Entertainment system**	Bose
Sail areas: (mainsail)	444m² (4,777ft²)		**Security system**	Infra-red passive beams &
(genoa)	317m² (3,411ft²)			Provilight camera system
(staysail)	99m² (1,065ft²)		**Paint system**	Awlgrip
(gennaker)	882m² (9,490ft²)		**Hull construction**	Alustar
Propulsion	1 x 570hp MTU 6R183TE93 diesel		**Classification**	Germanischer Lloyd
Fuel capacity	12,000 litres		**Project management**	Jens Cornelsen
Generators	2 x MTU 6R099 AZ51		**Naval architecture**	Bill Tripp Design
Bow and stern thrusters	Max Power, 60hp		**Styling**	Andrew Winch Designs
Watermaker	HEM 30/3200, 12,000 l/d		**Interior design**	Andrew Winch Designs
Water capacity	3,950 litres		**Builder/Year**	Abeking & Rasmussen/2002

Balaju

Right: Balaju, built from composite, was designed as a series production yacht.
Below: The pilothouse.

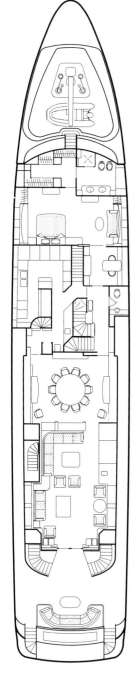

In general, European yacht builders have been slower than those in America to adopt composite plastics as a building material for hulls over 30m (98ft) in length. This is, in part, because of the large investment in tooling required, and in part because it was felt that purchasers of yachts in this size range have usually expected a totally custom design. But things are changing and the success of semi-custom designs built from composite materials, such as the Benetti Classic, shows that there is a growing market for such yachts.

In Italy, no shipyard has greater experience of very large composite hulls than the Sarzana-based Intermarine, which for a very long time has built mine hunters and patrol boats in this material for the Italian and other governments. Some years ago the yard set up a subsidiary in Savannah, USA to build mine hunters for the US Navy, although this company is now completely independent of its original parent. More recently the Italian company decided to diversify into the yacht market and its own naval architects drew up a very attractive displacement hull of 44.5m (146ft) overall and appointed the well-known Italian designer François Zuretti to create a layout and interior design.

Having no real experience of the yacht market,

Intermarine took the sensible decision to work with one of the top international brokerage agencies, Camper and Nicholsons, who created a specification for a charter yacht to MCA certification standards, the expectation being that Intermarine would in due course build up to ten of these yachts. But in the unexpected way that things often turn out, the first hull from these moulds has been completed as a private yacht, with its specification rewritten for the owner by Inigo Nicholson of Silver

Yachts, whose father George is the head of Camper and Nicholsons. To stretch coincidence even further, Camper and Nicholsons has since become part of the Rodriguez Group while Intermarine now comes under the Rodriquez Group – the one that builds ferries.

In spite of this rather complex background, it is clear that a great deal of experience has gone into the planning and building of *Balaju*. The hull is constructed from a single skin of solid GRP laminate, while the decks and

Above left: *A bar is built into the aft side of the sun deck's pool.*
Above: *Alfresco dining on the bridge deck.*

superstructure are sandwich construction GRP. Although sandwich construction is stiffer and lighter than solid laminate, it is often considered unsuitable for hull construction because of the risk of water penetration following damage to the outer skin. Solid laminate, on the other hand, is tough and straightforward to repair. For the superstructure, there is every argument in favour of sandwich construction, including low weight, stiffness, good heat and sound insulation, and the ability to build in curvature without additional building expense.

Being rather lighter than an equivalent steel hull, *Balaju* has turned out to be relatively lively in her motion at sea but very responsive to helm and power inputs. Her motion under way is well controlled by the Koop Nautic stabilisers but the owners are considering upgrading to the latest type, which is also effective in damping motion

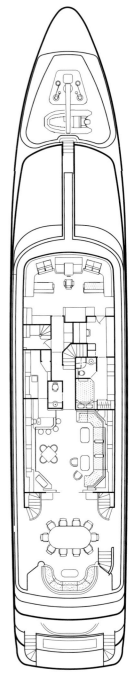

while at anchor. Everyone agrees that she is exceptionally quiet, both under way and at anchor.

The exterior styling is very successful as *Balaju* appears graceful and well proportioned in spite of being a high-volume hull with full-beam superstructure for about half of her length. Although she has three full decks plus a sun deck, the 'wedding cake' look has been avoided completely. No tenders are visible, as they are stowed in a capacious aft garage. In fact, the only boat carried on deck is the obligatory MCA rescue boat that nestles out of sight on the foredeck.

Useful deck area is strongly emphasised in *Balaju's* exterior design. On the well-planned sun deck, the raised spa pool is almost centrally placed, so that it is just clear of the shade created by radar arch, while the bar stools around its aft side are just out of the sun, assuming the sun is roughly overhead. Right forward, a row of sunpads are tucked in behind the streamlined glass windscreen that protects them from the inevitable breeze,

while a sweeping semicircle of settees follows the aft rail.

Curving stairs drop down to the upper deck, where a large oval teak table provides the favourite venue for an outdoor meal for as many as a dozen people, while a smaller table surrounded by seats offers space for a more intimate group. In addition to being partly shaded by the deck above, there are roller blinds that pull down at each side. On this level there are full side decks that meet in front of the pilothouse, from where a Portuguese bridge descends to the foredeck.

The main deck provides a further small seating area and table right aft but, more important, it is from here that one descends stairs to the teak-planked aft platform, either to swim or to board one of the tenders. Boats, waveriders and other sports equipment are lifted out by an overhead crane which extends aft over the platform.

A feature to which Inigo Nicholson attaches great importance is the aft engine room, which has many advantages, including the fact that there are no shafts,

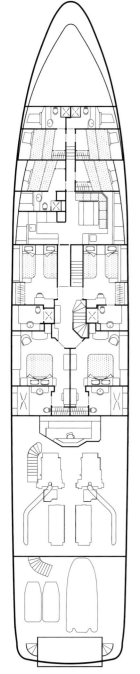

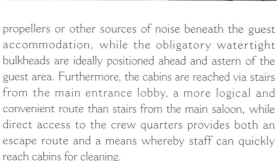

propellers or other sources of noise beneath the guest accommodation, while the obligatory watertight bulkheads are ideally positioned ahead and astern of the guest area. Furthermore, the cabins are reached via stairs from the main entrance lobby, a more logical and convenient route than stairs from the main saloon, while direct access to the crew quarters provides both an escape route and a means whereby staff can quickly reach cabins for cleaning.

In designing the décor for *Balaju*, Zuretti decided to step back a little from his usual decorative style towards a simple, modern look that appears clean and unobtrusive. The keynote timber used throughout the guest accommodation is lime-rubbed oak with radiused corners that are echoed on virtually all the furniture. Cabinets and tables are all burl oak, normally with marble tops. All carpets are plain off-white wool, while the saloon seating is either off-white silk brocade or royal blue velvet.

This calm decorative style positively invites the addition of artwork, and the owner of *Balaju* has responded with a very interesting selection of modern paintings from his own collection, while the yacht is certain to acquire some more ornaments on her travels. For instance, the translucent sliding screen that separates the main saloon from the dining room would provide an ideal background for a mural.

The owner's suite, forward on the main deck, is also simple and modern, though it is noticeable that Zuretti has included a few of his favourite art deco touches such as glass uplighters on a gold sconce. In addition to wooden venetian blinds, which can be used to adjust the amount of daylight entering, all the windows have roman blinds in various fabrics that add colour and interest at night. When originally designed for charter, the owner's cabin had twin bathrooms, but as she was replanned as a private yacht one of these was replaced by a large walk-in wardrobe. The remaining bathroom has wash-basins and a steam shower but no bath is fitted,

Left: Spacious and modern in its design, the owner's suite comprises a study, bedroom, shower room and a large walk-in wardrobe.
Far left above: A double guest cabin. Each of the cabins has a subtle colour variation.
Far left centre: One of the twin guest cabins. Noise levels are kept low because their position, forward of the engine room, means that they are remote from shafts and propellers.
Far left below: The master suite's shower room.

being a feature that the owner does not especially desire.

On the lower deck there are four very comfortable en suite guest staterooms – two doubles and two twins – grouped around a central lobby, all having subtle colour variations on the decorative theme that runs throughout the yacht. It should be added that all the cabins have first-class entertainment systems, with a very wide selection of satellite television channels available in addition to a huge choice of recorded sound and video.

The upper saloon shows a more carefree style, the large corner settee being upholstered in sea blue enlivened by leaping goldfish. A glamorous white marble bar occupies one corner of the room, while a wide-screen television rises on command from a hidden stowage. Throughout the yacht, the service routes have been carefully planned. This bar, for instance, backs into a pantry which has a food lift from the galley and a doorway onto the side deck, so that it can be used as the servery when meals are being taken at the outdoor table. A service stairway leads down from this pantry to the main one below, so that crew can move from deck to deck invisibly.

Mechanically, *Balaju* is relatively conventional, with twin Caterpillar diesels giving a maximum speed of around 16 knots. A special feature is that additional fuel tanks are fitted to provide a transoceanic range of

3,800 miles at 10 knots if required. For normal cruising with the standard tanks of 36,000 litres in use, a range of 2,000 miles at 12 knots will be more than adequate.

In addition to being a most attractive yacht in her own right, *Balaju* provides the evidence of a very well planned semi-custom production series. Whether further examples are built remains to be seen, but it would certainly be surprising if they were not.

SPECIFICATIONS

LOA	44.50m (146ft)
LWL	37.40m (112ft 8in)
Beam	8.60m (28ft 3in)
Draught	1.86m (6ft 1in)
Displacement (with standard fuel tanks)	275 tonnes
Propulsion	2 x 1,300hp Caterpillar 3508B diesels
Gearbox	ZF
Steering	Marsili
Speed (max & cruise)	16 knots
Fuel capacity (standard/extended)	36,000l/46,000l
Range (standard tanks at 12 knots)	2,000nm
(extended tanks at 10 knots)	3,800nm
Generators	2 x 125kW Northern Lights
Watermakers	Idromar
Fresh water capacity	8,000 litres
Sewage treatment	Evac Systems
Stabilisers	Koop Nautic
Bowthruster	Koop Nautic
Crane & passerelle	Motomar
Air-conditioning	Condaria
Fuel separator	Veronesi
Radars	Furuno
Owner & guests	10 in 3 x double & 2 x twin cabins
Crew	10 in 1 x double & 4 x twin bunk cabins
Construction	Solid GRP hull, GRP sandwich decks & superstructure
Interior designer	François Zuretti
Naval architect	Intermarine Spa
Classification	ABS ⊕A1 Yachting Service. MCA Code
Builder/Year	Intermarine Spa/2002

Bart Roberts

Below: Converted from a Canadian Coastguard vessel, the 80.7m Bart Roberts *is now a charter vessel with an unusual pirate theme.*

Over the years, *The Superyachts* has featured a number of outstanding conversions of commercial vessels into privately-owned yachts, with ocean-going tugs providing the most popular raw material to work with. However, none of these projects has been quite as ambitious or intriguing as the conversion of the 80.77m (265ft) Canadian Coastguard icebreaker into the unique 'pirate-themed' charter vessel *Bart Roberts*.

Almost everything about the story is surprising. It began when Arnie Gemino, whose business is in the aviation industry in Florida, was looking for a suitable vessel to convert for his own use. When the Canadian Coastguard declared their ship *Narwhal* surplus to requirements and put her up for auction, it was immediately apparent that she was far too large for his personal use, but she presented such a tempting opportunity that he decided to put in a bid anyway.

Although she is an old ship, having been built in 1963 by Canadian Vickers at Montreal, three facts made the *Narwhal* especially attractive. The first was that in 1986 she had been given a $20 million refit, amounting to a virtual rebuild that included completely new machinery and equipment throughout and, secondly, that the Coastguard were offering to include a huge spares inventory with the sale due to the fact that *Narwhal* was the last ship of her class in service. Thirdly, she is beamy with a shallow draught, having an average draught of only 3.8m (12.5ft) – roughly what one would expect of a 60m (197ft) motor yacht rather than an 80m (262ft) ship – and this helps to make cruising a practical proposition.

In the event, there were only two bidders, Gemino's company, Tradepower International, and the Russian Government, which was simply looking to acquire an ice-classed supply ship cheaply. To Gemino's considerable surprise, his bid was successful. The immediate task was to decide what to do with the ship and Gemino quickly came up with an imaginative and

unusual plan to convert her into a luxury charter vessel with a pirate theme.

It soon became obvious that she could not be registered as a yacht because she was too big to be economic with the usual limit of 12 paying passengers. As a result, she was converted under full Lloyd's supervision into a SOLAS-approved passenger vessel, licensed to carry up to 36 passengers, although in reality she is

Above: Using the crane's 23.8m extended reach, Bart Roberts' *tenders and storage boxes can easily be lifted aboard.*

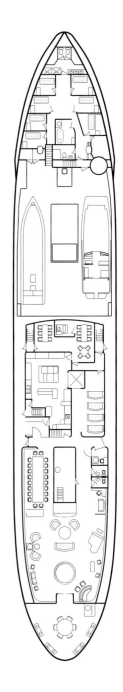

turbo-diesel landing craft, large enough to carry a full-sized sports utility vehicle and fendered so that it can double as a pusher-tug if required. Coming alongside the port side, one steps out onto a broad platform that hinges down from the ship's side just above water level. From here, stairs lead up to the main deck, the whole access route having been built within a steel casing so there is no risk of accidental flooding.

The stairway leads out onto the large open main deck that is planked, not with teak but with mature Douglas fir, in the centre of which is a 3m by 6m (20ft by 10ft) swimming pool: not the usual little 'splash-about' pool that one finds on yachts, but a proper pool in which one can swim up and down. This is fitted flush with the deck in the position originally occupied by the main cargo hatch and has been engineered in an ingenious way so that when not required, it can be lowered down into the hold and moved to one side on rollers, enabling large items, including a 6m (20ft) standard shipping container, to be hoisted up or down.

The pool, the stores and the tenders are all lifted by a 30-tonne hydraulic crane, with a maximum reach of 23.8m (78ft). In addition to the landing craft, *Bart Roberts* carries a 15m (49ft) Thriller Cat in which 25 passengers can experience a white-knuckle ride at speeds up to 113kph (70mph). For more mundane tasks, a RIB tender and a rescue boat are carried. One of the drawbacks of a commercial ship is that the accommodation is normally concentrated at one end of the hull but at least in the case of *Bart Roberts* it is the best end – aft. The existing superstructure was extensively remodelled to provide luxurious accommodation, including the addition of a second deck forward of the superstructure, to form a balcony for the VIP suite.

The most difficult task was to create the large open area needed for the main saloon, which basically takes up the whole of the aft section of the superstructure. Its very large floor area of 185.8m² (2,000ft²) demands a correspondingly large headroom, and to achieve the 3m (10ft) that was deemed necessary, two decks were opened into one, using a massive new deck beam to

Far left: *The fireplace centrepiece is inset with two halves of an authentic bronze cannon, and topped by a portrait of the pirate, Black Bart Roberts.*
Left: *Settee seating in the on-board cinema.*
Far left below: *The Yamaha self-playing piano is linked into the yacht's sound system.*
Left below: *The main lobby.*

luxuriously configured to carry 20 guests. In some ways this was not as high a hurdle as it sounds because the ship was already built and equipped to the highest standards, and had no difficulty in passing the survey on a technical level. To give just one example, in Coastguard service the galley was equipped to serve up to 160 meals per day, and so easily meets all hygiene and safety requirements. The big challenge was to give her completely new and attractive accommodation.

The work was carried out, not by a conventional shipyard but by direct labour, with the ship lying alongside a disused ferry berth in Victoria, British Columbia. Naval architect Lennart Edstrom turned Arnie Gemino's ideas into engineering drawings and then hired the shipwrights and craftsmen as required, with up to 100 people on the payroll at the peak of activity. No one could have called the old *Narwhal* beautiful, but by extending the bow, cleaning up the profile and rebuilding the superstructure, *Bart Roberts* has emerged as a handsome, purposeful vessel.

Guests can board her from a boat, having been ferried from the shore by the ship's custom-built twin

support the structure. The saloon is one of the most incredible rooms ever seen afloat, being entirely floored with antique bricks set in a herringbone pattern. To avoid loss of headroom, each of several thousand bricks was carefully sawn in half and set in cement that had been levelled to eliminate the deck camber. The centrepiece is an enormous fireplace built up from 14 tonnes of natural

stone and topped off with a mantlepiece made from an authentic bronze cannon, sliced in two lengthways.

On the port side of the saloon is a bar with a collection of 'treasure' set in the clear resin counter, while to starboard is a Yamaha self-playing grand piano that is linked to the main sound system. Between these is a seating area and a dance floor, complete with a pillar that

heads and a small but very comfortable movie and sound room. Just by the entrance to the theatre is a passenger lift that links all decks.

A further deck up brings one to the level of the five principal guest suites, all of which have outside views. The VIP suite stretches right across the forward side of the superstructure with its own private balcony outside, the very large central bedroom being flanked by a lavishly equipped en suite bathroom on one side and a walk-in wardrobe and separate head on the other. The three other doubles and one twin cabin also have en suite bathrooms with full-sized tubs, each cabin being named after the pirate whose portrait adorns the wall. All the beds and other furniture are in a Spanish colonial style, rather as if the rascally Black Bart Roberts had ransacked them from passing galleons. Five more cabins of roughly equal size are positioned on the lower deck, forward of the engine room, and although they are

Above left: A bar sits in the corner of the main saloon.
Above: 'Treasure' has been inlaid into the bar's resin counter.
Below: Sound and disco lights are concentrated upon the circular hardwood dance floor in the saloon.

retracts into the ceiling. The dining room, with its gigantic oak table – large enough for more than 20 diners – is on the port side, separated from the saloon by an aquarium filled with piranha fish. Along the dining room wall is a large painting by Jeff Maltby, one of a number that were specially commissioned for the ship. In the corresponding position on the starboard side are an office, a pair of day

Right: The VIP suite, which opens to a balcony deck that was added to the forward part of the superstructure.
Below: Luxurious bathroom facilities in the master stateroom.

Above: Each of the guest cabins is named after a pirate, with an appropriate theme and portrait to match.

compartment. The tankage and storage dimensions are sufficiently large for *Bart Roberts* to cruise for many months without resupply. And although she has been decorated and equipped with the Caribbean in mind, in fact she could cruise without problem anywhere in the world, hot or cold. The crew live in roomy quarters in the forecastle, while officers have cabins abaft the bridge.

The conversion of *Narwhal* into *Bart Roberts* could have been done quickly and on the cheap, but in fact the whole process has been completed to a very high standard. Although the whole 'pirate' theme is light-hearted, it does not lack taste in view of the high quality of both the materials and the workmanship. Cruising aboard *Bart Roberts* should be a very special experience and a great deal of fun. Without doubt, she is the most extreme and unusual vessel ever to grace these pages.

equipped and decorated to the same high standard, they do not have sea views.

Bart Roberts has a reasonable, if not huge, amount of open deck in addition to the tender deck. From the saloon, doors open onto a sheltered aft deck where an outside dining table can be set, an area that can be protected by side-screens or be air-conditioned if required. A sun deck, protected by windscreens, has been created on top of the bridge and this is fun to visit because it is high above the ship and has excellent views. Aft of the funnel is the helicopter deck and hangar. Fitted during her Coastguard career, this fully approved heli-deck and heated telescopic hanger seemed too good a facility to throw away, particularly as there is even a 18,925 litre (4,163gal) jet refuelling system that could be brought back into service if required.

To anyone used to looking over motor yachts, the technical areas of *Bart Roberts* seem huge, with vast main engines that one can stroll around with plenty of space to spare, the generators being located in an entirely separate

SPECIFICATIONS

LOA	80.77m (265ft 0in)	Cranes	Aurora 30 ton, hydraulic
LWL	67.00m (219ft 10in)	Air-conditioning	ASAC 240,000Btu (120 tons)
Beam	12.80m (42ft 0in)	Tenders	15,2m (50ft) Thriller Cat &
Draught	3.80m (12ft 6in)		11.6m (38ft) WE Munson landing craft
Displacement	2,425 tonnes	Communications	Skanti Inmarsat Mini M, SSB
Propulsion	2 x 2,000hp Ruston 6RKC diesels	Radars	Raytheon
Gearbox	Ulstein	Chart plotter	Raymarine
Propellers	Ulstein, variable pitch	Wind instruments	Raymarine
Speed (max)	13 knots	Construction	Steel hull & superstructure
Fuel capacity	416,394 litres	Classification	Lloyd's ✠100A1, LMC
Range at 12 knots	10,000nm		SOLAS Commercial Code for 36 passengers
Generators	3 x 250kW Baudouin &	Refit naval architect	Lennart Edstrom
	1 x 200kW Baudouin emergency unit	Refit interior design	Tradepower International
Bowthruster	0min, 400hp		& Karen Bamford
Watermaker	Seagold, 13,250l/d	Artwork	Jeff Maltby
Water capacity	22,144 litres	Brokerage	CNI Palm Beach
Sewage treatment	St Louis Ship D5, Evac	Builder/Year	Canadian Vickers/1963
Ballast water capacity	311,000 litres	Refit/Year	Tradepower International/2002

Borkumriff IV

Below right: Borkumriff's *owner united design teams from America and Europe, employing Niels Helleberg of Alden Design and Gerry Dijkstra as naval architects, while John Munford was responsible for the interior.*

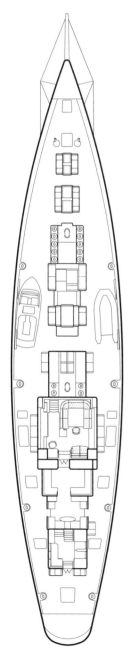

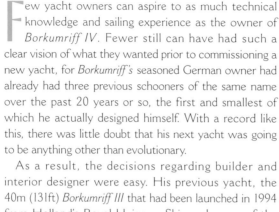

Few yacht owners can aspire to as much technical knowledge and sailing experience as the owner of *Borkumriff IV*. Fewer still can have had such a clear vision of what they wanted prior to commissioning a new yacht, for *Borkumriff's* seasoned German owner had already had three previous schooners of the same name over the past 20 years or so, the first and smallest of which he actually designed himself. With a record like this, there was little doubt that his next yacht was going to be anything other than evolutionary.

As a result, the decisions regarding builder and interior designer were easy. His previous yacht, the 40m (131ft) *Borkumriff III* that had been launched in 1994 from Holland's Royal Huisman Shipyard – one of the world's most impressive and revered builders of aluminium sailing yachts – had served him well. Engaging Royal Huisman's considerable services once again was, therefore, a safe bet.

He was also keen for John Munford to recreate a similarly peaceful and traditionally panelled environment below decks in what, by this time, he clearly envisaged as a scaled-up version of *Borkumriff III*. The new yacht, *Borkumriff IV,* was to be a long-keeled aluminium schooner of 50m (164ft) or so in length, that would be capable of extended cruising with the owner and no more than four guests, supported by a crew of up to nine.

However, when it came to selecting a principal firm of naval architects, a keystone in any new-build programme, his choice proved rather more difficult. Over the years he had established a real rapport with two highly accomplished firms on two different continents. Niels Helleberg of Alden Design in Boston, Massachusetts had particularly impressed him with the wealth of schooner wisdom held in his long-established office, particularly that relating to the much admired Gloucester fishing schooners of the late 19th- and early 20th-centuries, craft whose capabilities had evolved as skippers and crews sought speed advantage in what was then not only a potentially very lucrative industry but also a highly competitive one. But then he had also got to know Gerard Dijkstra and his Amsterdam studio, whose track record is unrivalled in respect of large traditional sailing vessels, and particularly their sail plans and sail-handling systems.

In the event, deciding between them proved too much, and this dictated an alternative solution. After much consultation and deliberation, the design team was finally completed by a quite unique design co-operation between Alden Design and Gerard Dijkstra & Partners, recalls *Borkumriff IV's* captain and project manager, Malcolm

Bromilow, who drew up the necessary design parameters for the owner and eventually rewrote the specifications.

Although the idea of two such well known and capable design firms, either of which could have easily carried the brief alone, being united in a collaborative project appeared somewhat strange, the association apparently worked perfectly. The practicalities were simple enough. Both firms communicated very closely with the owner and with each other on the overall scheme, before taking individual responsibility for specific areas – such as the bow, the sheer line, deck layout, hull apertures and so on. Alden Design led on the long-keel form and the attached

Left: Borkumriff IV *has already exceeded her theoretical hull speed of 14.6 knots.*

Far left: Aesthetically, Borkumriff IV *is all-classic, from her clipper bow to her counter stern, but she is also a yacht that abounds with high technology.*

rudder, so it is no coincidence that her underwater profile bears more than a passing resemblance to some of the best Gloucester schooners. Dijkstra, on the other hand, took greater responsibility for the sail and deck plans, while both were equally involved with weight and stability calculations.

From the decision to initiate the project in mid-1998, when a building slot was secured at the Royal Huisman Shipyard, it took nine months of rigorous design work – a process that included tank testing at the Delft Institute in Holland and wind-tunnel testing at the Southampton-based Wolfson Institute in the UK – until metal was finally cut in the spring of 1999.

The chosen hull material was Alustar, a relatively new alloy from Corus that Royal Huisman embraced as soon as it became available over five years ago and which they have used exclusively ever since. Alustar is said to provide 20% more tensile strength and significantly better corrosion resistance than the conventional marine choice of AA5083 aluminium, for only a slightly greater expense. Such benefits give designers and builders the option of going for either lighter yachts for a given strength or stronger yachts for a given weight. With her fuel and water tanks half full,

Borkumriff IV ended up with a displacement of just under 300 tonnes, which suggests her designers optimised with regard to strength and durability.

Outwardly Borkumriff IV is indeed a scaled up version of her earlier namesakes, another distinct evolutionary step for the twin-masted topsail schooner whose origins lie in north-east America. Aesthetically, she is certainly a classic – from her clipper bow, complete with finely raked and scalloped stem and belligerent bowsprit, to that high arc-like transom and its long clear counter. Indeed the differential between her overall length of 50.58m (165ft 11in), including her bowsprit, to her waterline length of 35.81m (117ft 6in) is quite dramatic. Never forget, however, that these bygone looks conceal the fact that her engineering and superyacht systems are firmly rooted in the 21st-century – Borkumriff IV is, without doubt, a state-of-the-art ocean cruising yacht.

Above deck and aft of her mainmast she sports first a deckhouse and aftmost a pilothouse, all made from beautifully varnished teak, as are the cappings that define her sheers. The cockpit sits between, where the focus of the aft working area is the classic brass binnacle and a wonderfully traditionally helm position in which the spoked wooden wheel is set on the forward side of its gearbox and the latter set against the pilothouse. Flanked by a pair of seats, the helmsman has the choice of either standing beside one side or other of the wheel, sitting outboard on either of the seats and steering with one hand, or of sitting astride the support box, directly behind the wheel. Interestingly, the steering aboard this yacht relies on a mechanical rod and gear mechanism, to which a Tenfjord Segatron autopilot system is also connected.

Although all the usual modern navigation instruments are to hand, they are located discreetly so as not to detract from that classic yachting experience – not only for the helm but also for those in the guest seating that occupies the area immediately forward of the steering cockpit and behind the deckhouse.

Between her mainmast and foremast, Borkumriff IV sports two yacht tenders beneath canvas covers, both of which sit on deck cradles and launch from davits of traditional appearance, but made from carbon. To port is the owner's 6m (19ft 8in) pilot boat, an interpretation of a 1935 Alden-designed 'commodore's launch' that was built using a wood core and GRP sheathing by Walsted in Denmark. To starboard is a more contemporary 4.5m (14ft 9in) Avon RIB with a 30hp Honda outboard for crew use. Beyond the usual foredeck equipment, there are several box lockers and two separate companionways that connect with crew and galley areas below.

As for her rig, which demands a massive 50m (164ft) air draught, Borkumriff IV's two tapered masts are made from Alustar plate, but her Park Avenue booms are carbon, as is her gaff pole and staysail boom. The bowsprit is fabricated from a high-tensile Duplex stainless steel. Unsurprisingly, all her spars, hydraulic headsail furlers, captive reel and drum winches, and much of her deck hardware were supplied by Rondal, a daughter company of Royal Huisman. Ocean Yacht Systems supplied the rigging, and the running rigging was a mix of Dyneema and Vectran ropes.

Her already fairly extensive sail wardrobe is actually the work of three lofts. Hood Sails UK was responsible for the 'working' Dacron sails, while Doyle USA produced one of its new OceanWeave Vectran mainsails and Doyle France made all the 'lightweights', such as the topsail, the fisherman and a snuffled MPS, the tack of which hooks to a snout ring on the tip of the bowsprit.

Under sail Borkumriff IV is quite awesome. Beyond the

Below: The main saloon, panelled in mahogany, has an abundance of natural light to illuminate its artwork, which includes paintings of Kaiser Wilhelm's schooner Meteor and four half models showing the evolution of the Borkumriff hulls.

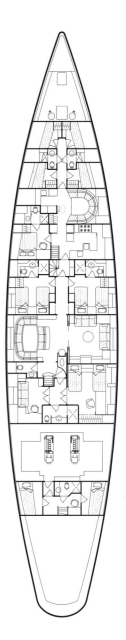

Above: The master cabin features twin beds, divided by an inbuilt armchair. *Right:* John Munford's quintessential style is seen in one of the two twin-bedded guest cabins.

occasional glimpse of technology, such as radar and communications antennae, her dramatic white hull and cream spars and sails are nostalgia at its high-powered best. Her theoretical hull speed is 14.6 knots, but in 50 degrees of apparent wind, with no topsail set, she has already exceeded that comfortably. The topsail, which is particularly useful for pointing, is only carried to around 25 knots apparent. Having sailed away from the yard in May 2002, she spent her first few months enjoying the western end of the Mediterranean – the Balearics in June and July, and Sardinia and Corsica during August, before returning to her home port of Antibes for September.

Under power she is propelled by her 1,072hp MTU/DDC Series 2000 diesel, driving a four-blade 1.2m-diameter variable-pitch LIPS propeller that is hooked up to an automatic control system developed by Royal Huisman engineers. The maximum speed under engine alone is around 12 knots, but the normal cruising speed would be nearer 10 knots, a speed at which her range would be around 2,500 nautical miles. However, by motor sailing – normal during delivery trips – that range could effectively be doubled.

The main guest entrance to *Borkumriff IV*'s interior is by means of the deckhouse. From the cockpit, a couple of steps take one down to a delightful deck saloon that

cathedral dome-style skylight on deck, located just forward of the mainmast. The walls are particularly interesting – not only is there a set of half models showing the evolution of all four *Borkumriff* hulls, but there are also many sail plans of Kaiser Wilhelm's *Meteor* racing schooners, not to mention some fine marine paintings and the antique octant presented to the owner by the three designers.

The lobby also gives acess to the guest day head and the entrance to the owner's suite. The suite consists of a twin-bedded cabin with a dressing area on the starboard side, a combined study and sitting room to port, and a hall and shower room in between.

Forward of the main saloon, a corridor leads to the guest cabins which lie to port and starboard, mirror images of each other, each with an en suite shower room. As the owner generally likes to sail with his wife and family, or occasionally with one or two close friends, two guest cabins were considered sufficient. Sensibly, one of the cabins has one of its beds lower than the other so that it can be used as a sofa when the cabin only has a single occupant.

Beyond the guest corridor is a small lobby from which a stairway rises to the deck. A second, watertight door opens forward to the yacht's service areas and crew quarters; an impressive galley, the captain's double cabin, crew mess, utility area, and four single crew cabins, two of them with Pullman bunks for additional passage crew.

Either side of the engine room door, two further crew cabins – for the engineer and mate – are accessed from steps from the aft pilothouse, while the pilothouse itself also offers a pilot berth in addition to being the yacht's navigation station and office.

By combining the efforts of some of the world's most experienced craftsmen and sailing yacht designers, coupled with a passionate feel for sailing, the owner of *Borkumriff IV* has created a modern yacht of great style and beauty that is sure to be hugely admired, both by traditionalists and by enthusiasts of modern technology.

Above: *The owner's suite incorporates a large study-cum-sitting room, attractively panelled in Brazilian mahogany.*

provides a small sofa, a dining table and a writing desk, creating a perfect day room while sailing or at rest, and an alternative location for informal meals if conditions are unsuitable on deck. Its particularly noteworthy features include a pair of custom-made, eight-gauge signalling cannons, working replicas of those used aboard the historic *USS Anson*, which are said to be capable of a considerable bang when the occasion demands.

Borkumriff IV's accommodation is quintessential John Munford, widely acclaimed for his 'gentleman's yacht' interiors, with their raised and fielded panelling, and beamed, white-painted deckheads. This classic deckhouse scheme aboard *Borkumriff IV* is carried throughout the yacht, although the satin-varnished veneers here are teak and those below Brazilian mahogany. In style and feel, it is similar to *Borkumriff III's* interior, although hers was dressed in cherrywood. All the veneers aboard this latest yacht are beautifully offset by blue buttoned-leather and quality cotton upholstery.

Stairs descend forward from the deckhouse to a lobby which opens forward to the saloon. Occupying the yacht's whole beam, a vast dining table fills the port side and a lounge the starboard, while fore and aft sliding panel doors offer the possibility of dividing the two. Natural light is abundant, thanks to a simply massive

SPECIFICATIONS

LOA 50.58m (165ft 11in)	**Propeller** . . Lips (auto variable pitch system by RHS)
LWL 35.81m (117ft 6in)	**Generators** . . . . . . 2 x 70kW, 1 x 30kW & 1 x 40kW
Beam (max) 9.24m (30ft 4in)	. . . . MTU/Leroy Somer
Draught 4.30m (14ft 1in)	**Fuel capacity** . . . . 21,760 litres
Air draught 50m (164ft 0in)	**Speed under power (max)** . . . . 12 knots
Displacement (half load) . . . . 298.8 tonnes	**Range at 10 knots** 2,500nm
Ballast . . . . 93.9 tonnes	**Deck hardware** . . . . Rondal
Spars . . . . Rondal, aluminium masts & carbon booms	**Autopilot** . . . . Tenfjord Segatron
Sails . . . . . Hood Sails UK/Doyle Superyacht Group	**Hydraulic system** . . . . Bosch Rexroth/RHS
Sail areas (mainsail) 403m² (4,336ft²)	**Bowthrusters** . . . . HRP 200-65, 68kW, hydraulic
(foresail) . . . . 252m²(2,711ft²)	**Watermaker** . . . . 2 x HEM 30/3200, 12,000 l/d
(outer jib) 226m² (2,432ft²)	**Owner & guests** . . . . 6 in 3 x twin cabins
(inner jib) 141m² (1,517ft²)	**Crew** . . . . 9 in 1 x double & 6 x single/twin
(staysail) 77m² (828ft²)	**Construction** . . . . . . Alustar aluminium hull & deck
(topsail) 65m² (699ft²)	**Classification** . . . . Lloyd's Hull Certificate
Rigging . . . . Ocean Yacht Systems	**Interior design** . . . . John Munford Design
Propulsion . . . 1 x 1,072hp MTU/DDC 12V2000 diesel	**Naval architecture** . . . Gerard Dijkstra/John G Alden
Gearbox . . . . ZF BW255, 2.75:1	**Builder/Year** . . . . . . Royal Huisman Shipyard/2002

Campbell Bay

Right: Designed by Diana Yacht Design and built by Hakvoort Shipyard, Campbell Bay is a classic displacement motor yacht with a top speed of 13 knots.

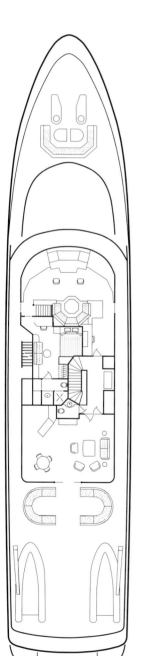

The trick that every yacht owner, naval architect and designer would like to achieve is a boat that is much roomier on the inside than she appears to be on the outside. In the search for more volume, extra decks can be added, the superstructure extended almost to the bow, side decks eliminated, the hull made beamier and more straight-sided until one ends up with something that looks like a car ferry. Not pretty!

Stanley and Peggy Bey have, however, pulled off the trick with their new 44.7m (146ft 8in) Hakvoort-built motor yacht *Campbell Bay*, creating a deceptively roomy interior within an attractive yacht with a well-balanced profile and a seaworthy hull, while incorporating traditional touches such as walk-around decks.

Stanley Bey's own experience includes ownership of a series of sailing yachts and then two motor yachts, the first the innovative triple-jet *Pegasus* built for him by Broward, and the second a refitted Feadship. His objective with *Campbell Bay* (Peggy is the Campbell, while he is the Bay) was to create the best yacht possible without exceeding 500 tonnes displacement and without spending a ridiculous amount of money. To do this, he assembled an exceptional team: Ken Denison of Broward Yacht Sales, to create the specification; Diana Yacht Design as naval architect; Andrew Winch as designer; Hakvoort as builder; and Rusty Allen as captain and owner's agent. Hakvoort is a relatively small, family-owned shipyard that builds one yacht at a time and gives each one its full attention. Stanley and Peggy Bey found them to be extremely thorough and a pleasure to deal with.

The basic hull design had already been used twice by Hakvoort, the previous example being *Lady Duvera*, a yacht which Bey liked because its large 8.8m (28ft 10in) beam made it possible to have all-round decks without unduly compromising internal space. However, he felt that she looked a little bulky, so he asked Diana Yacht

Far left: The spa pool on the forward part of the sun deck is edged with sunbathing cushions.
Left: On the bridge deck, a delightful alfresco dining area is positioned just aft of the sun lounge.
Below left: The pilothouse.

*Top: The main saloon
and dining room.*
*Above left: A laid teak floor
adorns the bridge deck landing.*
*Above right: The sky lounge
is decorated in Cuban style.*

Design to increase the reach of the bow and extend the stern to provide a boarding platform and lazarette.

A major influence was Winch's design for the interior of *Cakewalk*. By sheer coincidence the Beys bumped into the owner of this yacht, Charlie Gallaher, while on a trip to Holland. In spite of their being complete strangers, Gallaher insisted on sitting down with them for over an

hour while he went over their plans minutely before thumping his fist on the table and declaring 'You gotta stretch!' And stretch they did, just as much as they dared, while staying within the crucial 500 gross registered tonnes, whereafter the regulatory hoops suddenly get a lot tighter.

The layout is conventional in the best sense, with the engine room amidships and all the guest staterooms aft on the lower deck. The owner's bedroom, library and bathroom are forward on the main deck, with the main saloon and dining room aft. On the upper deck are the pilothouse, captain's cabin and sky lounge, while the boats are stowed aft on the open deck, rather than in a stern garage, so as to maximise the yacht's internal volume.

It was always the Beys' intention to have a traditional wood-panelled interior but it took a long time to settle on the 'keynote' timber which inevitably sets the tone for the rest of the decorative scheme. Finally, after a meeting with Andrew Winch in London, Peggy Bey noticed that the reception desk at the Ritz Hotel had just the colour and grain she was looking for – French walnut. This wood has been used throughout *Campbell Bay*,

Or rather, there appear to be two glass doors: the one to starboard is real and opens into the main hallway but the multiple bevelled panes on the port side are actually mirrors and conceal the door to the galley.

The beautiful table in the dining room extends to accommodate 12 and a nice practical touch is that the leaf stows inside the pillar of the table. Immensely comfortable Peter Dudgeon settees dominate the saloon, which has a pop-up television concealed in a cabinet at the head of the stairs down to the accommodation deck.

Walking forward via the marble-floored entrance hall, one reaches the library, one of the yacht's most attractive rooms. Abandoning the rather sterile concept of the typical owner's study, this delightful room, complete with wood-panelled walls and a fireplace surrounded by Dutch tiles, is really cosy and welcoming – the ideal place to spend a quiet time away from the crowd.

The owner's bedroom, decorated with a mixture of wood and silk panels, is as large and gracious as it is well lit through the large windows either side. One reason that many modern yachts do not have side decks is that people do not like the idea of crew or guests walking past their bedroom windows. Stanley and Peggy Bey have a simple solution: tell them not to! Meanwhile, *Campbell Bay* enjoys the many practical advantages of walk-around decks. Among a number of features which make this yacht suitable for both private and charter use is a pair of unobtrusive wardrobes, where the owners can lock away their own clothes so that charterers can enjoy full use of some rather more visible ones. The spacious and beautifully appointed en suite bathroom has a full-sized spa bath and a shower with optional steam.

The guest cabins are reached via a stairway from the aft end of the main deck saloon, and after just one glance into any of them, one has to agree that the *Campbell Bay* team really has found a lot of space for these very attractive rooms. The hull is beamy and does not taper much aft but, just as important, is the fact that the rooms have been pushed right out to the hull sides without the usual deep window sills. This is because the services, including ducted air-conditioning, are routed above or below the rooms rather than along the sides. Also, because the tenders are not stowed in a garage, the whole of the space between the engine room and lazarette is used for accommodation.

So much space is available that, in addition to the usual four double en suite guest staterooms, it has been

Above: *The dining table extends to seat 12. The spare leaf is conveniently stowed within the table's pedestal.*

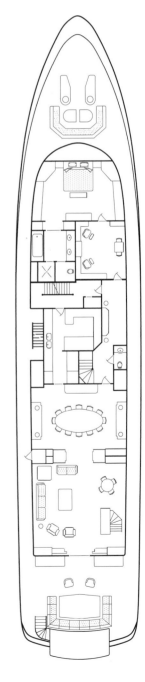

coloured with a light stain, and a satin varnish finish which leaves a semi-open grain. Although not quite as exuberant as some mahogany, it has very pleasant figuring and is also available in a burl version to give heightened interest to key areas.

Alarmingly, there was a major setback during the build when the almost-completed guest staterooms and crew quarters were destroyed in a fire that had spread to the joinery shop from an adjacent building. People in the small town of Monnickendam were so upset that many rushed to offer whatever assistance they could, but the whole project was put back by about six months. By the time it was completed, however, hardly a minute had been wasted from three years.

On the main deck, the combined saloon and dining room is large and gracious, with an enormous one-piece carpet by Lacey Champion into which various insets and pillar designs are woven. Wide windows on either side bring a flood of light, against which the French walnut appears restful and cool. To avoid having too large an area of dark wood at the end of the room, Winch positioned two glass doors on either side of a central sideboard.

Right: *The master suite comprises bedroom, bathroom and a library. Designed by Andrew Winch, all display the undoubted elegance of a byegone era.*

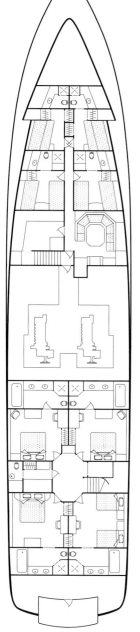

possible to include a smaller fifth stateroom, with upper and lower single berths, that is ideal for children. This brings the number of guests up to 12 without relying on folding Pullman berths. The four large guest staterooms have the added luxury of a bath as well as a shower and each have an individual theme, with decoration to match. The aftmost portside 'Monnickendam' stateroom has a twin-bed arrangement that can be converted to a queen-sized double by joining the beds and moving the bedside tables. Naturally, each stateroom has a television and sound system.

Being an MCA-approved yacht, *Campbell Bay* required a sliding watertight bulkhead, and this has been incorporated with exceptional care so that one really does not see it when it is stowed away. If the door is activated, alarms sound and arms attached to it peel back the carpet

and overhead lining as it moves. If someone squeezes through at the last moment, the hydraulically powered door stops, then tries again, like an elevator door. Furthermore, the major pipes that pass through the bulkhead are fitted with powered valves that close when the door moves, so the yacht will not flood as a consequence of a fractured pipe. If you are caught on the wrong side of the door when it is closed, MCA approved escape routes to the deck are available from every stateroom. These things do matter: charter yachts have both sunk and caught fire in the past.

The sky lounge has been given a Cuban theme which is a good-natured pastiche of the Hemingway era. Dappled sunlight entering through the venetian blinds falls on an aged rattan sofa and distressed leather armchairs which, in spite of their well-used appearance, are

Above: *The master suite is entered through the delightfully cosy library.*
Below far left: *The master bathroom.*
Below left: *By moving the beds together and repositioning the bedside tables, this twin-bedded guest cabin will convert to a queen-sized double.*

wonderfully comfortable. A walk-up bar and teak-planked floor reinforce the masculine atmosphere, while a glass-topped table displays a fascinating collection of postage stamps, each one featuring some kind of ship or yacht. A big television screen can swing around to face the seating area, backed by a full stereo surround sound system, making this a perfect place to watch a film: *The Old Man and the Sea*, perhaps. Very practically, the bar is fitted with a lift from the galley so that it can be used as a servery for alfresco dining at the extending double tables in the sheltered seating area aft of the sky lounge.

Guests are spoilt with three further choices as to where their meals can be served in the open. The second option is a large oval table in the shade of the radar arch on the sun deck, next to the spa pool with built-in fountain. Food here can be served from the barbecue and bar, which also has a food lift. Alternatively, one might decide to dine aft on the main deck, where a giant banquette curves around behind two big teak tables. Of course here you can be watched from the quayside if the yacht is moored stern-to, while for those who want peace and quiet, there is a very private seating area and two tables right forward on the foredeck.

So, what is wrong with beamy motor yachts? Well, they can look pretty chunky if they are also slab-sided, but *Campbell Bay's* walk-around decks go a long way towards breaking up the mass of the superstructure and help to impart a refined and classic look. An extra-beamy

yacht also calls for more power to drive it through the water but, provided one accepts the limitations of a full-displacement hull, their performance is actually much the same as other vessels of the same waterline length. *Campbell Bay's* Caterpillar main engines are only rated at 970hp each but she cruises quietly along at 13 knots, burning just 200 litres of fuel per hour, a figure which at 10 knots drops to a miserly 151 litres/hour to give her a range of some 5,000 nautical miles. To put it another way, she will cover 100 miles between dinner and breakfast in complete silence and comfort, which means you can cover a considerable number of destinations during a two-week holiday.

Campbell Bay, well conceived and built, seems an exceptionally professional piece of work with a very beguiling interior that, for both private and charter use, provides a high standard of luxury. It would be very hard indeed to find a better yacht in her particular size range.

SPECIFICATIONS

LOA	44.70m (146ft 8in)
LWL	37.50m (123ft 0in)
Beam	8.80m (28ft 10in)
Draught	2.80m (9ft 2in)
Displacement (half load)	435 tonnes
Propulsion	2 x 970hp Caterpillar 3508B diesels
Gearboxes	Reintjes 3.955:1
Propellers	Lips 5-blade
Shafts	Exalto
Speed (max/cruise)	14 knots/12.5 knots
Fuel capacity	58,000 litres
Range at 10 knots	5,000 nautical miles
Generators	2 x 99kW Northern Lights
Watermakers	2 x HEM 15,000l/d
Fresh water capacity	15,000 litres
Stabilisers	Koop Nautic
Bowthruster	55kW Cramm DCP75/150
Windlass	Steen, hydraulic

Fire control system	Heinen & Hopman
Exterior paint	Awlgrip
Hull insulation	Rockwool
Crane & passerelle	Cramm
Air-conditioning	Heinen & Hopman
Autopilot & gyrocompass	C. Plath
Radar	Furuno
Communications	Nera Inmarsat Mini M
Monitoring system	de Kaizer
Wind instruments	B&G
Guests	11 in 3 x double, 2 x twin & 1 x single cabin
Crew	10 in 1 x double, 2 x twin & 2 x twin bunk cabins
Construction	Steel hull & aluminium superstructure
Classification	Lloyd's ✠100A1 SSC Yacht, mono G6, ✠LMC. MCA Code
Naval architect	Diana Yacht Design International
Interior design	Andrew Winch Designs
Builder/Year	Hakvoort Shipyard/2002

Duke Town

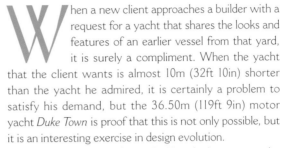

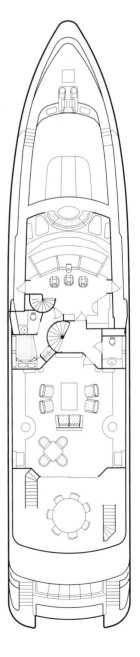

Main picture: Built by Heesen Shipyards, the 36.5m Duke Town *is named after the owner's home town of s'Hertogenbosch.*

Far left: Open-air dining on the aft of the bridge deck.

Left: The sun deck is a well thought out living space incorporating a bar, dining area, barbecue, spa pool and sunbathing area.

When a new client approaches a builder with a request for a yacht that shares the looks and features of an earlier vessel from that yard, it is surely a compliment. When the yacht that the client wants is almost 10m (32ft 10in) shorter than the yacht he admired, it is certainly a problem to satisfy his demand, but the 36.50m (119ft 9in) motor yacht *Duke Town* is proof that this is not only possible, but it is an interesting exercise in design evolution.

The starting point for *Duke Town's* design was the 45.86m (150ft 3in) *No Escape*, a blue-hulled, semi-displacement yacht, designed by Frank Laupman of Omega Design that had been launched from Heesen Shipyard in 1999. It was no wonder that the client admired her, for she is a particularly elegant vessel featuring a high bow that blends seamlessly into a curvaceous superstructure, while her interior packs in two saloons, five guest cabins and a stern garage. In the process of creating *Duke Town*, Laupman carefully pared down *No Escape's* key features, reducing the foredeck length and moving the superstructure forward, a change that was carefully concealed with a high foredeck bulwark so as to preserve the elegant sheer line as well as to give the impression of a longer foredeck.

At the same time, Laupman lowered the height of the pilothouse to create a more smoothly flowing silhouette as it rose from the bows to the sculptured arch mast, while the corresponding slope at the yacht's stern was made less steep by reducing the length of the bridge deck aft. With every intervening line precisely and sympathetically readjusted, the result became the harmonious whole that is *Duke Town*. Following this exterior styling exercise, the dimensions of the interior compartments were carefully modified so that those with a knowledge of both vessels do not feel restricted within the smaller one.

Interestingly, Bram Jongepier, the naval architect in Heesen's in-house Diaship Design Team, chose not to adopt the lines of *No Escape* because the shortening exercise had moved the position of the new yacht's centre of gravity further forward. One other significant design difference between the two vessels is that *Duke Town* has been built and certified so that she can be readily equipped to comply with the British MCA regulations for charter vessels. This will preserve her resale value in the future.

The starting point was, therefore, a clean sheet of paper, from which emerged a well-balanced, easily driven aluminium hull, whose running surfaces warped gently

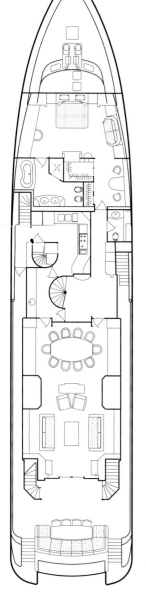

from a fine bow to a relatively flat aft body that is scalloped by two shallow propeller tunnels. The transom opens out and down, powered by hydraulic rams, thus creating a splendid teak-clad bathing platform, forward of which is a garage for the Novamarine 5.2m (17ft) tender, 850cc two-person Yamaha Waverunner and other watersports gear. This very useful feature clears the decks of clutter while the 6m (19ft 8in) or so of length that it puts between the engines and transom allows an efficiently shallow angle for the propeller shafts. Unusually, the tender and Waverunner are not launched by a crane but pulled seawards by a hydraulic winch via an ingenious system of turning blocks, with their keels sliding along a Teflon skid and over rollers that are temporarily mounted on the bathing platform. They are recovered in the same manner – a fast and easy operation with the added advantage that it avoids the need for a costly and relatively heavy crane. *Duke Town* does have a crane, however, but it is a small one positioned on the sun deck where, in future use under MCA regulations, it will launch a deck-stowed rescue boat. Today it is used to lift a second, smaller Waverunner into its stowage position across the aft of the sun deck.

The garage has enabled *Duke Town* to retain the same spacious deck areas that were a feature of *No Escape*. Aloft, there is a well laid out sun deck with a huge oval dining area, full service bar, spa pool and ample space for seating, while the aft ends of both the bridge and main decks offer further dining and lounging areas that adjoin the yacht's two saloons. While most designers ensure that good use is made of a yacht's aft decks, only a few take the trouble to develop a guest area forward. It is a delightfully private spot to take breakfast when the yacht

is stern-to in harbour. Laupman, therefore, made sure that *Duke Town* had a cluster of seating, a table and sunpads built into the sloping superstructure forward of the pilothouse. These four distinct deck areas will certainly ensure that any of *Duke Town*'s guests can find some personal open-air space should they wish it.

During the design of a yacht, co-ordination between the interior designer and the decorator can be rather blurred. The artistic flair of a decorator is often expressed in sketches and swatches, rather than in precise drawings, and this can cause problems of scale and fit during the final stages of the vessel's construction. In addition, even the most experienced decorator will run into problems with marine safety regulations and with awkwardly sized compartments when they first work with yachts. *Duke Town*'s owner had asked the very highly regarded Bert Quadvlieg, famous for his interiors of European castles and villas but a newcomer to yachts, to decorate his yacht and an effective method of working developed

between the designer and decorator. When Laupman finalised his design of the interior, a full set of drawings were sent to Quadvlieg, who then prepared his comments and materials in the usual way and returned them directly to Laupman, who incorporated the decoration in a final set of fully inclusive construction drawings that were delivered to the yard. Everything fitted into its designated place and the Heesen joiners were saved the problem of rationalising two different sets of plans.

The resulting interior is splendid. The owner had asked Quadvlieg to create a practical, modern-classic ambience in which he and his family would feel comfortable at all times. Quadvlieg started with a background of cherrywood panelling – part plain and part raised and fielded – that is surmounted by a classical moulding. The cherry is perhaps the yacht's only universal feature, as each room was given its own distinct personality, but, in the manner of a composer, Quadvlieg was careful to ensure that his symphony of decoration was endowed with overall harmony.

The main deck saloon – a gathering place for evenings or during dull weather – has a palette of muted straw, taupe and beige. The furnishings are bold but simple – two rattan chairs and a pair of settees facing each other

across a low table in the sitting area aft, while forward, past a narrows created by an antique Venetian chest of drawers flanked by cabinets filled with glassware, the oval-ended Georgian style dining table is overlooked by a splendid gallery of oils on the forward bulkhead, all with a food-related theme. The other art is eclectic – an Etruscan torso, a pair of 2,000-year-old Chinese jade discs, whose mystic purpose has long been lost, and a

Top: Extending forward to the dining room, the main saloon has a palette of muted straw, taupe and beige.
Above: *Oil paintings with a food-related theme decorate the dining room's forward bulkhead.*

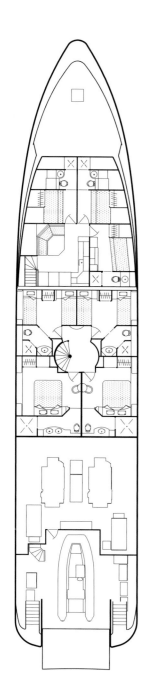

modern bronze disc, its pure line inspired by the jade. Most noticeable is the magnificent collection of early prints, not just in the saloon but throughout the yacht, that depicts the same heavily fortified medieval town. It is the Dutch city of s'Hertogenbosch, the home town of the owner and the key to the yacht's name, as loosely translated it means 'Duke town'.

At the head of the aromatic untreated teak stairway that winds up from the starboard side entrance hall, the upper saloon has quite a different character. Lined on three sides with windows, this bright and cheerful room has been primarily designed for daytime use and is decorated in a sporty style that leans heavily on natural materials from Asia, such as the untreated teak of the walls, the sharkskin Majilite of the deckhead and the crushed bamboo that faces the cupboard doors. A tactile, coarsely woven carpet in a mix of chunky white, beige and black jute, wicker furniture and accessories – a swordfish spear, a nut from a rare coco de mer palm and a polished turtle shell – could all have been gleaned from some sun-washed Indian Ocean beach. For comfort's sake, a settee upholstered in a silky velvet joins the wicker chairs around a low table to provide an ideal viewing spot for the plasma television screen concealed behind the bamboo doors while, further aft, a square, high-low table is available for a breakaway group to take coffee or play cards.

Duke Town has five en suite cabins, the owner's forward on the main deck and the remaining four – two twins and two doubles – found at the foot of the yacht's main stairwell, clustered around a hall that is adorned with a giant clam shell. Despite the scaling down process, all are comfortably sized and elegantly outfitted, with delightful and individual decoration.

The master suite is entered through a dressing room fitted with a desk and easy chairs, so it is also an area where the children can occupy themselves with games. The bedroom itself is a classically elegant room with walls clad in a raised damask that is dominated by its aft-facing king-sized bed. To port is a dressing table and fitted drawers, while to starboard a sitting area ensures that the owners have a convenient private retreat. A scattering of antique furniture adds to the homely, eclectic nature of the room. The en suite bathroom, extending aft on the port side, offers a huge shower, bidet, head, and a bath set within a delicately toned *lava rosa* marble surround and filled from a splendid lion's head tap.

Without doubt, Quadvlieg and Laupman did a fantastic

job in creating a modern, relaxing and stylish interior, with the help of high quality construction by Heesen, not only in the yacht's interior, but also throughout the yacht. The same high standard can be found in the equipment and installation in *Duke Town's* pilothouse, crew areas and technical spaces.

This is particularly apparent in the engine room, where the Diaship Design Team was given the difficult task of accommodating what is, with the exception of slightly smaller engines, almost identical machinery to that installed in the significantly larger compartment found in *No Escape*. Certainly, this is not a place for a portly engineer, but the layout is flawless and every

Left: *The classically elegant owner's stateroom with its walls clad in a raised damask.*
Above: *A shower room adjoining one of the four guest cabins. Each has an individual decorative scheme.*
Below left: *The starboard aft guest cabin has a blue and white Mediterranean theme.*

There is no doubt that *Duke Town* is a little miracle of design – a compact, high quality superyacht with an excellent mix of top calibre accommodation and expansive deck spaces. Just as *Duke Town* was inspired by another yacht, this yacht is surely bound to inspire future clients.

item of equipment is readily accessible for inspection and maintenance.

Such is the nature of semi-displacement yachts, that the twin 2,285hp MTU diesels are infrequently taken to their full power (which, incidentally, drives *Duke Town* to a highly respectable 21 knots) so a carbon build-up in the lubricating oil is inevitable. In this respect, the engineer's pride and joy is the centrifuge-style oil filtration system, an optional extra from MTU, that is inserted in the oil line to remove this excess carbon. It keeps the engines in tip-top form and increases the servicing interval from 250 to 500 hours, a worthwhile saving of effort which pays for itself in a very short time.

SPECIFICATIONS

LOA	36.50m (119ft 9in)	**Marble supplier**	Stone bv
LWL	30.70m (100ft 8in)	**Exterior paint**	Awlgrip
Beam (max)	7.95m (26ft 1in)	**Air-conditioning**	Heinen & Hopman
Draught (max)	2.10m (6ft 11in)	**Radars**	Furuno
Displacement (to DWL)	185 tonnes	**DGPS**	Leica
Propulsion	2 x 2,285hp MTU 12V396TE94 diesels	**Chartplotter**	Transas
Gearbox	ZF, BW465P	**Wind instruments**	B&G, Hydra
Propellers	Shaffran, nibral 4-blade	**Autopilot**	C. Plath
Shafts	130mm	**Gyrocompass**	C. Plath
Speed (max/cruise)	21 knots/16 knots	**Communications**	Seatel 4094E Satcom-C & B
Fuel capacity	44,100 litres	**Owner & guests**	10 in 3 x double & 2 x twin cabins
Range at 12 knots	2,800nm	**Construction**	Aluminium hull & superstructure
Electricity generation	2 x 66kW Northern Lights	**Classification**	ABS ✠A1, AMS. MCA
Stabilisers	Koop Nautic 353	**Interior design**	Omega Design – Frank Laupman
Anchors	2 x SHHP Pool-TW, 167kg	**Interior decoration**	Bert Quadvlieg
Bowthruster	Dane, 80hp	**Exterior styling**	Omega Design – Frank Laupman
Watermakers	2 x HEM, 3,000l/d	**Naval architecture**	Diaship Design Team
Sewage treatment	Hamann	**Builder/Year**	Heesen Shipyards/2002

Eleonora

Top: *Enclosed within low bulwarks, Eleonora's teak planking curves gracefully from stern to bow.*
Above: *The spoked wheel and binnacle, created by the French company Dryade, is historically perfect.*
Right: *Eleonora flies almost 890m² of canvas as she roars along at 15 knots.*

When it comes to classic yachts, Ed Kastelein is a total enthusiast. He once owned the 36.5m (120ft) Alfred Mylne-designed gaff ketch *Thendara*, which was first launched in 1937, and later built *Zaca a te Moana*, a modern-classic 38m (125ft 5in) schooner inspired by the lines of Errol Flynn's *Zaca*. He enjoyed the build, and learnt so much from it that he felt he needed to tackle the re-creation of another classic yacht. The question was, which one?

His quest, pursued among old yachting books and magazines, lasted several years, during which time the name of one yacht – *Westward* – occurred with regularity. Launched in 1910, *Westward* was a design from the board of the legendary American naval architect, Nathaniel Greene Herreshoff – the Wizard of Bristol – who in his 91-year lifetime (1848-1938) designed and built a host of highly successful racing yachts, steam yachts, and even a racing catamaran. The steel-hulled gaff schooner *Westward* was built in Bristol, Rhode Island and measured 41.6m (136ft 6in) on deck, with a waterline length of (96ft) 29.3m and a displacement of some 323 tons. She was designed for New Yorker, Alexander S Cochrane,

who sailed her to Europe for the 1910 regatta season, with the redoubtable Charlie Barr as captain. Her performance created a sensation in both Kiel and Cowes, where she soon built up a reputation for her pointing ability, as well as her speed in heavy weather, winning 11 out of 11 races at the former regatta and, at the latter, losing only one race out of nine – that to the King's yacht *Britannia*. Following the death of Charlie Barr in 1911, she was sold to the Norddeutscher Regatta Verein in Germany, an ownership which lasted just two years until she was seized as a prize at the outbreak of the First World War. After the war, *Westward* was acquired by TBF Davis and distinguished herself repeatedly over two decades of racing but, sadly, when Davis died his heirs were unable to find a buyer and they followed the course set by her rival *Britannia* and scuttled her in Hurd Deep, off Alderney, in 1947. With a pedigree like this, *Westward* seemed the ideal candidate for re-creation, especially as Kastelein was aware that her construction details were held in the Hart Nautical Museum in Cambridge, Massachusetts.

But Kastelein did not wish to build a replica. *Elena*, a second yacht to the same design as *Westward*, had been

Above: Eleonora *is a modern re-creation of Nat Herreshoff's legendary steel-hulled gaff schooner* Westward.
Left: A dining table, removable when the yacht is at sea, is positioned on deck beneath the foresail boom. In the distance are the davits that launch her anchors.

Top: *Displaying raised and fielded mahogany panelling and exquisite cabinet making skills, Eleonora's main saloon is a real delight.*
Above: *Detailing, such as this Corinthian column, was taken from original Herreshoff drawings.*

constructed in 1911 for William S Bell, so it made sense to continue the breed and build the third yacht in the series which, where practicable, would replicate *Westward*, but where necessary, would be updated to modern standards. Thus, *Eleonora* was conceived. Kastelein flew to Boston, where he spent almost a week in the museum. *Westward* was incredibly well documented – 600 to 700 folios on microfiche and about 350 drawings, all of which he copied before returning to Europe. The next task was to find a naval architect, and although this might seem strange as the yacht had already been built and all the plans existed, it was essential for two reasons. First, Herreshoff worked from sketches, hull models and a table of offsets, and unexpected problems could be solved as the yacht was being built – a far cry from today's precise computer-aided yacht construction. Nowadays, the steel hull plates are cut to millimetric accuracy by computer controlled plasma cutters and the hull must be faired to a very high degree before this takes place. Secondly, today's safety standards and building regulations are extremely rigid and many calculations are needed to obtain hull approval, including those for stability, chainplate design, framing, watertight compartments and bulkheads. Ship Design Gaastmeer, a highly technical naval architecture practice in Gaastmeer, Holland, was engaged to undertake this work, while the

hull construction and machinery installation was placed in the hands of the Van der Graaf Shipyard in Hardinxveld-Giessendam, Holland, a specialist hull builder and technical outfitter, to which several of the leading Dutch yacht yards regularly sub-contract work. On 30 March 2000, exactly 90 years after the launch of *Westward*, *Eleonora's* elegant hull slipped into the cold waters of the River Merwede.

With a then undefined major project in mind, Kastelein had purchased the teak used on *Eleonora's* decks some 10 years previously, and he had also purchased a massive 19m-long (62ft 4in) mahogany log of 2.5m (8ft 2in) diameter, a particularly fine specimen with a highly prized reddish tint. In due course, the timber was consigned to marine joiners, Vedder Jachtbetimmering in Rotterdam, who constructed the yacht's decks and interior. It was clear from the start that although *Eleonora's* decks, with just a few modern additions, would be almost identical to those of *Westward*, her original interior layout would not serve modern standards of living. In addition to the necessity of incorporating today's essentials, such as air-conditioning and en suite washing facilities, *Westward's* beds were just 1.8m (6ft) long, and resizing them would have upset the entire floor plan. Because of this, a totally new general arrangement plan and interior design to suit

Left: On the starboard side of the main saloon a settee curves around a pair of low coffee tables.
Below: The navigation desk is located at the foot of the companionway in the main lobby.

quartering breeze of 30 knots, and later behaved perfectly in gusts of 48 knots as she passed Gibraltar.

On deck, the only modern touches are her powered drum winches and her electric anchor windlass – items that necessarily replace the muscle power of 20 crew – and, less obviously, her stainless steel forestay, which prevents excess wear from the jib hanks. Otherwise she is the image of her period, her 7.4m-long (24ft 4in) bowsprit underhung with a bobstay and dolphin striker, massive spruce masts and topmasts, and her lengthy main boom, stowed on a crutch, overhanging the transom by a good 2.4m (7ft 9in). Standing proud on the open deck, the spoked wheel and binnacle, recreated by the French company Dryade, is historically perfect, as is every detail of the deck fittings, most of which were cast from bronze by the Fonderie Nivet to the original design of Herreshoff. The two tenders are stowed amidships, outboard of a large dining table positioned on the centreline between the masts. One, a magnificent near replica of the original motor tender that used to tow the otherwise engineless *Westward* in and out of harbour, is built from mahogany and fitted with an inboard diesel, while the second is a necessarily modern Novamarine 460 RIB. At the forward end of the long curving sweep of teak, the twin anchors are stowed in the style of the period, with stocks overboard and flukes on deck, a position from which they are launched and recovered using davits, their traditional blocks and tackles now led to a winch.

Eleonora's interior might be quite different from *Westward's* but it would surely take Nat Herreshoff to pick out any flaws in its character. Decoratively, it follows the same classic style throughout: mahogany raised and

modern requirements was drawn up by Kastelein but he was careful to use the same style of joinery and detailing shown on Herreshoff's original drawings.

Three years after the project started, the newly completed *Eleonora* sailed from Holland to the Mediterranean, an authentic picture of classic elegance under a veritable cloud of sail – main, main-topsail, foresail and fore-topsail, jib, flying jib and staysail, and a fisherman set high aloft between the masts. Offwind, she readily proved that she could equal the 15-knot performance for which *Westward* was famous, touching 16 knots in a

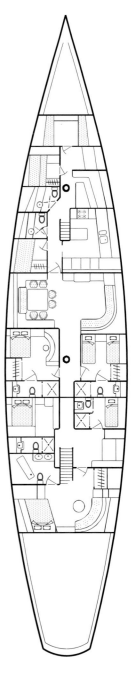

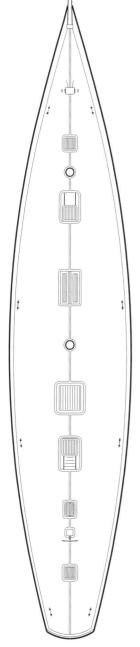

fielded panelling, its upper elements painted white to create a brighter atmosphere in the cabins; white painted beamed deckheads backed by tongue and groove planking; and floors made from harder wenge wood. Again, the detailing is excellent: fluted Corinthian columns carved from mahogany; silver plated drawer pulls and hinges cast from brass to an original design, and tiny 'taffrail' fiddles that edge the shelves and cabinet tops.

At the base of the companionway that sweeps down from the deck is a small lobby, where the navigation station is conveniently positioned against the starboard hull side – a kneehole desk bordered by a tallboy and a chest of drawers, its facia displaying a computer/chart plotter, radar, Navtex, DSC and Mini-M Satcom. Just forward is a single cabin for the captain. The remainder of *Eleonora's* interior layout is classically straightforward –

from the lobby, a passageway leads aft to the master accommodation and also reaches forward, passing between the three guest cabins to the main saloon and the crew quarters in the bow.

The accommodation in the aftermost habitable portion of the yacht, where the motion is at its best, would have been the ladies cabin but, following modern fashion, this position is occupied by *Eleonora's* master cabin. Well lit by five portholes and a skylight to the deck, it follows the general style of a ladies cabin, with a bed to port, albeit a double rather than the single of earlier times, and a large settee that wraps around the cabin's starboard aft quarter to abut the desk. Authentic period details abound, with particularly pleasing touches being the carving on the dressing table mirror and in the decorative cut-outs that adorn the edge of the bed. Adjacent is a bathroom, well endowed with marble and a teak parquet floor, that offers a full bath, a head and twin washbasins.

The three guest cabins, two further doubles and a twin-berthed cabin, are also delightfully in keeping with the yacht's period. All are adjoined by very practical and highly attractive shower rooms, the showers themselves featuring teak gratings, marble and engraved glass, while the basin is set in a charming washstand, behind which twin cupboards flank a recessed shaving mirror. All provide an enviable standard of accommodation, but one in particular, the forward port side cabin, stands out. This is slightly larger and, apart from its large bureau-style writing desk, it has two delightful built-in armchairs that offer the

Above: *The master bathroom, lit through twin portholes and well endowed with marble, offers a bath, head and twin washbasins.*

most comfortable and secure seating – the very place to relax and read a book as a storm rages outside.

Proceeding forward towards the main saloon, one cannot fail to be impressed by the huge girth of the mainmast, a raw pillar of spruce that stabs through the passageway between deck and keel. Again, the classic panelling, hung with a collection of Tim Thompson's America's Cup prints, takes one back a hundred years to the Golden Age of yachting. Well lit from portholes and a skylight, the dining table is to port, set athwartships against a settee and surrounded by six chairs while, opposite, a settee fronted by a pair of low tables curves between the aft bulkhead and the perfect joinery of the cupboard and drawers on the forward bulkhead.

The crew and service areas occupy the bow of the yacht and include a huge galley – probably the largest and best equipped on any sailing yacht of this size. 'When racing we feed up to 35 crew, so it must be big, while my catering background drove me to equip it properly', explained Kastelein. And this he has done with a full range of professional stainless steel equipment. Just forward is the mess, laundry room and quarters for six further crew in three cabins that share two shower rooms.

An advantage that *Eleonora's* truly classic hull form has over the lighter and shallower hulls of modern classics is that there is sufficient space and depth in her hull for the engine room to run beneath the floor of the yacht, rather than being squeezed into a tiny space beneath a raised deckhouse. Divided into three compartments and united by watertight doors, *Eleonora's* engine room is a model of accessibility, with the forward compartment racked for storage, the middle containing a workshop, pumps, watermakers and air-conditioning plant. The aft compartment carries the main engine – a 460hp Baudouin diesel, chosen for its slow running qualities and hence its low vibration and sound transmission – and a pair of 42kVA Lister Stamford generating sets positioned between the fuel tanks. Engineers accustomed to life in the cramped conditions of a modern sailing yacht would weep for joy!

Inevitably, *Eleonora's* heavy displacement, deep hull and its consequentially large wetted surface will mean that her performance will not equal that of the modern classics, being slow to accelerate and reluctant to surf. On the plus side, *Eleonora* offers the comfortable motion in a seaway that is only found on a heavy displacement yacht, while her long 29.3m (96ft 2in) waterline, which rises to around 36m (118ft 1in) when she is heeled, will give her long legs in an ocean passage. But her most positive asset of all is her totally authentic appearance – the sheer romance of seeing such an historic design powering through the seas beneath a cloud of perfect white sail is a truly emotional experience that somehow cannot be matched in a modern yacht of this size. We owe a debt of gratitude to her owner and all of his construction team for creating such a magnificent craft.

SPECIFICATIONS

LOA (including bowsprit)	49.00m (160ft 9in)	**Propeller**	S.P.W. Sailpropeller
LOD	41.60m (136ft 6in)	**Fuel capacity**	7,500 litres
LWL	29.30m (96ft 2in)	**Electricity generation**	2 x 42kVA Lister Stamford
Beam (max)	8.20m (26ft 11in)	**Winches**	14 x Meissner bronze, 6 x electric
Draught	5.28m (17ft 4in)	**Windlasses**	Orvea, 400V electric
Ballast	45 tonnes, lead	**Watermakers**	Dessalator, 240l/h
Displacement (to DWL)	213 tonnes	**Exterior paint**	International, 2 part
Rigging	F. Langrenay	**Air-conditioning**	Cruisair, chilled water
Sail areas: (main & foresail)	570m² (6,133ft²)	**Owner and guests**	8 in 4 x cabins
(staysail)	70m² (753ft²)	**Crew**	7 in 4 x cabins
(jib)	85m² (914ft²)	**Construction**	Steel hull & deck
(flying jib)	95m² (1,022ft²)	**Classification**	Bureau Veritas I3/3E, ✠CY, MACH
(fore & main topsail)	112m² (1,204ft²)	**Modern naval architects**	Ship Design Gaastmeer
Sailmaker	Bryt Sails, Poland	**Naval architect**	N.G. Herreshoff
Engine	1 x 460hp Baudouin 6R124SR diesel	**Builder/Year**	van der Graaf bv, Holland

Gran Finale

Far right: Gran Finale *is a 44.8m composite-hulled motor yacht built by Delta Marine.* **Right:** *Monitor screens dominate the pilothouse.*

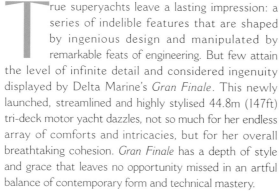

True superyachts leave a lasting impression: a series of indelible features that are shaped by ingenious design and manipulated by remarkable feats of engineering. But few attain the level of infinite detail and considered ingenuity displayed by Delta Marine's *Gran Finale*. This newly launched, streamlined and highly stylised 44.8m (147ft) tri-deck motor yacht dazzles, not so much for her endless array of comforts and intricacies, but for her overall breathtaking cohesion. *Gran Finale* has a depth of style and grace that leaves no opportunity missed in an artful balance of contemporary form and technical mastery.

Prior to construction, the owner himself worked at considerable length on the hull design. On this yacht, his fourth vessel, he undertook tank testing of four hull designs at the University of British Columbia, Canada. 'I didn't want any surprises, and the boat needed to be seaworthy,' he said, having finally settled on Delta Marine's design. This easily driven hull met its weight target by utilising a lightweight cored composite sandwich that made generous use of high modulus carbon-fibre in the superstructure. This reduced the need for obstructive pillars and, hence, greatly enhanced spaciousness and openness. All of the moulds for the composite parts were designed by the Delta Design Group and JC Espinosa and machined by Janicki Machine Works. Following the owner's wishes, all moulds, other than those for the hull, were destroyed after use so as to ensure a unique vessel.

Even when walking on board *Gran Finale*, it is difficult to gain a true sense of the scope of a project that responded so comprehensively to the client's exacting and evolving requirements. *Gran Finale* epitomises the modern approach to yacht design, with its rakish bow, clean exterior lines, spacious private and communal areas, walk-around side decks and a sophisticated, European-influenced interior layout.

Entering the main saloon, one is struck not only by an aesthetically pleasing interior that has been created from deep, rich bevelled woods and elegant curves, but also by the wide panoramic views through the windows, a recurring theme throughout the vessel. From the preliminary design stages it was the owner's insistence that all furnishings and cabinetry be kept as low as possible so as not to obstruct the outside view. The result is a spacious yacht that feels considerably larger than her 44.8m (147ft) overall length.

JC Espinosa's design team relished the fact that the owner pushed the limits of design. For every project finalised, several options were explored by him in respect of what might or might not work. Often, these required lateral thinking to solve challenges that might at first have seemed impossible. 'By pushing, the client got what you see,' said Jeff Langs, project co-ordinator with Espinosa. 'It was amazing how he fought for every square inch, and as a result he now has the spacious interior of vessels far larger in size to show for it.'

Throughout *Gran Finale*, such attention to detail becomes apparent: the panorama from the sunken, circular aft saloon bar, looking out to the sea over two inlaid mother-of-pearl aft deck tables and a seating area

warmed by radiant heat, while the main deck saloon lounge area is dominated by three sumptuous settees and an expanse of rich lacewood and sapele panelling that was inspired by the owner's home dining table.

The dining saloon, with its Dakota Jackson lacewood table for 12, is defined by a sapele-trimmed oval ceiling detail that is framed by slender mahogany pillars to provide a subtle divide from the lounge. A discreet, port side sliding door offers access to the commercially equipped galley. Over a Brueton bow-fronted cabinet, a

striking six-part installation, commissioned from the renowned Seattle glass artist Dale Chihuly, dominates a central stairwell to the sky lounge. Sensibly, the oyster-toned Chihuly glass artwork can be removed and stored in anticipation of rough weather. Access to all three levels can be gained by an elevator, whose etched glass doors, in keeping with the panels throughout the vessel, were made by another Seattle artist, Jim Francis.

The galley boasts every amenity, including a relaxed, informal dining area from which there is access below and

Far left: Alfresco dining on the bridge deck.
Left: The spa pool on the sun deck offers the best views aboard.

owner's elegant office opens forward into the bedroom, where its superb bed is set back against a curving wall. A 127cm (50in) flat-screen television elevates smoothly from the half-height divide between the bedroom and the forward positioned bathroom, its stereo surround-sound speakers, part of the Bose home entertainment system, concealed in adjacent mahogany pillars. When the television screen is raised, the two backlit sinks, the luxurious spa bath and the shower are concealed from view. Beyond the bath, the onyx wall, crafted from meticulously bookmatched onyx panels by Jeff Holmchick, is backlit by fibre optics to accentuate the grain of the stone and cast a warm glow when the room is darkened, an effect which, together with the gold-leaf ceiling, provides a soft and relaxing backdrop to the entire area. Of this area's many practical design points, two stand out in particular. Blending well with the other metalwork in the spacious 'rain' shower, some additional rungs have been fitted to the wall – they are actually a ladder to the forward escape hatch, while, for barefoot comfort, heating elements are installed within all of the vessel's stone floors.

Top: Vivid colour styling in the sky lounge.
Above: Sculpted and etched glass is to be found throughout the yacht.
Below: A lacewood table and sapele-trimmed ceiling detail grace the dining room.

forward to the accommodation for the yacht's six crew. A Vulcan six-burner range, Kosploch refrigerators and freezers (two in the lazarette) and four ovens (including a baking oven) ensure that *Gran Finale*'s guests will always enjoy the best in cuisine and hospitality. Conveniently, a concealed stairway with a pedal-activated sliding door rises from the galley to allow prompt, behind-the-scenes service to the sky lounge.

Forward, past the starboard side of the main stairs leading up to the bridge deck, is a day head and forward again is the entrance to the master suite, an area that fully brings home the remarkable individuality of this vessel. Much more than just an elegant stateroom, this is a complete living and sleeping area, wholly separate from the formal public areas and designed to offer the maximum in comfort and necessities while under way. Every detail has been thoughtfully considered and every opportunity to add space has been explored. The 2.7m (9ft) high raised ceiling adds spaciousness and light. Expansive glass affords dramatic views from every angle, while a flick of a switch lowers blinds and deploys the skylight blackout screen. Just beyond the entrance the

To port, aft of the bedroom, a spacious walk-in wardrobe is fitted with a treadmill so that it can double as an exercise room. On the opposite side of the bedroom is an exquisite and unusual goatskin dressing table with a hinged top and concealed, fully lit mirror, made in Italy for Carriage House Design of Florida. Here, and throughout the yacht, the level of craftsmanship is excellent, a view that has been endorsed by *Gran Finale's* owner, who considers that Delta performed far beyond the usual standards of construction and finish.

Moving down to the accommodation deck, it is immediately apparent that the thoroughness of design extends to the guest quarters, which are reached through a lacewood-panelled lower foyer whose oval ceiling is adorned with gold leaf. Opening aft from here, two VIP staterooms offer ingenious use of space, with their diagonally offset king-sized beds set on curved pedestals against mahogany headboards that reach upwards to the ceiling. The metallic paint colours reflect the owner's affinity with automotive finishes. *Shoji* screens filter natural light and afford privacy, while a small love seat

Left: In the aft portion of the main saloon, the circular bar has outstanding views of the sea and a heated seating area.
Below: Furnishings and cabinetry were kept low in the saloon so as not to obstruct the outside view.

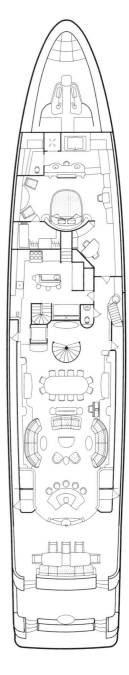

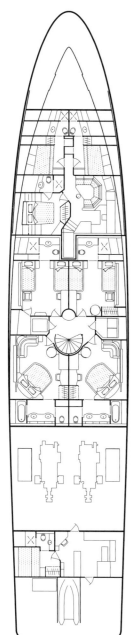

and the slim wall cabinets and shelves continue the theme of abundant (but often cleverly hidden) storage. Entertainment systems are revealed by sliding aside bow-fronted panels in a mahogany floor-to-ceiling column that mimics the headboard treatment. En suite bathrooms are finished with contrasting granite and marble countertops and are provided with a separate head and shower stall, double backlit basins, and concealed laundry drawers.

When children are aboard, the two forward twin bedded staterooms equipped with Pullman beds offer additional sleeping space, while the entertainment quotient is raised considerably by built-in flat-screen televisions and PlayStations. For adult guests with less time to play, small desks also double as dressing tables.

The level of comfort continues. The foyer, adorned with a dramatic Craig French sculpture, houses a small panelled night bar, while (in addition to more hidden luggage storage) an entire ceiling-high door serves as a niche to frame the sculpture. Amazingly, this whole assembly opens hydraulically to reveal a sound-insulated and air-conditioned laundry centre.

The more formal dining and sleeping areas are marked by a gently traditional, sometimes even an Italianate feel, perhaps. By contrast, the bridge deck sky lounge and pilothouse are more effervescent and contemporary, denoted by a riot of vivid blues, maroons and purples. The captain's cabin, which would typically occupy this prime space, was placed on the lower accommodation deck, affording the designers the

opportunity to create a wonderful open space with 360-degree views. And, again, the owner's desire for a multi-functional area met with surprising results. A low, curved 6m-long (19ft 8in) leather settee aft of the stairwell, padded stools, and a games table with armchairs provide a number of seating choices – either for the wrap-around outside panorama or for viewing films on the home

Gran Finale's capacious engine room houses twin 2,450hp Caterpillar 3512B diesels that run remarkably quietly – low decibels being another requirement from the owner's brief. A sophisticated combination of thrust bearings and isolation mounts for noise and vibration reduction allow for a much softer installation. Other precautions include custom-made stainless steel sound shields over the 99kW Northern Lights generators. *Gran Finale*'s impressively low acoustics owe much to the sound and vibration supression technology engineered by Willem Van Cappellen, who claims that this is the smoothest and quietest vessel that Delta has yet built.

Displacing a total of 252 tonnes, *Gran Finale* enjoys an ideal cruising speed of 15 knots at 1,250rpm, a speed at which she burns only 242 litres of fuel per hour. Such relative economy is testament to the extensive tank-testing carried out on her slippery hull. Her top speed, fully loaded, is 20.6 knots.

With four on-board spa baths, fresh water needs can be substantial, but are easily met with two 22,275 litres per day Filtration Concepts watermakers. Extensive backup systems, including one for fuel transferral, significantly reduce the possibility of a disabling breakdown, while the presence of the chief engineer's twin berth cabin in the stern adjacent to the engine room will ensure that he is right on the spot in any emergency.

When it comes to details, despite the sometimes seemingly impossible demands, Delta was more than able to deal with all that was required. Five years in the making, including two in design, *Gran Finale*'s owner was quietly amazed at the final result. 'I like something shapely,' he said. 'The feel of contemporary and streamlined design, with harmonious spaces to attain those vital 360-degree views. I have a passion for detail and design and Delta always found a solution to my crazy ideas.' He adds, 'This is a vessel built entirely on a time and materials contract. Best of all, I didn't have to buy the shipyard to finish the boat!'

entertainment system. A giant screen lowers on the starboard side, while the customised projector emerges from a 25cm (10in) ceiling cavity.

The pilothouse, dominated by seven 44cm (17in) monitors set in its control panel, has a visitor settee at its aft side so that guests may watch the action. Aft of the settee, it is open to the sky lounge, but to avoid the watchkeeping officer being distracted by the latest Hollywood blockbuster playing on the room's satellite television, it can be closed off by a curved glass panel that is electrically raised from the settee back.

But not all the fun is to be found inside the yacht. Ceiling-high curved glass sliding doors (claimed to be the largest of their kind so far built) lead aft from the sky lounge to the bridge deck. This well-equipped outside area contains a six-seater bar, barbecue, wet bar and an additional galley with a complete set of appliances. Forward and up a flight of circular stairs, the best view on the yacht may well be from the six-person spa pool, set into the forward part of the deck and surrounded by sunbathing cushions. This area is encircled by particularly elegant protective guardrails made from oval-section stainless steel by Malcolm Cole of Dorset, England.

The preservation of clean lines is paramount – so much so that often the more practical equipment is completely concealed. A custom-made Nautica FLA diesel jet tender is launched by a concealed davit built into the bulwark, while the crew tender, windsurfers, and kayaks are all garaged forward of the bathing platform.

SPECIFICATIONS

LOA	44.80m (147ft 0in)	**Comms installation**	Harris Electric
LWL	39.90m (131ft 0in)	**GPS/DGPS**	Northstar, WAAS 952XD & 914XD
Beam	8.70m (28ft 7in)	**Radar**	Furuno
Draught	2.10m (7ft 0in)	**Chartplotter**	Transas
Displacement (loaded)	252 tonnes	**VHF**	Icom & Furuno
Propulsion	2 x 2,450hp Caterpillar 3512B diesels	**SSB**	Furuno
Speed (max/cruise)	21 knots/15.4 knots	**Wind instruments**	B&G
Fuel capacity	56,018 litres	**Autopilot**	C. Plath
Range at 12 knots	4,000nm	**Entertainment systems**	Cello Technologies
Generators	2 x 99KW Northern Lights	**Security systems**	Elbex/Servowatch
Stabilisers	Koop Nautic, 3050	**Specialist furniture**	Michael O/Brueton
Windlass	Muir	**Technical equipment**	Harris Electric
Bowthruster	American, 125hp	**Construction**	Cored composite
Watermakers	2 x FCI, 15,519l/d	**Owner & guests**	10 in 2 x double & 3 x twin cabins
Fresh water capacity	8,327 litres	**Crew**	8 in 1 x double & 3 x twin bunk cabins
Exterior paint	Awlgrip	**Naval architecture**	Delta Design Group
Air-conditioning	Marine Air	**Exterior styling**	JC Espinosa
Communications eqpt	KVH Mini-M & Ocean Cell	**Interior design**	JC Espinosa
Satellite television	SeaTel, 4094	**Builder/Year**	Delta Marine/2002

Lady Ann Magee

Right: The fourth yacht in Codecasa's 50m series, Lady Ann Magee *offers the highest quality at very reasonable cost.*
Below right: The aft deck has been enclosed to form a cosy deck saloon.

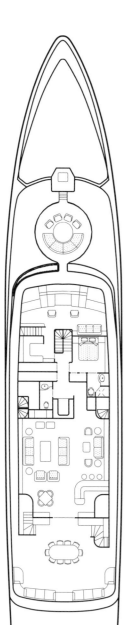

High levels of design customisation in a yacht are usually the signs of an experienced owner with a distinctive taste and lifestyle, who often intends to use his vessel in a specialised manner. Customisation offers convenience of use and a high level of tailored comfort to the owner who commissioned the vessel as well as the pleasure of creating something which will exactly meet one's needs. But there is also a downside to customisation: it is rare that highly customised vessels will suit the exact requirements of a subsequent owner, and the need for modifications will certainly lower the resale value. Reliability can suffer, too. By their nature, highly customised vessels are prototypes, often with innovative mechanical systems and layouts that can take a good deal of tinkering and modification to get some elements running – indeed, some of the more ambitious systems never, ever work satisfactorily.

But such highly customised vessels only account for a small proportion of today's new builds. The needs of the vast majority of superyacht owners are very similar, and most of the bespoke design that is carried out to the interior layouts and exterior styling is only done to create a distinctive, personalised vessel that will stand out from the crowd. Potential owners who are happy to create

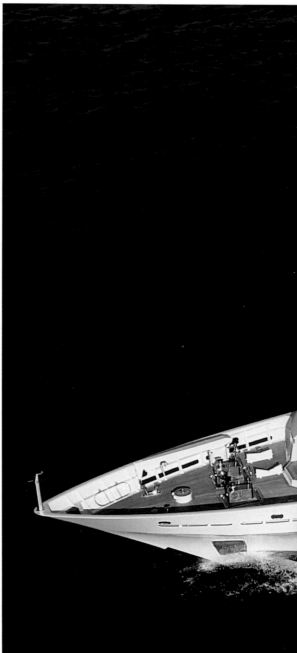

individuality with interior design rather than interior layout – by the selection and use of choice woods, fabrics and furniture – would be well advised to explore the advantages of purchasing a proven stock design with no opportunity for layout customisation.

The Viareggio-based Codecasa Shipyards, owned and run by the Codecasa family since 1825, were among the

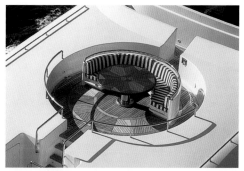

Far left: *The bridge deck aft offers formal alfresco dining.*
Left: *While under way, guests can feel the cool breeze in this ideal sitting area built into the forward slope of the superstructure.*

earliest superyacht builders to spot the benefits of this approach. *Andale*, a 49.6m (162ft 9in) steel-hulled motor yacht with an aluminium superstructure, was launched in 1998. Its size, just below the critical 50m (164ft) size where regulations begin to make construction and crewing of a yacht more complex, is a popular choice with owners, while its overall design and general arrangement also impressed Fulvio Codecasa, the yard's owner. Seeing the potential of this craft, he laid down a second hull to complete and build as a speculative project, thus taking full advantage of the economies offered by the side-by-side construction of two identical yachts. *Andale* was not even launched when buyers arrived to view this second hull. They were offered little choice:

Main picture: *Interior designers, Franco and Anna Dellarole assembled a sumptuous collection of fabrics and furniture in rich Italian style.*
Above: *The sky lounge.*

they could take this second hull with the possibility of making minor changes, or they could walk away. In fact, the design, construction quality and, above all, the price of this yacht were too good to miss, and the offer was accepted. The resulting yacht, *Invader*, was launched in 1999 and the process was repeated with *Moneikos* in 2000, and *Lady Ann Magee* in 2001.

Lady Ann Magee is not only the most recent, but also probably the best example of the series so far launched, as one of the most telling arguments for series production is the continual improvement in design and construction that can be incorporated into successive yachts. So successful is this technique that *Lady Ann Magee's* captain, Roger Mills, had no major items listed for warranty attention after his shakedown cruise – just a couple of pieces of cracked marble, a few unreliable light switches, and a sticking door – an amazing record for a complex motor yacht of this size.

But one cannot market a successful series of 50m (163ft) yachts on reliability alone. *Lady Ann Magee* is a remarkable yacht on many fronts, in particular the layout of her interior and decks; the quality of her construction; her mechanical installation; her quietness of operation; and her excellent performance. All of these combine to create a yacht so special that there is little demand from owners for any serious design change – not that Fulvio Codecasa would, in any case, permit change without being absolutely certain that it represented significant improvement.

Designed in-house by Codecasa Shipyards, its 50m-series (163ft) hull is perhaps the starting point of the yacht's success story. With a beam of 9.50m (31ft 2in), this design offers a greater internal volume than most

yachts of this length, a factor that is also enhanced by the raised foredeck and a knuckle in the bow sections that permits the beam to be carried well forward, at the same time allowing a fine entry at the waterline. Weighing in at 480 tonnes displacement (light ship) the steel-hulled *Lady Ann Magee* is clearly a full displacement vessel but, powered by a pair of Caterpillar 3516B diesels that develop a total of 4,400hp, she is slippery enough to deliver a very respectable 18-knot top speed and a continuous cruising speed of 16 knots. She is reasonably economic, too, with her tank capacity of 120,000 litres providing a cruising range of 5,500nm at 14 knots.

The owner of *Lady Ann Magee*, who had previously chartered yachts on a regular basis, was first attracted to Codecasa after having chartered *Andale*. His principal fascination with the vessel was its quietness compared with other yachts. While this is, in part, a result of experience from the earlier yachts in the series, the aft position of the engine room is the major factor, concentrating the noise from machinery and propellers in a part of the ship where sound and vibration can be readily isolated. Continuous design development has also resulted in a well ordered, beautifully engineered engine room, its walls and deckhead finished in white-painted perforated zinc sheet, while a particularly spacious

engineer's office and control room is the icing on the cake. Ancillary machinery includes twin Northern Lights 125kVA generating sets, two Idromar 9,000 litres per day watermakers and, more unusually, the power pack for the yacht's Otis lift, positioned alongside the fuel centrifuge between the main engines.

In the stern, just aft of the engine room, is another element that has contributed to the design success of this yacht – a huge garage with an upwards hinging door that opens out to the bathing platform moulded into the stern of the yacht. Here, there is ample space to store the yacht's Novurania Equator 600XL tender flanked by a pair of jet-skis, all of which are launched by a beam crane that extends aft through the open door.

This garage is the key to the success of *Lady Ann Magee's* exemplary deck spaces, all of which are beautifully laid with teak. With the tenders and jet-skis tucked away in the stern and the small rescue tender (required by the British MCA regulations, with which the yacht complies) positioned on the foredeck, the yacht's prime deck areas are left to the full enjoyment of the owner and guests. Aloft, her extensive sun deck provides everything that one could possibly wish for the full enjoyment of outdoor living. Easily accessible, even for infirm guests who can take the lift from any of the yacht's three enclosed decks, it offers sunbathing, lounging, and a large spa pool, as well as a bar, barbecue and dining area. Unlike the earlier yachts in the series, *Lady Ann Magee's* sun deck is shaded by awnings set over a very solidly built, curving stainless steel frame that is as attractive as it is practical. Just below, the bridge deck aft is devoted to more formal entertainment, being provided with an expanding table that will seat either six or 12 guests and an aft bulwark ringed by settees. Main decks aft are often under-utilised, being overlooked in port and sometimes flooded with exhaust fumes while the yacht is at sea and, because of this, it is one of two areas where Fulvio Codecasa has relented regarding customisation. *Andale's* aft deck was largely enclosed to form a lounge, *Invader's* owner chose an open deck space, while on *Lady Ann Magee* the area reverted to a lounge. This results in a relatively small aft deck, but it is still of ample size to meet and greet guests, or to use in conjunction with the bathing platform as a watersports base.

The last arrow in the quiver of design success for the Codecasa 50m (163ft) series is that the yachts' interior arrangements are particularly well balanced, with every need catered for and no compartment uncomfortably

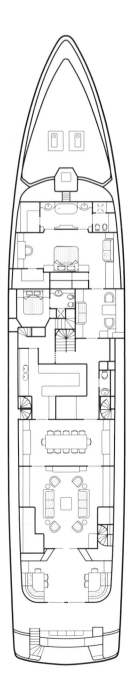

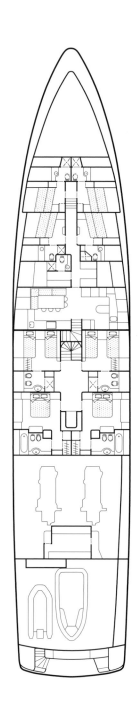

large or cramped. The aft deck lounge, with its wooden floor and huge vista, is an airily bright and relaxed room where two quadrants of seating fronted by circular tables offer a great breakfast venue. Beyond sliding stainless steel doors – MCA required the same solid quality as if the aft deck had been open – the main saloon is a richly formal reception room delightfully furnished with overstuffed settees and easy chairs. At its forward end, a central cabinet flanked by sliding doors allow the dining saloon to be closed off or opened at will, especially as the upper part of the cabinet can be closed off with a pop-up television or a solid panel. The yacht's fourth saloon is on the bridge deck, this time a classic upper deck lounge with panoramic seascapes that can be readily united with the open deck through wide doors – always the most popular gathering place for guests. Here, there is a full service bar, two more conversation areas and a variety of entertainments including an electric organ, large-screen television and a games table.

Lady Ann Magee's owner knew exactly what he wanted in terms of decorative style – he called it 'rich Italian' – and the yard's in-house decorators, Franco and Anna Dellarole, who have been responsible for the interiors of the whole series, seemed the ideal team to achieve this. Working closely with the owner, they put together a selection of sumptuous furniture and grandiose floral furnishing fabrics, tempered by plain colours and embellished with a range of classical table lamps, that perfectly matched the backdrop of red pear panelling and the occasional Italianate mural. Carrara marble graces hallways, bathrooms and heads, its distinguished grey and white tone lifted by a selection of more exotic stone. The finish, be it the gloss varnish of the woodwork, the way the gold fittings are cut into the doors, the fit of the marble, or the build of the furnishings, is perfection itself – however much one spent or wherever one went, it would be difficult to better.

Lady Ann Magee has a full-beam master suite forward on the main deck that, entered through a study, offers a superb bedroom with a simply enormous double bed created from two queen-sized doubles joined together, a particularly sumptuous marble-lined bathroom with an inbuilt sauna, and two large, well-fitted dressing rooms. To this is added four guest cabins – two excellent doubles with en suite bathrooms, and a pair of twins each with a third Pullman and adjoining shower room – which open

from a central passageway on the lower deck to take the guest complement to the usual maximum of 12. But this is a second area where Codecasa has allowed some flexibility. *Invader* featured a gymnasium, with its own bathroom, tucked alongside the master suite and entered from a crew corridor just beyond the main lobby. *Lady Ann Magee's* owner, however, chose to utilise this room as a VIP guest cabin to introduce an element of flexibility into the accommodation plan. Despite the location of its entrance, its grand double bed and magnificent furnishings will surely delight any future occupant.

On the working side of the yacht, *Lady Ann Magee's* owner chose to upgrade the standard equipment package

Left: The master stateroom occupies the yacht's full beam. Its enormous bed was created by uniting two queen-sized doubles. *Above:* The owner's bathroom, which incorporates a sauna, is lined with Carrara marble.

of the bridge to the highest possible specification, fitting an Anschütz autopilot, Leica GPS receivers, twin Furuno radars, a chartplotter, weather-sat receiver, Mannesman-Rexroth controls and an Antares monitoring system. The galley, as one might expect aboard an Italian-built yacht, is a solidly professional, well laid out compartment, fitted with excellent commercial equipment. In the forward part of the lower deck, there is a spacious, six-machine laundry, and a large reserve fridge/freezer, while the fully racked space that runs aft to the engine room between the tank tops and floor permits huge storage for vital spares and supplies. One criticism just has to be mentioned. Although the crew mess has all the facilities that one would expect, it is a little on the cosy side for modern standards – a design fault that is perhaps caused by the fact that many Italian boats are crewed on a live-ashore basis when the yacht is not actually at sea. Find a little more volume for this space, and both the standards of service and crew loyalty will certainly improve.

Lady Ann Magee is an attractive yacht of a popular size that has been built with consummate skill by one of the best Italian shipyards. It is arguable that, in terms of facilities, she offers slightly more than one would find in most other yachts of her size, while the price of a yacht in this series will inevitably be substantially lower than that of a newly designed, fully customised vessel.

If one is bothered that there are a handful of similar yachts in the oceans of the world, then the series production route should be avoided, but if one is ready to take the risk run by every female film star – of turning up at the Oscar ceremony with the same dress as someone else – then have a close look at the value which *Lady Ann Magee* offers, not just in terms of price, but also in terms of advanced design development and reliability.

SPECIFICATIONS

LOA 49.90m (163ft 9in)	**Bowthruster** . . . . Schottel
LWL 41.70m (136ft 10in)	**Watermakers** . . . . 2 x Idromar, 9000 l/d
Beam (max) 9.50m (31ft 2in)	**Fire control system** . . . . Hi-Fog
Draught 3.10m (10ft 2in)	**Radars** . . . . Furuno S & X band radars
Displacement (to DWL) . . . . 480 tonnes	**Autopilot** . . . . Anschütz
Propulsion . . 2 x 2,200hp Caterpillar 3516B diesels	**Entertainment systems** . . . . Linn
Propellers . . . . Finnscrew, 5-blade S-Class	**Galley equipment** . . . . Baratta/Miele
Gearboxes . . . . Reintjes, WVS 930	**Owner and guests** . . 14 in 4 x double & 2 x twin cabins
Speed (max/cruise) . . . . 18/16 knots	**Crew** . . . . 10 in 1 x double & 4 x twin cabins
Fuel capacity . . . . 120,000 litres	**Construction** . . Steel hull & aluminium superstructure
Range at 14 knots 5,500nm	**Classification** . . . . Lloyd's ✠100A1, SSC Yacht,
Electricity generation . . 2 x 125kW Northern Lights	. . . . Mono G6, ✠LMC. MCA Code
. . . . & 1 x 50kW Northern Lights	**Interior designers** . . . Franco & Anna Maria Dellarole
Power converter . . . . Atlas	**Naval architect** . . . . Cantieri Navali Codecasa
Stabilisers . . . . Vosper/Koop Nautic	**Builder/Year** . . . . . . Cantieri Navali Codecasa/2001

Lady Lola

Main picture: Lady Lola, *the latest launch from Oceanco, is a yacht whose superb customisation was achieved by the extraordinary knowledge, interest and committment of her owner.*
Below: *On-deck and underwater lighting create a spectacular sight after dusk.*

eafing through the pages of this book, one might be astonished by the variety and style of interiors. Interior decorators of all persuasions, from minimalist to exotic and a multitude of styles in between, have spread their magic to the delight of yacht owners. But anyone studying the general arrangement plans of each of the yachts will discover that the interior layouts often show less adventure, with many conforming to a practical, but well used, stereotype. For such highly customised products this is, perhaps, a little surprising, so it is very refreshing when one comes across a yacht that differs from the norm. Duane and Lola Hagadone's new *Lady Lola*, built by Oceanco, is such a yacht.

Given a top quality builder and talented designers, the difference between what is merely a 'good' superyacht and a 'superb' one is often just the degree of knowledge and commitment with which the owner enters into the project. Hagadone had dreamed of owning a yacht since he was a child, living on the shore of Lake Coeur d'Alene in Idaho. Towards the end of a highly successful business career, his dream came true with the purchase of the 44.7m (147ft) *Ambrosia*, a pre-owned Benetti first launched in 1994, which he renamed *Lady Lola*. He very much enjoyed this yacht, using her extensively over a two and a half year period but, being a perfectionist, his next dream was to lay out his own design.

In fact, the interior of the first *Lady Lola* already had most things that he needed, and while some rooms were

perfect, some were under-used and others were, perhaps, a little small. The main saloon, for instance, was seldom used, nor were all of the guest cabins and, as a person who loves outdoor living, he resented the tenders cluttering up the decks. Lastly, he also wanted a much larger personal suite, as he intended to make even greater use of his new yacht.

With a firm idea of their needs, the Hagadones contacted interior designer François Zuretti, who had been responsible for *Ambrosia's* original interior as well as the post-purchase refit he carried out on her. They admired Zuretti's style, but were very clear in their insistence that the new interior should be clean and uncluttered, without over-embellishment. In respect of the interior spaces that were required, the brief was clear. The highest priority was for a whole deck dedicated to the owners, which would include a sizeable saloon, a study, and a large en suite bedroom. Elsewhere, the Hagadones wanted just four guest cabins, whose prime use would be for their children, a formal dining room and a guest saloon. It was not an extravagant request – one that, for sure, might have been

Right: An intimate dinner can be enjoyed by the owners on their private aft deck, but, should they wish for company, the table can expanded by an outer rim that is lowered from the deckhead.
Far right: The owners' deck features a terrace forward of the master stateroom.
Below right: The guest seating area aft on the main deck. At the press of a button, the tables rise, unite and move aft to create dining table.

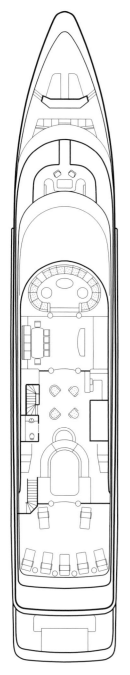

fitted into a yacht the size of the first *Lady Lola* – but they wanted to do things properly, without compromises that might later cause regret. This new design was also to incorporate ample storage space to cope with world-encompassing voyages, together with efficient working areas and comfortable crew quarters. When the plans were finalised, *Lady Lola* was 62m (205ft) in length.

The starting point for the interior layout had been the owners' deck. This could only be positioned on the upper deck and, because the Hagadones wanted a bedroom in the fore part of the superstructure, this meant that the pilothouse had to be located on a lower deck. As the yacht was to comply with Lloyd's Commercial rules as well as MCA regulations, getting approval for such positioning was a hurdle, but this was eventually achieved by creating a mezzanine level, which raised all the levels in the forward third of the yacht by half a deck. This, together with an exterior styling in which the bow lines fall slightly downwards, give the pilothouse excellent views forward, while providing the same mezzanine level on the upper deck, where the owners' stateroom is positioned. At the same time, the crew quarters, on a similarly raised portion of the lower deck below the pilothouse, now occupied a beamier portion of the bows, which, in turn, created room for a bilge deck below, where there is a dry foods larder, a beverage store and long-term refrigeration.

The next design challenge was to create a first class garage in the stern, so as to free up the deck space that the tenders would otherwise have occupied. The centrally positioned engine room left space aft for the four well-sized guest staterooms and a garage that could carry the two tenders, a classic 8.5m (28ft) Stan Craft and a 7.6m (25ft) Novurania, as well as a pair of Bombardier four-stroke jet-skis (quiet running, and without smoke), diving gear and other water toys, such as canoes. To ease the problem of launching large tenders via the stern, where the reach of the crane becomes extreme, it was decided to incorporate a door in the starboard side of the hull, while a stern door would fold down to create a bathing platform and tender dock. Calculations showed that when the 4-tonne side door was hinged open and a 2.2-tonne tender fully extended on the beam crane, the yacht would heel sufficiently to take in water over the door sill. Abandon the idea? No way. The matter was resolved by creating a knee-high dam, running fore and aft to port of the tenders, and by building a water ballast tank below the deck against the port side of the hull. When water comes in over the sill it is taken down drains and held in the ballast tank, thus serving to correct the heel. After the launching is complete it is pumped back into the sea. The diving centre was given a separate compartment, complete with a compressor and ample gear storage, while to port is a shore-power room.

Lady Lola has no permanent stern platform and this means that access to the deck can only be made through the garage and up a stairway, a solution which ensures that, with the stern door closed, unauthorised boarding of the yacht is particularly difficult.

With the outline design of the upper and lower decks complete, attention was focused on the main deck. In most yachts, guests have the run of two saloons, a more formal one on the main deck and a relaxed sky lounge – mainly for daytime use – aft on the upper deck. Clearly, the latter was not possible because this position had already been taken by the owners' private saloon and study. However, the designers still managed to incorporate both uses within a single main deck saloon, as well as adding a music area, while the remainder of the deck was taken up by a formal dining room and the galley. Everything that the owners

desired had been included, without the slightest hint of compromise. *Lady Lola's* steel hull and aluminium superstructure were built in Oceanco's South African yard and shipped to its European facility in Alblasserdam, for finishing under the watchful eye of her captain, Stan Antrim, a retired US Navy Commander.

For guests, the most used entry to the yacht will almost certainly be through the main deck aft, either from the stern dock or the passerelle and thence through the wide, fully glazed doorway leading into the guest saloons. The first is circular in shape with a full 270° of its walls glazed from deck to deckhead. In combination with the aft deck, and of course the sun deck, this is the guests' daytime area. The main deck offers a large settee against the aft bulwark fronted by twin coffee tables which, at the press of a button, rise to dining height as they close together and

Above: The spectacular heated pool on the sun deck features a waterfall, which cascades into two smaller pools.

Below: To compensate for the lack of a sky lounge, the magnificent main deck saloon has been designed to incorporate several different areas in which guests can converse and relax.

move aft to form a single table just the right distance from the settee. Aft of the settee, beyond the area shaded by the upper deck overhang, a broad sunpad is the ideal place to relax after water sports. Just forward, within the air-conditioned comfort of the circular observation lounge – its white wool carpet ringed with a border of honey onyx – a settee faces a bureau from which a television pops up, the latter probably more useful after dusk when this room becomes the guests' television lounge. The formal saloon is just forward, through a passage containing a bar cabinet and a Steinway grand piano. The latter is one of just 300 of this model that were specially designed by Dakota Jackson in 2002 to celebrate the 300th anniversary of the invention of the piano. Beyond, the saloon offers a large conversation area to port, in which settees and easy chairs are gathered around a low table, while to starboard is a games table. Decoratively, this area sets a splendid tone that is used, with minor variations, throughout the whole yacht.

Zuretti, in close collaboration with Lola Hagadone, combined materials that provide both formality and relaxation, as well as brightness and space. White is used for the carpet, deckhead and most of the furnishings, while solemnity is introduced by a magnificent band of dark apple mahogany that rings the lower portion of every wall. This is topped by the warmth and subtle texture of Norwegian birch burl, its highly glossed honey tone deliciously flecked with darkly interesting imperfections. The owners particularly wished to minimise fussy decoration. The shelves, which display a splendid collection of glass bowls, are modernly square-edged, while the cabinets also lean to the future, displaying an illuminated panel of sculpted glass set within their fronts. There is whimsy, too. Behind the bar the wall is clad in a diamond pattern, each segment being made from a fan of bamboo, while a beautiful silk waterfall-patterned wall covering acts as a backdrop to the Steinway piano.

Left: Mirrors on the inboard wall of the dining room allow all guests to have spectacular views through the large windows.
Below left: The conversation area in the guests' saloon.
Below right: The stairs rising from Lady Lola's entrance lobby to her owners' private deck can be completely closed off with a mirrored sliding door to ensure privacy.

This theme is carried forward into the spacious starboard side lobby, where the mahogany and birch now alternate in horizontal bands, broken only by a pair of fluted columns. Here, the focus of attention is an amazing glass waterfall that tumbles down the central column of the stairs to join an equally detailed glass stream that flows across the marble-floored lobby towards the massive side-deck doors. Almost totally frameless, these flood the hall with light and are the only glass elements in the yacht that need to be protected with a storm shutter while at sea – the remainder are all bulletproof. From here, a stairway descends to the four excellent en suite guest cabins – three doubles and a convertible twin/double, and rises to the owners' deck, the latter path protected by the unique privacy system. Its operation is simple. One of the fluted columns opens to reveal a control box (there is a similar box at the head of the stairs) and at the press of a button a mirrored panel slides across to close the upward flight of stairs so seamlessly that no one would guess that they exist. Simultaneously, a red light goes on in the crew quarters to signify that the owners are not to be disturbed.

Forward, past the entrance to the servery and a side table topped in red onyx, is the dining room. Running fore and aft, it is flanked on its outboard side by huge windows and inboard with equally large mirrors so that every guest seated at the long 12-seater table can see the view. This is, perhaps, best at night, when four two-million candlepower searchlights set in the hull side can reach out to illuminate a cove, attract a shoal of fish, or merely light up white-crested waves sweeping by.

At the top of the stairs from the lobby is the owners' landing. Aft is their saloon, which opens to a private deck, while forward is the master suite with a second private deck forward of it. To starboard is a study and to port a larder and kitchen – it is a totally self-contained living area. The deck's star attraction is certainly the master suite. Climbing the short set of stairs one enters behind the bedhead and it is difficult not to gasp as the semi-circular room opens up to reveal a spectacular 180° panorama with the bed at its focal point. How wonderful to wake in this room to a sunrise over some tropical atoll, especially when one can emerge onto the private deck, just forward, for breakfast. To port, a few stairs descend aft from the mezzanine to the lady's dressing room, which offers luxuriously fitted wardrobes

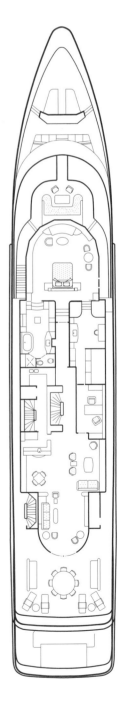

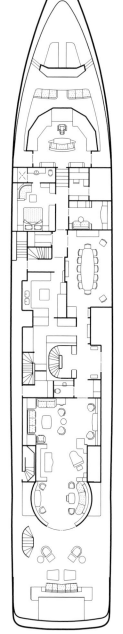

and drawers, beyond which is a delightfully marbled
bathroom with separate head and shower compartments.
Set by the large window, the bath has an unrivalled view,
while privacy can be ensured with an LCD panel that can
be made opaque at the flick of a switch. To starboard, the
equivalent position is filled with the gentleman's shower
room, this time with a huge shower lined with a stunning
blue Brazilian marble. A head compartment, a wash-basin
surrounded by the same blue marble, and a towel-warming
drawer complete the luxury of the shower room, while,
beyond a display of meteorological instruments, is a custom
tailored dressing room with spacious wardrobes and glass-
fronted drawers. Conveniently, a door opens aft from the
dressing room into the study – its desk fully fitted for private
communications and overlooked by a map-style world time
clock and flat-screen television, while its main door opens
onwards into the private lounge.

Of much the same size as the guests' lounge, its layout is quite reminiscent of the sky lounge in the former *Lady Lola*, but cleaner in its decoration and flooded with light and external views. A sitting area is to starboard, while the port side is filled with a games table and a marble-topped bar, adjoining which is a fully stocked private galley and pantry. One notable example of custom design is that a small, discreet serving hatch opens between the pantry and the owners' lobby, so that when the area is in privacy mode breakfast and papers may be slipped through. Aft of the lounge area, the narrow section contains a massive 137cm (54in) projection television opposite which is a hedonistically comfortable settee, whose seats can be powered to a reclining position. Beyond this circular observation saloon, which is furnished with side tables and easy chairs, is access to the open deck. Here, the owner wanted a dining table of a size where two could dine in intimacy but, at the same time, he could foresee occasions when eight might sit around the table. He solved the problem for himself by designing an intimate two-seater table which could be instantly enlarged by the addition of an outer ring that is stored in the deckhead and lowered into place by four cables. Ingenious – and it works perfectly. The thorny occasional problem of excessive breeze causing havoc with the table was also solved with elegance. On either side of the table are buffets, backed by a glass panel or, rather, three glass panels – two of which can be extended forward on a track to close the gap between buffet and superstructure, completely eliminating wind or even draughts.

In the past, many very large and splendidly decorated yachts were built without much consideration for the detailed design of their sun deck, a lapse which often resulted in large expanses of windswept, and hence under-used open space. Smaller yachts, however, with less deck area to play with, usually made use of every square inch available. *Ambrosia* was such a yacht, and she taught Duane Hagadone the value of having a variety of purpose-designed decks, valuable experience that was re-invested with enthusiasm in his new *Lady Lola*, whose sun deck is a veritable multi-functional outdoor living area. Forward on the rise of the mezzanine, behind an encircling bulwark raised by a glass windbreak, is a pleasant sitting area, while amidships beneath the shade of the mast is a dining area. A head and a bar are built into the legs of the arch mast. Just aft is a large heated pool, surrounded by seats, from which water cascades into two smaller pools, while the aftermost portion of the deck carries umbrella-shaded sunloungers. A large screen can drop from the mast for open-air movies. And then there is the golf course. A golf course? On a yacht? Yes, really. It works like this. With the yacht at anchor and a couple of aft rails removed, a small portion of

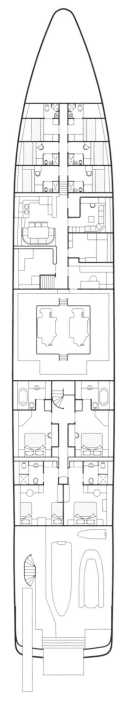

the teak-laid deck is mechanically replaced by a square of artificial grass that contains an automatic golf tee that presents ball after ball to the player. Set out in an arc at various distances up to about 200m (218yds) around the stern of the yacht are 18 'holes' – numbered floating flags – are anchored in position. The golfer plays each hole in turn, with just one shot, and the closest ball wins the hole. The balls, almost exactly the same weight as a regular golf ball, float, and are recovered by the tender. The nineteenth hole is handily close too! Then there is the floating tennis court – no, this time we are kidding!

Given the detail already described, it is almost needless to say that *Lady Lola's* service and crew areas are also well conceived, spacious and totally functional. The pilothouse shares the clean, uncluttered looks of the guest areas, with its control desk and facia dominated by seven monitor screens that relay information from radars, chart plotters, the monitoring system and the many instruments, the majority of whose black boxes are either beneath the desk or remotely positioned. Keyboards and mice are stowed away in custom compartments, manuals and documentation are hidden in cupboards, leaving only vital

controls on display. Guests can observe the action from the substantial settee. The captain has a large cabin and a separate lounge just aft of the bridge, a few steps down from the mezzanine level. The remaining 14 crew are housed in seven well-sized double bunked cabins. Also in the crew area are messes for officers and crew and a six-machine laundry. Up on the main deck, the galley boasts a full complement of professional equipment, while the adjacent storeroom for the yacht's tableware is perhaps the best organised on any yacht of this size.

The same can be said of the engine room, an immaculately laid out and constructed two-deck affair with its own control room. Twin 1,651hp diesels deliver *Lady Lola* with a 15 knot maximum speed and a cruising speed of 12 knots, which gives her a range of 4,500nm – ideal for her world cruising role that has already begun with a tour of the Mediterranean. To date, she has completed 5,000nm without mechanical problem.

Lady Lola is splendid in her exterior styling, decoration, and thoughtful customisation. But why did she turn out so much better than many other 'standard' yachts? The answer lies in the knowledge, interest and commitment of her owner, both before and during the build. Duane Hagadone is a man who thrives on projects, and during the two and a half year building period he visited the yard every 60 days and had 10 further meetings with Zuretti in his Idaho home. On top of this, he recalls that, during the build, not a day went by without his being involved in some design issue, which he resolved on the spot. Not everything was perfect first time, but Hagadone had the dogged persistence to retrace wrong paths and redesign troublesome items again and again until they looked right – the mast, for instance, was redrawn three times. 'There are no short cuts,' says Hagadone, 'You have to put in the time to get the design and quality that you want.' Good advice for anyone about to start a custom yacht-building project. Today, standing proudly on his completed yacht, if he is asked if he would change anything after six months' experience of living aboard, his answer is emphatically no: 'This is exactly the yacht I wanted, and I am really happy with her.' That is how customisation should be.

Above: *A highly-glossed hallway gives access to the four guest cabins on the lower deck.*
Below left: *The en suite guest bathrooms share the luxury of those on the owners' deck.*

SPECIFICATIONS

LOA	62.60m (205ft 5in)	**Fire control system**	Thorn
LWL	54.06m (177ft 4in)	**Exterior paint**	Awlgrip
Beam (max)	10.50m (34ft 4in)	**Air-conditioning**	Heinen & Hopman
Draught	3.65m (12ft 0in)	**Communications equipment**	Sailor/Radio Holland
Displacement (to DWL)	924 tonnes	**Navigation equipment**	Furuno/Radio Holland
Propulsion	2 x 1,651hp Caterpillar 3512B DI-TA	**Autopilot & gyrocompass**	C.Plath
Gearbox	2 x ZF, BW 466-G 4.063:1	**Entertainment systems**	Van Bergenhenegouwen
Propellers	Lips, 5-blade	**Passerelle & boarding ladder**	Yacht Tec
Speed (max/cruise)	15 knots/12 knots	**Owners & guests**	10 in 5 x double cabins
Fuel capacity	117,700 litres	**Crew**	15 in 1 x double cabin & 7 x twin cabins
Range at 12 knots	4,500nm	**Construction**	Steel hull & aluminium superstructure
Electricity generation	Northern Lights	**Classification**	Lloyd's ✠100 A1, SSC, YACHT (P),
Stabilisers	Koop Nautic, Searocq 4080		MONO G6, LMC, UMS. MCA Compliant
Bowthruster	Holland roerpropeller	**Interior design**	Zuretti Interior Designers
Watermakers	2 x HEM, 30/4000 15000l/d	**Naval architects**	Oceanco
Windlass & davits	Ascon	**Builder/Year**	Oceanco/2002

Northern Light

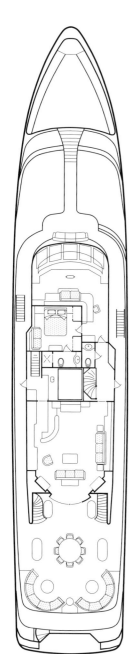

Right: The 46m Feadship, Northern Light features a classic interior by John Munford Design.

When someone who has previously owned two sailing yachts and two motor yachts commissions a new one, it is fair to assume that he has a very clear idea of what he wants. The 46m (151ft) Feadship *Northern Light* was designed to be thoroughly comfortable, beautifully appointed and capable of remaining independent of the shore for an extended period. And although 46m (151ft) is a very substantial vessel, one of the requirements was that she should 'not be too big'. This is because the owners understand that yachts over 50m (164ft) in length, according to Lloyd's formula, and 500 registered tons tend to face more regulatory hurdles and suffer higher charges as a result, so they specified a design with the maximum accommodation in a hull just 4m (13ft) shorter than the critical length.

Northern Light was designed primarily for the owner's personal use, both in the Caribbean and Mediterranean, but he may decide to offer her for charter in the future. In this respect the important decisions were to go for full Lloyd's certification and MCA approval, which will allow her to charter without further formalities and will also ensure that she finds a ready market when offered for sale at a later date.

In addition to their programme of extended cruises, the owners like to 'weekend' with family and friends as often as they can manage and, if all the Pullman berths are filled, up to 14 guests may sleep aboard. They are cared for by a permanent crew of 10, who live in the comfortable and spacious quarters forward.

The interior of *Northern Light*, designed by John Munford, is completely and richly traditional, featuring raised and fielded panelling in top-quality Honduras mahogany for all the guest compartments. The warm, chestnut glow of this beautiful timber is offset by pale-coloured carpets and ceilings, the latter being beamed and cambered to give an authentic nautical atmosphere.

Right: The 'family lounge' is furnished with handmade Peter Dudgeon settees and armchairs, complemented by an Arthur Brett mahogany and rosewood coffee table.
Below: Gold tones and stately traditional furniture embellish the formal dining saloon.

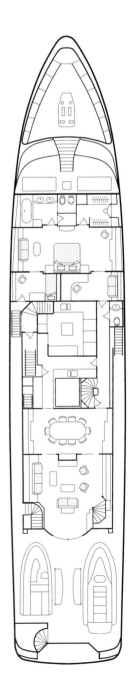

In a number of ways the tone for the whole yacht is set by the 'family lounge' on the upper deck, a large and well-lit open room, decorated in a library style, that radiates solid comfort. Deeply upholstered sofas and armchairs, handmade by Peter Dudgeon, look over a mahogany and rosewood Arthur Brett coffee table towards a 127cm (50in) plasma-screen television that is concealed behind a painting when not required. Discreet gold wire grilles hide the speakers of a comprehensive Linn stereo outfit. This, together with the television, the curtains, the lights and the air-conditioning, can be controlled at the touch of an icon on a Crestron wireless remote control – a system used throughout the yacht.

Occupying the forward port corner of this delightful room is one of *Northern Light's* unique features: a granite-topped bar complete with a tap for draught beer. Three kegs of the owner's favourite brew are stowed in a special temperature-controlled locker, which also features a purpose-designed davit for swinging the kegs aboard.

Double doors open onto the upper deck, a large teak-laid area, where the planking is mimicked by a superb teak and holly outdoor dining table with space for 14 to sit at in comfort. Against the stern rail, large curved settees provide the ideal spot to relax, glass in hand, to watch the sun go down.

From the upper saloon, a sliding door opens to the upper hallway, from where an elegant wooden stairway descends to the main deck, passing a very special antique stick barometer on the way. Also on the upper level is a day head, and although one does not normally linger over a description of such compartments, this one really is very special, with a stunning hand-painted blue and gold compass rose adorning the wash-basin, which is set in a swirling blue and white marble counter with hand-painted nickel-gold taps.

The main saloon and formal dining room are very gracious, with handmade Tai Ping carpets that have a diamond pattern of cut silk woven into the wool background. Pineapples, the symbol for welcome, are sculptured into the corners of a central panel, where the yacht's compass rose logo is embroidered. The superb oval dining table, again by Arthur Brett, has a burr madrona centre and borders of pearwood and mahogany, outlined with inset lines of brass. Unseen by guests, a tiny CCTV camera overlooks this table, the picture being visible on a small screen in the pantry. This enables staff to appear as if by magic when they are needed, instead of hovering behind guests and perhaps making them feel uneasy.

On such a comfortable yacht, one would naturally expect the owner's quarters to be particularly special and one would not be disappointed. Placed in the traditional position forward on the main deck, the overhead beams and mahogany furniture give a powerful impression of being aboard some classic yacht from the past.

The owner's study guards one entrance, emanating a strongly masculine feel with its green leather-topped desk, well-filled bookcases, aged leather sofa and racing yacht models on display. Like any gentleman's desk these days, this one has a PC on it, but one with an elegant black flat-screen monitor and wireless keyboard. Another nice touch is the small, unobtrusive B&G monitor to display information about the vessel's performance.

The owner's stateroom is large and elegant, the formal impression of the mahogany joinery being softened by pale carpets and overhead panels, and by the cheerful covering on the centrally placed king-sized bed. On one side of this well-lit room there is a comfortable sofa and side tables, and on the other a particularly attractive mahogany chest of drawers, where the top drawer is a false front concealing a slide-out writing desk and four small stationery drawers.

Off the bedroom is a smaller cabin designed around the needs of a young child, including a splendid built-in cot upholstered in baby-blue satin. A leather-topped ottoman serves as a toy box for this privileged infant, who can also play host to an older person, or perhaps his nanny, by making use of the cabin's folding Pullman berth.

Right: The king-sized bed in the owner's cabin is framed by immaculate Honduras mahogany panelling.
Below right: Off-white marble prevails in the master bathroom, which has an electically heated floor.
Below far right: One of the two twin bedded guest cabins.

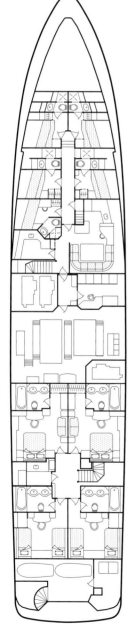

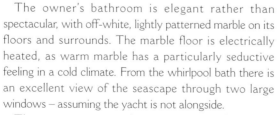

The owner's bathroom is elegant rather than spectacular, with off-white, lightly patterned marble on its floors and surrounds. The marble floor is electrically heated, as warm marble has a particularly seductive feeling in a cold climate. From the whirlpool bath there is an excellent view of the seascape through two large windows – assuming the yacht is not alongside.

The guest accommodation comprises four very comfortable and spacious cabins – two double and two twin – opening off a parquet-floored lobby on the lower deck. The sliding watertight door – an MCA safety requirement – is cleverly concealed between pairs of wooden pillars. In addition to the four cabins, the lobby has a hidden door to a luggage room and bonded store, and there is also a small guest pantry with coffee

machine, juicer, a fridge and a toaster in case guests should feel peckish during the night.

Panelled in the same superb Honduras mahogany as the owner's accommodation, the double cabins are particularly impressive, having marble bathrooms with double basins and a full-sized bathtub. Each cabin has a comprehensive entertainment system including a dedicated satellite television receiver giving an almost unlimited choice of live or recorded sound and vision, all controllable via Crestron touch screens.

Of the outdoor spaces, the sun deck is likely to prove the most popular, as it provides an immensity of space for outdoor relaxation. At the forward end is a spa pool with surrounding sun cushions, sheltered by a glass windscreen. Under the shade of the radar arch is a bar

and service counter where, once again, draught beer is on tap. Further aft, large settees shaded by giant umbrellas follow the curve of the aft rail. The aft portion of this deck is open to the skies but can be covered by an awning that slides along support wires.

The deck below, opening off the upper saloon, has already been mentioned and is the one used for slightly more formal entertainment and alfresco dining. Down again on the main deck are two substantial tenders on chocks, which are launched sideways by two horizontal beam cranes that extend from concealed stowages. Feadship does not believe that it is practical on a vessel this size to stow the tenders in a garage because their size and weight calls for substantial lifting gear and because they take up so much internal space. Instead there is a smaller lazarette with room for a couple of jet-skis, which are also launched sideways by a small crane that extends through a door in the side of the hull. As a result, there is no large transom door but instead a fixed bathing and boarding platform with access from the aft deck.

It is useless to talk about a long-range cruising yacht unless the crew and working spaces are appropriate for long-term use. For instance, *Northern Light's* galley is fully equipped with professional rather than domestic equipment. The Electrolux 'Therma' hobs and ovens – adequate for a small ship or restaurant – are backed up by a double fryer, a warming cupboard, two microwaves, two refrigerators and two sinks, all of it to catering standards. Better still, all of this is set within a pleasant, well-lit ambience with a view of the sea.

Forward, on the lower deck, the crew have a roomy mess deck with its own pantry, entertainment system and computer station. Opening off it is a fully equipped laundry with three washing machines, three dryers and a rotary presser. Below the mess deck and its five twin crew cabins is a storage deck, with dry stores, cool room and freezers.

The engine room is conventional in its design, with the twin V-8 Caterpillar main engines and three 85kW generators installed in a relatively uncrowded twin-level configuration. The engineers enjoy a separate air-conditioned and soundproofed control room, complete with a fully equipped work bench and other useful equipment, including a portable electro-welding set.

Northern Light is not spectacular in the conventional sense and she is certainly not ostentatious. On the contrary, she is well-designed, solidly built, superbly decorated, and finished with top-class materials and equipment. She is sure to give her owners and guests enormous satisfaction for very many years to come.

SPECIFICATIONS

LOA	46.00m (150ft 11in)	**Sewage treatment system**	Hamann
LWL	41.00m (134ft 5in)	**Fire suppression**	Hi-fog
Beam	8.80m (28ft 10in)	**Exterior paint**	Awlgrip
Draught	2.95m (9ft 8in)	**Communications**	Inmarsat Satcom-B
Propulsion	2 x Caterpillar 3508B-DI-TA	**Radar**	Furuno
	1014bhp at 1600rpm	**Autopilot & gyrocompass**	C. Plath
Gearbox	Reintjes Waf 541	**Echo sounder**	Furuno
Propellers	Fixed pitch, 5-blade	**Entertainment system**	Linn
Speed (max/cruise)	14.5 knots/13 knots	**Remote controls**	Crestron
Fuel capacity	73,000 litres	**Guests**	10 in 3 x double & 2 x twin cabins
Range at 13 knots	4,500nm	**Crew**	11 in 1 x double, 1 x single & 4 x twin cabins
Generators	3 x 85kW Caterpillar/Stamford	**Construction**	Welded steel hull &
Stabilisers	Koop Nautic		aluminium alloy superstructure
Watermakers	2 x HEM, 12,000 l/d	**Classification**	Lloyd's ✠100A1, SSC Yacht, G6, LMC
Fresh water capacity	16,400 litres		MCA compliant
Shore connection	2 x 50kVA Atlas	**Interior design**	John Munford Design
Tenders	Novurania Equator 660 & 530,	**Naval architects**	De Voogt Naval Architects
	Yamaha jet-skis	**Builder/Year**	Feadship – Royal Van Lent & Zonen/2001

Olympia

Right: *Olympia's exterior styling is modern-classic.*

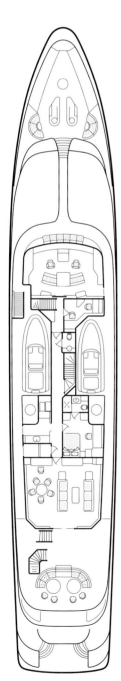

The story of the 57m (187ft) Feadship motor yacht *Olympia* is of a project with an interesting history during inception, design and construction that ultimately became an outstandingly beautiful and successful yacht.

Following discussions that went on for more than a year in late 1998, Feadship signed an agreement to build a 50m (164ft) modern-classic motor yacht for a very experienced yachtsman. From the outset the owners' wish was for airiness and transparency of styling and interior design, reflecting the style of their homes, which the design teams from the yard and De Voogt Naval Architects were able to visit.

Several well-known yacht designers were approached but finally the owners settled on the New York firm of Mark Hampton Inc, who had decorated some rooms in the White House in a classic but light design. This company had no experience of yachts, but with some coaching from the yard and De Voogt it was quickly able to grasp the essentials of designing the interior spaces aboard a yacht.

Just before the keel was due to be laid, about 10 months into the project, the owners decided that they needed rather more space than was available in the 50m (164ft) hull and asked the yard if it would be possible at this late stage to lengthen it. This is not unusual in custom yacht projects, but unfortunately it proved impossible to meet the additional space requirements within the existing hull shape. Instead, the yard proposed working from the hull lines of the 57m (187ft) *Barbara*

Jean (see *The Superyachts*, volume 15), which had recently been launched by Feadship's De Vries yard, optimising its lines to fit the exact requirements for the new yacht. Thanks to some fast work by De Voogt, which effectively drew up an entirely new hull in record time, the project was re-started without too much delay.

After this, work in all departments went ahead at a steady pace and, with Feadship busy booking follow-on orders at what was a very hectic time in the luxury yacht market, project 663 quietly approached completion.

Unexpectedly and suddenly, however, the yacht appeared for sale. Although the owners remained very involved with the design and construction process, they had a change of mind concerning the capacity in which the yacht would be used. The original plan was for a purely private yacht, but subsequently there was a tendency to regard her more as a charter yacht and, as the design was not suitable for this, she was discreetly placed on the market, about five months before the projected delivery date.

Fortunately, a new owner was found very quickly, attracted by the fact that he could have a brand new Feadship almost immediately instead of having to wait for three years or more. The Mark Hampton interior was already well-advanced in construction at the time of the sale. The new owner liked the bright, clean, open appearance but felt that it was almost dazzling and called in the firm of the well-known London designer Jon Bannenberg with the brief to add a little more colour and texture to the interior. The Bannenberg team, led by Jon's

Far Left: *The light-coloured interior is carried through to the pilothouse.*

Above: White-stained ash was chosen as the keynote timber. This was finished with an open grain to impart a natural feel.
Right: Lighting leads one up the grand central stairway.
Far right: The oval dining table has a central leaf that can be removed to create a pretty circular table for four.

son Dicky, had to work extremely fast as there was only limited time remaining in the build programme. In spite of this, they were able to make a considerable impact on the look of the interior.

The other unusual fact about *Olympia*, as she became named, is that she is the first yacht to be managed by the Cyprus-based company Unicom, whose normal business is managing a large fleet of Russian cargo and passenger ships including the famous cruise liner *Maxim Gorky*. Among the company's strengths is access to a large pool of highly qualified Russian officers and crew, an important asset when good crew are at a premium.

The layout of *Olympia* has been found to work very well. The only debatable point is whether the engine room is better placed amidships or aft. For good balance and weight distribution the amidships position is

favoured, while an aft engine room enables designers to work with central staircases connecting all decks.

In any case, *Olympia* has a central engine room with guest cabins aft and crew quarters forward on the lower deck. On the main deck, the saloon is at the aft extremity of the superstructure. Moving forward via the dining room, one passes through the main entrance lobby, leaving the galley on the port side, before entering the owner's suite, which uses the full width of the hull thanks to the fact that the side decks finish at this point.

At the upper level there are full walk-around decks and the two main tenders are stowed in 'docks' set into the side of the superstructure abaft the bridge. This arrangement results in the superstructure being lengthened and the top deck becoming longer, while still leaving a large and unobstructed aft deck. From the very

attractive upper saloon, based on the successful design used on *Excellence II*, a corridor runs forward past the captain's cabin and a larder, then between the tenders to the bridge. Above this level is a substantial sun deck, partly shaded by an overhanging roof.

The design brief was for a very light interior with the maximum number of transparent glass windows and the minimum obstruction to outside views. The intention was to eliminate as far as possible the barriers between the

Above: With the name Olympia, *it seemed only natural to decorate her with pictures from the Greek classical period and illustrations of classical buildings, as seen flanking the central stairway.*

Above: A quiet spot where guests can relax and indulge in a little conversation.

outside and inside worlds so that one seemed to flow naturally into the other. This is partly achieved by maximising the glazing. The main saloon has almost full-length windows, while the bulwark outside is dropped in height and replaced by an open rail so that the water is visible even from a seated position. The sky lounge takes this a step further with almost entirely glazed sides. To open up this deck even further, the aft portion of the bulwark has been replaced by glass and the stairway to the sun deck has been built as a freestanding structure using stainless steel tubes to make it appear transparent.

To translate this brightness to the interior, Hampton chose white-stained ash as the keynote timber, with an open grain finish to provide a natural feel. The actual architecture of the interior is quite formal, with raised and fielded panelling and classical pillars, but the effect is light and simple. To add further to the brightness, Hampton opted for white wool carpets and mostly light-coloured furniture plus white or off-white marble in the majority of the bathrooms.

Bannenberg's contribution to the overall decoration was to add a little more colour in the final fitting-out. His most important action was to replace some of the white ash with bird's-eye maple. Although it is also a light-coloured timber, the maple has a pale golden-brown tone and an unobtrusive but interesting grain texture that is restful on the eye. The De Vries joiners were also able to step these panels out from the background in order to give them more prominence.

The off-white carpets have been covered in a number of places by striped light brown JAB rugs, while settees that were to have been built in along the sides of the main and upper saloons were changed to free-standing furniture to offer a more informal look. After the yacht received the new name *Olympia*, it seemed quite natural to decorate her with pictures from the Greek classical period and illustrations of classical buildings. The main entrance lobby, in which the pillared base of the stairway is flanked by two large etchings of the Parthenon, seems

particularly appropriate. David Linley rushed through a special order for an oval dining table with a bird's-eye maple top and classical pillared plinth. This table has a central leaf that can be removed to create a pretty circular table for four. The seats, with woven cane backs, are a particularly impressive colour match for this table.

A special feature of *Olympia* is that she actually has two master staterooms, the owner's quarters on the main deck and an extra-large VIP suite on the lower deck. These two bedrooms are about the same size but the owner's has additional details. From the entrance hall, one first enters an elegant study on the starboard side and then the very spacious bedroom with a central double bed flanked on either side by comfortable seating areas and lit by large windows. Blue and light brown fabrics provide a cool, sophisticated look. With this layout it is possible to have two bathrooms but the owner preferred to fit out the starboard space as a gym with a treadmill

faced by a television to take away the tedium of running on the spot. Finally, a doorway beyond the bed opens into a large closet, with room for all the clothing most people could wish for.

Down on the lower deck, the VIP suite has wall panels of golden-brown fabric to give a warm and softer atmosphere. As in the owner's suite, an antique sea-chest and suitcase at the foot of the bed add an exotic touch. The white marble-trimmed bathroom is very similar to the owner's, with a full-sized tub and separate shower.

The three remaining cabins have been arranged for maximum flexibility with double beds and additional Pullman berths. The two aft cabins are large and have bathtubs, while the third is smaller and has a shower. All the cabins have first-class audio and video outfits with televisions that can tune into the satellite system. The two saloons and the owner's cabin have big screens and a top-quality Linn sound-and-vision system on demand.

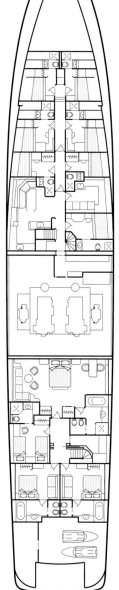

No modern superyacht would be complete without a sun deck, and a great deal of thought has gone into *Olympia's*. One difficulty with sun decks is that if the yacht is under way, there is certain to be a strong breeze blowing across such an exposed space. As protection against this, the forward curve of the deck, where a spa pool and sunbathing pads are situated, is fitted with a glass windscreen, while as a second line of defence there is a complete glass wall across the centre of the deck. This means that al fresco meals can be taken on the aft part of the deck in confidence that the plates and glasses will not be blown off the table.

Although the two main tenders are stowed on the upper deck, *Olympia* also has a capacious lazarette with a watertight door opening onto the aft bathing/boarding platform. Inside, an extending overhead hoist is rigged to lift either of the two waveriders or other water sports equipment. There is a compressor for diver's air bottles and scuba gear for qualified guests. Also fitted in the lazarette is a power pack for the various hydraulic equipment and a Marihoff Hi-Fog fire suppression system.

Mechanically, *Olympia* follows a well-established pattern that De Vries has followed many times, with

Caterpillar main engines driving high pitch, skew back, five-bladed propellers through Reintjes gears. There are just two Caterpillar generators (with Halyard exhaust-gas cleaning systems), either of which is able to carry the whole electrical load of the ship.

It would be fascinating to place *Olympia* alongside her near-sistership *Barbara Jean*. From the outside it might be difficult to tell them apart but on board they are totally different. *Barbara Jean* is perfectly finished in quiet, dignified dark mahogany that provides a complete refuge from the outside world. *Olympia*, on the other hand, is light, bright and, as far as possible, totally integrated with the outside world. The contrast could hardly be greater.

SPECIFICATIONS

LOA	57.00m (187ft 0in)	**Stabilisers**	Brown Brothers
LWL	49.90m (163ft 9in)	**Bowthruster**	HRP
Beam	10.10m (33ft 2in)	**Air-conditioning**	Heinen & Hopman
Draught	2.95m (9ft 8in)	**Autopilot**	Anschütz, digital Nautopilot D
Main engines	2 x 1,500hp Caterpillar 3512B diesels	**Fire supression**	Marihoff Hi-Fog
Gearboxes	ZF, BW466G	**Entertainment systems**	Linn
Speed (max/cruise)	15.5 knots/13 knots	**Owner & guests**	10 in 1 x twin & 4 x double cabins
Range at 13 knots	4,700nm	**Crew**	16 in 1 x double & 7 x twin bunked cabins
Generators	2 x 160kW Caterpillar 3306B	**Construction**	Steel hull & aluminium superstructure
Shore connection	2 x Atlas 75kVA	**Classification**	Lloyd's ✠100A1, SSC
Fuel capacity	100 tonnes	**Naval architects**	De Voogt Naval Architects
Watermakers	2 x HEM 10t/d	**Interior design**	Mark Hampton
Fresh water capacity	24,400 litres	**Interior furnishing and fit-out**	Jon Bannenberg
Windlasses	Steen, 8kW	**Builder/Year**	Feadship–De Vries/2002

Patricia

Three years ago, Benetti launched the first of a new series of semi-custom motor yachts with a glass-reinforced plastic hull and superstructure. The first model was the 35m (115ft) Benetti Classic, which has proved a spectacular success with 11 models delivered so far and another eight on order. Two further models are now in production – the 30m (98ft) Benetti Tradition, which attracted five orders before the first boat had even been launched, and now the 45m (148ft) Benetti Vision enters the stage.

To commission a 45m (148ft) composite construction motor yacht was a fairly bold decision, as the costs involved in constructing the moulds are very high, however if the success of the Classic is anything to go by, it was well justified. A huge advantage for the owner will be reduced maintenance, while the yard should eventually benefit from lower building costs and a simpler, faster construction process. European yards have been slower than those in the United States to adopt plastics as a hull material for superyachts, but there is undoubtedly a growing market.

Moulding is carried out at Cantiere Moschini in Fano on the east coast of Italy and the completed hulls are towed from there to Viareggio for completion. Since the existing Benetti shipyard is already fully committed to construction of its larger steel yachts, additional space has been found by taking over the former Lusben Craft premises, where a collection of old buildings has been knocked down to be replaced by brand new ones. Such was the enthusiasm for the project that in the beginning there was the remarkable sight of a new building shed being erected around the hull of a new Benetti Classic. This site has an extensive waterfront, where yachts can be launched or lifted by the 600-tonne mobile boat lift.

The Benetti Vision is a displacement motor yacht with a top speed of 15 knots and sufficient range to cruise the oceans of the world. The styling and layout have been established by Stephano Righini and can be varied within certain limits to suit the customer. This first model, *Patricia*, has an interior design by François Zuretti, but future customers could chose a different designer. The really interesting fact is that instead of an

Main picture: Benetti's all-composite Patricia *is the first of their Vision series.*
Far left: *A spa pool forward of the master stateroom provides absolute seclusion.*
Left: *The owner's private deck also features a small table on which to enjoy an alfresco breakfast.*
Below: *Curved glass screens shelter the sun deck.*

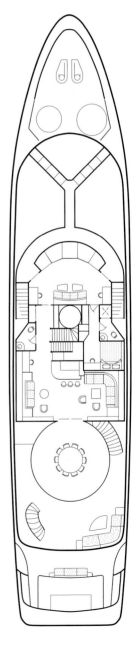

Right: Elegant dining for
10 on the main deck.
Below: The main deck
saloon has cherrywood as
its keynote, while café au lait
tub chairs surround
games tables from
Bradley of Folkestone.

average 'catch-all' design – the normal *mode d'emploi* on production yachts – Benetti has gone for a bold, innovative layout with interesting new features.

Several areas of the yacht have been designed to present panoramic views of the outside world. Perhaps the most striking of these is the circular sun lounge on the bridge deck. Opening off the bridge deck saloon, it has curved, floor-to-ceiling glass doors that can be set to any position, from completely closed to fully open and stowed out of sight. This adds a new dimension to the idea of alfresco dining, allowing the gastronomic experience to be enjoyed in any weather condition.

This circular theme has also been used in a most original way in the owner's stateroom, the forward side of which is a semicircular wall of windows overlooking a small private deck. In the centre of the cabin, the king-sized bed lies back-to-back with a comfortable sofa, both of which are set on a turntable so that, at the flick of a switch, they can turn to face either the view forward or a giant plasma-screen television on the bulkhead. It has to

be said that this cabin would not be the most comfortable place to sleep with the yacht butting into a lively head sea, but this would probably be the last thing that most owners would wish to do anyway.

Another dramatic circle is found on entering the main lobby, where a curved staircase encircles a glass-walled lift. This serves all decks except the sun deck, where the top of the shaft acts as both a skylight and a glass-topped table. A lift is a most unusual feature on a production yacht and makes it especially attractive to any passenger who has difficulty with stairs.

At the lower end of its journey, the lift opens into the circular guest lobby, from which four comfortable staterooms are accessed. This lobby contains a mini-bar, so that cold drinks are immediately available, and also a mini-laundry, in case guests would like to wash a few personal items for themselves.

Of the four guest en suite staterooms, two are VIPs in which the beds are set at a 45-degree angle to the centreline in order to add visual interest to the room. The forward twin-berthed pair are more conventional in layout but very spacious. The entire space forward of the guest staterooms is devoted to the crew quarters. Special care has been taken to allow the crew access to different areas of the yacht without intruding into guest areas, and this includes a crawl space beneath the guest staterooms that gives access to the tank tops.

Aft of the guest accommodation, the compact engine room holds the Caterpillar main engines, the generators and an impressive array of other technical equipment. The engineer enjoys a soundproof control room where the main electrical switchgear is installed. Right aft is a large garage for toys and tenders. The problem with storing tenders in this way is that one normally has to

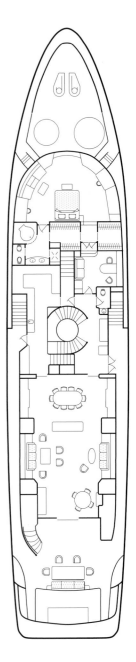

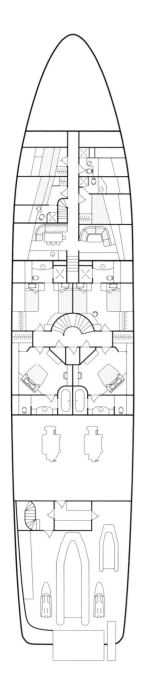

launch the main tender first, even if it is not needed, because it blocks the exit to the stern platform. Benetti have solved this difficulty rather neatly by fitting a second doorway, on the starboard side. A sizeable piece of the ship's side hinges down to act as a boarding platform and a small jib crane can be used to lift out the crew boat or jet-skis by this route.

François Zuretti has used fine timbers and exotic marbles to decorate *Patricia's* interior in a bright, eye-catching style. On entering the starboard-side lobby one steps onto an unusual marble combination floor and faces high-gloss cherrywood joinery, chromed handrails with gold trim and the polished stainless steel and glass of the lift.

The main saloon and dining room are open plan with very large rectangular windows on both sides. The keynote timber is cherrywood with a high-gloss finish, while burl maple is used for the locker doors and the elegant dining tables. *Café au lait* leather tub chairs and a pair of pretty games tables by Bradley of Folkestone are found at the aft end of the saloon, while a settee on each side provides the ideal spot from which to watch the giant plasma-screen television that pops up from the cabinet separating the saloon from the dining room.

The bridge deck saloon is the one that really surprises. It seems at first like a snug but comfortable bar area, with an attractive marble-topped servery, comfortable sofas and armchairs. From these club-like surroundings, double glass doors open into the completely different atmosphere of the circular sun lounge, which has so much glazing that the distinction between indoors and outdoors is abolished. By careful adjustment of the doors and curtains, any variation between open air and complete enclosure can be achieved. A stylish circular table with a rotating centre section transforms this compartment into a dining terrace of the utmost elegance.

Compared to this spectacular compartment, the decoration of the guest areas is relatively traditional with arched and panelled doors in solid cherrywood, contrasting with lighter toned maple in the cabins. The different choice of marbles for each of the en suite bathrooms is always interesting and sometimes quite arresting, as in the owner's bathroom. One certainly cannot accuse this yacht of being plain or bland.

A tour of the exterior should begin with the sun deck, which is spacious and sheltered from the wind by glass screens curving around its forward edge and shielding a settee. From the radar arch, a permanent awning frame extends over a circular table with built-in seats, which has

a barbecue, a bar and the top station of a food lift in adjacent lockers. For those who seek the sunshine without shade, a large area of sunpads is set inside the aft rail, surrounding a bubbling spa pool.

One level down from here, the bridge deck is dominated by the circular sun lounge, but there is still a substantial area of teak-laid deck with settees around the

Left: The owner's stateroom has an ingenious turntable that enables the bed to be manoeuvred to face the giant plasma-screen television or, alternatively, to provide a wonderful view out to sea.

aft rail. There are no side decks on this level so access to the bridge is internal or via steps from the main deck. In compensation, a Y-shaped Portuguese bridge descends forward, over the top of the owner's suite, and down to the special private deck that has a small breakfast table on one side and a spa pool on the other.

Unencumbered by boats, the main deck offers a generous open space aft, shaded by the upper deck, and here a rectangular teak table with a settee along one side and chairs on the other offers an alternative venue for alfresco dining. From this deck, stairs lead down to the boarding/bathing platform on one side, while the passerelle extends to the quayside on the other.

As well as being a big step forward towards larger moulded plastics hulls, *Patricia*, as the first Benetti Vision, has many interesting and attractive features. She is large enough to offer a great deal of choice in detailed layout and decoration and it is safe to predict that numerous variations on her theme will be seen in years to come.

SPECIFICATIONS

LOA	44.22m (145ft 0in)
LWL	37.90m (124ft 3in)
Beam	9.40m (30ft 8in)
Draught	2.65m (8ft 7in)
Displacement (loaded)	390 tonnes
Propulsion	2 x 1,300hp Caterpillar 3508B diesels
Gearbox	ZF
Propellers	2 x 5-blade (Benetti design)
Speed (max/cruise)	15 knots/14.5 knots
Fuel capacity	67,000 litres
Range at 12 knots	4,000nm
Generators	2 x 99kW Northern Lights
Stabilisers	Vosper/Koop Nautic
Windlass	Muir
Bowthruster	Vosper/Koop Nautic
Watermakers	2 x Village Marine, 12,112l/d
Fresh water capacity	11,000 litres
Crane	Motomar
Fire control system	Flexifog
Lift	AIEC, Genoa
Air-conditioning	Condaria/Marine Air
Communications	Thrane Satcom-C & Mini-M
Autopilot	C. Plath, Model 10
Galley equipment	Miele
Entertainment systems	Sony, Sharp, NEC, JVC
Owner & guests	10 in 3 x double & 2 x twin cabins
Crew	9 in 2 x double, 1 x single & 2 x twin cabins
Construction	composite
Classification	Lloyd's ✠100A1, LMC
	MCA compliant
Interior design	François Zuretti
Exterior styling & concept	Stephano Righini
Naval architect	Benetti
Builder/Year	Benetti/2002

Primadonna

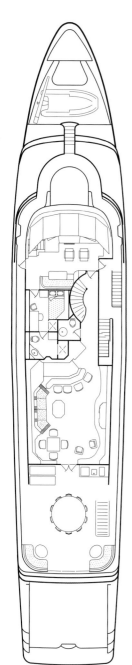

Main picture: The aft cockpit, with its fighting chair, bait tank and tackle preparation area.
Below right: The sun deck is dominated by a deep spa pool.

Superyachts can come to fruition in just as many ways as there are yachts themselves. Sometimes they are the result of years of patient planning by the owners, while in other cases they spring to life over a casual cup of espresso.

In the case of the 44.20m (145ft) Christensen *Primadonna*, it was from intriguing glimpses of other yachts that led to the new project being commissioned. The owners, with extensive superyacht experience, had seen *Namoh*, a 43.28m (142ft) built by Christensen in 1995, and had liked the modern but classic tri-deck styling. A spacious aft cockpit was considered essential for the vessel, since the owner is an avid sport fisherman and, in spite of the yacht's bulk, was intent on pursuing his passion while on board.

Having settled on which yard was going to be responsible for the construction of the yacht, the next challenge was to find a suitable designer. Several were interviewed by the owners, but everything came together when Paola D Smith showed them her ideas. Once again, they had already been impressed by Smith's earlier designs, such as *Neninka* (ex-*Azzura*), the 47.50m (156ft) CRN yacht. By the end of the afternoon, contracts had been signed.

The brief given to Smith for the project was to provide a timeless look, yet one that would be both opulent and dramatic. They wanted a yacht that was, according to Smith, 'over the top'. Christensen's project manager, Robert Emerson, adds that the two words most frequently used were 'unique' and 'colourful'. A glance at the photographs on these pages will undoubtedly prove that these goals were achieved.

Christensen has thus far established its reputation by using semi-production methods to construct more composite yachts of over 36m (120ft) than any other builder. However, with *Primadonna* the yard has delved much deeper into the territory of fully custom builders. Although it had provided a basic interior layout, Smith was able to modify it extensively, and her space planning allowed for extremely spacious living areas in addition to incorporating the grand staircase, which is the focal point of the yacht.

Far left: Aft of the sky lounge, a large dining table with inlaid marquetry provides ample seating for alfresco dining.
Left: The uncluttered pilothouse is placed forward on the upper deck, its twin helm seats facing an array of monitors.

Above: Madrona wood, animal print upholstery and glass in the main deck saloon set the tone for the interior styling throughout Primadonna.
Right: The dance floor, lit from beneath to enhance the colours of its marble and honey onyx, is overlooked by a black mirror with pin-point lighting and illuminated zodiac signs.

Striking red madrona burl has been used extensively throughout the interior for the furniture and bulkheads, creating a stark contrast to the cream upholstery and carpeting, but a *mélange* of cherrywood, ash, sycamore and tulipwood also contribute to the finish. The guest staterooms use woods from Tabu, an Italian company with a proprietary method of dyeing wood to ensure that the delicate colours penetrate deeply, rather than just staining the surface.

The saloon sets the style for the entire yacht, with animal print fabrics covering the free-standing chairs and an extravagant use of glass. The entertainment centre has a large, calla lily-shaped inlay of etched and chipped glass in the madrona burl cabinet, which is accented by

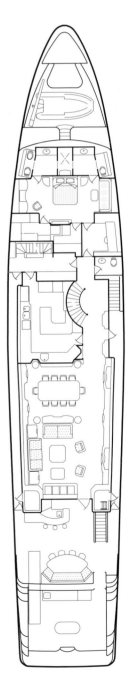

The dining table, which seats 10 on silver-leafed chairs, continues the theme of glass that was both etched and chipped by Glass Deco of Holland. Highlights from real shells are set in its glass edges. The forward bulkhead has two more of the leafy *torchére* lamps on either side of a large painting of a moonlit sailing boat. When required, however, the painting slides upwards into a pocket to reveal a hatch that opens through to the galley.

The galley is no less unusual, with carefully antiqued cabinetry and hand-painted tiles on the hood above the oven. The bulkheads are tiled with underwater scenes, the Pergo floors have tile inlays, and the ceiling has a high-gloss finish. Divided into separate cooking and food preparation areas, the galley benefits from having two dishwashers, dual ovens, and a built-in food smoker. Forward, a separate larder has two SubZero freezers and a refrigerator, to back up the under-counter freezers and the stand-up SubZero refrigerator in the galley.

For guests boarding *Primadonna* through the formal entry foyer to starboard, the first impression is of unrestrained elegance, from the inlaid marble by Jeff Homchick – who has contributed to many previous Christensens – to the silver-leafed table. Most of all, however, they will marvel at the extravagant stairwell of crystal, gold and stainless steel, again created by Belina and Savoy. The walls of the curving stairway are inlaid with backlit glass ropes and, overhead, recessed lighting illuminates a silver-leafed dome in the foyer's deckhead.

The master suite fills the forward area of the main deck, thus taking advantage of the full beam of the yacht. Bookshelves and a computer desk mark the simple office at the entrance to the suite, with SubZero under-counter refrigerators providing refreshments when required. Doors to this area can be closed if extra privacy is needed.

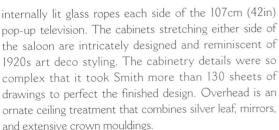

internally lit glass ropes each side of the 107cm (42in) pop-up television. The cabinets stretching either side of the saloon are intricately designed and reminiscent of 1920s art deco styling. The cabinetry details were so complex that it took Smith more than 130 sheets of drawings to perfect the finished design. Overhead is an ornate ceiling treatment that combines silver leaf, mirrors, and extensive crown mouldings.

Dividing the dining and entertainment areas is a transparent glass panel etched with scallop shells, standing between four columns of gold-banded stainless steel and blown glass. Adding a further accent are twin *torchére* lamps with madrona trunks, stainless steel trims by Belina Interiors and glass leaves from Savoy Studios.

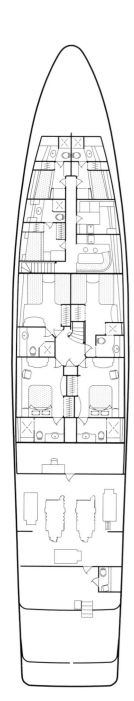

The master bed is ornate, with foot posts and an arch over the headboard that continue the stainless steel, gold and crystal theme of the stairwell. A large walk-in wardrobe is located aft, with Lucite-fronted drawers and a compact washer/dryer for the personal use of the owners. Built-in desks also carry forward the unusual cabinetry of the saloon, and ornate reading lamps are set into tall mirrors on either side of the bed.

However, no matter how pleasant the bedroom area is, it is the master shower room that will be memorable for those fortunate guests invited to view it. 'I wanted it to feel like you were inside a diamond,' remarks Smith, who created a dazzling glitter from countless facets of mirror and glass. His-and-hers areas lie on either side of a spacious shower with bevelled, etched and inlaid glass doors. Inside the cubicle, one entire bulkhead is devoted to a waterfall made up of diamond-shaped crystal and stainless steel catch basins that spill one to the next down the entire wall. It will be a jaded visitor who is not impressed by this spectacular display. To either side of the shower are his-and-hers wash-basins surrounded by white onyx surfaces with stainless steel inlays, while the look is completed by ornate marble floor patterns with chipped glass inlays by Homchick.

Guests have the lower deck to themselves, which is reached via a stairway leading to a *giallo reale* and *rossa* marble foyer featuring an intricate Homchick sun pattern. A pair of mirrored staterooms are located aft, again with the art deco-styled desks, 107cm (42in) flat screen televisions, and private marble shower rooms. A set of identical twin-berthed cabins are forward, also with marble heads and 107cm (42in) televisions. Each guest cabin is distinguished by a different colour of the Tabu-stained woods, ranging from pale greens to silvery blue.

The stairwell continues up from the main deck to the sky lounge, where it ends under twin silver-leafed oval ceiling coves. If any visitors were unsure of exactly what the phrase 'over the top' meant, the sky lounge would define it clearly. The animal print carpet is striking, but so is the ornate dance floor inlaid with chipped glass, various colours of marble, and honey onyx, all outlined in stainless steel and lit from underneath. Overhead, a black mirror features pin-point lighting as well as four zodiac symbols in lights, while the madrona on the bulkheads and cabinets marks a contrast to the ebony games table

and chairs aft. Forward, the curved bar features a one-piece worktop of chipped amber glass, and the mirrored bulkhead holds a full complement of crystal. For entertainment, another 107cm (42in) pop-up television is placed under the starboard buffet counter. Double doors open to the aft deck, which is protected by the overhang of the deck above and dominated by a 2.4m (8ft) alfresco dining table with exquisite inlaid marquetry.

The sun deck, served by a dumb waiter from the galley, has a helm station forward with a settee, and a marble-topped wet bar. However, much of the space is taken up by a large and deep German spa pool. Aft, a 6.7m (22ft) Zodiac RIB and four WaveRunners are launched by the

Christensen-built 1.9-tonne crane, while a large Lynx barbecue is to starboard.

Crew quarters are very civilised, with the captain having a double cabin on the upper deck, just off the pilothouse, that is finished in the same madrona burl as the guest staterooms. The pilothouse is uncluttered and straightforward, with an array of Samsung monitors in front of a pair of Stidd helm chairs, twin doors to the side decks, and wing controls for manoeuvring. Since fishing is important aboard *Primadonna*, another control station is positioned aft, so that the skipper can overlook the cockpit. The remainder of the crew cabins and the crew mess are forward on the lower deck, with stairs leading to the larder and giving direct access to the side decks.

The aft cockpit is immense by sport fishing standards, with an illuminated bait tank in the centre and a tackle preparation area forward. The large Murray Brothers fighting chair fits into a flush mounting plate on the teak deck and the stainless steel rails on the transom are removable while fishing. When the fighting chair is not in use, the crane lifts it to a storage mount on the upper deck.

Between the fishing cockpit, which is almost at water level, and the saloon is what sport fishermen call the California deck – a raised area with a dining table, where refreshments can be served from the bar. Here, guests can enjoy the fishing action without being in the way.

A hatch from the fishing cockpit leads to a compartment with extensive storage for wetsuits and diving equipment, fishing tackle, and a work bench. A sound-insulated control room houses all the electrical panels, while a desk and window enables the engineer to keep an eye on the engines.

Said to be the most expensive Christensen ever built, it is obvious that *Primadonna* is far from the original semi-production design. Extravagantly decorated, opulent and dramatic, she is exactly what her owners wanted.

SPECIFICATIONS

LOA	44.20m (145ft 0in)
LWL	40.00m (131ft 6in)
Beam	8.38m (27ft 6in)
Draught (light)	1.98m (6ft 6in)
Displacement (light)	196 tonnes
Propulsion	2 x 1,826hp DDC/MTU 8V4000M90 diesels
Speed (max/cruise)	20 knots/18.5 knots
Fuel capacity	45,420 litres
Range	4,500nm
Water capacity	7,570 litres
Generators	2 x 99kW Northern Lights & 1 x 65kW Northern Lights
Stabilisers	Naiad, 510
Bowthruster	American Bow Thruster, 100hp
Watermakers	2 x 7,570l/d
Marble supplier	Jeff Homchick
Entertainment electronics	Sound Solutions
Navigation electronics	Harris Electric
Owner & guests	10 in 3 x double & 2 x twin cabins
Crew	8 in 1 x double & 3 x twin cabins
Hull construction	Cored composite
Classification	ABS ✠A1, AMS
Interior design	Paola D Smith
Exterior styling	Christensen Shipyards
Naval architect	Christensen Shipyards
Builder/Year	Christensen Shipyards/2002

Salperton

When the 53m (174ft) ketch *Salperton* slipped into the upper reaches of Auckland Harbour in January this year, she claimed the record as the largest launch ever from Alloy Yachts, as well as being the biggest sailing yacht ever to be built in New Zealand. She is also a notable vessel for her naval architect and designer Ed Dubois, being both his largest sailing yacht and his first design to incorporate a flying bridge helm station. But despite *Salperton's* size and the impressive statistics that she generates – her two masts, for instance, soar some 60m (197ft) and 45m (148ft) into the sky and can set a massive total of 1,572m² (16,920ft²) of fore and aft sail and 2,324ft² (25,015ft²) downwind – she is also a yacht of exceptional beauty. Her long, low hull, topped by the flowing lines of a sexily sleek superstructure that incorporates Dubois' trademark of dark wrap-around deckhouse windows, results in a vessel of such harmonious proportions that, from a distance, it is difficult to judge just how large she is. A quality that is, surely, the true mark of a distinguished design.

Having chartered sailing yachts for many years before owning a 37m (121ft) Perini Navi, also named *Salperton*, on which he regularly spent 16 weeks a year, English businessman Barry Houghton knew exactly what he required of his new yacht. He liked his Perini very much, and his new yacht would have to have an equally gracious and stylishly understated interior of the same superlative quality, but she would also need improved sailing performance and be large enough to incorporate an owner's suite, four guest cabins and generous crew quarters. This new *Salperton* was also to be built under

ABS classification as well as to comply with the MCA Code of Practice, albeit as interpreted by the Cayman Islands Authority, which seems to adopt a more pragmatic approach to the intent of the regulations. During the formative stages of the project Houghton took the opportunity of visiting as many building yards as he was able and discussed his thoughts and ideas with several naval architects before selecting Ed Dubois. 'Ed just clicked', recalls Houghton. 'As soon as I met him, I knew that he was the one I would work with.' Houghton's manufacturing and design background had taught him that it was important to get the specification correct at the very outset of any project, so the next year was spent working closely with the Dubois office, preparing a design and detailed bid package that was eventually offered to five builders. It is now history that Alloy Yachts won the contract and delivered the new *Salperton* – 400,000 man hours of work – within a remarkably short 25-month period.

In a sailing vessel, high speed is a function of low weight and large sail-carrying power, so good stability and lightness were two of Dubois' design objectives. In terms of weight, the largest savings were made by specifying an aluminium hull, rather than the steel of her earlier namesake, while savings in the rig offered double-value economies as, for a given stability figure, weight saved in the masts is also saved in the keel. A lightweight carbon-fibre rig was, therefore, a natural choice, while further weight aloft was saved by selecting in-boom furling, rather than the in-mast system fitted to the earlier *Salperton*. Both of these were built by the specialist Auckland company Marten Spars. In-boom furling also improved performance directly, as it allowed the use of fully-battened sails of perfect aerodynamic shape. While no special savings were sought in respect of the weight of the interior furnishings, a single engine was specified rather than the twin engines usually found on yachts of

Above: The guest cockpit is sheltered by waist-high bulwarks and a solid overhang extended by a canvas awning.
Below: An intimate bar greets visitors entering the saloon. To its left, stairs descend to the guest cabins.
Far right below: The dining area in the guest cockpit.

this size, a choice that also emphasised that this was a pure sailing yacht rather than a motor sailer.

Draught is important both to sailing performance and stability but one practical consideration is that it should not be so large as to restrict access to harbours. After a study of the limiting depths of many popular harbours around the world, a maximum desirable draught of 4.85m (15ft 11in) was established. Tank tests at the Wolfson Unit in Southampton served to optimise the complex relationship between the chosen draught, stability, ballast, beam and sailing performance, finally settling on a maximum beam of 10.35m (33ft 11in), a figure that would

provide more than adequate interior volume, and a fin and bulb keel with 93 tonnes of ballast. These resulted in a calculated half-load displacement that was in the region of 360 tonnes. One indicator of performance is a yacht's displacement to length ratio, and although *Salperton's* figure, based on a finished light load displacement of 374 tonnes, is not in the same league as ultra-high performance sailing superyachts such as *Mari Cha III*, where fanatical efforts were made to minimise weight, it is, nevertheless, as much as 40% better than many yachts of this type, size and complexity.

Since her launch, these calculations have been more than validated. Eleven knots to windward with 40° apparent wind angle has been readily achieved in moderate airs, while 14 to 15 knots is the norm in 25 knots of true windspeed. Dubois, who was present on her shakedown cruise from Auckland to the Marlborough Sounds in northern South Island, noted that in a steady wind of 28 knots at 60° apparent she achieved 16.5 knots, and he is convinced that 20 knots is obtainable in heavy weather conditions once the crew get to know her better. Under power, she will reach 15.2 knots for short periods and cruises comfortably at 14 knots with extremely low noise levels. Perhaps most significant is her ability to sail in a breeze of less than 12 knots, sometimes with her own speed approaching that of the true windspeed — performance that should ensure that her motor will see less use than those of many sailing yachts of this size.

Salperton's deck crew speak glowingly of her sailing

systems and her ease of control. Although the large wheelhouse, located behind the sweep of windows at the forward end of the deck saloon, affords facilities for paper chartwork together with a comprehensive range of communications systems, the yacht's prime helm station is aloft on the flying bridge. With 360° visibility and wind on the helmsman's face, this is the sensible place from which to steer a sailing yacht. All the sailing controls, together with the monitoring and navigation systems, are logically divided between three panels and a pair of control boxes on wander leads, which hoist and furl the main and mizzen using captive reel winches. The reacher, blade and staysail are all set and furled using hydraulically powered Reckmann furlers, while eight further captive winches, operated by a forest of joysticks on the central control panel, take care of the sheets, with the speed of individual winch drums being proportional to the physical displacement of the stick. Minimising complexity and maintenance were principles that guided the design of *Salperton's* mechanical and control equipment, so, unlike the Perini Navi's sail control system, no attempt was made to automate the complete tacking process. As the reacher and blade must be furled prior to a tack, the task of releasing and sheeting in the staysail using two joysticks, together with any slight adjustment to the main and mizzen sheets that may be necessary, was, in any case, not considered a challenge. Both the gennaker – tacked down to the bow – and the mizzen staysail are trimmed using manually operated Lewmar drum winches.

Sensors, positioned to measure the loads in critical elements of the rig, display their readings on the B&G displays but again, in the interest of simplicity, there is no automatic response other than to a critical load.

Naturally, the decks of a 53m (174ft) sailing yacht are very spacious, but good design has made *Salperton's* particularly easy for one to move around without the need to dodge standing rigging and sheets, or to avoid toe-stubbingly painful fittings. The foredeck is particularly clear, with its many hatches (like all the stainless fittings, made in-house by Alloy Yachts) smooth to the deck, while the anchors – stowed and launched from flush-

Above: The pilothouse. Guest seating is to port.

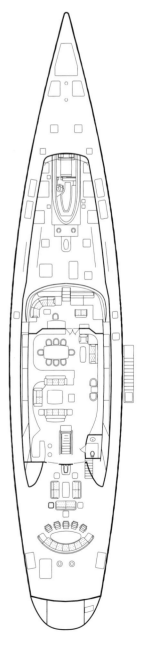

Above: *The yacht's high level of finish is seen in the cutlery drawer.*
Right: *The saloon and dining room offer extensive views whether standing or sitting.*

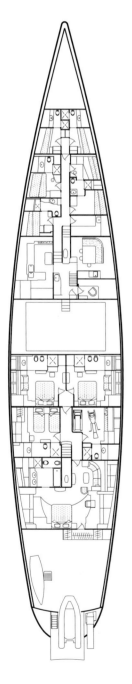

topped underdeck lockers using an up-and-over whipstock – have underdeck chain runs to their windlasses. The furlers have also been partially sunk into the deck, both a cosmetic move to minimise their bulk as well as to lower the feet of the headsails closer to the deck for improved performance. The yacht's main tender, a Castoldi 6.25m RIB with water-jet propulsion, is stowed forward of the mast within a sunken well in the deckhouse, which lowers its profile so as to make it near invisible when the canvas cover is closed.

Other examples of good design include the thoughtfully positioned teak gratings, placed just before the side decks descend a couple of steps into the guest cockpit. These swallow those buckets of spray water that always seem to accumulate on the windward side deck and thus keep the cockpit sole dry. At the foot of the steps, the guest cockpit is a truly luxurious domain that offers fresh air and wide open views, yet it is also well sheltered from the sun and elements by the combination of its waist-high bulwarks and a solid overhang combined with a soft awning that shade the whole cockpit. In high latitudes or poor weather the cockpit can be completely enclosed by fitted side curtains made from transparent material. Furnished with a 10-seater dining table set against an arc of seating along the aft bulwark and a cluster of three teak sofas, guests can lounge or dine in total comfort. From the cockpit, a stairway rises to the flying bridge (passing through a horizontal hatch that can be closed with a pneumatic bi-fold door to eliminate rain and draught) where sunbathing, a barbecue, and more casual dining and lounging are on offer in the open deck area aft of the control station.

At anchor, the prime means of boarding *Salperton* is by way of the starboard side ladder. This pops out from the

platform, so that the latter may be opened when moored stern-to in a dock. Another nice point of detail is that, when she is so moored, the lazarette, which also houses a workshop, is kept private by means of a door.

Being a designer who cut his teeth on racing yachts, Dubois was keen to concentrate the weight of the engine room in the centre of the yacht, where it would act to reduce pitching and also be a positive asset to the stability equation. This meant that the owner's and guest accommodation could be positioned on the lower deck between the lazarette and the engine room – the most comfortable part of the yacht – while the combined saloon and dining saloon are located in the sizeable deckhouse, and the generous crew quarters fill the forward third of the hull.

A pair of delicately curved sliding doors on either side of the mizzen-mast open from the guest cockpit into the deckhouse. Notably, and laudably, this is achieved without a change in floor level, a feature of which the Dubois design office, which was also responsible for the division of the interior volume and the layout of the yacht, is proud to point out. Once inside, the overriding impression is of huge volume combined with wide exterior views that can be appreciated both from a standing or sitting position. Flanked by large windows set above storage cabinets topped with a rosewood inlay, and undivided by any furniture above waist level, this is one huge saloon, completely open from its aft entrance doors right through to the wheelhouse windscreen at its forward extremity. *Salperton's* owner very much liked the elegant decoration of his previous yacht and he decided to develop the same style of interior for his new yacht, flying Alloy's own interior designer to visit and make notes. The result is a pleasantly understated decorative scheme, built entirely in Alloy Yachts' own workshop,

Above: *The master suite is entered through a private lounge, beyond which the owner's desk is at the entrance to the bedroom.*
Below: *The dining saloon. If required, a vertically sliding panel can be raised from within the sideboard to close off the room from the wheelhouse, offering privacy to the diners and protecting the watchkeepers from excess light.*

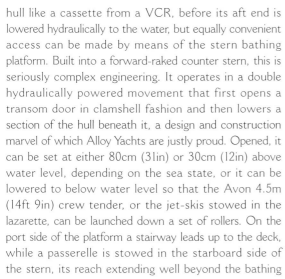

hull like a cassette from a VCR, before its aft end is lowered hydraulically to the water, but equally convenient access can be made by means of the stern bathing platform. Built into a forward-raked counter stern, this is seriously complex engineering. It operates in a double hydraulically powered movement that first opens a transom door in clamshell fashion and then lowers a section of the hull beneath it, a design and construction marvel of which Alloy Yachts are justly proud. Opened, it can be set at either 80cm (31in) or 30cm (12in) above water level, depending on the sea state, or it can be lowered to below water level so that the Avon 4.5m (14ft 9in) crew tender, or the jet-skis stowed in the lazarette, can be launched down a set of rollers. On the port side of the platform a stairway leads up to the deck, while a passerelle is stowed in the starboard side of the stern, its reach extending well beyond the bathing

Top: *The master bedroom offers a king-sized bed, desk and walk-in wardrobe.*
Above: *The private sitting room at the entrance to the master suite.*

trimmed with white Carrara marble, a games table with an inbuilt backgammon board and a sumptuous horseshoe of comfortable settees arranged around a low table. In the forward portion of the room is a particularly attractive 10-seater dining table, its corners inlaid with the heraldic griffin emblem that adorns the main entrance to the owner's country estate in England, while to starboard is a further conversation area with a settee, easy chair and low table, the ideal setting for a casual breakfast or a place for children to dine separately.

So that the lights of the saloon do not intrude on the wheelhouse during night navigation or when guests in the saloon require privacy, the press of a button raises a wall of panelling from the low divide forward of the dining area, while the walkway forward is closed by doors. But the wheelhouse is not wholly dedicated to a command and control function, being divided between guests and the yacht's control station. To starboard of the central stairs leading forward and down to the crew quarters is the wheelhouse proper. Like most modern wheelhouses, computer screens on the facia offer plotter and radar displays, while information from Alloy Yachts' own alarm and diagnostic system is displayed on a separate touch screen. The autopilot, thrusters and wheel are centrally positioned, while the chart table and communications equipment fill the starboard side. The guest area is to port – a quarter circle of beige leather seating and a desk, whose computer gives access to the internet and to the ship's network hub to provide a useful amenity for visitors. Watertight pantograph doors, custom

that showcases warm cherrywood panelling and classically styled furniture from the same material, the latter embellished with delicate reeded highlights. Pale cream deckheads, a light taupe wool carpet and choice table lamps complete the effect. Easily rivalling the size and facilities of a motor yacht of this size, the saloon offers a cherry-topped full service bar, a day head

designed and built, give access to the deck on both sides.

Salperton's guest accommodation opens off a lobby at the base of a stairway descending from the aft end of the saloon. The master is aft, set across the yacht's full beam and entered through a private lounge with a comfortable sofa and a television that descends into a wall cabinet. Around the corner in the bedroom, a second pop-up television set is located in a cabinet at the foot of the king-sized bed, while other amenities include a desk and a walk-in wardrobe fitted with clear-fronted drawers. The splendid bathroom luxuriates in twin wash-basins set in a white Carrara marble counter and both a spa bath and a shower cubicle, while a separate compartment houses a head and bidet. Opening forward from the lobby, through a watertight door, two identical queen-sized guest cabins offer their occupants sublime comfort, providing them with settee, desk and entertainment system and an en suite shower room. The fourth cabin, a convertible twin/double, is positioned in the central area opposite the gymnasium, adding flexibility to the sleeping arrangements, while further versatility is offered by the gymnasium itself. Adjoined by a shower room, this has been provided with a pair of Pullman bunks and a single fixed bunk, thus creating a useful overflow cabin for children and staff.

Little decorative distinction has been made between the guest accommodation and the crew working and living areas. Positioned in the bows and entered either from the wheelhouse or down a deck companionway just aft of the mainmast, this area contains the galley – equipped with top-of-the-range domestic appliances and ample storage space for dry, fresh and frozen produce – a ship's office, a laundry with two pairs of commercial washers and dryers and a rotary iron, six en suite crew cabins, and the crew mess. The latter, comfortable and well sized in normal use when the yacht will be run with nine crew, might seem crowded when all 12 crew bunks are filled. Such occasions will, however, be limited to charters or when there is a full guest complement – busy times when crew members will either be working or sleeping, so it will be a rare occasion when more than half the crew will be together in the mess.

The main entrance to the engine room is through a control room at the foot of stairs leading from the crew quarters. One cannot fail to be immediately impressed by the size of the mast foot, on either side of which is a pair of huge 120-tonne hydraulic jacks used for rig tensioning – this is serious engineering! Captive winches for the main halyard and the mainsheet are also located in this compartment, their weight kept low in the yacht, but the room's main function is to house the electrical distribution system and provide an engineer's office, from where all aspects of the yacht's systems are monitored. The compartment also carries refrigeration plant for the fridges and freezers and, more unusually, a 'spring water' tank which supplies the icemakers and several drinking fountains around the yacht with the gourmet water. The engine room itself, aft through a watertight door, is notable for its neatness and ready access to all important items. The main engine, a single Caterpillar 3412E diesel

delivering 1,400hp at 2,300rpm, is dwarfed by the twin 104kW Northern Lights generating sets. This serves to emphasise that, even though *Salperton's* sails provide its main motive power, a sailing superyacht requires a huge amount of electricity for its sheet-handling systems and the output of it's generators is frequently more than on a motor yacht of the same size.

Barry Houghton wanted a yacht of greater size and improved sailing performance, with an equally elegant, well constructed interior built under ABS survey and complying with the MCA safety regulations. The measure of the success of the yacht's designers, her builder, mastmaker and sailmakers – indeed, everyone involved with the project – is that he is totally delighted with the finished product. And it is not just the owner who is pleased – his captain, mate and engineer are also delighted – and that is an all too rare situation during the early life of a yacht of this size and complexity. With her blend of excellent sailing ability, her outstanding comfort, her style and her amenities, *Salperton* will surely impress and astonish everyone who sails aboard her.

Above: The gymnasium, which is adjoined by a shower room, provides the accommodation with a degree of flexibility as it is fitted with a single bed as well as a pair of Pullman berths – very handy for children or household staff.

LOA 53.03m (174ft 0in)	Jib & staysail furling systems . . . . Reckmann
LWL 44.62m (146ft 5in)	Captive winches . . . . Nilsson, (Alloy Yachts' design)
Beam (max) 10.35m (33ft 11in)	Drum winches . . . . Lewmar
Draught 4.85m (15ft 11in)	Windlasses . . . . 2 x Maxwell, VWC 11000
Ballast . . . . 93 tonnes	Thrusters . . . . American Bow Thruster, 90hp
Displacement (half load) . . . . 374 tonnes	Watermakers . . . . 2 x HEM S30, each 10,000l/d
Spars . . . . Marten Spars, carbon fibre	Exterior paint . . . . Awlgrip
Rigging . . Ocean Yacht Systems, discontinuous rod	Air-conditioning . . . . Condaria, 360,000Btu/hr
Sailmaker . . . North Sails (NZ) & Vela 2000 (Spain)	Autopilot & gyrocompass . . . . C. Plath
Sail area (main & mizzen sails) . . . 706m² (7,597ft²)	Owner & guests . . . . 8 in 1 x twin & 3 x double cabins
(reacher) 658m² (7,080ft²)	Crew . . . 12 in 2 x double & 4 x twin bunk cabins
(gennaker) 1,298m² (13,973ft²)	Construction . . . . Aluminium alloy
Engine . . . . . 1 x 1,400hp Caterpillar 3412E diesel	Classification . . ABS ✠A1 Yachting Service; MCA Code
Range at 10 knots (power) 8,000nm	Naval architect & stylist . . . Dubois Naval Architects
Generators . . . . 2 x 104kW Northern Lights M6108T	Builder/Year . . . . . Alloy Yachts International/2002

Sarah

Below: Sarah *cruises at an effortless 16 knots and has transoceanic range.*
Above right: *The owner was persuaded to opt for a hull colour part-way between royal and deep-sea blue.*

Big, blue and beautiful, the 62m (203ft 5in) Amels motor yacht *Sarah* is undoubtedly one of the most impressive new launchings of 2002. The sheer professionalism involved in planning, designing, building and running this vastly complex machine is quite breathtaking in its scope. With a full-time crew of 22, she is virtually a small luxury liner, with all the comfort and facilities that one would expect from a ship of that class, the big difference being that she is entirely private.

The owner had not previously owned a large motor yacht but had a number of years' experience of chartering and therefore had a fairly clear idea what he wanted. *Sarah* was to be a purely private yacht for the enjoyment of the owner's family and friends but at the same time, because

he is a man of standing, some rooms, especially the main saloon, are rather more formal in character than normal.

The owner entrusted the task of developing this concept to the London-based designer Donald Starkey, who was responsible for the exterior design, in addition to the layout and design of the interior. The requirement was for a modern-looking yacht that would be extremely comfortable but not ostentatious. The owner likes the best quality mahogany, marble and other beautiful natural materials, so it should come as no surprise that *Sarah* is richly endowed with these. He was attracted to the idea of a dark blue hull but Starkey persuaded him to try a slightly lighter tone than the usual dark navy, the result being that *Sarah* glows with a colour that is part-way between royal and deep-sea blue.

Several yards were invited to tender for the project and Amels, well-known for its high standards and meticulous attention to detail, was awarded the contract. Five years ago, *The Superyachts* published details of the Amels motor yacht *Tigre d'Or*, which was the very first to receive certification under the MCA Code of Practice for commercial yachts. From July 2002, all commercial vessels over 500 gross registered tons were required to operate with a valid Safety Management Certificate (SMC) under the terms of the ISM protocol. Although a private yacht, *Sarah* is believed to be the first yacht to leave her builder's yard with an SMC. This new certificate does not deal with the construction or equipment of the vessel but with its management. It has involved the officers of *Sarah* and their shore-based consultant Marine

Safety Services in months of work to define the vessel's working practice and prepare the documentation.

Amels is one of several Dutch yards that has recently acquired additional capacity to enable it to build more and larger hulls. Being part of the Damen Group made it easier for Amels to take over an existing yard in the Rotterdam area that builds large steel hulls. These are then floated to the original Amels shipyard in the north of Holland for completion. Once the contract was awarded, Wim Koersfelt of WK Yacht Projects had been appointed project manager and deserves a great deal of credit for bringing it to a successful conclusion.

As *Sarah* is not designed to meet the usual charter stereotype of 12 guests, she has a generous amount of accommodation for the owner, his family, his friends and

Above left: The forward section of the sun deck features a spa pool.
Above: Stylish loungers and a bar provide an ideal spot to while away the afternoon in the shade of an awning.

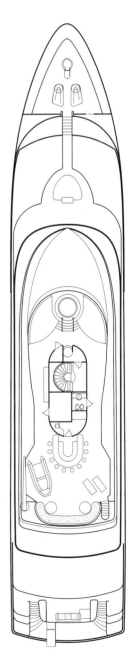

Above: The main hallway provides access to the owner's suite forward on the main deck.
Above right: The 14-place dining table is inlaid with a giant double-ended version of the 'lamp' motif that is used in many parts of the yacht.
Below: The main saloon.

his staff. The owner's personal accommodation has been designed for the maximum flexibility of use, depending on who is on board. In addition to his own full-beam suite, there are two further en suite cabins within the private area. Each of these has a double bed that folds into the wall when not required. When not in use as accommodation, the cabin on the starboard side is furnished and equipped as an office, while that on the port side can be used as a gymnasium, including a treadmill that can be folded away into a purpose-designed locker in the lobby.

On the upper deck there are two particularly delightful VIP guest staterooms that enjoy superb views from the large rectangular windows right along one side. The luxurious en suite bathrooms have full-sized tubs and are panelled in very attractive marble. In fact every bathroom aboard has a different marble, onyx or granite, including some of the most spectacular stone effects ever seen afloat. These special double staterooms would normally be used by members of the owner's family or close friends.

On the lower deck, there is a more conventional arrangement of four very comfortable guest staterooms opening from a lobby, which is accessible from the crew quarters as well as via the grand spiral staircase from the main entrance hall. On a yacht that boasts a number of spectacular displays of marble, the main hallway is something really special, with radiating panels of stone flooring that are extravagantly figured, flawed and

cracked so that one expects to feel a broken surface beneath one's feet when in reality it is perfectly smooth.

Double doors open into the main saloon and dining room. The 14-place dining table is inlaid with a giant double-ended version of the 'lamp' motif that is used in many parts of the yacht and is woven into the border of the huge oval carpet on which the table stands. The very large and open main saloon has inward-facing sofas and individual armchairs forming a square. In the centre of the square is a sizeable mahogany-framed coffee table that appears to stand on a cross of heavy stainless steel

Top: *The vista lounge is decorated in the style of a Balinese beach house.*
Above: *A rug in the vista lounge can be taken up to reveal a dance floor.*

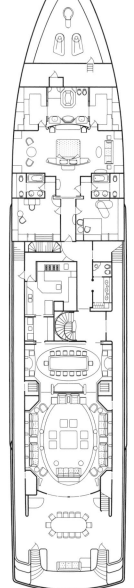

Above: The spacious pilothouse would keep any captain satisfied.

hinge down to the horizontal and then the boat slides out sideways on supporting beams. A pair of beam hoists then appear from the main deck overhead and take the weight of the boat, while its cradle is drawn back inboard before it is finally lowered into the water.

The central part of the garage is filled with a huge collection of water-sports equipment such as jet-skis, canoes, windsurfers, and fishing and diving gear, all of which can be unloaded across the aft boarding/bathing platform. Certainly this yacht has one of the most capacious toy-boxes so far seen afloat.

This idea of a drop-down door is also used in the crew area to create a loading platform in order that stores can be brought directly into the lower deck, so it is not necessary for everything to be carried aboard and then taken down below.

Two more special features are the bulbous bow, to reduce running resistance at cruising speed, and the special Koop Nautic stabilisers, which are effective in reducing roll when the yacht is stopped as well as under way. When at anchor, these stabilisers act like large paddles that push the water up or down to produce a counter-rolling force. That is easier to say than do, of course, and a great deal of research and sophisticated

engineering has gone into making these stabilisers work.

With her long waterline and Caterpillar V16 engines of 1,866kW each, *Sarah* can make around 20 knots when displacement is light but, more to the point, she cruises at an effortless 16 knots and has transoceanic range. It would take a whole book to list all the systems and services that are fitted aboard *Sarah*; the electronics alone need a whole shelf of technical manuals, while in the engine room there is a computerised maintenance system which has literally thousands of items in its inventory.

Of course, one must never forget the outstanding design, engineering and craftsmanship that went into the construction of this yacht, as well as the dedicated efforts of a large and highly trained crew, who are devoted to creating a totally tranquil and comfortable environment for the owner and his guests. *Sarah* is a magnificent achievement by all those involved.

SPECIFICATIONS

LOA	62.00m (203ft 5in)	**Stabilisers**	Koop Nautic
LWL	55.30m (181ft 5in)	**Fire control**	Marioff Hi-Fog
Beam	11.80m (38ft 9in)	**Satcom**	2 x ABB Nera Saturn Satcom-B
Draught	3.65m (12ft 0in)	**SSB & VHF radios**	Sailor
Displacement (half load)	950 tonnes	**Radars**	Jotron
GRT	1,370 tons	**Satellite television**	Sea Tel
Fuel capacity	120 tonnes	**Chartplotter**	Transas
Fresh water capacity	35 tonnes	**Owner & guests**	18 in 5 x double & 4 x twin cabins
Main engines	2 x 2,502hp Caterpillar 3516B	**Crew**	22 in 1 x double, 8 x twin & 4 x single cabins
	HD-DITA diesels	**Construction**	Steel hull & aluminium
Gearbox	Reintjes		alloy superstructure
Speed (max/cruise)	17 knots/16 knots	**Classification**	Lloyd's ✠100A1, SSC Yacht (P),
Range at 16 knots	6,000nm		✠LMC, G6
Shore power converter	Atlas	**Interior design**	Donald Starkey Designs
Generators	2 x 215kW Caterpillar 3406/Leroy Somer	**Exterior styling**	Donald Starkey Designs
	& 1 x 160kW Caterpillar 3306	**Naval architects**	Amels Holland
Bowthruster	Jastram 140kW	**Builder/Year**	Amels Holland/2002

Teleost

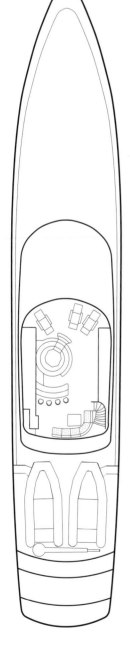

Right: *Launched as* Ulysses *from Feadship's Royal Van Lent Shipyard,* Teleost *was renamed by her new owner, a keen naturalist, after a species of fish with external skeletons.*

Readers probably understand that some of the finest yachts to emerge from the world's shipyards are never written about for the simple reason that they are the property of owners who value their privacy. This was certainly the case with the 49m (161ft) Feadship *Ulysses*, which was completed by the Royal Van Lent Shipyard in 1998.

In the past two years, though, her circumstances have changed. In 2000, *Ulysses* was sold and renamed *Teleost*. Rather amazingly, she was purchased sight unseen, a decision that her new owner has not since regretted. Her new captain, Nigel Burnet, collected her from Auckland, New Zealand and motored across the Pacific to Seattle. Almost immediately she departed on a cruise to Alaska as her new owner, passionately interested in ecology, wildlife, fishing and diving, was keen to embark on his aim of visiting the world's wildlife outposts in the complete comfort and security afforded by a top-class motor yacht such as *Teleost*.

Another unusual aspect of her story is that *Teleost* was involved in a docking accident in the United States: she fell partially off the keel blocks in a dry dock. As a result there was some damage to the hull and paintwork, although she remained seaworthy and in class – a testimony to the strength of her construction.

Naturally, repairs were needed, and the owner's first thought was to return to *Teleost's* builder, the Royal Van Lent Shipyard in Holland. The yard was already fully committed and could not accept the work, although they

Far left: The alfresco dining area on the bridge deck, aft of which there is still room to stow two tenders.

Centre left: At main deck level, the side decks rise over the master suite to allow it privacy and greater volume.

Left: Teleost's sun deck offers facilities for lounging and sunbathing, as well as a spa pool and bar.

Right The formal dining room just forward of the main deck saloon. The spectacular table, seating 12 with ease displays exquisite marquetry.
***Below:** The sky lounge has the comfortable atmosphere of a London gentleman's club.*

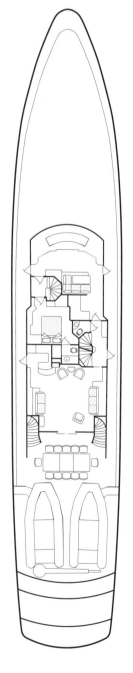

contributed invaluable technical assistance throughout. Lürssen of Bremen, however, made a very convincing bid, proposing to place the work with its wholly owned subsidiary Krögerwerft, which has a modern, undercover facility near Kiel.

The actual hull repair was not incredibly demanding, but because it required access to the inside of the hull, the repair process resulted in two of the guest cabins being dismantled and later rebuilt. This called for exceptionally careful work by the joinery contractor, Metrica, which not only had to restore the woodwork to the original high standard, but also had to match all colours and finishes exactly.

Knowing that the yacht would be in the yard for some time, the owner took the opportunity to carry out a mini-refit, making some improvements resulting from the experience of his Alaskan cruise. The most substantial engineering change was to add catalytic exhaust cleaners to the generators – as a lover of the natural environment, he absolutely hated the idea of diesel smoke drifting

across a quiet anchorage. With these in place, *Teleost* is not only silent in the anchorage but also squeaky clean.

At this time her galley was also substantially upgraded with the latest culinary equipment, including a steam oven, induction burners, and an amazing gadget that can make perfect ice sorbet in minutes. Given half a chance, French-Polynesian chef Gabriel Levionnois will wax lyrical about the dishes he can now produce from his gleaming stainless steel domain.

When the refit/repair was under way, the owner also decided to place *Teleost* on the charter market for part of the year, and as she flies the Red Ensign, this entailed obtaining MCA certification. She was built to the highest Lloyd's classification only four years ago, so this was mainly a matter of grinding through the paperwork and ensuring that all the crew had the right stars and asterisks on their licences. This also meant that the veil of privacy was necessarily lifted, as a charter yacht needs to set out its stall just like any other business. At the time of writing, *Teleost* expects to get her MCA Certificate of Compliance in the near future.

At the time of *Teleost's* conception, the original idea was to create a yacht with European style and some

Above: *Teleost's interior is decorated in European style, blending strong lines with satin-finished raised and fielded mahogany panelling and overstuffed settees covered in rich fabrics.*

Above: *The full-beam owner's lounge and study is divided from the master bedroom by a pair of sliding doors.*
Below right: *The master bathroom luxuriates in gold-veined Portoro marble.*

American features, the most noticeable of which is the fishing cockpit aft. There cannot be many 48.9m (160ft) yachts that have successfully landed marlin directly onto the main deck, but *Teleost* is certainly one of them. She can cruise with outriggers in place, and although there is nothing quite as specialised as a fighting chair, she does have a particularly snug and secure fishing position right aft by the mooring bitts. Amazingly, one is able to see exactly what has taken the bait as there are tiny television cameras on the fishing lines. Any fish successfully reeled-in can be whisked straight onto the barbecue, and any guests who might be watching from the security of the aft deck can, within minutes, find the catch-of-the-day on a plate in front of them.

The other sport that is strongly emphasised is diving: not only is a full outfit of scuba gear carried, but there is also an upgraded bottle refill system using tanks topped up by a high-capacity compressor. Guests who are qualified can dive with the resident dive-master, while in the remote possibility of an accident, the yacht carries an air-portable decompression chamber. The main tender is a sturdy 6.4m (21ft) sportsboat that is equally useful as a fishing boat or diving tender.

Teleost's European influence begins with the interior. John Munford designed this with strong traditional lines

using a background of raised and fielded mahogany panelling in a satin finish. This is an ideal yacht for a lover of fine woodwork – in fact, it's hard for anyone to avoid reaching out to fondle the fluted pillars, curved locker fronts, and crisply carved decorative details. The absolute perfection of colour, fit, and finish almost defies belief.

An example is found in the formal dining room on the main deck, which has the most beautifully curved, glass-fronted tableware cabinets on either side of the lovely marquetry dining table. One of these cabinets has a 'secret' compartment that contains several large mahogany panels that fit together to form an additional

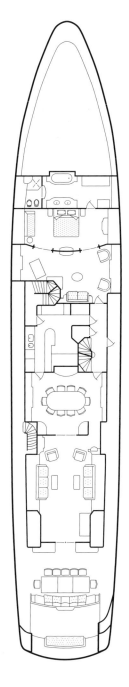

Left: The stately touch of interior designer John Munford can be seen in the decoration of the master stateroom.

side wall if the room is needed for private meetings. Without it, the dining room is open to the saloon.

The main saloon, with giant, overstuffed sofas along each side, embodies solid comfort rather than flashy design and, notably, it has no television. But addicts need not worry – a set is to be found in every cabin, and there is an extra-large screen in the sky lounge on the upper deck. Another pleasing touch are the large, opening windows in the saloon, upper saloon, and dining room – in case guests prefer not to breathe conditioned air.

The upper saloon, with its cosy bar and distressed leather armchairs, has a real 'club' atmosphere and there

could not be a better place to enjoy a drink and watch a movie on the home theatre system, or to curl up with a book on one of those hugely comfortable sofas. The neat little three-seater bar, with its brass rail and leather-topped stools, fills a secondary role as a pantry when food is served on the upper deck. A dumb waiter from the galley is concealed behind a panel, while a door to the side deck allows immediate crew access.

Because of her aft cockpit, *Teleost* does not have a tender garage, so the boats are stowed in the traditional position on the upper deck, from where they are launched by a crane that is neatly concealed in the aft bulwark.

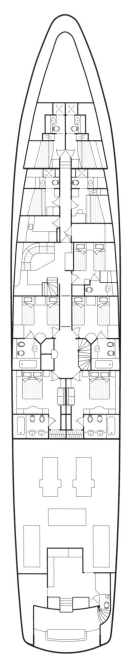

With the boats in place, there is still ample room for an outdoor dining table but, when more space is needed, the boats are launched and the chocks swung aside or stowed away. One level up, there is abundant open-air space on the sun deck, which boasts its own bar and barbecue served by the dumb waiter, and a large spa pool as well as superb sunbathing and lounging areas.

The owner's suite is in the traditional position – forward on the main deck – but it does not follow the traditional layout. By slightly rearranging neighbouring compartments and reversing the crew stairway, *Teleost's* designers found sufficient floor area to provide the owner with a particularly spacious suite that includes a full-beam lounge and study, as well as a full-beam bedroom. A pair of sliding partitions make it possible to open or divide the two rooms so that the occupants can create exactly the level of privacy they prefer.

The joinery is in the same style as the rest of the yacht, while the choice of furniture and fabrics give this whole area a feeling of elegance, refinement, and luxury. Beyond the bedroom, with its king-sized double bed and elegant *chaise longue*, lies the bathroom, which features a spectacular display of marble. The full-sized bathtub and twin basins have counter tops in a splendid *Portoro Maccia Oro Fino* marble, while behind the bath and lining

control, a fully comprehensive audio-visual entertainment system, a direct dial satellite telephone and a data plug for connecting to the internet. Decoratively, each displays beautiful woodwork, soft carpets, and a marble bathroom, while the two larger twin cabins also have additional Pullman berths for added flexibility of use. Except for the captain, whose cabin is in the traditional position abaft the bridge, the crew of 10 are accommodated in four comfortable twin-bunked cabins positioned forward on the lower deck.

Mechanically, *Teleost* is conservative, in the Feadship tradition, with twin Caterpillar 3508 diesels rated at an undemanding 905hp. Her top speed is around 15 knots, while at the economy cruise speed of 12 knots, fuel consumption drops from 208 litres per hour to a moderate 150 litres hour, giving a range of more than 4,500 nautical miles.

Ulysses was a magnificent motor yacht, and in her reincarnation as *Teleost*, she has been improved still further. Those who are lucky enough to spend some time aboard can look forward to an unforgettable experience.

Above: *One of the three twin-bedded guest cabins, the forwardmost of which can also be used for personal staff when required.*

the shower an amazing golden onyx is arranged in book-matched panels. On either side of the basins are fluted mahogany pillars – a typical Munford touch – and if one knows where to look, these open up to reveal conveniently positioned toiletry lockers.

Down a stairway from the main foyer, five guest cabins – two doubles and three twins – open off a hallway. The forwardmost of these, a slightly smaller twin fitted with an en suite shower rather than a bath, opens from the service passageway between the guest and crew quarters, a position which enables it to be used either by guests, or by personal staff. This corridor, soundproofed by a set of doors at each end, allows the cabins to be serviced easily, as well as providing a second fire escape route, right through to the crew escape hatch that opens onto the foredeck.

Each of the two double cabins occupies half the width of the hull and they are, thus, the largest and most beautifully appointed. Every cabin has individual climate

SPECIFICATIONS

LOA	48.90m (160ft 5in)	**Air-conditioning**	NR Koeling
LWL	42.30m (138ft 9in)	**Entertainment systems**	Van Berge Henegouwen
Beam	8.65m (28ft 5in)	**Communications**	1 x Furuno Sat Com, 1 x SSB
Draught	2.70m (8ft 10in)		2 x Sailor VHF, Model RT-4801 DSC
Displacement	468 tonnes	**Radars**	1 x Kelvin Hughes ARPA &
Main engines	2 x 905hp Caterpillar 3508 diesels		1 x Kelvin Hughes True Motion radar
Speed (max)	14.7 knots	**Autopilot**	C. Plath, Model NAVIGAT X
Range at 12.5 knots	4,500nm	**Fire control system**	Thorn
Fuel capacity	57,290 litres	**Exterior paint**	International Paint
Fresh water capacity	16,154 litres	**Construction**	Steel hull & aluminium superstructure
Watermaker	2 x HEM, 12,000l/d	**Classification**	Lloyd's ✠100A1, SSC, G6, LMC
Stabilisers	Vosper	**Owner & guests**	12 in 3 x double & 3 x twin cabins
Generators	2 x 125kW Caterpillar	**Crew**	9 in 1 x double & 4 x twin cabins
Gearbox	Reintjes, type WAF 541L reduction 3,955:1	**Interior design**	John Munford Design
Propellers	Teignbridge, 150cm	**Naval architect**	De Voogt Ship Design
Windlass	Steen, Model 19	**Builder/Year**	Feadship – Royal Van Lent/1998
Bowthruster	Jastram, 55kW Model BU-10F	**Refit/Year**	Krögerwerft/2002

Tueq

Top left: *Tueq illuminated at dusk is a stunning sight.*
Top centre: *The main deck aft features two circular seating areas and a large sunpad.*
Top right: *The owner's private aft deck with similar seating.*

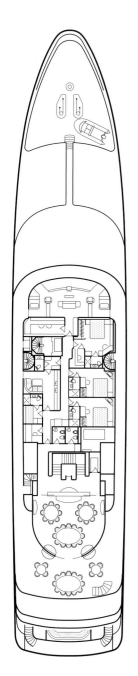

Conventional wisdom dictates that it takes at least a year to plan a large yacht and another two years to complete her construction, while extra delay results from the fact that the top yacht-building yards often have a waiting list of a year or more. However, the Athens-based management and design company, SETE Yachts accomplished the delivery of the 72m (236ft 3in) *Tueq* in just two years.

The owner had, in fact, been discussing a new yacht for some time with SETE Yachts, which is one of the most experienced yacht management companies in the business, with around 30 superyachts on its books. SETE had prepared the concept design, a general arrangement plan and exterior styling and, as soon as these were agreed upon, was ready to go ahead at full speed. An advantage of working with SETE Yachts, which is part of the Latsis Group, is that it is a relatively large company and was able to form a management team of around 10 professionals and specialists who saw the whole task through from start to finish.

It began work immediately on commissioning a naval architect and designer, while simultaneously searching for a shipyard able to take on such a project without delay. This was the hardest part, as all the well-known firms were unwilling to undertake such a short delivery. So, SETE chose the Rotterdam commercial shipyard GNS, that was able to offer the space, the labour and the facilities. Although it had virtually no experience of yacht building, its metalwork and engineering were excellent, and thus the yard was engaged for this challenging task.

Cutting of metal began at the end of September 2000, and advanced extremely quickly thanks to the advanced CAD techniques used by GNS as well as the fact that the vessel was built in vertical sections, each of approximately 15m (49ft 2in) in length. This technique allows more areas to be worked on at the same time and results in a section that embraces everything from the keel to the sun deck, complete with decks, bulkheads, piping and wiring conduits, all ready to be welded together to form the complete hull.

Above: A yacht of Tueq's size requires propulsion and auxiliary machinery on a commercial rather than yacht scale. Two 3,600hp Wartsila diesels provide an impressive top speed of 19 knots.

Right: The dining saloon has been placed aft on the bridge deck and can accommodate 28 people around three tables.
Below right: The main saloon offers seating on a selection of settees and armchairs around a centrally positioned table. Forward of this saloon is the main lobby.

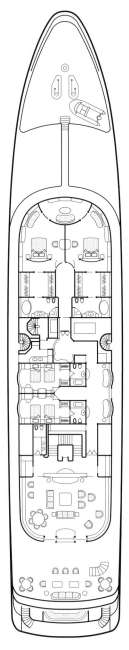

Design and construction of the interior began as soon as contracts were signed, and continued right up to the date of completion. In order to meet the deadlines, the interior was cleverly designed to be prefabricated as much as possible, so SETE co-ordinated not just one but several of the best-known fitting-out companies in Greece, Germany and Holland, each of which was given a different section of the yacht on which to concentrate. This allowed much of the elaborate work to be carried out in workshops away from the shipyard and then assembled very quickly towards the end of the building programme under the strict supervision of SETE Yachts.

With a relentless pressure on all the contractors maintained by the SETE Yachts management team, *Tueq* sailed from the yard in June 2002, just two years from the signing of contracts and a mere 21 months from the first cutting of metal. Considering the size of the vessel and the high quality of all the work involved, this was an extraordinary achievement.

With a vessel of this size, it is possible to have four complete accommodation decks, plus a sun deck on top and a storage deck below. The hull is beamy and the main emphasis is on interior space rather than deck space so that the internal volume available is very large, with 1,100m² (11,836ft²) of deck space allocated to guest areas and 800m² (8,608ft²) to crew. This allows the upper deck to be devoted entirely to the owner's private accommodation, including a comfortable saloon and private deck area aft, in addition to spacious bedroom suites for the owner and his family.

The main deck is dominated by the saloon, which accommodates at least 20 people in comfortable armchairs and settees that are grouped around a central table. Although this saloon is located in its usual position at the aft end of the superstructure, that is the point where traditional layout plans are torn up, because the next major compartment forward of the lobby is yet another saloon. The whole of the forward part of the main deck is devoted to guest accommodation, with no fewer than eight beautifully appointed double or twin staterooms. There are also four guest staterooms on the lower deck, which brings the total number of double rooms to 12, or 16 if one were to include the two staterooms that are positioned on the owner's deck.

Above: *A quiet corner of the main saloon where guests can choose to play cards or read a book.*

Above: The starboard-side owner's stateroom, which is mirrored on the port side by the lady's stateroom.
Above right: One of the VIP staterooms on the main deck.
Far right: The owner's saloon is similar in styling to the main saloon, but with checked rather that striped upholstery.
Right: The observation lounge is positioned forward of the master suite's two staterooms.

The dining room, which is on the bridge deck, above the owner's deck, has three tables with places for 28 people. Provided the weather is suitable, sliding glass doors open onto the deck, where 24 more diners can be seated at three outdoor tables. A passenger lift for up to four people has a broad stairway wrapped around it and provides access to all five decks. Meanwhile, an additional service lift is used to transport food in heated trolleys from the main galley on the lower deck to a large and fully equipped pantry forward of the lobby.

The main lobby stretches across the full width of the superstructure, with access to the each of the side decks. The designer, Mick Leach, was very anxious to prevent the lift and stairs from dominating it as a solid mass,

especially as there was the technical requirement for sliding fire doors on either side. He achieved this by giving the structure of the lift a bronze lacquer finish with very carefully drawn outlines, which affords it a floating appearance against the dignified wood panelling around it. In fact bronze – either real metal or bronze coloured lacquer – is used in a number of places aboard *Tueq*.

Concerning the style of the interior, the dominant timber is limed oak, which is used for raised panelling and many architectural forms such as pillars, window frames and tables. Carpets are a pale beige in all areas, usually outlined with a rope border. This detail is also used in carved timber to define the dado and architrave. Above the dado level, walls are mostly covered with Novasuede, which adds a contrastingly softer look to the more formal appearance of the oak panelling. Every stateroom has at least one original painting, usually landscapes of mainland Greece and the Greek islands. In several places there are also large murals with classical themes.

With so many guest staterooms, it would have been extremely easy to fall into a dull uniformity, but each one has individual colour themes, both in the soft furnishings and the marble or Corian used in the bathrooms. Coloured leather details around the beds and Roman blinds in a variety of materials also give individuality. Two staterooms on the owner's deck have been made especially cheerful with painted 'blue sky' ceilings, featuring kites in one case and balloons in the other.

The two owner's staterooms are reached via a central corridor and curved and fluted oak doors. Identical in size and shape but quite different in style and colouring, both have beds that face a curve of windows offering splendid views towards the bow. One of the beds is backed by a screen of green glass with sculptured waves that appear particularly attractive when they are edge-lit by concealed lamps, while the other screen has a mural painting of an undersea scene. In each case, these screens conceal the entrance to the large walk-through dressing area and splendid marble-trimmed bathroom. These two master-suite bedrooms meet at their forward end in a charming observation lounge, whose windows have an unobstructed view over the bows.

Television, video and music form an important part of the pleasure of being on holiday and away from the pressures of life. There is, therefore, a very complete television outfit with two satellite dishes and numerous receivers, providing the widest possible choice of channels in addition to DVD and recorded music. The three saloons each has a 157cm (62in) plasma-screen, the largest currently available, and while not in use these are concealed behind oak 'roll-top' screens. Each of the guest staterooms has a plasma television screen of a more normal size as part of a full entertainment system.

In addition to the open-air sections of the main, owner's and dining decks, there is a very pleasant sun deck, which, in spite of its name, is mostly shaded. In the forward part is a pair of circular tables and settees, while further aft, under the roof overhang, is a selection of seats and small tables plus a bar. The central island contains the top station of the lift and powder rooms. The aft section of this deck is used for tender storage.

Such a large vessel as *Tueq* calls for propulsion and auxiliary machinery on a commercial rather than yacht scale. Accordingly, the main engines are 3,600hp Wartsila diesels, while the three MAN/Leroy-Somer generators supply 480kW each – enough energy in total to power a small town. Although the Wartsila engines would normally be found in commercial or military vessels, in

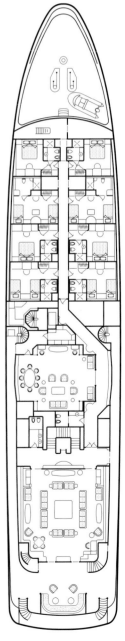

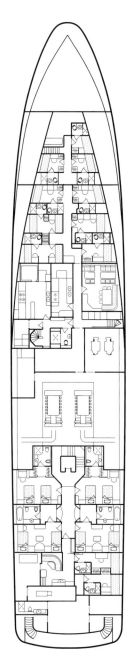

this case they have been beautifully prepared with white-enamelled blocks and chromed cylinder covers so that they positively gleam in the spotless engine room.

Tueq was designed with a particular berth in mind, which she fits into with centimetres to spare. To make this practicable, she has been given an exceptional degree of manoeuvrability with Lips controllable-pitch main propellers and both bow and stern side-thrusters. All of these are integrated by a computer and can be controlled from the pilothouse using a 'Lips-stick', which can cause the vessel to move in any direction, including sideways. Furthermore, when turning, the captain can select any of three turning centres so that the vessel will pivot around a point three-quarters forward, amidships, or three-quarters aft. She will certainly not require the assistance of a tug. The fun of watching this and other manoeuvres can be enjoyed by guests thanks to a pair of settees on either side of the bridge.

The tenders and a selection of jet-skis are stowed on the sun deck and launched by a pair of cranes. They were not given a garage because, although *Tueq* is large, there is a great deal to be fitted in and the space right aft on the lower deck was needed as staterooms and a mess deck for staff, although there is a lazarette with storage for additional sports equipment adjacent to the combined boarding and bathing platform at the stern. Meanwhile, the whole of the lower deck forward of the engine room is devoted to the crew and technical spaces. Despite the size of *Tueq* and its massive engines, the noise and vibration levels achieved are considerably lower than the recommended Lloyd's guidelines, and in this respect she is probably one of the quietest yachts afloat.

On the port side of the lower deck is the main galley, adjacent to the stairs and lift that carries food to the pantries on each deck above. Opposite is the crew mess with three tables of different sizes to accommodate the 21 crew in various groups. Forward of this, nine crew cabins, each with its own shower room, open off a central corridor. The captain and two other senior officers have cabins abaft the bridge. Below the crew mess and galley is a sub-deck containing a sizeable and fully-

Far left: Tueq's *captain can easily manoeuvre the vessel with the combined help of the Lips controllable-pitch main propellers as well as bowthrusters and sternthrusters, all of which are fully integrated.*
Left: *The second, smaller saloon on the main deck.*
Below left: *Hot-air balloons mark the theme of one of the beautifully designed twin-bedded guest staterooms.*

equipped laundry as well as extensive freezers and storerooms. With some 50 people aboard, the daily requirement for clean linen and towels is formidable.

Tueq, a vessel built to accommodate 30 people in the owner's party who are attended by 21 crew and seven staff, is a private city away from the world, conceived and built with the utmost professionalism by the highly skilled and dedicated SETE Yachts team.

SPECIFICATIONS

LOA	71.80m (235ft 6in)	**Cranes**	King Metaal
Beam	13.50m (44ft 3in)	**Passerelle and boarding**	Cramm
Draught	4.30m (14ft 2in)	**Fire control system**	Marioff Hi-Fog
Displacement	1,979 tonnes	**Ship's monitoring system**	CSI
Construction	Steel hull & aluminium superstructure	**Navigation & communication installation**	Litton
Main engines	2 x 3,600hp Wartsila diesels	**Entertainment systems**	Linn, Sony
Gearboxes	Reintjes	**Air-conditioning**	Heinen & Hopman
Propellers	Lips, 5-bladed	**Owner & guests**	30 in 6 x double & 10 x twin cabins
Speed (max/cruise)	19 knots/16 knots	**Crew**	21 in 1 x double & 10 x twin cabins
Fuel capacity	234 tonnes	**Classification**	Lloyd's ✠100A1, SSC Yacht (P),
Range at 15 knots	5,500nm		Mono G6, ✠LMC, UMS
Generators	3 x 480kW MAN/Leroy-Somer	**Naval architect**	De Voogt Naval Architects
Fresh water capacity	90 tonnes	**Exterior styling**	SETE Yachts/Mick Leach Design
Watermakers	2 x 30 t/d Hatenboer	**Interior design**	Mick Leach Design
Bow & stern thrusters	Veth Marine	**Project management**	SETE Yachts
Stabilisers	Rolls-Royce	**Builder/Year**	GNS/SETE Yachts, Holland/2002

Windrose

Main picture: Windrose is a modern classic of 40.3m LOA. Design inspiration was drawn from the schooners Heartsease *and* Meteor V, *built in 1903 and 1914 respectively.*

Above right: *The owner, Chris Gongriep, at the wheel.*

Right: *In May 2002,* Windrose *claimed the trans-atlantic record for schooners, on the Sandy Hook to Lizard course.*

Five years ago, Chris Gongriep, a Dutch property developer and owner of Holland Jachtbouw, was racing *Sapphire*, his 30.5m (100ft) Spirit of Tradition sloop, in the Antigua Classic Regatta. *Sapphire* is an elegant and supremely comfortable yacht – perfect for world cruising – but, in his eyes, her only downside was that she lacked the competitive edge that Gongriep, a keen racing yachtsman, would have liked. Another yacht at the event, however, seemed to combine the excellent performance and the good looks to which he aspired. She was the steel-hulled, *Adela*, a schooner of 42.4m (139ft 1in) LOA that had recently been launched from the Pendennis Shipyard. *Adela* had been recreated in the modern idiom by Dutch naval architect Gerard Dijkstra from the classic wooden-hulled, William Storey-designed schooner *Heartsease*, built by JG Fay & Co. in Southampton in 1903. So, two years later when his thoughts were turning towards a new yacht, he commissioned Dijkstra to prepare a preliminary design for a modern classic which should draw its inspiration both from *Adela* and a second schooner admired by Gongriep, the 39m (128ft 2in) LOA *Meteor V* designed by Max Oertz and built in 1914 for the German Kaiser, Wilhelm II.

The size of this new yacht, named *Windrose*, was to be limited to 43m (141ft) on deck and, while she was to have good performance in all wind conditions, she was to be optimised for light weather as Gongriep planned to race her in the Mediterranean, where summer breezes rarely exceed 15 knots. The ability to excel for family cruising and the occasional charter were also to be incorporated

in her deck layout and interior design, in which respect a large and protected guest cockpit was required, together with a large saloon and dining saloon, a master stateroom and three further guest cabins.

Dijkstra defines the term 'modern-classic' as a yacht with the appearance of a classic vessel, but modern in respect of its underwater profile and materials, its hydrodynamically efficient appendages, its sailing systems and its efficient rig. With light weather performance in mind, Dijkstra's design team, led by Thijs Nikkels, created a vessel of particularly light displacement, which used Alustar aluminium for the hull and deck – a material that offers 10% less weight and equal strength to a regular boatbuilding alloy, while ballast in the keel was reduced to a minimum by creating heavy weather stability with ballast tanks holding up to seven tonnes of water beneath each side deck. Naturally, the rig was to be made from carbon fibre, which offers a tube weight that is about 50% lighter than aluminium, while the interior joinery was to be foam cored to further reduce weight.

Built under ABS survey and, with charter use in mind, in compliance with MCA regulations as interpreted by the Cayman Islands authorities, *Windrose's* construction started in October 1999 at the yard of specialist hull builder Bloemsma, after which it was moved to Holland Jachtbouw in Zaandam, near the mouth of the Noordzee Canal. The rig was sub-contracted to Carbospars, a specialist composite sparmaker, while Tom Dodson of North Sails (New Zealand) won the contract for the sails, which were to be made from Gatorback Spectra. As it turned out, the mainsail and foresail were made at North's English loft due to pressure of America's Cup work in New Zealand. All these elements were united just before the launch in November 2001, and *Windrose*, weighing in at a remarkably light 150 tonnes, subsequently underwent sailing trials in the North Sea and was delivered to her owner in January 2002.

In appearance, *Windrose* reflects the two yachts that inspired her. Elements of *Adela* can be seen in her rig, while *Meteor V* can be seen in her fore and aft overhangs that were united with a delicately curved sheerline, a powerful 6m (19ft 8in) bowsprit and an elegant counter stern. Beneath the waterline is a modern skeg-hung rudder and a fin and bulb keel, the 4m-long (13ft) bulb finished with a flattened 1.5m-long (5ft) beaver-tail and weighing in at some 45 tonnes, providing a draught of 4.3m (14ft 1in). Her towering rig features a foremast rising 39.2m (128ft 7in) above the waterline and a 45.6m (149ft 7in) mainmast, the former with three spreaders

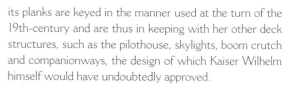

its planks are keyed in the manner used at the turn of the 19th-century and are thus in keeping with her other deck structures, such as the pilothouse, skylights, boom crutch and companionways, the design of which Kaiser Wilhelm himself would have undoubtedly approved.

Surrounded by high wooden bulwarks, the cockpit is dominated by the huge wooden wheel that is mounted on a wooden pedestal topped with a delightful glass and chrome six-sided binnacle. From the helmsman's point of view, however, the wheel's most delightful feature is without doubt the Whitlock Mamba steering system that connects it rigidly to the rudder using a series of universal joints and gear wheels. The result is silky smooth steering combined with a full feedback of information from the rudder to indicate clearly the balance of the yacht – a helmsman's dream. Other than the binnacle's magnetic compass, all of the helmsman's instrumentation and controls are mounted on a pair of short peninsulas that jut out into the cockpit just forward of the wheel, each of them carrying B&G wind instruments. The Segatron autopilot and its joystick controller, the proportional joystick for the bowthruster, and a slave screen for the Furuno radar are to starboard, while the engine controls

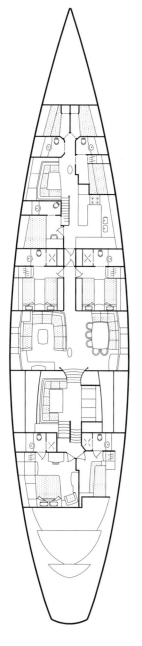

and the latter with four, both fitted with Navtec discontinuous rod rigging and running backstays. The mastheads are united by a triatic stay in addition to a lower triatic running from the foremast head to the attachment point of the mainmast's running backstay. To reduce loading in the booms, they are free to rotate at the gooseneck and have no vangs fitted, although the twin Spectra loops emerging from the undersides of the booms can be braced down to the gunwales when necessary.

The sail plan will certainly have some traditionalists clucking over their beer. Fully-battened foresails and mainsails espouse the latest America's Cup thinking in their heavily roached heads – not a sight that one would have seen in the Golden Age – but as Chris Gongriep points out: 'Other modern classics use carbon reinforced fabrics that are far removed from the sail cloth of their eras and, surely, if the technology to make a heavily roached sail head existed at that time and it was shown to be fast, they would certainly have adopted it.' Following the same thinking, *Windrose* also displays a powerful collection of Lewmar drum winches on her deck, 18 of them hydraulically powered (the six handling her runners are, for safety reasons, hand ground) and apart from a modest number of Dorades, her deck is otherwise staunchly authentic. Beautifully laid with teak,

are to port. The only unfamiliar controls are the three buttons that operate the ballast tanks. Once the port or starboard tank is loaded up with sea water by the pump – a 30-minute operation – three-quarters of the water is transferred by gravity in the three minutes prior to a tack, and the remainder pumped up over about 10 minutes after the tack is completed. A full tank will lessen the yacht's angle of heel by around four degrees, sufficient to cause a noticeable increase in boatspeed and comfort.

Forward of the wheel, the cockpit becomes guest territory – a huge space with its central table ringed by cushioned seating for at least 16 people. From here, doors open forward into the pilothouse, where a cosy dining area on the port side faces the twin navigation and communications desks to starboard. Here, the yacht's deeply traditional interior is introduced. Mahogany raised and fielded panelling, often with its upper areas white-painted, together with beamed and planked deckheads and a pale maple floor – the exemplary work of the Dutch specialist furniture manufacturer, Dorr. Edging every horizontal surface are beautifully moulded upstands, while a pair of banister rails, their extremities terminating in neat curlicues, frame the stairs that descend to the saloon. The interior layout of *Windrose* was created by Thijs Nikkels in conjunction with Maggie Russell-Smith, the captain's wife and a highly experienced yachting professional, who concentrated on its decoration and functional practicalities. They aimed for the same hardwearing, time-enduring, classical appearance that had proved so successful on *Sapphire*.

No attempt was made to conceal that this is a sailing yacht. This is clearly exemplified by the lower section of the mainmast which, passing through the saloon, has only its lower element encased in panelling that terminates in a useful handgrip. To port of the mast is a huge U-shaped settee upholstered in white Clarence House fabric and scattered with contrastingly colourful Turkish cushions. To starboard is the dining area, where a splendid flame-cut mahogany table nestles into an L-shape of inbuilt seating upholstered in a Paisley design, its 10-seater complement finished with a scattering of loose dining chairs outboard. The room's other amenities include a huge flat-screen television for DVD and video, which swings out from its concealed stowage within a cupboard to port. The cupboards and drawers that surround the starboard-side writing desk hide a

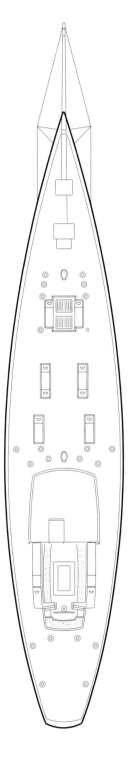

Far left above: The deckhouse, with dining to port and the navigation desk to starboard, sets the decorative tone of the interior.
Far left below: The dining area in the saloon.
Below left: Mahogany panelling provides a hardwearing yet traditional background to the saloon which, when racing, becomes a sail store.

computer and printer attached to the yacht's network. Of particular note is a cabinet fitted with lattice doors and bevel-edged glass that is positioned against the bulkhead aft of the seating area. In perfect keeping with its position, it has been built so that its corniced top follows the rise of the deck, resulting in a beautifully crafted asymmetric shape that surely tested the skill of Dorr's most experienced cabinetmaker.

The owner's accommodation is in the stern of the yacht, opening off a lobby at the foot of a short stairway descending aft from the deckhouse. Rather than a full-beam owner's suite, Chris Gongriep chose to have a family area comprising a roomy owner's cabin to port with desk and easy chair, while the starboard side has a separate twin bunk childrens' cabin. Both have delightful en suite head compartments, trimmed with understated marble and a large shower floored with a teak grating. The remaining two guest cabins open off the passageway leading forward from the saloon. Mirror images of each other, these occupy a similar floor area as the owner's cabin while, with charter in mind, they are fitted with beds that can be made up as twins or doubles. They are also provided with a Pullman berth that is particularly useful while *Windrose* is in racing mode, when each cabin would accommodate a total of six 'hot-bunking' crew – half on watch while the other half sleep. On these occasions, the cabin's large showers have a second purpose as wet oilskin storage, while the suitably protected saloon becomes the yacht's sail packing centre.

Apart from her design skills, Maggie Russell-Smith's daytime job is chef aboard *Windrose*, so she naturally paid particular attention to the galley's layout and equipment. Although compact, it would delight any chef in its ergonomic layout and practical division of storage and work surfaces that, where necessary, can be accessed from both sides by chef and stewardesses without

Above: The twin bunk children's cabin in the stern of the yacht.
Below: Forward of the binnacle, the guest cockpit contains cushioned seating and a large dining table.

interfering with each other's function. Opposite the galley is the captain's cabin, with double bed and en suite shower which, like the rest of the crew area, is decorated in the same style as the rest of the yacht. Forward, is a crew mess, the engineer's en suite cabin, and two twin-bunked crew cabins that share a shower room.

The engine room, positioned beneath the pilothouse, is entered from the owner's lobby. Lined in glistening white aluminium, this is a fairly large compartment for a sailing yacht of this size, offering near standing headroom and ample space to move easily around its main machinery – a centrally positioned Lugger 425hp straight-six diesel that will power *Windrose* at a continuous cruising speed of 12 knots, and two 33kW Northern Lights generating sets. The compartment itself is very well insulated against the transmission of noise and vibration, while the generators, one or both of which must be running at all times while the yacht is under way to provide hydraulic power to the sailing systems, are also cased in soundboxes that render them near inaudible from the deck.

Of course, the real thrill of *Windrose* is in her stunning performance under sail. Since her delivery in January 2002, she first proved herself with a transatlantic

crossing, while her racing prowess was demonstrated in Antigua Classic Week's hotly contested Spirit of Tradition class, where she regularly finished ahead of two J-Class yachts, *Shamrock* and *Velsheda*, as well as the larger Abeking & Rasmussen-built ketch *Hetairos* designed by Bruce King. Racing in winds of up to 26 knots, she romped along the close reaches at anything between 12 and 14 knots and took off when the wind came further astern, at times logging 15 and 16 knots with her big asymmetric spinnaker aloft. It was only to windward that she was outpaced by the J-Class sloops – ultimate windward machines – whose deep keels combined with the perfect aerofoils of their carbon-fibre sails gave them a higher pointing ability and marginally greater speed in these windy conditions.

The climax of the first year's racing for *Windrose* undoubtedly came when she passed the Lizard Peninsula on England's south coast on her return passage from the New World in mid-May 2002. She had been pitted against the much larger 58m (190ft) schooner *Adix* in a two-boat match race across the Atlantic starting at Sandy Hook – a classic re-run of the 1905 race won by the legendary Charlie Barr, when in command of the 57m

(187ft) *Atlantic*, during which he set a remarkable course record of just over 12 days. Amazingly, Barr's schooner record remained in place until *Windrose* completed the course 97 years later in a time that was 17 hours, 37 minutes and 9 seconds faster. Mission accomplished!

SPECIFICATIONS

LOA (including bowsprit)	46.32m (152ft 0in)	Jib furling system	Reckmann
LOA	40.36m (132ft 5in)	Halyard runner & sheet winches	Lewmar
LWL	29.30m (96ft 2in)	Windlasses	Ascon
Beam (max)	8.00m (26ft 3in)	Communications	Nera Mini M Satcom
Draught	4.30m (14ft 1in)	Gyrocompass	C. Plath, Navigat 2100
Ballast keel	45 tonnes	Owner and guests	8/10 in 4 cabins
Displacement (to DWL)	150 tonnes	Crew	7 in 4 cabins
Spars	Carbospars, carbon-fibre	Hull tank testing	Delft University
Rigging	Navtec discontinuous rod	Wind tunnel testing	Wolfson Unit
Sail areas (upwind)	1,067m² (11,481ft²)	Construction	Aluminium hull & deck
(downwind)	2,317m² (24,931ft²)	Classification	ABS. MCA (Cayman Islands)
Sailmaker	North Sails (NZ & UK)	Interior design	G Dijkstra & M Russell-Smith
Engine	1 x 425hp Lugger 6-cylinder diesel	Exterior styling	Gerard Dijkstra & Partners
Propeller	Hundested variable pitch	Naval architect	Gerard Dijkstra & Partners
Electricity generation	2 x 33kW Northern Lights	Builder/Year	Holland Jachtbouw/2002

A PLACE TO DREAM

INTERIOR DESIGN

Creators of exclusive interiors for luxury yachts and prestige projects worldwide.
Whatever and wherever your dreams are, we specialise in making them come true.

L

LOHER

INTERIORS

45м

44м

50м

COR D ROVER DESIGN
WWW.COR-D-ROVER.COM
MAIL : CDRD@EURONET.NL
TEL.+31 78 6133822
FAX. +31 78 6390293
VEERSTEIGER 2, DORDRECHT, HOLLAND
CURRENTLY UNDER CONSTRUCTION:122M REFIT, 45M MONDOMARINE, 44M DIASHIP, 43M REFIT, 40M MONDOMARINE, 39M HIGH SPEED

Excellence III. Abeking and Rasmussen 57.3m (188'). Winner of the 2002 ShowBoats Awards, Best Motor Yacht Interior.

Linn Marine Entertainment Systems

Proven at sea and supported right around the world by Linn Approved Marine Affiliates

LINN

UK Tel: +44 (0)141 307 7777 UK Fax: +44 (0)141 644 4262
USA Tel: +1 904 645 5242 USA Fax: +1 904 645 7275
e-mail: **info@linnmarine.com** internet: **www.linn.co.uk** or **www.linninc.com**

Photograph courtesy of Abeking & Rasmussen.

PROJECT: 155FT (46m) HIGH PERFORMANCE SLOOP
DESIGNER: LP ARCHITECTS + YACHT DESIGNERS
NAVAL ARCHITECT: PEDRICK YACHT DESIGNS
YACHT BUILDER: PENDENNIS SHIPYARD LTD
PROJECTED LAUNCH: AUTUMN 2003
CONFIGURATION: GROUNDBREAKING

THE BEST IDEAS EARLY

LIEBOWITZ   PRITCHARD

LP ARCHITECTS + YACHT DESIGNERS   info@LParch.com
THIRTEEN ERISEY TERRACE   FALMOUTH   TR11 2AP   ENGLAND

Tim Heywood

Tim Heywood Designs Limited
Tel: 44 (0) 207 481 8958

SUMMIT

Summit Furniture (Europe) Ltd.   3/24 Chelsea Harbour Design Centre, London SW10 0XE   *ph* +44 (0)20 7795 3311   *fx* +44 (0)20 7795 3322
Summit Furniture, Inc.   5 Harris Court, Monterey, CA 93940   *ph* 831.375.7811   *fx* 831.375.0940   **www.summitfurniture.com**

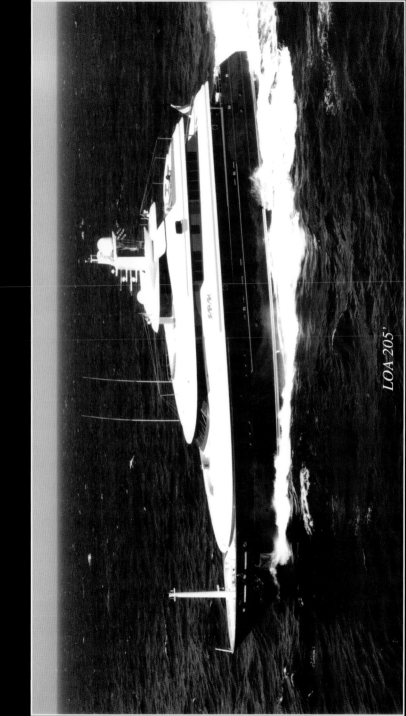

SARAH

LOA 205'

QUALITY
WITHOUT QUESTION

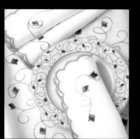

OUTFITTED IN EXCESS OF 130 SUPERYACHTS

DUBOIS
Naval Architecture & Yacht Design

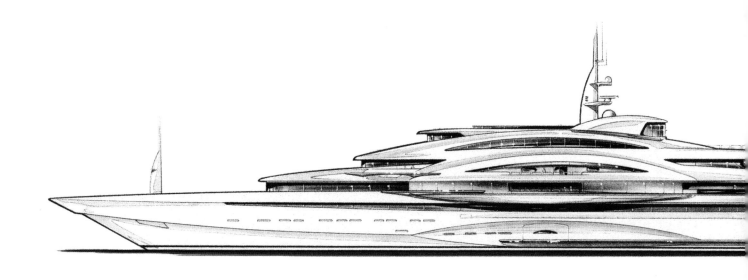

The complete
yacht design service

Yacht design

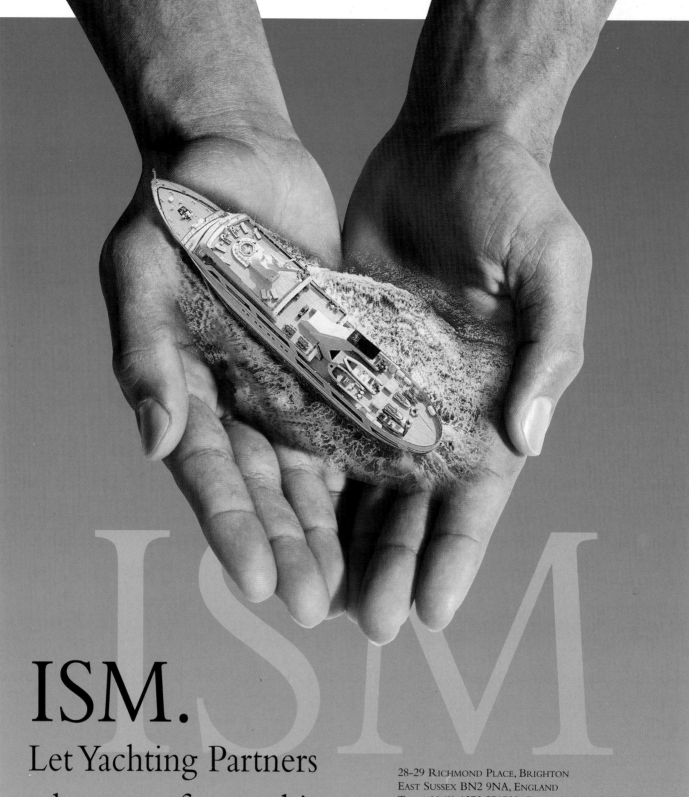

ISM.

Let Yachting Partners take care of everything...

The International Safety Management Code becomes compulsory for commercial yachts over 500GT in 2002. Yachting Partners International understands every aspect of the ISM Code – so you don't have to. Simply talk to Nigel Studdart at YPI, and you, your captain and your crew can sail easy – knowing that the complexities of ISM compliancy have been taken care of by a professional team.

IN SAFE HANDS SINCE 1972

francisdesign.com

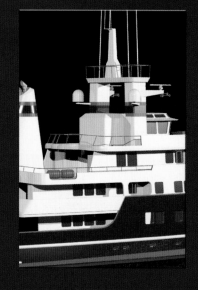

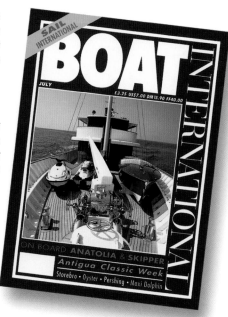
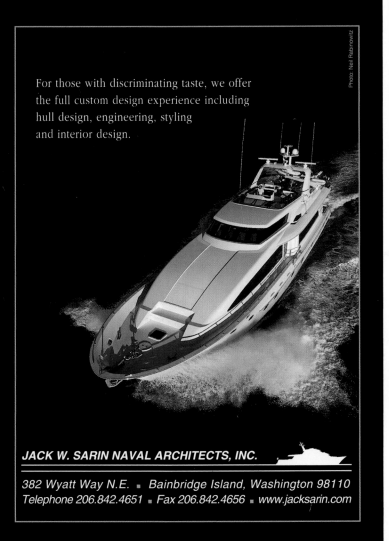

EØ

SPEN ØINO
aval architects

Espen Oeino Naval Architects - 10 Avenue de la Libération - 06600 Antibes - France
Tél. +33 (0)4 9291 0777 - Fax +33 (0)4 9291 0718 - mail@espenoeino.com - www.espenoeino.com

Création : www.lencrenoire.com - Crédits Photos : Klaus Jordan

New Projects

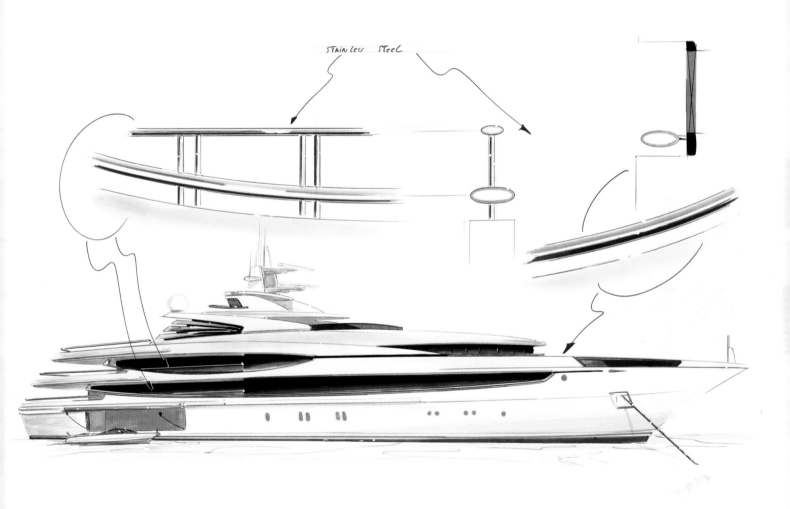

STAINLESS STEEL

A Preview of the Latest Superyachts
in Design and Build Around the World

Acubens

Luiz de Basto

ACUBENS

The 36.27m (119ft) Mustang 119 is a very high-speed, hard-top sports boat that has been developed by **Acubens** for the Spanish shipyard **Izar San Fernando**, which has extensive experience in the construction of high-speed craft. Designed by **Iñigo Echenique**, the Mustang has a deep-V monohedron hull and will be available with various power installations including up to three **MTU** 16V diesels which, delivering a total output of 11,100hp, will provide a top speed of 50 knots using either surface drives or waterjets. With a tank capacity of 27,000l, the range at 40 knots will be 650nm. Several layouts are available, accommodating up to eight guests.

LUIZ DE BASTO

An exciting 34m (112ft) raised-pilothouse fast motor yacht has been developed by **Luiz de Basto Designs**. The yacht's innovative layout features a pilothouse design that sits inside the main saloon like an open island. The upper part of the windshield is for the helmsman

Acubens

DONALD BLOUNT

Donald L Blount and Associates is currently developing a 52m (172ft) fast motor yacht with a maximum speed of 36 knots, a cruising speed of 29 knots and excellent sea-keeping characteristics. The owner has requested shallow draught to accommodate some of the

JON BANNENBERG

Among the most interesting of several large projects in the **Jon Bannenberg** office is a 115m (377ft) motor yacht **(BELOW)** that has been commissioned by a leading broker for one of their existing clients. As well as having unmistakable Bannenberg looks, this vessel, which provides accommodation for 22 guests and 46 crew, is truly state of the art in its systems, design and construction. Also under development is a 75m (246ft) yacht designed for maximum owner enjoyment, housing a wealth of toys. In spite of this, no compromise has been made

in the looks department – even the helicopter landing pad retracts into the deck. Following the success of the recently launched 50m (164ft) motor yacht *Multiple* from **Benetti**, the two companies are joining forces once again on a ground-breaking project whose details remain highly confidential.

John Bannenberg

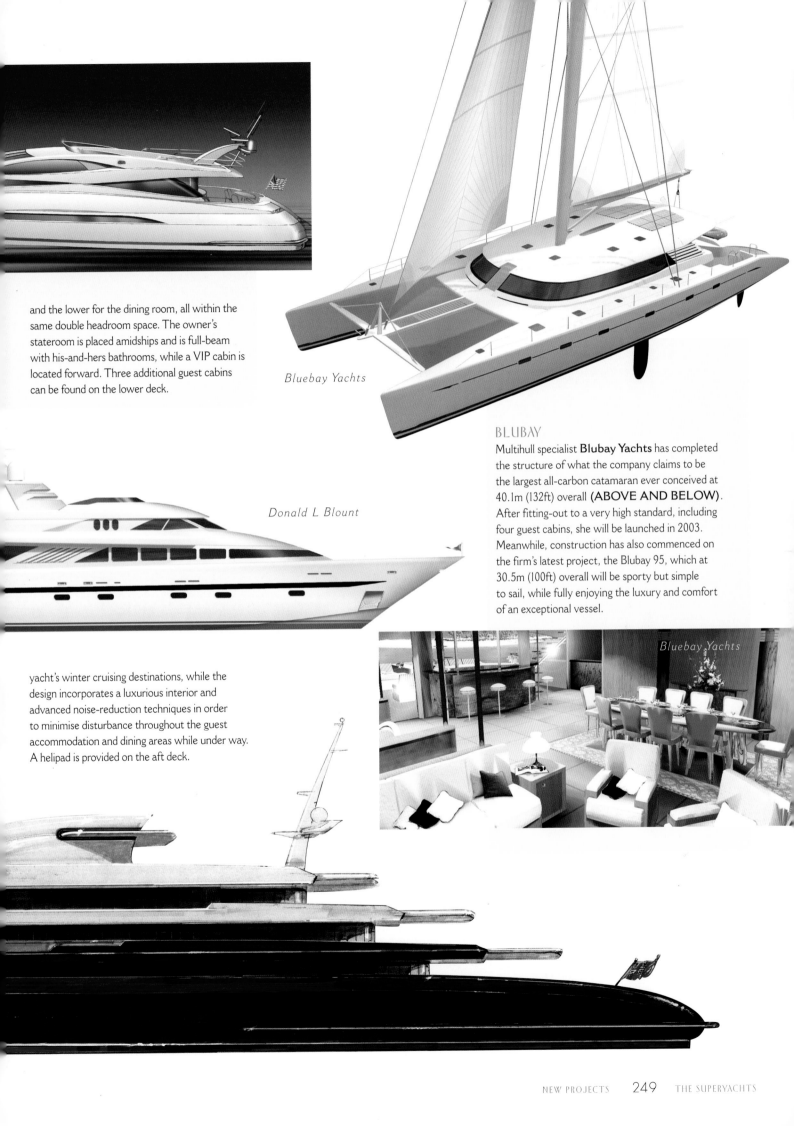

and the lower for the dining room, all within the same double headroom space. The owner's stateroom is placed amidships and is full-beam with his-and-hers bathrooms, while a VIP cabin is located forward. Three additional guest cabins can be found on the lower deck.

Bluebay Yachts

Donald L Blount

BLUBAY

Multihull specialist **Blubay Yachts** has completed the structure of what the company claims to be the largest all-carbon catamaran ever conceived at 40.1m (132ft) overall **(ABOVE AND BELOW)**. After fitting-out to a very high standard, including four guest cabins, she will be launched in 2003. Meanwhile, construction has also commenced on the firm's latest project, the Blubay 95, which at 30.5m (100ft) overall will be sporty but simple to sail, while fully enjoying the luxury and comfort of an exceptional vessel.

yacht's winter cruising destinations, while the design incorporates a luxurious interior and advanced noise-reduction techniques in order to minimise disturbance throughout the guest accommodation and dining areas while under way. A helipad is provided on the aft deck.

Bluebay Yachts

Philippe Briand

PHILIPPE BRIAND

Currently under design development by **Philippe Briand Yacht Design** is a 40m (132ft) cruiser-racer that will be one of the most high-tech of her size and, with a mast rising 48m (157ft) above the deck, one of the world's largest sloops. The client has asked for everything needed to carry on work and business aboard, and for this reason both a private office and a meeting room have been included. Although slightly smaller than *Mari-Cha III*, similar windward performance is anticipated.

CARBOSPARS

What is believed to be the tallest free-standing rig yet seen is being constructed by **Carbospars SL** in Llucmajor, Mallorca for the 48m (157ft 6in) sloop *Erica*, designed by **Ted Fontaine** and **Gerry Dijkstra**, which is due to be launched from its Dutch builder in the spring of 2003. This semi-balanced freely rotating mast, built to Carbospars' own design, will be the largest AeroRig® in existence, being 60m (197ft) tall, with a 1.5m (5ft) deep wing section, a weight of seven tonnes and a massive 36m (118ft) boom. It will be constructed of high-strength T800 carbon fibres to give maximum strength and minimum weight. Thanks to the extreme ease and safety of handling conferred by this system, the owner of this yacht intends to cruise with only two crew to assist him.

BURGER BOAT COMPANY

The **Burger Boat Company** of Manitowoc, Wisconsin has signed contracts to build a 34m (112ft) full-displacement, expedition-style motor yacht. This will be the third custom tri-deck yacht order taken within 18 months. *Top Times* will feature a modern classic interior to complement her striking exterior lines. Amenities will include a sun deck with hot tub and helm station, a family room/sky lounge, gourmet galley, a full-beam deck-level master suite, and four large guest cabins.

TONY CASTRO & JONGERT

The long-standing collaboration between designer **Tony Castro** and Dutch yacht-builder **Jongert** continues to be fruitful. A client who saw a model of the Jongert 3200M performance cruising sloop at the Düsseldorf Boat Show has ordered a larger version, which will be 41.00m (134ft 6in) overall **(RIGHT)**. A development of Jongert's 'Modern Line' with enhanced performance, the new yacht will make use of the yard's patented folding keel to reduce draught from 6.45m to 3.20m (21ft to 10ft 6in). Jongert has also commenced construction of the fifth yacht in the highly successful 40T semi-custom series. This will be the second yacht in this series to be built for the same owner, who has this time requested MCA certification so that the yacht can be used for charter. As well as the owner's cabin, there will be three spacious guest cabins.

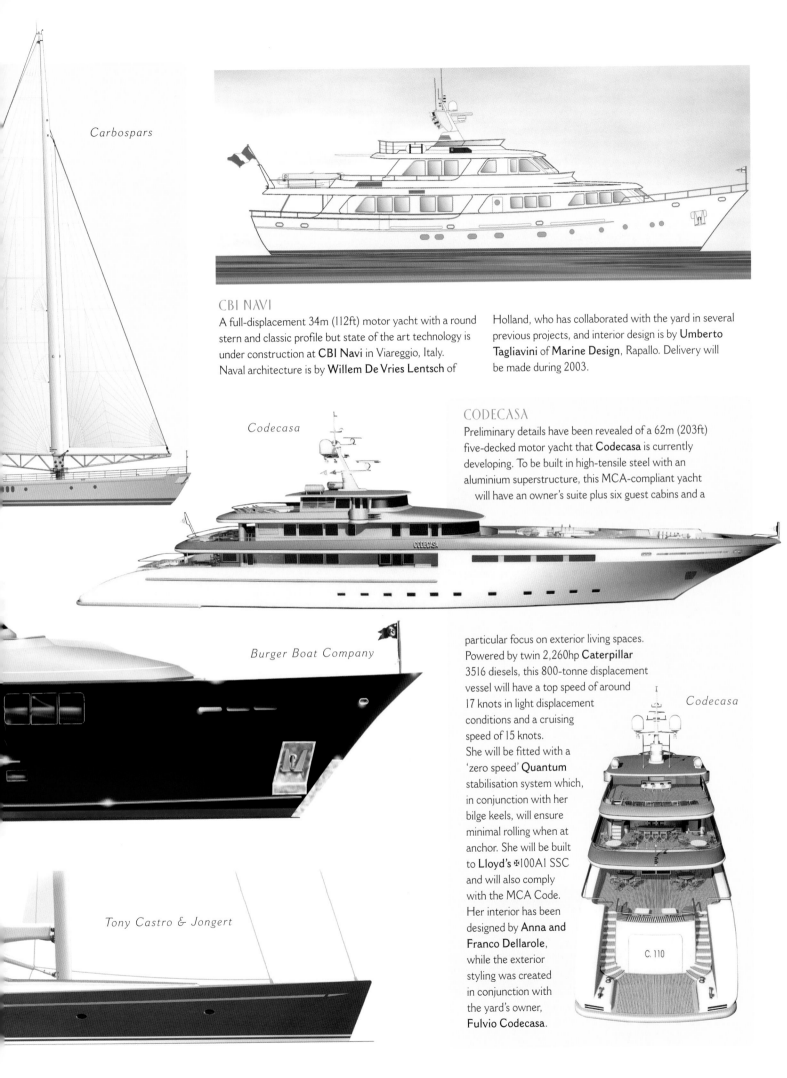

Carbospars

Codecasa

Burger Boat Company

Tony Castro & Jongert

Codecasa

CBI NAVI

A full-displacement 34m (112ft) motor yacht with a round stern and classic profile but state of the art technology is under construction at **CBI Navi** in Viareggio, Italy. Naval architecture is by **Willem De Vries Lentsch** of Holland, who has collaborated with the yard in several previous projects, and interior design is by **Umberto Tagliavini** of **Marine Design**, Rapallo. Delivery will be made during 2003.

CODECASA

Preliminary details have been revealed of a 62m (203ft) five-decked motor yacht that **Codecasa** is currently developing. To be built in high-tensile steel with an aluminium superstructure, this MCA-compliant yacht will have an owner's suite plus six guest cabins and a particular focus on exterior living spaces. Powered by twin 2,260hp **Caterpillar** 3516 diesels, this 800-tonne displacement vessel will have a top speed of around 17 knots in light displacement conditions and a cruising speed of 15 knots. She will be fitted with a 'zero speed' **Quantum** stabilisation system which, in conjunction with her bilge keels, will ensure minimal rolling when at anchor. She will be built to **Lloyd's** ✠100A1 SSC and will also comply with the MCA Code. Her interior has been designed by **Anna and Franco Dellarole**, while the exterior styling was created in conjunction with the yard's owner, **Fulvio Codecasa**.

BERNIE COHEN DESIGN

Currently under construction at **Shipworks Brisbane** is a 56m (183ft) steel and aluminium motor yacht designed by **Bernie Cohen Design**. The brief stipulated that the craft had to exude 'timeless style and character' with a visual balance between innovation and classic design. She has superlative accommodation for the owner and 10 guests in six staterooms plus three lounges, a gymnasium and four outside deck areas. Four main decks are served by a spiral staircase and lift.

Bernie Cohen Design

CRESCENT CUSTOM YACHTS

The largest project to date at **Crescent Custom Yachts** is also the most interesting, as this 50m (163ft) motor yacht will have a steel hull and composite plastics superstructure, a most unusual combination that the client, naval architect **Jack Sarin** and the builder agree is perfect for this project and expect to see used more often in future. Materials for the interior, designed by **Robin M Rose**, include light woods with a mix of high-gloss and semi-gloss finishes, bamboo and stone flooring, coffered ceilings and selected soft furnishings, giving the impression of Asian grace. The owner and guests will share five staterooms on the lower deck. The project is scheduled for completion in December 2004.

Crescent Custom Yachts

DESIGN Q LIMITED

Best-known for its automotive, aviation and interior designs, **Design Q Limited** has designed a 35m (115ft) luxury sports cruiser whose sleek, powerful appearance is derived from the exterior lines of the Aston Martin *Vantage*, a vehicle much loved by the client. The interior is just as inspiring, with an unique helmstation that is more akin to a luxury sports car cockpit.

Design Q Limited

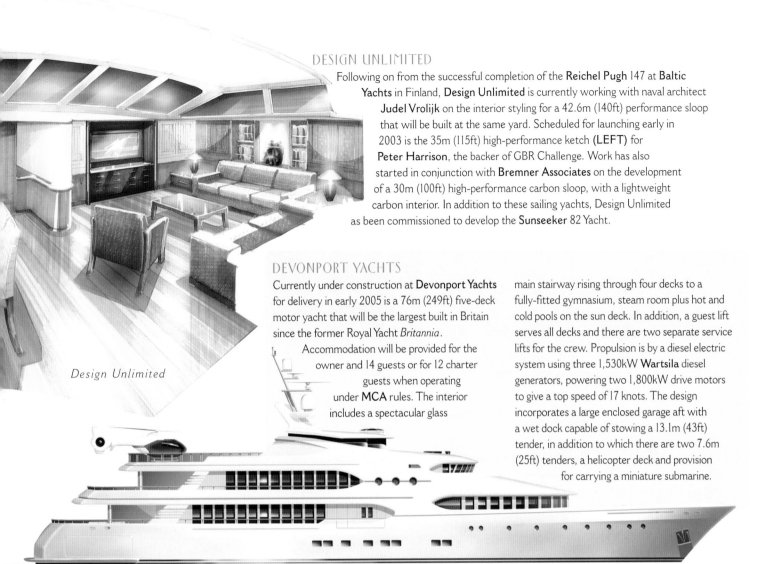

DESIGN UNLIMITED

Following on from the successful completion of the **Reichel Pugh** 147 at **Baltic Yachts** in Finland, **Design Unlimited** is currently working with naval architect **Judel Vrolijk** on the interior styling for a 42.6m (140ft) performance sloop that will be built at the same yard. Scheduled for launching early in 2003 is the 35m (115ft) high-performance ketch **(LEFT)** for **Peter Harrison**, the backer of GBR Challenge. Work has also started in conjunction with **Bremner Associates** on the development of a 30m (100ft) high-performance carbon sloop, with a lightweight carbon interior. In addition to these sailing yachts, Design Unlimited as been commissioned to develop the **Sunseeker** 82 Yacht.

Design Unlimited

DEVONPORT YACHTS

Currently under construction at **Devonport Yachts** for delivery in early 2005 is a 76m (249ft) five-deck motor yacht that will be the largest built in Britain since the former Royal Yacht *Britannia*.

Accommodation will be provided for the owner and 14 guests or for 12 charter guests when operating under **MCA** rules. The interior includes a spectacular glass main stairway rising through four decks to a fully-fitted gymnasium, steam room plus hot and cold pools on the sun deck. In addition, a guest lift serves all decks and there are two separate service lifts for the crew. Propulsion is by a diesel electric system using three 1,530kW **Wartsila** diesel generators, powering two 1,800kW drive motors to give a top speed of 17 knots. The design incorporates a large enclosed garage aft with a wet dock capable of stowing a 13.1m (43ft) tender, in addition to which there are two 7.6m (25ft) tenders, a helicopter deck and provision for carrying a miniature submarine.

Devonport Yachts

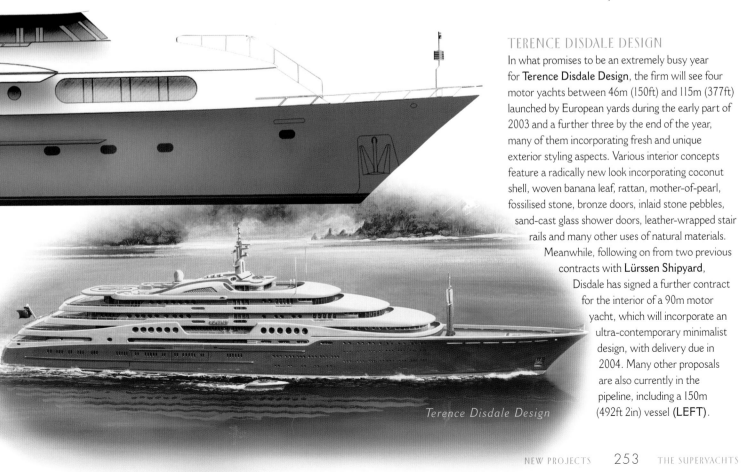

TERENCE DISDALE DESIGN

In what promises to be an extremely busy year for **Terence Disdale Design**, the firm will see four motor yachts between 46m (150ft) and 115m (377ft) launched by European yards during the early part of 2003 and a further three by the end of the year, many of them incorporating fresh and unique exterior styling aspects. Various interior concepts feature a radically new look incorporating coconut shell, woven banana leaf, rattan, mother-of-pearl, fossilised stone, bronze doors, inlaid stone pebbles, sand-cast glass shower doors, leather-wrapped stair rails and many other uses of natural materials. Meanwhile, following on from two previous contracts with **Lürssen Shipyard**, Disdale has signed a further contract for the interior of a 90m motor yacht, which will incorporate an ultra-contemporary minimalist design, with delivery due in 2004. Many other proposals are also currently in the pipeline, including a 150m (492ft 2in) vessel **(LEFT)**.

Terence Disdale Design

DIXON YACHT DESIGN

The most significant signing of the year by **Dixon Yacht Design** is the 40m (131ft) ketch *Antares* (RIGHT), which has recently commenced construction at **Royal Huisman Shipyard**. Another exciting project is a 36.5m (120ft) aluminium performance sloop that will start building early in 2003. Of modern concept, both in and out, she promises to offer an unique blend of style and performance. The company, as well as working on a variety of large production motor yachts, has been developing designs up to 50m (164ft) in length for individual clients.

Dixon Yacht Design

Dubois Naval Architects

DUBOIS NAVAL ARCHITECTS

Dubois Naval Architects continues its strong association with New Zealand builders: the 39.5m (130ft) fast cruising sloop *Janice of Wyoming* will be the 12th yacht built to the company's designs by **Alloy Yachts**. The accommodation allows for a large owner's suite, two guest cabins, one of which is convertible to a gym, and particularly roomy crew quarters. Special attention has been given to refined appearance and high performance. Meanwhile, **Fitzroy Yachts** is building two more 37m (122ft) fast cruising sloops in aluminium, *Midnight* (ABOVE LEFT & ABOVE RIGHT) and *Zulu*. The latter has been designed for charter use and will be **MCA** compliant. Her **Redman Whiteley Dixon** interior provides four guest cabins. *Midnight*, which will be the 15th Dubois yacht in excess of 33m (108ft 3in) to be built in New Zealand, will be launched in the second half of 2003 and will be followed in 2005 by *Zulu*. Launched by Alloy Yachts in time for the 2003 Millennium Cup is another Dubois/Redman Whiteley Dixon collaboration: the 40m (131ft) *Harlequin,* which has a dramatically-styled flame mahogany interior.

ESPINOSA

Current projects at **Espinosa** include exterior styling and a complete interior package for a 46m (151ft) three-deck motor yacht (BELOW) to be built by **Palmer Johnson**. The owner's suite is on the main deck, while the lower deck guest accommodation includes two equally-sized VIP suites in addition to a pair of generous doubles. With her Portuguese bridge and her sheltered, unencumbered upper deck made possible by the tender garage aft, and an extensive flying bridge with hard top, this yacht has a special emphasis on outdoor spaces. However, these do not outdo the luxury of her interior. Also under construction by Palmer Johnson, at its Savannah yard, is a 29m (96ft) cockpit motor yacht, also with a full interior by Espinosa.

Feadship

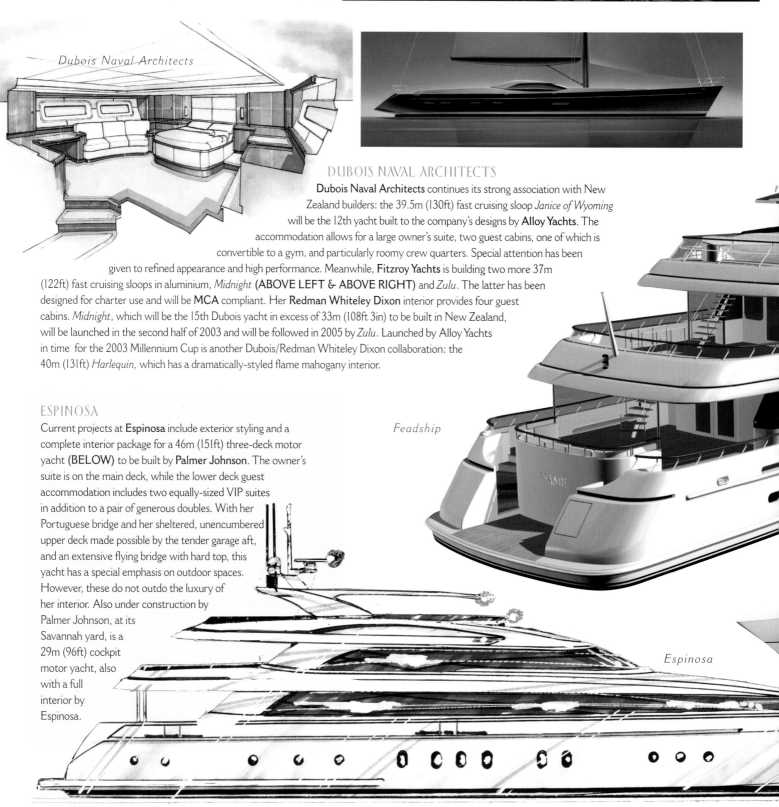

Espinosa

FEADSHIP

Among the many projects that **Feadship** is currently working on is a completely new system for storing and operating an 'embarked' helicopter (one that is based

aboard). Previously, helicopter hangars have been sited on the aft deck but this uses precious outdoor space, so this one is fitted beneath the foredeck, where the machine is stored with rotors folded in a fully-protected environment (**ABOVE**). When required, two large doors slide out sideways and the aircraft is raised on a lift that fills the gap between the doors to form the take-off/landing platform. The first yacht to use this system has yet to be announced.

The Feadship yards currently have 10 yachts under construction, ranging from 38m (125ft) to over 80m (262ft) in length. During summer 2002, the keel was laid for a 55.5m (182ft) **De Voogt** design (**BELOW**) that will be a new, innovative and sleek interpretation of the classic walk-around Feadship design with flowing lines and elegant proportions.

FRANCIS DESIGN

Shipyard negotiations with a view to delivery in 2005 are going ahead for a classical high-volume moderate-displacement motor yacht of 120m (394ft) designed by **Francis Design**. The integrated approach offered by this office, including concept, hull design, naval architecture, engineering and interior design, was one of the major factors in the owner's choice to use this firm. The owner's brief was for extensive periods at sea without the need to enter port to refuel or re-provision. She is a truly autonomous worldwide cruising yacht designed to comply with **SOLAS** requirements; she carries purpose-designed lifeboats and also has two-compartment damage status.

Francis Design

KEN FREIVOKH

The most exciting sailing yacht project currently under development is surely that of *Maltese Falcon* (**RIGHT**), the 87m (286ft) full-rigged vessel with a three-masted Dynarig concept. Developed by **Gerard Dijkstra**, this interesting yacht has engineering by its builders, **Perini Navi**, styling and interior design by **Ken Freivokh**, while the ultra-light outfitting of guest areas is by the Stuttgart-based specialist furniture maker **Sinnex**. This promises to be a ground-breaking project in many ways. On the power front, Ken Freivokh Design has provided the styling and interior design for a range of yachts being developed by **Ocean Classic**. The initial 58m (190ft) model (**ABOVE LEFT**) is to be followed by a 70m (230ft) and two 33m (108ft) high-speed yachts. Work is also progressing at **Penzance Dry Dock** on the ice-classed 45m (148ft) exploration yacht *Vega*, also with styling and interior by Ken Freivokh Design.

Ken Freivokh

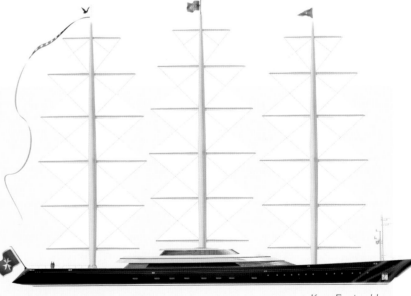

Ken Freivokh

HEESEN SHIPYARD

The ever-busy **Heesen Shipyard** has six yachts under construction, one of which has not yet been sold – a 36.3m (119ft) aluminium vessel (**FAR RIGHT**) with a full-beam master stateroom on the main deck and three doubles and a smaller twin-berthed cabin on the lower deck. Four of the other projects are also fast aluminium motor yachts, with top speeds of 25 knots or above, while another yacht is a steel-hulled displacement design of 46.7m (153ft) (**RIGHT**), which will have a cruising speed of 15 knots. All have naval architecture by **Diaship Design Team** with interior designs from a variety of firms including **Omega Architects**, **Peter Beeldsnijder** and **Terence Disdale**.

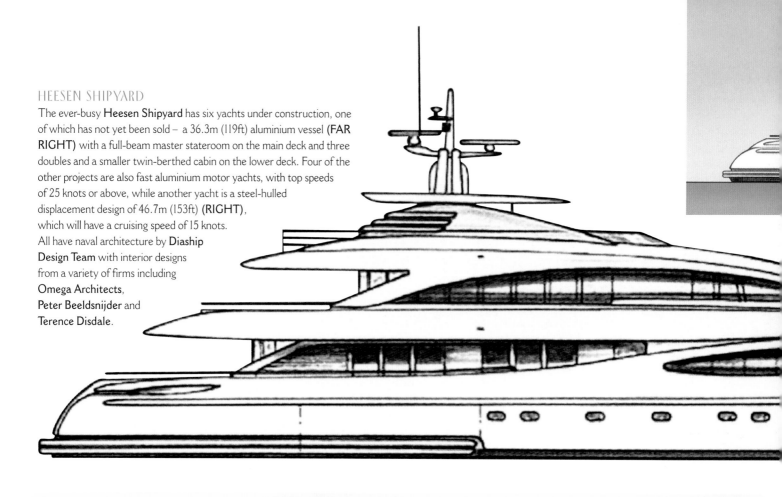

LIEBOWITZ & PRITCHARD

A very striking 46m (151ft) sailing superyacht designed by **Liebowitz & Pritchard** is currently under construction at **Pendennis Shipyard** in Falmouth. Exterior features include an aggressive *retroussé* stern, integral roof vents for expelling engine air, large plate glass windows for the guest staterooms and a wide array of protected exterior spaces. Two large tenders are carried, and the cockpit is covered by a motorised canopy that can be retracted for open-air sailing. Launching is scheduled during 2003.

Liebowitz & Pritchard

LÜRSSEN YACHTS

Two major projects have recently begun construction at **Lürssen Yachts**. The first is the 61m (200ft) *Phoenix* (**LEFT**), with interior design by **Andrew Winch** and exterior details by **Espen Oino**. The second project, *Capri,* (**BELOW**) is 58.5m (192ft) in length with an interior designed by **Glade Johnson**. Very shallow draught was a requirement for cruising in the Bahamas, and to ensure stability at anchor she will be fitted with a stabilising system by **Quantum Marine**. She will be built to full **Lloyd's** class and **MCA** certification.

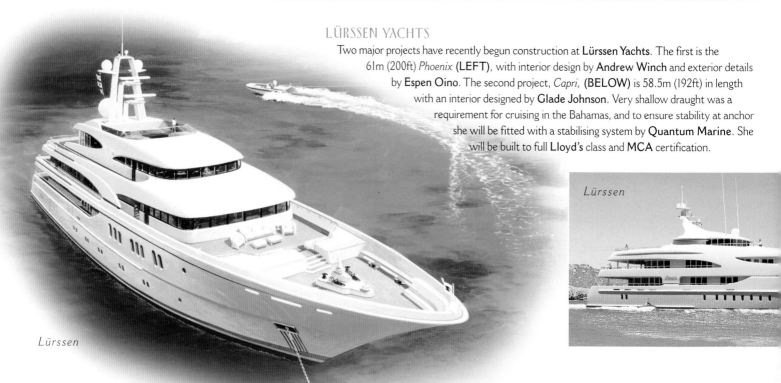

Lürssen

Lürssen

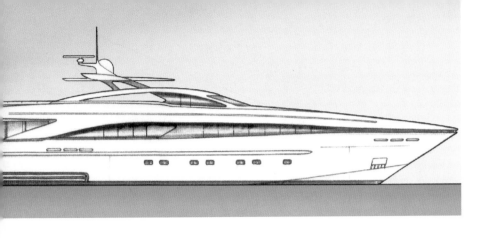

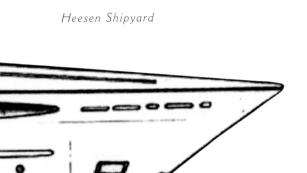

Heesen Shipyard

EVAN K MARSHALL

Among a fascinating variety of work passing
through the **Evan K Marshall** design office
is the exterior styling and interior design of
the motor yacht *Maratani X* (**BOTTOM**), which
has been built in New Zealand by **Sensation
Yachts**, with naval architecture by **Phil Curran**.
The owner is a prominent Bahamian who
will use the yacht extensively for entertainment.
Among many striking features is a three-level,
glass-enclosed lift and a master stateroom
that is spread over both the upper and sky
decks creating some unique spaces for
the owner to enjoy.

Marshall is also heavily involved with
Millenium Superyachts, most of which
are built in Dubai, except for smaller boats
and special projects, such as the **John Staluppi**
super-fast vessel, which are built in Holland.
Currently, 36m (118ft) (**BELOW**) and 35m (115ft)
yachts are building in the Dubai yard with naval
architecture by **Frank Mulder**. Just
commencing design for a Russian client is
a 47m (154ft) motor yacht with interior and

Evan K Marshall

exterior design by Marshall and naval architecture
by **Paolo Scanu**. One of the special features
of this yacht, which will be named *Terra*, is
a master suite on two levels, connected by
a sumptuous spiral staircase.

Evan K Marshall

Mulder Design

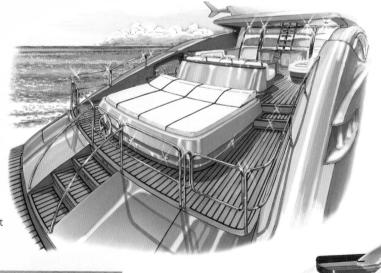

MULDER DESIGN

Among several projects for very high speed yachts with naval architecture by **Mulder Design,** the Millenium 140 stands out as being the latest project by **John Staluppi** in his quest to create the fastest ever superyacht, this time with a target speed in excess of 70 knots. Power for this 42.44m (139ft 3in) Alustar-built vessel **(ABOVE RIGHT)** will come from a pair of 4,000kW 18V **Paxman** diesels and a **Lycoming** TF80 gas turbine driving **Lips** water jets. The lightweight interior has been designed by **Evan K Marshall**. Launching is expected from **Millennium Super Yachts'** new yard in Holland by the end of 2003.

A similar power package has been specified for another high-speed yacht, whose concept, styling and interior design is by **Luiz de Basto Designs** with engineering and naval architecture by Mulder. The hull shape has been extensively tested to ensure a comfortable ride and the yacht will have a range of 3,000nm at 12 knots and a top speed of 50+ knots. A pair of **MTU** 16V diesels of 3,648hp driving Lips water jets will be installed in the 35m (115ft) sportsboat that Mulder has developed in cooperation with **Devonport Yachts**, giving a speed of around 46 knots. **Art-Line** of Holland are responsible for the interior design of this fast and sophisticated yacht.

A quite different emphasis of long range and comfort at sea characterises a 43.8m (143ft 8in) steel motor yacht **(BELOW)** that Mulder has designed for a European owner. With a displacement of 260 tonnes, this vessel will have the enormous range of 9,000nm at 10 knots, powered by twin **Caterpillar** diesels of 1,000hp each.

Mulder Design

NUVOLARI-LENARD

Now under construction by **Palmer Johnson** is a 36.6m (120ft) express motor yacht **(RIGHT)** with naval architecture by **Ray Hunt and Associates** and design by **Nuvolari-Lenard**. The yacht is designed as a mix between elegant Mediterranean lines and the superb technical construction quality achieved by the American yard. Interiors are classic 'old English' in contrast to the streamlined exterior; a comfortable and relaxing ambiance that protects guests after a day in the open air. Nuvolari-Lenard are also fully involved with the 46m (151ft) motor yacht **(BELOW)** for **CRN-Ferretti** that will be the second of the *Magnifica* line. The very modern exterior styling is dominated by the sizeable radar arch on the sun deck that provides shade for a large panoramic dining area and bar. The interior is also very modern with a considerable use of mahogany, rosewood and ebony. Meanwhile a 53m (174ft) full-displacement motor yacht is being designed for a European owner with accommodation for 12 guests in 6 suites.

Nuovolari-Lenard

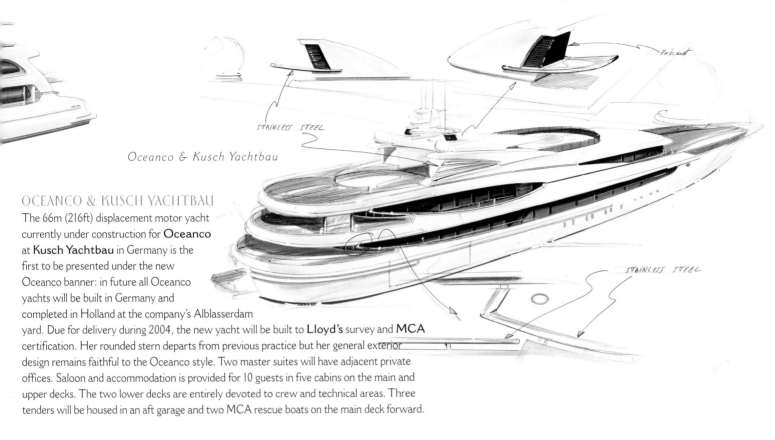

Oceanco & Kusch Yachtbau

OCEANCO & KUSCH YACHTBAU

The 66m (216ft) displacement motor yacht currently under construction for **Oceanco** at **Kusch Yachtbau** in Germany is the first to be presented under the new Oceanco banner: in future all Oceanco yachts will be built in Germany and completed in Holland at the company's Alblasserdam yard. Due for delivery during 2004, the new yacht will be built to **Lloyd's** survey and **MCA** certification. Her rounded stern departs from previous practice but her general exterior design remains faithful to the Oceanco style. Two master suites will have adjacent private offices. Saloon and accommodation is provided for 10 guests in five cabins on the main and upper decks. The two lower decks are entirely devoted to crew and technical areas. Three tenders will be housed in an aft garage and two MCA rescue boats on the main deck forward.

Redman Whiteley Dixon

REDMAN WHITELEY DIXON

A 73m (240ft) motor yacht **(BELOW LEFT)** is now under construction at **Amels Shipyard** with both interior and exterior design by **Redman Whiteley Dixon**. The smooth exterior disguises the impressive ability to house a helicopter in the aft deck as well as two bathing decks which fold out from the yacht's side. The contemporary mahogany and lacquer interior has six guest staterooms, a cinema, gymnasium and separate owner's deck, complete with forward-facing observation lounge. The pilot house is located on the sun deck, which is largely shaded by an overhang. Also under way are two very different interior designs for two motor yachts, a 70m (230ft) and a 55m (180ft), now building at the **Feadship-De Vries Scheepsbouw**. The office has been busy with the 40m (131ft) sailing yacht *Harlequin* which **Alloy Yachts** of New Zealand are building to a **Dubois** design. This vessel, fitted with a dramatic flame mahogany interior, is the fourth large sailing yacht from this partnership and is to be launched in time for the 2003 Millenium Cup in Auckland.

REYMOND LANGTON DESIGN

Among six motor yachts and one sailing yacht from the drawing board of **Reymond Langton Design**, a collaboration with **Izar** has resulted in an eye-catching 42m (138ft) motor yacht **(LEFT)** in which great attention has been given to ensure a coherent and harmonius design that links the exterior profile to a striking modern interior. In the interior, **(RIGHT)** the palette is restrained and restful, balancing soft natural colours and materials against dark leather upholstery. Accents of exotic woods such as ebony and rosewood are used sparingly on specific pieces of furniture.

Reymond Langton Design

Reymond Langton Design

Cor D Rover

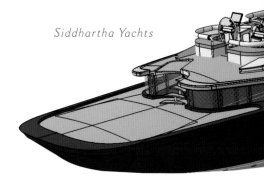

Siddhartha Yachts

COR D ROVER

A 45m (148ft) full-displacement steel hulled motor yacht with a beam of 9.25m (30ft) has been designed by **Cor D Rover** with naval architecture by **Sydac** of Genoa. It is to be constructed at **Mondomarine** in Savona, Italy. Powered by a pair of 2,500hp **Caterpillar** diesels, her top speed is projected to be 17 knots in half loaded condition, giving a range of 3,000nm. Fully loaded, the yacht displaces 425 tonnes.

SIDDHARTHA YACHTS

Substantial savings in time and cost in construction are claimed by **Siddhartha Yachts** thanks to use of the advanced CATIA system of computer-aided design, which makes it possible to view the whole vessel in three dimensions and to plan all systems before work begins. The company's 29.30m (96ft) cruising sloop **(ABOVE)** has been designed in this way and has many unusual features, including a raised deck with large windows around its aft end and a recessed seating area on the foredeck.

SAM SORGIOVANNI

With several superyacht projects either under construction or recently launched, **Sam Sorgiovanni Designs** continues to expand into every facet of the industry. An innovative style shows equally well on a 50m (164ft) high-speed expedition vessel or on the world's first 60m (197ft) trimaran yacht, currently under construction at **North West Bay Ships**. Also being developed is a 53m (174ft) high-speed motor yacht with contemporary lines. In collaboration with **Jonathan Quinn Barnett** of Seattle, Sorgiovanni is continuing to work on a 120m (394ft) vessel under construction in Europe and due to be launched in 2003.

SENSATION NEW ZEALAND

Together with **Arthur M Barbeito**, **Sensation New Zealand** has developed a lightweight medium-displacement express motor yacht of 33.5m (110ft) **(BELOW)**, which will have shallow draught and a GRP hull. Powered by a pair of **Caterpillar** 3512 diesels, this new design is expected to reach 35 knots. Accommodation includes a master and three en suite guest cabins. At the same time as building this yacht, Sensation and Barbeito are developing a 38m (125ft) raised pilothouse variation and a 43m (140ft) three-deck motor yacht, both of which will be of composite construction and will appeal to American buyers looking for a sleek, eye-catching yacht. More conventional construction is being used for the 60m (200ft) classic motor yacht **(RIGHT)** that will become the largest private yacht so far built in New Zealand. Interior designs for this and two smaller versions are by **François Zuretti**.

Donald Starkey Designs

Sensation New Zealand

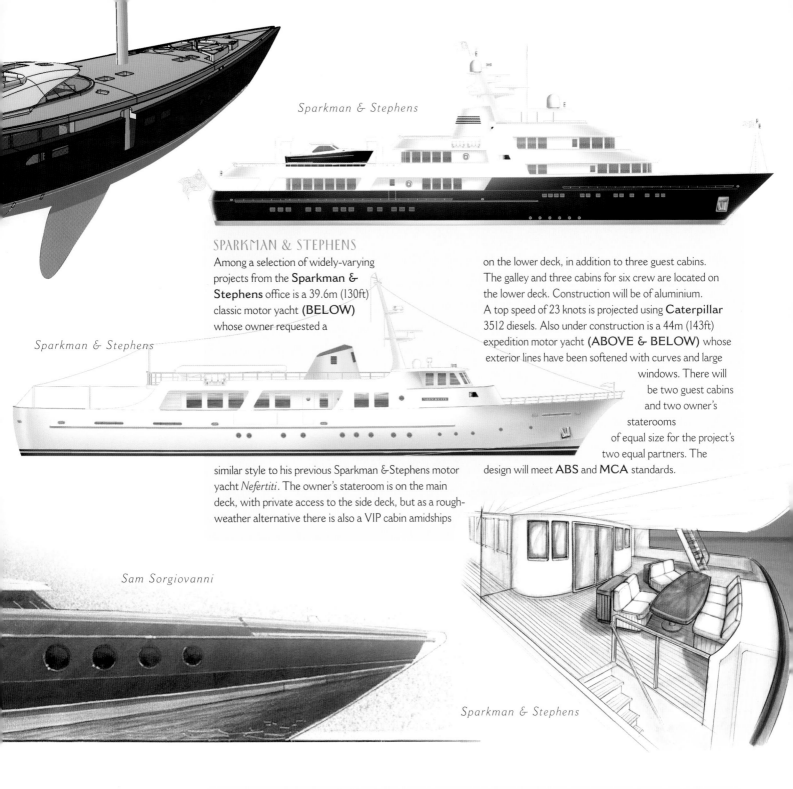

Sparkman & Stephens

Sparkman & Stephens

SPARKMAN & STEPHENS

Among a selection of widely-varying projects from the **Sparkman & Stephens** office is a 39.6m (130ft) classic motor yacht **(BELOW)** whose owner requested a similar style to his previous Sparkman & Stephens motor yacht *Nefertiti*. The owner's stateroom is on the main deck, with private access to the side deck, but as a rough-weather alternative there is also a VIP cabin amidships on the lower deck, in addition to three guest cabins. The galley and three cabins for six crew are located on the lower deck. Construction will be of aluminium. A top speed of 23 knots is projected using **Caterpillar** 3512 diesels. Also under construction is a 44m (143ft) expedition motor yacht **(ABOVE & BELOW)** whose exterior lines have been softened with curves and large windows. There will be two guest cabins and two owner's staterooms of equal size for the project's two equal partners. The design will meet **ABS** and **MCA** standards.

Sam Sorgiovanni

Sparkman & Stephens

DONALD STARKEY DESIGNS

Sensation
New Zealand

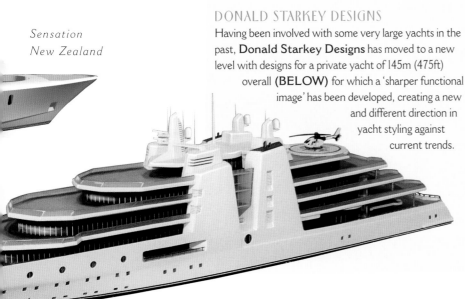

Having been involved with some very large yachts in the past, **Donald Starkey Designs** has moved to a new level with designs for a private yacht of 145m (475ft) overall **(BELOW)** for which a 'sharper functional image' has been developed, creating a new and different direction in yacht styling against current trends.

The extensive accommodation has been arranged over eight decks in an area of 8,000m² (86,080ft²), comprising 15 large suites, two VIP suites with private aft decks, an owner's suite with private forward and aft decks, a large covered entertainment deck with swimming pool, and waterfall feature overlooked by the main saloon. The formal dining room will accommodate 50 people and there is also a 20-seat cinema and large gymnasium. Access to the yacht is over a recessed dock in the stern so that visitors and guests may step aboard under cover from tenders, which literally drive into the yacht. There is extensive accommodation for 50 officers and crew plus personal staff. The vessel will have a beam of 23m (75ft), 5m (16ft) draught and will be capable of cruising at 20 to 25 knots powered by four 7,375hp diesels.

STUDIO VAFIADIS

Scheduled for delivery in June 2003, classified by **Bureau Veritas** and complying with **SOLAS** and **MCA** rules, the 82m (270ft) motor yacht *O'Mega* **(BELOW)** has five decks, two dedicated to crew and service and five to the owner and guests. Conceived for private and charter use in response to the continually raised standards requested by charterers, she has been designed with soft and slender lines by **Studio Vafiadis**. Fourteen cabins and VIP suites are located forward on the main and upper decks in addition to a huge owner's suite in the forward part of the main deck. Each deck has wide side decks inspired by the promenades of the old ocean liners. Among the many special features are a large and well-equipped exercise room and an elegant saloon that can be converted into a ballroom, conference room or theatre. Also designed by Vafiadis is the 78m (256ft) motorsailer *O'Dyssey* **(RIGHT)**, which is intended for corporate and charter use and has 24 cabins and VIP suites on the main and upper decks. The luxurious interior is built to **SOLAS** rules with a dining room and two large saloons in the aft sections of the main and upper decks. Delivery is scheduled by the end of 2003.

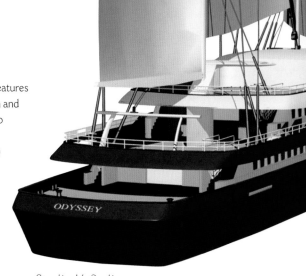

Studio Vafiadis

Studio Vafiadis

VITTERS SHIPYARD

A trio of exceptionally interesting sailing yachts are under construction at **Vitters Shipyard**. A very high-performance carbon-fibre speed machine designed by **Luca Brenta** has been planned so that structural elements also form the internal partitions for a comfortable interior. The owner has placed equally high demands on speed, comfort and style.

A very different concept is the 43m (141ft) **Dubois** sloop that will be specially equipped for circumnavigation. The interior design by **Dick Young** is contemporary with the use of light coloured wood and modern hardware. Unlike her two previous near-sisters *African Queen* and *Whirlaway*, the new yacht will have a cutter rig.

Thirdly, the largest yacht so far undertaken by the yard, is the re-started *Adèle* project **(RIGHT)**. Designed by **Hoek Design Naval Architects**, this extremely impressive 55m (179ft) retro ketch has thoroughly classic lines with long overhangs and a very detailed deck that includes three well-proportioned deckhouses. Both the main and owner's cockpits are built in teak. The interior is also by Hoek Design and will be in a style that fully matches the exterior, and will be executed in stained mahogany.

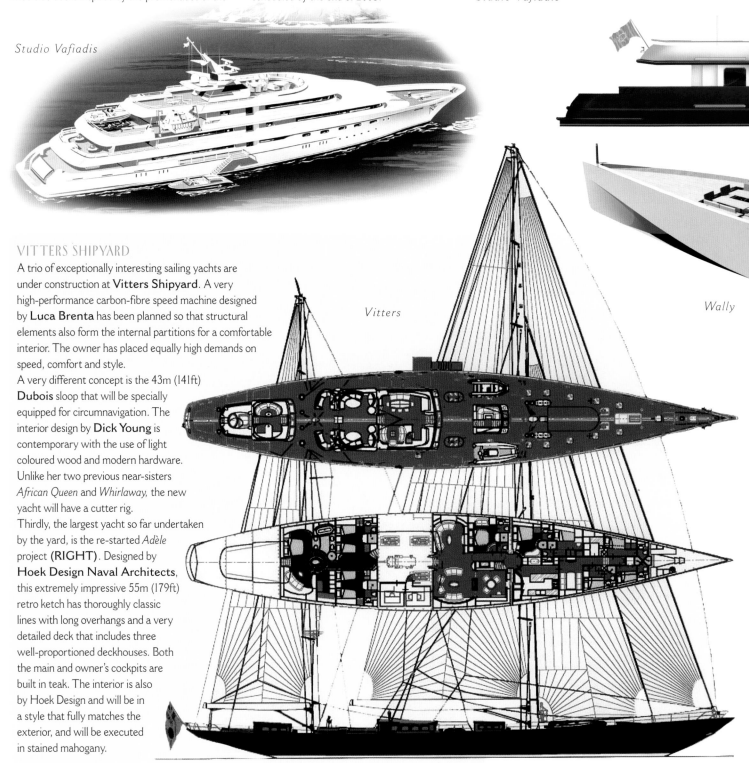

Vitters

Wally

Vripack/Jasmin/RMK

VRIPACK/JASMIN/RMK

Vripack continues to concentrate on explorer yachts, a concept that
the company virtually invented and has been widely copied. Recent projects
include an 85m (279ft) vessel with a strongly commercial style that
carries a helicopter on the aft deck and a 40m (132ft) ocean-
going explorer that has smoother, more yacht-oriented lines.
For the Turkish company **Jasmin Marine**, Vripack has
designed a 36.8m (121ft) explorer **(LEFT)** with a full luxury
interior **(ABOVE)**, that is currently under construction at **RMK
Marine** in Tuzla for launching during 2003. Interior styling is by **Act
Studio** and **Mrs Birgul Vargi**.

WALLY

The new **Wally** 98 SA is a 30.60m (98ft) sloop designed by **Javier Soto Acebal**
currently under construction in Italy for launching in summer 2003. This will
be a very high performance yacht built in high-tech composites and
incorporating, for the first time on a Wally, a water ballast
system. The owner intends to race in the maxi
circuit but also to live comfortably with
an owner's and two guest cabins
forward and crew aft.
Even more spectacular will
be the 158 TR, a 48m (158ft)
performance sloop **(RIGHT)** designed by **Bill
Tripp** for exceptional offshore performance, safety,
comfort and ease of handling and incorporating both a water ballast system and a lifting keel.
Bill Tripp is also responsible for the design of 36m (119ft) Wally 119 TR currently under construction
in Italy and due to launch in 2004. This will have a highly unusual arrangement with a deck layout
resembling a city loft building and strongly emphasising the Wally concept of inside-outside living areas.
The second example of the WallyPower 118 **(ABOVE)** is under construction at **Intermarine** in
Italy and will be fitted with twin **MTU** diesels of 4,000hp each, giving a top speed of 40 knots.

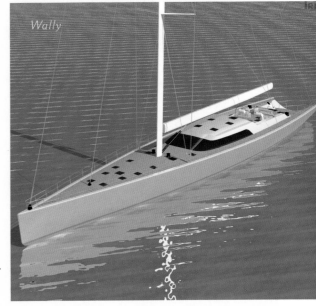

Wally

Andrew Winch Designs

ANDREW WINCH DESIGNS

During 2003, **Andrew Winch
Designs** is looking forward to
the launch of the 61m (200ft)
Lürssen motor yacht _Phoenix_,
the 35m (115ft) sloop _Whisper_
at Holland Jachtbouw, the 47m
(154ft) ketch _Scheherezade_ at
Hodgdon Yachts and a
Boeing business jet. Winch has
been involved with both the interior and
exterior of _Phoenix,_ which has a huge volume and has
been developed for maximum comfort both under way and at rest. Special features include a saloon
and dining room separated by a piano rotunda with sliding lacquer screens concealed behind curved
leather panels **(ABOVE)** and an owner's suite on two decks with a private terrace deck.

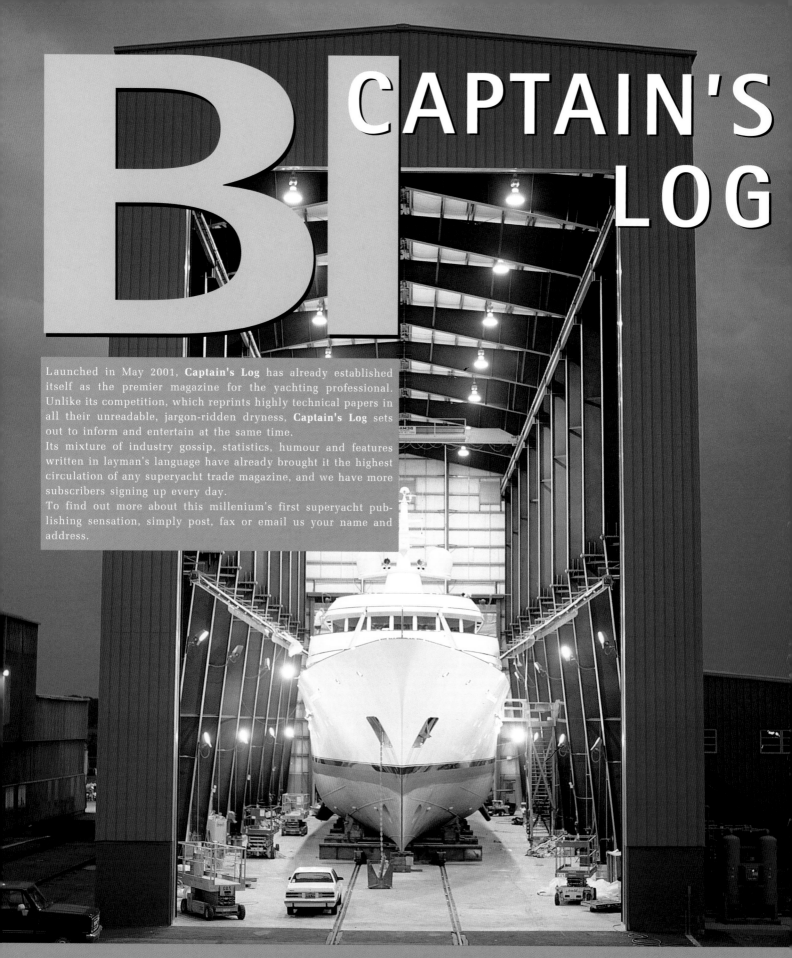

BI CAPTAIN'S LOG

Launched in May 2001, **Captain's Log** has already established itself as the premier magazine for the yachting professional. Unlike its competition, which reprints highly technical papers in all their unreadable, jargon-ridden dryness, **Captain's Log** sets out to inform and entertain at the same time.

Its mixture of industry gossip, statistics, humour and features written in layman's language have already brought it the highest circulation of any superyacht trade magazine, and we have more subscribers signing up every day.

To find out more about this millenium's first superyacht publishing sensation, simply post, fax or email us your name and address.

Boat International Publications, 5/7 Kingston Hill, Kingston upon Thames, Surrey, KT2 7PW England
tel: +44 (0) 20 8547 2662 fax: +44 (0) 20 8547 1201
email: info@boatinternational.co.uk

www.boat-international.com

 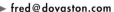

Fascination
of **Power**

Power can impress. Elegance can inspire.
When power and elegance meet intelligence
and precision, inspiration turns into
admiration. Feel the fascination with any of
our yacht propulsion engines.

www.mtu-online.com

DaimlerChrysler Off-Highway

The Register

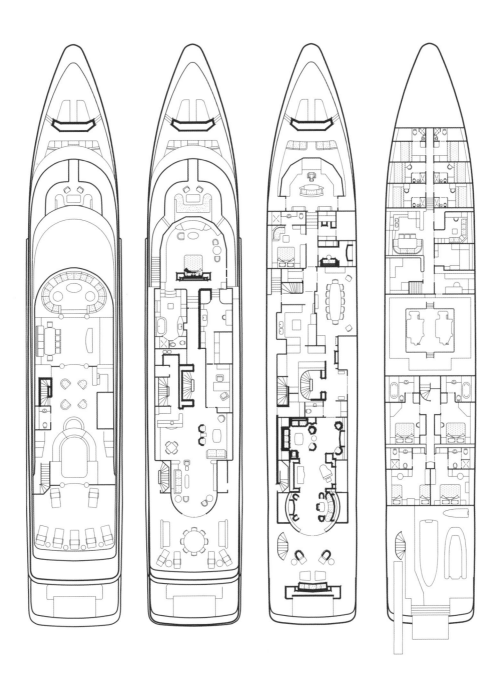

The World's Superyachts
Listed in Order of Size

INDEX TO THE REGISTER

An alphabetical index of yachts appearing on the following pages

NUVOLARI LENARD™

naval design · Venezia Italia

YACHT'S NAME ex-name(s)	PROPULSION TYPE CONSTRUCTION	BUILDER NAVAL ARCHITECT/STYLIST/ INTERIOR DESIGNER WHERE/YEAR	DIMENSIONS LOA/LOA including spars / Length water line m (ft)	Beam (Maximum) Draught m (ft)	ENGINES Number & Cylinders Horse Power Maker/Type	REMARKS
PRINCE ABDUL AZIZ ex-Abdul Aziz	Twin Screw Motor Yacht Steel	Helsingor Vaerft A/S Maierform GmbH Copenhagen/Denmark/1984	147.01 (482.31) 131.45 (431.26)	18.30 (60.04) 4.87 (15.97)	2 x 12 cylinder 15382hp Pielstick diesels	Saudi Arabian Royal Yacht Lloyd's ✠100A1, ✠LMC
EL HORRIYA ex-Mahroussa	Triple Screw Motor Yacht Iron	Samuda Bros O Lang London/UK/1865	145.69 (478.00) 128.47 (421.50)	12.98 (42.60) 5.33 (17.50)	2 x Ansaldo Steam Turbines	Originally built for HM The King of Egypt. Lengthened 1872 Lengthened and converted to Paddle Steamer in 1905 Rebuilt 1950. Now Egyptian Presidential Yacht
AL SALAMAH	Twin Screw Motor Yacht Steel	HDW Kiel/Lürssen Werft Lürssen/Disdale/Disdale Kiel & Bremen/Germany/1999	140.00 (459.34)	23.50 (77.10) 5.00 (16.40)	2 x 20 cylinder 8046hp MTU diesels	
SAVARONA	Twin Screw Motor Yacht Steel	Blohm & Voss/Kahraman Sadikoglu Cox & Stevens/Starkey Hamburg/Germany/1931	136.03 (446.19)	16.00 (52.50) 6.10 (20.00)	2 x 8 cylinder 3600hp Caterpillar 3608 diesels	Built for Emily Cadwalader. Later purchased by Turkey as presidential yacht for Kemal Atatürk. Total rebuild in Istanbul in 1992 Featured in The Superyachts, Volume 6
ALEXANDER ex-Regina Maris	Twin Screw Motor Yacht Steel	Flender Werft Flender Werft Lübeck/Germany/1976	121.11 (397.36) 104.60 (343.19)	16.90 (55.45) 5.55 (18.21)	2 x MAN 4050hp G10V52/74 Turbo-charged diesels	Owned by John Latsis. Lloyd's ✠100A1, ✠LMC Rebuilt Flenderwerft 1986
ATLANTIS II	Twin Screw Motor Yacht Steel	Hellenic Shipyards Co Maierform GmbH Skaramanga/Greece/1981	115.82 (380.05) 104.40 (342.51)	14.40 (47.45) 4.29 (14.08)	2 x 12 cylinder 4800hp No Stops Pielstick diesels	Owned by Stavros Niarchos. Lloyd's ✠100A1, ✠LMC
AL SALAMAH ex-Prince Abdulaziz ex-Atlantis	Twin Screw Motor Yacht Steel	Hellenic Shipyards Co Maierform GmbH Skaramanga/Greece/1973	115.76 (379.80) 105.20 (345.16)	14.40 (47.25) 4.29 (14.07)	2 x 12 cylinder 4360hp No Stops Pielstick diesels	Lloyd's ✠100A1
PELORUS	Twin Screw Motor Yacht Steel	Lürssen Werft Tim Heywood/Terence Disdale Bremen/Germany/2003	115.00 (377.29)	17.20 (56.43) 4.50 (14.76)	2 x Wärtsilä	
LE GRAND BLEU	Twin Screw Motor Yacht Steel	Bremer Vulkan Kusch Design/Kusch Design/Da Pilla Germany/2000	106.39 (349.00)	17.68 (58.00)	2 x 16 cylinder 4570hp Deutz-MWM SBV 16-M diesels	
LADY MOURA	Twin Screw Motor Yacht Steel	Blohm & Voss Diana Yacht Design/Sturchio/Di Pilla Hamburg/Germany/1991	105.00 (344.05) 89.62 (294.04)	18.50 (60.70) 5.50 (18.04)	2 x 12 cylinder 6868hp MWM TBD 510 BV12 diesels	Lloyd's ✠100A1, ✠LMC
AL SAÏD	Twin Screw Motor Yacht Steel	Picchiotti Picchiotti Viareggio/Italy/1982	103.85 (340.73)	16.20 (53.15) 5.00 (16.40)	2 x 6 cylinder 4200hp Detroit TA 420-6 diesels	Owned by the Sultan of Oman. Refitted by DML in 1989 Lloyd's ✠100A1, ✠LMC
CHRISTINA O ex-Argo, ex-Christina ex-HMCS Stormont	Twin Screw Motor Yacht Steel	Canadian Vickers/Howaldt Werke Pinmau (conversion) Canada/Germany/1943/1954	99.14 (325.25)	11.12 (36.50) 4.26 (14.00)	2 x 6 cylinder 2775hp MAN diesels	Built as an Escort Frigate, she served in the North Atlantic during WWII on anti-submarine duties. Converted to a yacht in 1954 by Aristotle Onassis. Refitted 2001. Now owned by JP Papanicolaou Featured in The Superyachts, Volume 15
CARINTHIA VII	Motor Yacht Steel	Lürssen Werft Tim Heywood Bremen/Germany/2002	97.00 (318.24)	15.95 (52.33) 4.80 (15.74)	4 x MTU	
SEA CLOUD ex-Patria, ex-Antara ex-Angelita, ex-Sea Cloud ex-Hussar II	Auxiliary Twin Screw Four Masted Barque Steel	Fr Krupp Germania Werft Cox & Stevens Kiel/Germany/1931	96.50/109.50 (316.60/359.20) 77.20 (253.29)	14.94 (49.01) 5.13 (16.83)	4 x 8 cylinder 1250hp Enterprise diesels	Built for Edward Hutton as a wedding gift to his wife Featured in The Superyachts, Volume 3 Rebuilt Bremerhaven 1978
LIMITLESS	Twin Screw Motor Yacht Steel/Aluminium	Lürssen Werft De Voogt/Lürssen/Catroux Bremen/Germany/1997	96.25 (315.77) 86.50 (283.79)	12.50 (41.01) 4.00 (13.12)	2 x 16 cylinder 15000hp Caterpillar 3616 diesels	Built to ABS Classification. A combined diesel and diesel-electric propulsion package. Her conventional diesels can be boosted with a further 6607hp from 2 x 16 cylinder Caterpillar 3516 and 2 x 12 cylinder Caterpillar 3412 diesels powering electric motors

Name	Type / Construction	LOA m (ft)	Beam / Draft m (ft)	Builder / Designer / Place / Year	Engines	Notes
AL MIRQAB	Triple Screw Motor Yacht / Steel/Aluminium	95.00 (311.00)	15.15 (49.70) / 4.50 (14.70)	Oceanco / The 'A' Group / Alblasserdam/The Netherlands/1999	3 x 20 cylinder 10000hp MTU 20V1163TB93 diesels	Lloyd's ✠100A1 SSC, Yacht(P), mono, G6, ✠LMC, UMS
TATOOSH	Twin Screw Motor Yacht / Steel	92.42 (303.16)	14.94 (49.00)	HDW Nobiskrug / Kusch/Studio 8/Disdale / Bremen/Germany/2000	2 16 cylinder 4350hp Deutz-MWM SBV 16-M diesels	
EVERGREEN	Twin Screw Motor Yacht / Steel/Aluminium	92.10 / 82.20 (302.16) (269.68)	12.80 (41.99) / 4.00 (13.12)	Evergreen Shipyard / Diana Yacht Design/Buytendijk / Japan/1998	2 x 12 cylinder 6598hp Wärtsilä 12V32E diesels	Featured in The Superyachts, Volume 13
NAHLIN ex-Libertatea, ex-Luceafarul ex-Nahlin	Twin Screw Motor Yacht / Steel	91.44 (300.00)	10.97 (36.00) / 6.40 (21.00)	John Brown & Co / GL Watson & Co / Clydebank/UK/1930	2 x Brown-Curtis turbines 4000hp	Currently being rebuilt
ASEAN LADY	Single Screw Outrigger Motor Yacht / Steel	88.15 / 82.46 (289.20) (270.53)	21.20 (69.55) / 3.50 (11.48)	Yantai Raffles Shipyard / Mitchell / Singapore/2002	1 x 12 cylinder 2000hp Caterpillar 3516B	ABS
ARCTIC	Twin Screw Motor Yacht / Steel	87.58 (287.35)	14.73 (48.33) / 7.30 (23.95)	F Schichau / Schichau/Kusch Yacht Agentur / Bremerhaven/Germany/1969	2 x 12 cylinder 6508hp Deutz SBV12M640 diesels	Ocean-going, ice-class tug converted by Malta Drydock Company in 1995 with project management by Claus Kusch
KINGDOM 5KR ex-Trump Princess ex-Nabila	Twin Screw Motor Yacht / Steel	86.01 / 76.25 (282.18) (250.16)	13.20 (43.31) / 4.67 (15.32)	Fratelli Benetti / Benetti/Bannenberg/Di Pilla / Viareggio/Italy/1980	2 x 16 cylinder 3000hp AB Bofors	Lloyd's ✠100A1, ✠LMC Featured in The Superyachts Volume 2 Refitted at Amels 1992
ANNALIESSE	Motor Yacht	85.30 (279.85)	14.00 (45.93)	Neorion, Greece / Alpha Marine/Poulias / Greece/2003	Caterpillar	
AL YAMAMAH ex-Quadissiyat Saddam	Twin Screw Motor Yacht / Steel	82.04 / 73.04 (269.15) (239.62)	12.99 (42.61) / 3.50 (11.48)	Helsingor Vaerft / Helsingor Vaerft / Helsingor/Denmark/1981	2 x 12 cylinder 3000hp MTU diesels	Lloyd's ✠100A1, ✠LMC Formerly owned by Government of Iraq–now owned by Saudi Arabia
BART ROBERTS ex-Narwhal	Twin Screw Exploration Vessel / Steel	80.77 / 67.00 (264.99) (219.81)	12.80 (41.99) / 3.80 (12.46)	Canadian Vickers / Edstrom/Tradepower Intl/Bamford / Montreal/Canada/1963	2 x 2,000hp Ruston 6RKC	Lloyd's ✠100A1, ✠LMC, SOLAS Conversion from Canadian Coastguard vessel in 2002 Featured in The Superyachts, Volume 16
GOLDEN ODYSSEY	Twin Screw Motor Yacht / Steel/Aluminium	80.47 / 68.01 (264.00) (223.13)	12.80 (28.21) / 4.05 (13.29)	Blohm & Voss / Platou/Pinto / Hamburg/Germany/1990	2 x 12 cylinder 5820hp MWM Deutz SBV diesels	Lloyd's ✠100A1, ✠LMC Major refit and lengthened by 4.3m in 1995 by Campbell Shipyard, San Diego, USA
NORGE ex-Philante	Twin Screw Motor Yacht / Steel	80.16 (263.00)	11.58 (38.00) / 4.41 (14.41)	Camper & Nicholsons Ltd / C E Nicholson / Southampton/UK/1937	2 x 8 cylinder 1760hp Bergen diesels	Norwegian Royal Yacht. DNV ✠1A1, ✠MV
CONSTELLATION	Twin Screw Motor Yacht / Steel/Aluminium	80.00 (262.46)	13.00 (42.65) / 4.00 (13.12)	Oceanco / Oceanco/The 'A' Group / Alblasserdam/The Netherlands/1999	2 x 20 cylinder 8160hp MTU 1163TB74L diesels	
STARGATE	Twin Screw Motor Yacht / Steel/Aluminium	80.00 (262.46)	13.00 (42.65) / 4.00 (13.12)	Oceanco / The 'A' Group/Constantini / Alblasserdam/The Netherlands/2001	2 x 20 cylinder 8160hp MTU 1163TB74L diesels	Lloyd's class contemplated
AL DIRIYAH ex-Massarrah, ex-Serendipity ex-Ultima II, ex-Danginn	Twin Screw Motor Yacht / Steel	78.65 / 71.67 (258.03) (235.13)	11.30 (37.08) / 4.20 (13.77)	National Bulk Carriers Inc Ltd / McClusky / Kure/Japan/1960	2 x 10 cylinder 1800hp Fairbanks Morse diesels	Lloyd's ✠100A1, ✠LMC
DELPHINE ex-Dauntless ex-USS Dauntless ex-Delphines	Twin Screw Steam Yacht / Steel	78.61 / 76.40 (257.75) (250.66)	10.80 (35.43) / 4.50 (14.76)	Great Lakes Engineering Works / Henry J Gielow / USA/1921	2 x 4 cylinder Great Lakes Engineering Steam Turbines	Built for auto magnate Horace Dodge. A major rebuild was planned, but she remains laid up
LONE RANGER ex-Simson S	Twin Screw Motor Yacht / Steel	77.73 (255.00)	13.20 (43.40) / 6.50 (21.30)	Schichau-Unterwasser AG / Setton/Vollers / Bremerhaven/Germany/1973	2 x 12 cylinder 4400hp Deutz RBV12M350 diesels	Lloyd's ✠100A1, ✠LMC Ocean-going, ice-class tug converted by Malta Drydock Company in 1994 with project management by Claus Kusch Featured in The Superyachts, Volume 9

YACHT'S NAME ex-name(s)	PROPULSION TYPE CONSTRUCTION	DIMENSIONS LOA/LOA including spars Length water line m (ft)	Beam (Maximum) Draught m (ft)	BUILDER NAVAL ARCHITECT/STYLIST/ INTERIOR DESIGNER WHERE/YEAR	ENGINES Number & Cylinders Horse Power Maker/Type	REMARKS
LADY SARYA ex-Lady Sarah I ex-La Belle Simone, ex-Sarah	Twin Screw Motor Yacht Steel	76.37 (250.55) 68.53 (224.83)	11.65 (38.22) 4.17 (13.68)	Cantiere Navale Apuania Gastaldi Marina de Carrara/Italy/1972	2 x 12 cylinder 3004hp MTU diesels	Lloyd's ✠100A1, ✠LMC
TALITHA G ex-Jezebel ex-Reveler, ex-Chalena ex-Carola, ex-Elpetal	Twin Screw Motor Yacht Steel	75.28/82.60 (247.00/271.00) 75.33 (206.00)	10.37 (34.02) 5.80 (19.02)	Fr Krupp Germania Werft Cox & Stevens Kiel/Germany/1930	2 x 16 cylinder 1400hp Caterpillar 3516 TA diesels	Rebuilt at Devonport Yachts in 1993 with interior by Jon Bannenberg. Lloyd's ✠100AL, ✠LMC, UMS
PHOCEA ex-Club Mediterranée	Four Masted Auxiliary Schooner Steel/Aluminium	75.12 (246.47) 66.50 (218.18)	9.58 (31.43) 6.11 (20.05)	DCAN Toulon Bigoin/Pierrejean/Heywood/Beiderbeck Toulon/France/1976	2 x 12 cylinder 1056hp MTU 12V2000M90 diesels	Single-handed racer converted into a cruising yacht in 1986. Rebuilt at Lürssen Werft, 1999 with interior design by Jörg Beiderbeck and exterior styling by Tim Heywood. Featured in The Superyachts, Volume 14
MONTKAJ	Twin Screw Motor Yacht Steel	75.00 (246.06)	13.90 (45.60) 3.60 (11.81)	Amels BV Amels/Disdale Makkum/The Netherlands/1996	2 x 12 cylinder 2525hp Caterpillar 3516 DI-TA diesels	Lloyd's ✠100A1, ✠LMC
LEANDER	Twin Screw Motor Yacht Steel/Aluminium	74.80 (245.41) 65.20 (213.92)	12.80 (41.99) 4.10 (13.45)	Peene Werft Kusch Yacht Agentur/Nunns Wolgast/Germany/1992	2 x 12 cylinder 2013hp Deutz SBV 12M 628 diesels	Lloyd's ✠100A1, ✠LMC, UMS Featured in The Superyachts, Volume 7
GIANT ADVENTURER ex-Giant	Single Screw Motor Yacht Steel/Aluminium	74.70 (245.01)	13.30 (43.63) 5.90 (19.35)	EMC Holland EMC Holland The Netherlands/1974	2 x 8 cylinder 3400hp Smith Bolman diesels	Former tug. Rebuilt in Ensenada, Mexico, 1999
DANNEBROG	Twin Screw Motor Yacht Steel	74.60 (244.76) 63.10 (207.03)	10.39 (34.10) 3.70 (12.14)	Danish Royal Dockyard Danish Royal Dockyard Denmark/1931	2 x 6 cylinder 870hp 6T23L-KVO B & W Alpha diesels	Danish Royal Yacht
KATANA ex-Eco	Triple Water Jet Motor Yacht High Tensile Steel/GRP	74.50 (244.43) 68.05 (223.27)	11.20 (36.74) 3.20 (10.49)	Blohm & Voss Martin Francis/François Zuretti Hamburg/Germany/1991	2 x MWM Deutz BV16M628 5000hp diesels & 1 x GE LM1600 18500hp Gas Turbine	Propelled by three KaMeWa water jets, Lloyd's ✠100A1 Yacht, ✠LMC, UMS Featured in The Superyachts, Volume 11
SALEM ex-Cumulus	Twin Screw Motor Yacht Steel	73.50 (241.12) 63.50 (208.31)	12.50 (41.00) 4.60 (15.09)	NV Scheepswerf NV Scheepswerf Numegen/The Netherlands/1964	2 x 12 cylinder 3942 hp MAN B&W Alpha 2882A diesels	Former ocean weathership rebuilt by Devonport Yachts in 1998
CORAL ISLAND	Twin Screw Motor Yacht Steel	72.00 (236.23) 61.25 (200.96)	12.40 (40.68) 3.25 (10.66)	Lürssen Werft Lürssen/Bannenberg/Bannenberg Bremen/Germany/1994	2 x 16 cylinder 1877hp Caterpillar 3516 DI-TA diesels	Lloyd's ✠100A1, ✠LMC
TUEQ	Twin Screw Motor Yacht Steel/Aluminium	71.80 (235.56)	13.50 (44.29) 4.30 (14.11)	GNS, Rotterdam De Voogt/Mick Leach Rotterdam/The Netherlands/2002	2 x Wärtsilä 3600hp	Lloyds ✠100A1 SSC Yacht (Mono), G6, ✠LMC, UMS Featured in The Superyachts, Volume 16
CARINTHIA VI	Triple Screw Motor Yacht Steel	71.06 (233.14) 66.70 (218.82)	9.36 (30.70) 2.92 (9.57)	Lürssen Werft Lürssen/Bannenberg Bremen/Germany/1973	3 x 20 cylinder 2700hp MTU diesels	Lloyd's ✠100A1, ✠LMC
SKAT	Twin Screw Motor Yacht Steel	71.00 (232.91) 62.50 (205.03)	13.50 (44.29) 3.70 (12.14)	Lürssen Werft Lürssen/Espen Øino/Marco Zanini Bremen/Germany/2002	2 x 16 cylinder 2682hp MTU 2000 16V diesels	
BOADICEA	Twin Screw Motor Yacht Steel	70.50 (231.28) 62.50 (205.03)	14.00 (45.93) 3.70 12.14	Amels BV Amels/Terence Disdale Design Makkum/The Netherlands/1998	2 x 16 cylinder 2636hp Caterpillar 3516 DI-TA diesels	Lloyds ✠100A1 SSC, ✠LMC, UMS MCA Code
REVERIE	Twin Screw Motor Yacht Steel/Aluminium	70.00 (229.67)	12.50 (41.01) 4.00 (13.12)	Benetti Shipyard Benetti/Benetti/John Munford Design Viaraggio/Italy/1999	2 x 16 cylinder 1500hp Caterpillar 3516	DNV classification
AUSSIE RULES	Twin Screw Motor Yacht Aluminium/Composite	69.95 (229.46)	11.50 (37.72) 3.00 (9.84)	Oceanfast Oceanfast/Sam Sorgiovanni Perth/Australia/2002	2 x 16 cylinder 2000hp Caterpillar 3516B diesels	Lloyds register
ALWAELI ex-Awal ex-Awal II	Twin Screw Motor Yacht Steel/Aluminium	68.00 (223.07) 58.10 (190.62)	11.50 (37.73) 3.50 (11.48)	CRN CRN/Disdale/Disdale Ancona/Italy/1990	2 x 16 cylinder 2448hp MWM Deutz diesels	Lengthened by CRN in 1999. Lloyd's ✠100A1, ✠LMC

Name	Type / Construction	Length (ft/m)	Beam / Draft	Builder / Designer / Year	Engines	Notes
AMAZON EXPRESS ex-Kisuca, ex-Amazon Express ex-Crustamar, ex-Albacora	Single Screw Motor Yacht Steel	66.75 59.01 (219.00) (193.60)	10.61 4.81 (34.80) (15.78)	CN Officine Meccaniche CNOM/Dwinger Venice/Italy/1966	1 x 6 cylinder 1260hp Wichmann diesel	Converted at Horton Werft/Germany/1984 Lloyd's ✠100A1, ✠LMC
GOLDEN SHADOW	Twin Screw Motor Yacht Steel	66.75 61.84 (219.00) (202.89)	11.80 6.00 (38.71) (19.68)	Campbell Shipyard Campbell/Francis & Francis San Diego/USA/1994	2 x 9 cylinder 2665hp Deutz SBV 9M 628 diesels	Lloyd's ✠100A1, ✠LMC
HAIDA G ex-Rosenkavalier, ex-Sarina ex-USS Argus, ex-Haida	Twin Screw Motor Yacht Steel	65.88/66.44 (216.15/217.98)	9.10 3.80 (30.00) (12.06)	Fr Krupp Germania Werft Cox & Stevens Kiel/Germany/1929	2 x 6 cylinder 750hp Krupp diesels	Used as US Navy patrol ship during World War II
ASTARTE II ex-Katalina	Twin Screw Motor Yacht Steel	65.20 57.50 (213.90) (188.64)	11.20 4.00 (36.74) (13.12)	Blohm & Voss Ross Industrie/Thwaites/Inchbald Hamburg/Germany/1987	2 x 12 cylinder 2992hp Deutz diesels	Featured in The Superyachts, Volume 1 Lloyd's ✠100A1, ✠LMC
WEDGE TOO	Twin Screw Motor Yacht Steel/Aluminium	65.00 56.62 (213.25) (185.76)	11.40 3.35 (37.40) (10.99)	Feadship/De Vries Scheepsbouw De Voogt/Philippe Starck Aalsmeer/The Netherlands/2002	2 x 16 cylinder 4000hp Caterpillar 3516B DI-TA	
OLYMPIAKOS ex-Arctic Gael ex-Benjamin Bowring ex-Martin Karlsen, ex-Kista Dan	Twin Screw Motor Yacht Steel	64.90 (212.94)	11.21 6.00 (36.78) (19.69)	Aalborg Vaerft A/S Aalborg Aalborg/Denmark/1952	2 x 6 cylinder 1184hp Oil Engines	Converted to yacht 1988
AL RIYADH	Twin Screw Motor Yacht Steel	64.69 59.74 (212.23) (195.99)	9.72 3.01 (31.88) (10.25)	Feadship – C Van Lent & Zonen BV De Voogt/De Voogt/Tanter Kaag/The Netherlands/1978	2 x 16 cylinder 2860hp MTU diesels	First yacht built for Saudi Arabian royal family Lloyd's ✠100A1, ✠LMC
SHEMARA	Twin Screw Motor Yacht Steel	64.66 59.40 (212.16) (194.89)	9.22 3.96 (30.25) (13.00)	J I Thorneycroft & Co Thorneycroft Southampton/UK/1938	2 x 6 cylinder 960hp Atlas diesels	
VAN TRIUMPH	Twin Screw Motor Yacht Steel	64.59 59.32 (211.90) (194.61)	11.27 5.42 (36.98) (17.78)	Supercraft (Hong Kong) Ltd Tseng Van Lieu Hong Kong/1984	2 x 6 cylinder 1400hp Yanmar diesels	Lloyd's ✠100A1, ✠LMC. MCA Code
FELICITA WEST	Auxiliary Twin Screw Sailing Ketch Aluminium	64.00 50.11 (210.00) (164.40)	12.70 3.94/9.24 (41.66) (12.92/30.31)	Perini Navi Ron Holland/Nuvolari & Lenard Viareggio/Italy/2003	2 x 8 cylinder 1251 Caterpillar 3508	Lloyd's ✠100A1, ✠LMC, MCA Code
SANS PEUR ex-Trenora, ex-Sans Peur ex-Trenora	Twin Screw Motor Yacht Steel	64.00 59.44 (210.00) (195.00)	9.27 3.96 (30.40) (13.00)	Thorneycroft J I Thorneycroft Southampton/UK/1933	2 x 6 cylinder 870hp Atlas diesels	
LADY MARINA	Twin Screw Motor Yacht Steel/Aluminium	63.95 56.70 (209.10) (186.00)	11.20 3.50 (36.74) (11.15)	Feadship – De Vries Scheepsbouw De Voogt/Starkey/Starkey Aalsmeer/The Netherlands/1999	2 x 16 cylinder 2000hp Caterpillar 3516B diesels	Lloyd's ✠100A1, SSC, ✠LMC. Featured in The Superyachts, Volume 14 MCA Code
SIRAN	Twin Screw Motor Yacht Steel/Aluminium	63.68 54.93 (208.93) (180.21)	10.28 3.30 (33.75) (10.82)	De Vries Scheepsbouw De Voogt/Bannenberg/Bannenberg Aalsmeer/The Netherlands/1991	2 x 16 cylinder 1592hp Caterpillar 3516 DI-TA diesels	Lloyd's ✠100A1, ✠LMC, UMS
CEDAR SEA II	Twin Screw Motor Yacht Steel	63.63 57.20 (208.77) (187.66)	10.20 3.20 (33.46) (10.50)	C Van Lent & Zonen BV De Voogt/Bannenberg Kaag/The Netherlands/1986	2 x 12 cylinder 1630hp MAN diesels	Lloyd's ✠100A1, ✠LMC Featured in The Superyachts, Volume 3
LADY HAYA ex-Shahnaz ex-El Bravo of Cayman ex-El Bravo	Twin Screw Motor Yacht Steel/Aluminium	63.50 53.20 (208.34) (174.55)	11.00 3.20 (36.09) (10.50)	Nuovi Cantieri Liguri Studio de Jorio Genoa/Italy/1991	2 x 2250hp SBV M628 Deutz MWM diesels	Lloyd's ✠100A1, ✠LMC. Featured in The Superyachts, Volume 5
SOKAR ex-Jonikal	Twin Screw Motor Yacht Steel/Aluminium	63.50 56.30 (208.34) (184.71)	9.40 3.00 (30.84) (9.84)	Codecasa Codecasa/Manfredo & Sforzi/Cerruti Viareggio/Italy/1990	2 x 12 cylinder 3760hp Wärtsilä Nohab diesels	Featured in The Superyachts, Volume 4 ABS classified Lengthened and refitted at Abeking & Rasmusen in 1998
BIG ROI	Twin Screw Motor Yacht Steel	63.22 55.60 (207.41) (182.41)	11.40 3.20 (37.40) (10.49)	Royal Denship Ole Steen Knudsen/Ole Rune Design Denmark/2002	2 x 12 cylinder 1850bhp Caterpillar 3512B DITA	Lloyds ✠100A1 ✠LMC, UMC, MCA Code
SHAHNAZ ex-Pegasus IV	Twin Screw Motor Yacht Steel	63.02 58.02 (206.75) (190.35)	10.40 3.90 (34.12) (12.79)	Mitsubishi Heavy Industries Disdale/Jones Shimonoseki/Japan/1981	2 x 2100hp Daihatsu diesels	Lloyd's ✠100A1, ✠LMC

YACHT'S NAME ex-name(s)	PROPULSION TYPE CONSTRUCTION	DIMENSIONS LOA/LOA including spars Length water line m (ft)	Beam (Maximum) Draught m (ft)	BUILDER NAVAL ARCHITECT/STYLIST/ INTERIOR DESIGNER WHERE/YEAR	ENGINES Number & Cylinders Horse Power Maker/Type	REMARKS
ESMERALDA ex-Taouey, ex-Luisella ex-Maria Alexandra	Twin Screw Motor Yacht Steel	62.50 (201.78) 53.30 (174.88)	10.00 (32.81) 3.40 (11.16)	Codecasa Codecasa/De Iorio Viareggio/Italy/1982	2 x 6 cylinder 1500hp MAK diesels	Rebuilt and refitted in 1985
CAKEWALK	Twin Screw Motor Yacht Steel/Aluminium	62.30 (204.40) 55.10 (180.77)	10.80 (35.43) 3.20 (10.49)	Feadship – Van Lent & Zonen De Voogt/Andrew Winch/Liz Dalton Kaag/The Netherlands/2000	2 x 16 cylinder 2000hp Caterpillar 3516B diesels	Lloyd's ✠100A1 MCA Code Featured in The Superyachts, Volume 15
VIRGINIAN	Twin Screw Motor Yacht Steel/Aluminium	62.22 (204.14) 54.72 (179.54)	10.20 (33.46) 3.25 (10.66)	Feadship – Van Lent & Zonen De Voogt/Easton Kaag/The Netherlands/1990	2 x 12 cylinder 1630hp MAN diesels	Featured in The Superyachts, Volume 4 Lloyd's ✠100A1, ✠LMC
ANDALE	Motor Yacht Steel/Aluminium	62.00 (203.42) 53.24 (174.67)	11.20 (36.74) 3.50 (11.48)	Codecasa Della Role Viareggio/Italy/2003	2 x 16 cylinder 4520hp Caterpillar 3516B	
LADY AVIVA	Twin Screw Motor Yacht Steel	62.00 (203.42) 54.86 (179.99)	11.00 (36.09) 3.20 (10.50)	Feadship – Van Lent & Zonen De Voogt/Winch/Winch Aalsmeer/The Netherlands/1998	2 x 16 cylinder 2028hp Caterpillar 3516BDI-TA diesels	
SARAH	Twin Screw Motor Yacht Steel/Aluminium	62.00 (203.42) 55.30 (181.41)	11.80 (38.71)	Amels Holland Amels/Donald Starkey Design Makkum/The Netherlands/2002	2 x 16 cylinder 2028hp Caterpillar 3516BDI-TA diesels	
AL MENWAR	Twin Screw Motor Yacht Steel	61.78 (202.68) 56.28 (184.64)	9.77 (32.05) 2.42 (7.93)	Cantiere Navale Nicolini Cantiere Navale Nicolini Ancona/Italy/1987	2 x 16 cylinder 4170hp MTU diesels	Qatar Royal Yacht Lloyd's ✠100A1, ✠LMC Featured in The Superyachts, Volume 2
NEW SUNRISE ex-Numptia	Twin Screw Motor Yacht Steel/Aluminium	61.50 (201.74) 53.00 (173.89)	11.00 (36.09) 3.50 (11.48)	CRN Ancona Studio Scanu/Studio Scanu/Zuretti Ancona/Italy/2000	2 x 16 cylinder 2000hp Caterpillar 3516 diesels	Featured in The Superyachts, Volume 14
SOLEMAR	Twin Screw Motor Yacht Steel/Aluminium	61.50 (201.74) 55.50 (182.01)	10.60 (34.77)	Amels Holland Amels/Michael Leach Design Schelde/Belgium/2002	2 x 16 cylinder 2028hp Caterpillar 3516BDI-TA diesels	
CLAIRE T ex-Lara A ex-Nefertiti	Twin Screw Motor Yacht Steel	61.30 (201.12) 53.37 (175.10)	9.45 (31.00) 2.89 (9.48)	Astilleros Tolleres Celayo Sparkman & Stephens Spain/1973	2 x 16 cylinder 1125hp Caterpillar diesels	
IL VAGABONDO AGAIN ex-Majestic ex-Il Vagabondo	Twin Screw Motor Yacht Steel	61.27 (201.01) 54.45 (178.63)	10.98 (36.02) 3.29 (10.79)	CRN CRN/Disdale & Jones Ancona/Italy/1987	2 x 12 cylinder 3283hp Deutz MWM SBV628 diesels	Lloyd's ✠100A1, ✠LMC
MYLIN IV	Twin Screw Motor Yacht Steel/Aluminium	61.00 (200.14) 53.20 (174.50)	9.75 (32.00) 3.00 (9.15)	Feadship – Van Lent & Zonen BV De Voogt Kaag/The Netherlands/1992	2 x 12 cylinder 3755hp MTU 1163TB63 diesels	Lloyd's ✠100A1, ✠LMC, UMS Featured in The Superyachts, Volume 6
LADY LOLA ex-Anthelion	Twin Screw Motor Yacht Steel/Aluminium	62.60 (205.38)	10.50 (34.44) 3.45 (11.32)	Oceanco The 'A' Group/Zuretti Alblasserdam/The Netherlands/2002	2 x 12 cylinder 1650hp Caterpillar 3512 B diesels	Lloyd's ✠100A1 SSC Yacht mono G6, ✠LMC, UMS Featured in The Superyachts, Volume 16
MEDUSE	Twin Screw Motor Yacht Steel/Aluminium	60.60 (198.82) 53.65 (175.95)	10.55 (34.61) 3.20 (10.50)	Feadship – De Vries Scheepsbouw De Voogt/McMillen Aalsmeer/The Netherlands/1996	2 x 16 cylinder 1734hp Caterpillar 3516DI-TA diesels	Lloyd's ✠100A1, ✠LMC
NARA ex-Dianamare ex-Diana II	Twin Screw Motor Yacht Steel	60.54 (198.42) 54.93 (180.21)	9.69 (31.79) 2.98 (9.77)	Feadship – Van Lent & Zonen BV De Voogt Kaag/The Netherlands/1979	2 x 16 cylinder 3155hp MTU diesels	Lloyd's ✠100A1, ✠LMC
PALOMA	Twin Screw Motor Yacht Steel	60.10 (197.20) 53.65 (176.00)	8.87 (29.10) 3.11 (10.20)	Ishikawajima-Harima Tokyo/Japan/1965	2 x 12 cylinder 870hp GM diesels	

Name	Type / Construction	LOA / LWL (m)	LOA / LWL (ft)	Beam / Draft (m)	Beam / Draft (ft)	Builder / Designer / Place / Year	Engines	Notes
PARAFFIN	Twin Screw Motor Yacht Steel/Aluminium	60.10 / 53.00	(197.15) / (173.86)	10.50 / 3.25	(34.44) / (10.66)	Feadship – Royal Van Lent Shipyard De Voogt/Owner Kaag/The Netherlands/2001	2 x Caterpillar 3516 DI-TA 2000hp	Lloyds ✠100A1, SSC Yacht G6, ✠LMC, MCA Code
LADY BEATRICE	Twin Screw Motor Yacht Steel/Aluminium	60.00 / 53.50	(196.63) / (175.53)	10.50 / 3.20	(34.45) / (10.49)	Feadship – Van Lent & Zonen BV De Voogt Aalsmeer/The Netherlands/1993	2 x 16 cylinders 1633hp Caterpillar 3516DI-TA diesels	Lloyd's ✠100A1, ✠LMC
NEW HORIZON L	Twin Screw Motor Yacht Steel	59.95 / 54.59	(196.69) / (179.10)	9.70 / 3.00	(31.10) / (9.10)	Feadship – Van Lent & Zonen BV De Voogt/Sturchio/Di Pilla Kaag/The Netherlands/1983	2 x 12 cylinder 3000hp MTU diesels	Owned by Prince Leo de Lignac Lloyd's ✠100A1, ✠LMC Featured in The Superyachts, Volume 1
FREQUENCY ex-La Baronessa	Twin Screw Motor Yacht Aluminium	59.44 / 50.29	(195.00) / (165.00)	10.46 / 3.47	(34.33) / (11.40)	Palmer Johnson Incorporated Sparkman & Stephens/Nuvolari & Lenard Sturgeon Bay/USA/1997	2 x 12 cylinder 1950hp Caterpillar 3512 diesels	Featured in The Superyachts, Volume 13
AMBROSIANA	Twin Screw Motor Yacht Steel/Aluminium	59.10	(193.87)	10.00 / 3.40	(32.80) / (11.15)	Oceanco The 'A' Group/Zuretti Alblasserdam/The Netherlands/2002	2 x 12 cylinder 1650hp Caterpillar 3512 B diesels	
PEGASUS	Twin Screw Motor Yacht Steel/Aluminium	59.10	(193.87)	10.50 / 3.40	(34.45) / (11.15)	Oceanco The 'A' Group/Oceanco/Marc Michaels Alblasserdam/The Netherlands/2000	2 x 12 cylinder 1650hp Caterpillar 3512B diesels	
ALTAIR	Triple Screw Motor Yacht Steel	59.00	(193.58)	10.80 / 3.80	(35.43) / (12.47)	Amels BV Sorgiovanni/Bannenberg Makkum/The Netherlands/1974	3 x 12 cylinder 1875hp Paxman HPH-CE Mk7 diesels	Bureau Veritas Yacht ✠ Rebuilt by Oceanfast Marine in 1998 Diesel electric propulsion
CAPELLA C	Single Screw Motor Yacht Steel	59.00 / 54.00	(193.58) / (177.17)	10.60 / 3.70	(34.77) / (12.13)	Scheepsbouwerft Gerb Pot SGP Bolnes/Denmark/1968	3 x 8 cylinder 600hp Deutz diesels	Lloyd's ✠100A1, ✠LMC. Built as pilot vessel and converted to a yacht in 1985
INTUITION II	Single Screw Motor Yacht Steel	59.00 / 54.50	(193.58) / (178.78)	10.60 / 4.00	(34.77) / (13.12)	Amels BV Amels/Indart/SYS Makkum/The Netherlands/1974	3 x 1094hp Deutz SBA 8M diesels 3 x Heemaf 3-phase alternators 1 x 1330hp Smit Electric Motor	Converted pilot vessel with diesel-electric propulsion. Rebuilt at Vosper Thorneycroft in 2000 with interior design by Indart and SYS. Featured in The Superyachts, Volume 14
MARALA ex-Gaviota IV, ex-Evadne	Twin Screw Motor Yacht Steel	58.86 / 54.90	(193.12) / (180.11)	8.08 / 3.78	(26.50) / (12.50)	Camper & Nicholsons Ltd CE Nicholson Southampton/UK/1931	2 x 8 cylinder 750hp MAN diesels	Lloyd's ✠100A1, ✠LMC Featured in The Superyachts, Volume 11
CALIXE ex-Cacique A, ex-Belle France, ex-Cacique	Twin Screw Motor Yacht Steel/Aluminium	58.82 / 52.37	(193.00) / (171.10)	9.50 / 3.30	(31.16) / (10.82)	Feadship – De Vries Scheepsbouw De Voogt/Disdale Aalsmeer/The Netherlands/1986	2 x 6 cylinder 1500hp Deutz diesels	Featured in The Superyachts, Volume 1 Lengthened in 1993 Lloyd's ✠100A1, ✠LMC
ULYSSES	Twin Screw Motor Yacht Steel	58.53 / 51.61	(192.00) / (169.30)	(11.58) / 2.90	(38.00) / (9.50)	Trinity Yachts Trinity Yachts/Ricky Smith New Orleans/USA/2002	2 x 12 cylinder 1500hp Caterpillar 3512B diesels	
LIBERTAD ex-Sakura ex-October Rose, ex-Puka Puka	Twin Screw Motor Yacht Steel	58.51 / 51.06	(191.97) / (167.50)	8.90 / 3.17	(29.16) / (10.41)	Elsflether Werft Elsflether Werft/Disdale Elsfleth/Germany/1986	2 x 16 cylinder 1720hp Caterpillar diesels	Lloyd's ✠100A1, ✠LMC. Total refit and lengthening by Trinity Yachts in 1992 with design by Doug Sharp and Donald Starkey
CAPRI	Twin Screw Motor Yacht Steel/Aluminium	58.50 / 49.60	(191.92) / (162.73)	10.83 / 3.30	(35.53) / (10.83)	Lürssen Werft Glade Johnson Design, Inc Bremen/Germany/2003	2 x 1877hp Caterpillar diesels	Lloyds, MCA Code
KATANA ex-Izanami	Twin Screw Motor Yacht Aluminium	58.50 / 53.60	(191.93) / (175.85)	9.00 / 2.50	(29.53) / (8.20)	Lürssen Werft Gilgenast/Foster Bremen/Germany/1993	2 x 16 cylinder 5793hp MTU diesels	Featured in The Superyachts, Volume 11
HENRIETTE ex-Henrietta II ex-Argo, ex-Danginn	Twin Screw Motor Yacht Steel	58.28 / 51.08	(191.21) / (167.58)	9.39 / 4.50	(30.80) / (14.76)	Welding Shipyard Inc John H Wells Inc Norfolk/USA/1950	2 x 6 cylinder 663hp Suizer-Busch diesels	Lloyd's ✠100A1, ✠LMC
SEAWOLFE ex-Clyde	Single Screw Converted Tugboat Steel	58.05	(190.45)	11.22 / 4.80	(36.81) / (15.75)	J & K Smit Hoghton/Paulo-Piano Kinderdijk/Holland/1957	2 x 1500hp Smit-MAN RB666 diesels	Refitted Varadero Palma 2002 MCA Code
CREOLE ex-Mistral ex-Creole, ex-Vira	Auxiliary Three Masted Schooner Wood/Composite	58.01/65.30 / 42.70	(190.33/214.20) / (140.09)	9.44 / 5.00	(31.00) / (16.40)	Camper & Nicholsons Ltd CE Nicholson Gosport/UK/1927	2 x 450hp MTU diesels	Featured in The Superyachts, Volume 8 Refitted in 1985 by Shipyard Ferrari with naval architecture by Giorgetti & Magrini and interior design by Russo

YACHT'S NAME ex-name(s)	DIMENSIONS LOA/LOA including spars Length water line m (ft)	Beam (Maximum) Draught m (ft)	BUILDER NAVAL ARCHITECT/STYLIST/ INTERIOR DESIGNER WHERE/YEAR	ENGINES Number & Cylinders Horse Power Maker/Type	REMARKS	PROPULSION TYPE CONSTRUCTION
TAOUEY	58.00 (190.28) 46.68 (153.15)	11.54 (37.86) 3.60 (11.81)	Perini Navi Perini Navi Viareggio/Italy/1994	2 x 8 cylinder 1312hp Deutz MWM TBD604B diesels	Featured in The Superyachts, Volume 8	Auxiliary Twin Screw Ketch Steel/Aluminium
ISLANDER ex-The Other Woman	57.95 (190.00) 45.45 (149.00)	10.37 (34.02) 2.01 (6.60)	Australian Yacht Builders Laurent Giles/Bold Craft/Glade Johnson Brisbane/Australia/1990	2 x 12 cylinder 2800hp DDEC 4000 Series diesels	Featured in The Superyachts, Volume 5 Refitted by Palm Beach Yacht Brokerage in 2000	Auxiliary Twin Water Jet Ketch Aluminium
OCEAN ONE	57.95 (190.00) 49.00 (160.76)	9.70 (31.82) 2.50 (8.20)	Ocean Classic International SSPA/GVA Sweden/Ken Freivokh Design Suez/Egypt/2003	3 x 2000hp Caterpillar 16V 3516B diesels	Germanischer Lloyd, 10 A5 Motor Yacht, MCA Code	Triple Water Jet Motor Yacht Aluminium
PRINCESS TANYA ex-Radiant II ex-Lisboa II	57.60 (189.00) 51.80 (170.00)	8.80 (28.87) 3.60 (11.81)	Austin & Pickersgill A&P 1961/Stylianou 1991/Jojima Sunderland/UK/1961/Greece/1993	2 x 8 cylinder 840hp Sulzer TAD24 diesels	Complete rebuild by Intermarine Enterprises Inc in 1993. Featured in The Superyachts, Volume 7 Lloyd's ✠100A1, ✠LMC	Twin Screw Motor Yacht Steel
EXCELLENCE III	57.30 (188.00)	10.70 (35.10) 3.50 (11.50)	Abeking & Rasmussen Abeking & Rasmussen/Donald Starkey Lemwerder/Germany/2001	2 x 16 cylinder 1998hp Caterpillar 3516 B-DITA	Lloyds ✠A1 SSC G6 Yacht, UMC	Twin Screw Motor Yacht Steel/Aluminium
ULTIMA III	57.30 (188.00) 50.20 (164.70)	10.30 (33.79) 3.50 (11.48)	Abeking & Rasmussen Abeking & Rasmussen/Donald Starkey Lemwerder/Germany/1998	2 x 16 cylinder 1500hp Caterpillar 3516DI-TA diesels		Twin Screw Motor Yacht Steel/Aluminium
ZENOBIA	57.30 (187.99) 50.20 (164.69)	10.70 (35.10) 3.50 (11.48)	Abeking & Rasmussen Albert Pinto Lemwerder/Germany/2002	2 x 16 cylinder 1877hp Caterpillar 3516 B-DI diesels	Lloyds, MCA Compliant	Twin Screw Motor Yacht Steel/Aluminium
MAWASA ex-Midnight Saga ex-Majestic M	57.20 (187.67) 50.32 (165.09)	9.60 (31.50) 3.25 (10.73)	Cammenga Shipyard Feadship – De Vries Lentsch/Bannenburg Amsterdam/The Netherlands/1978	2 x 8 cylinder 1350hp Ruston Paxton diesels	Featured in The Superyachts Volume 2 Lloyd's ✠100A1, ✠LMC	Twin Screw Motor Yacht Steel
SAGITTA	57.00 (187.01)	10.50 (34.45)	Oceanfast Jon Bannenberg Ltd Fremantle/Australia/2001	2 x 16 cylinder 3700hp MTU 16V 4000 M90		Twin Screw Motor Yacht Aluminium/Composite
SENSES	57.00 (187.01) 51.50 (168.94)	12.70 (41.66) 3.20 (10.50)	Stahl Bau Nord/Fr Schweers Shipyard Lasse & Pache/Setton & Martin Francis/M&H Weser/Germany/1999	2 x 12 cylinder 1600hp Deutz MWM 620 diesels	Lloyd's ✠100A1, SSC Yacht (P) G6, ✠LMC, CCS Featured in The Superyachts Volume 14 MCA Code	Twin Screw Motor Yacht Steel
TACANUYA ex-Defiance, ex-Swiftship ex-Intrepid	57.00 (187.00) 52.00 (170.60)	9.35 (30.60) 2.18 (7.08)	Swiftships Inc Robinson/Puléo Morgan City/USA/1992	2 x 16 cylinder 2800hp Caterpillar 3516DI-TA diesels	Lengthened 9m in complete refit to the designs of Studio Scanu at Lusben Shipyard 1997	Twin Screw Motor Yacht Aluminium
OLYMPIA ex-Netanya	57.00 (187.00) 50.20 (164.69)	10.10 (33.13) 2.95 (9.67)	Feadship – De Vries Scheepsbouw De Voogt/Mark Hampton/Jon Bannenberg Aalsmeer/The Netherlands/2002	2 x 12 cylinder 3000hp Caterpillar 3512B series diesels	Featured in The Superyachts, Volume 16.	Twin Screw Motor Yacht Steel/Aluminium
CHAMAR	56.74 (186.16) 47.00 (154.20)	9.70 (31.82) 1.80 (5.90)	Brooke Yachts International Shead/Sturchio Lowestoft/UK/1992	3 x 16 cylinder 2775hp MTU 396TB84 diesels	Lloyd's ✠100A1, ✠LMC. Featured in The Superyachts, Volume 6. Propulsion system includes 2 x KaMeWa S90 & 1 x KaMeWa B80 water jets. Extensively refitted by Abeking & Rasmussen in 1996	Triple Water Jet Motor Yacht Aluminium
CLEOPATRA C ex-My Gail III	56.73 (186.13) 49.53 (162.49)	9.21 (30.21) 3.04 (9.97)	Amels BV Diana Yacht Design/Bannenberg Makkum/The Netherlands/1985	2 x 16 cylinder 1430hp Caterpillar 3516DI-TA diesels	Lloyd's ✠100A1, ✠LMC	Twin Screw Motor Yacht Steel
BARBARA JEAN	56.50 (185.36)	9.60 (31.49) 2.79 (9.15)	Feadship – De Vries De Voogt/De Voogt/Munford Alsmeer/The Netherlands/2001	2 x 12 cylinder 1500hp Caterpillar 3512B DI-TA diesels	Lloyd's ✠100A1 SSC Yacht, ✠LMC Featured in The Superyachts, Volume 15	Twin Screw Motor Yacht Steel/Aluminium
MERCEDES III	56.50 (185.36)	10.00 (32.80)	Oceanfast Jon Bannenberg Ltd Fremantle/Australia/2003	2 x 1600hp Caterpillar diesels		Motor Yacht Steel/Composite

Name	Type / Hull	LOA (m)	LOA (ft)	Beam / Draft (m)	Beam / Draft (ft)	Builder / Naval Architect / Location / Year	Engines	Notes / Classification
DREAM ex-Samantha Lin	Twin Screw Motor Yacht / Steel	56.38	(185.00)	10.97 / 2.74	(36.00) (9.00)	Halter Marine Inc / Trinity Yachts / Louisiana/USA/1999	2 x 16 cylinder 2100hp Caterpillar 3508 B diesels	Expeditionary yacht / MCA Code / ABS ✠A1, ✠ AMS
LADY J ex-Quest	Twin Screw Motor Yacht / Steel	56.38	(185.00)	12.19 / 3.9	(40.00) (13.00)	Halter Marine Inc / Quest Inc/Quest Inc / Louisiana/USA/1976	Wärtsilä Nohab G-28V-D825	ABS classified
PARIS I ex-Katamarino	Twin Screw Motor Yacht / Steel/Aluminium	56.20	(184.39)	10.30 / 3.10	(33.79) (10.17)	Amels BV / Hargrave/Garzouzi / Makkum/The Netherlands/1991	2 x 12 cylinder 1521hp Caterpillar 3512 DI-TA diesels	Featured in The Superyachts, Volume 5 / ABS classified
ADIX ex-XXXX ex-Jessica	Auxiliary Three Masted Schooner / Steel	56.02/64.53 (42.09)	(183.70/211.6) (138.00)	8.63 / 4.90	(28.31) (16.08)	Astilleros de Mallorca / Arthur Holgate/Dijkstra/Munford / Palma de Mallorca/Mallorca/1984	1 x 8 cylinder 650hp MAN diesel	Featured in The Superyachts, Volume 1 / Modified by Pendennis Shipyard 1991 / Lloyd's ✠100A1, ✠LMC
BURRASCA	Sailing Yacht / Aluminium	55.70 / 45.93	(182.74) (150.68)	11.52 / 3.83/9.61	(37.79) (12.56/31.53)	Perini Navi / Ron Holland/Perini Navi / Viareggio/Italy/2003	2 x 12 cylinder 1257hp Deutz TBD616V12	ABS ✠AMS, MCA Code
LADY CHRISTINE	Twin Screw Motor Yacht / Steel/Aluminium	55.63 / 49.80	(182.52) (163.38)	10.00 / 3.51	(32.80) (11.51)	Oceanco / The 'A' Group/The 'A' Group/Villate / Alblasserdam/The Netherlands/2001	2 x 16 cylinder 2201hp Caterpillar 3516B DI-TA diesels	Lloyd's ✠100A1, SSC Yacht, mono G6, ✠LMC, UMS / Featured in The Superyachts, Volume 15
HANSE	Twin Screw Motor Yacht / Steel	55.50	(182.09)	8.83 / 2.90	(28.97) (9.51)	Elsflether Werft / Elsflether Werft / Elsfleth/Germany/1979	2 x 12 cylinder 1685hp MTU diesels	Extensively refitted and extended by Insignia Yachts in 2002. / Refit design by Angelo Kiliadonis/Luiz de Basto.
VARMAR VE	Twin Screw Motor Yacht / Steel	55.50 / 49.50	(182.09) (162.39)	9.35 / 3.00	(30.80) (9.10)	Feadship – Van Lent & Zonen BV / De Voogt/Disdale / Kaag/The Netherlands/1986	2 x 16 cylinder 1572hp Caterpillar 3516DI-TA diesels	Lloyd's ✠100A1, ✠LMC
SOUTHERN CROSS III	Twin Screw Motor Yacht / GRP	55.16 / 44.73	(181.00) (147.00)	11.78 / 4.20	(38.66) (13.78)	Sterling Yacht & Shipbuilders / Sterling/Bannenberg/Jujima / Mie/Japan/1986	2 x 20 cylinder 4680hp MTU 583TB93 diesels	Featured in The Superyachts, Volume 3 / Stern extension by Devonport Yachts 1997
AMNESIA	Twin Screw Motor Yacht / Steel/Aluminium	55.00	(180.45)	10.20 / 3.00	(33.46) (9.84)	Benetti Shipyard / Benetti/Benetti/Natucci / Viareggio/Italy/2003	2 x 12 cylinder 2262hp Caterpillar 3512 diesels	
HUNTRESS ex-Kahalani ex-Sea Sedan	Twin Screw Motor Yacht / Steel/Aluminium	55.00 / 47.50	(180.45) (155.83)	9.60 / 3.20	(31.50) (10.50)	De Vries Scheepsbouw / De Voogt/Disdale / Aalsmeer/The Netherlands/1997	2 x 12 cylinder 1298hp Caterpillar 3512DI-TA diesels	Featured in The Superyachts, Volume 11 / Lloyd's ✠100A1, ✠LMC
LA MASQUERADE	Twin Screw Motor Yacht / Steel/Aluminium	55.00 / 48.50	(180.45) (159.12)	9.60 / 3.10	(31.49) (10.17)	Amels Makkum / Amels/Terence Disdale / Makkum/The Netherlands/2003	2 x 12 cylinder 3502hp Caterpillar 3512 B DI-TA	Lloyds ✠100A1
LE PHARAON	Twin Screw Motor Yacht / Steel	55.00 / 48.05	(180.45) (157.65)	9.45 / 3.15	(31.00) (10.40)	Feadship – Van Lent & Zonen BV / De Voogt/Tanter / Kaag/The Netherlands/1989	2 x 16 cylinder 1430hp Caterpillar 3516DI-TA diesels	Featured in The Superyachts, Volume 3 / Lloyd's ✠100A1, ✠LMC
TRUE BLUE ex-Maalana, ex-Bolkiah I ex-Oceana	Triple Water Jet Motor Yacht / Aluminium	55.00 / 43.50	(180.45) (142.72)	9.00 / 1.50	(29.52) (4.92)	Oceanfast Pty Ltd / Curran/Bannenberg / Perth/Australia/1992	2 x 3480hp 16V TB94 1 x 2610hp 12V TB94 MTU diesels	Propulsion system includes 2 x KaMeWa 9056 and x KaMeWa 80S62 water jets
SAMAX ex-Tits	Twin Screw Motor Yacht / Steel	55.00 / 49.00	(180.45) (160.76)	10.00 / 3.20	(32.81) (10.50)	C Van Lent & Zonen BV / De Voogt/Winch/Winch / Kaag/The Netherlands/1996	2 x 16 cylinder 2636hp Caterpillar 3516 DI-TA diesels	Featured in The Superyachts, Volume 12 / Lloyd's ✠100A1, ✠LMC
SHAF ex-Akitou	Twin Screw Motor Yacht / Steel	55.00 / 47.90	(180.45) (157.15)	8.30 / 2.50	(27.23) (8.20)	CRN / CRN/Mandron / Ancona/Italy/1981	2 x 16 cylinder 4425hp MTU 956TB92 diesels	Bureau Veritas 13/3E ✠Yacht, ✠MOT / Lengthened by 3m in a major refit at CRN Shipyard in 1997
LADY MONA K ex-Lady Ghislaine	Twin Screw Motor Yacht / Steel	54.96 / 48.00	(180.33) (157.47)	9.19 / 2.97	(30.16) (9.75)	Amels Makkum / Diana Yacht Design/Bannenberg / Makkum/The Netherlands/1986	2 x 16 cylinder 1430hp Caterpillar 3516 DI-TA diesels	Featured in The Superyachts, Volume 3 / Lloyd's ✠100A1, ✠LMC
PLATINUM ex-Pegasus II	Triple Screw Motor Yacht / Steel	54.65	(179.33)	8.99 / 2.66	(29.50) (8.75)	Lürssen Werft / Lürssen / Bremen/Germany/1962	3 x 16 cylinder 1750hp MTU diesels	
SARAFSA	Twin Screw Motor Yacht / Steel/Aluminium	54.50 / 50.00	(178.81) (164.04)	10.00 / 3.20	(32.81) (10.50)	Amels Makkum / Amels/Winch/Winch / Makkum/The Netherlands/1998	2 x 12 cylinder 1673hp Caterpillar 3512B DI-TA diesels	Lloyd's ✠100A1, ✠LMC, UMS / MCA Code

YACHT'S NAME ex-name(s)	PROPULSION TYPE / CONSTRUCTION	DIMENSIONS LOA/LOA including spars / Length water line (m)	(ft)	Beam (Maximum) / Draught (m)	(ft)	BUILDER / NAVAL ARCHITECT/STYLIST/ INTERIOR DESIGNER / WHERE/YEAR	ENGINES Number & Cylinders / Horse Power / Maker/Type	REMARKS
AMBROSIA II	Twin Screw / Motor Yacht / Steel/Aluminium	54.00 / 46.70	(177.16) / (153.21)	9.60 / 3.00	(31.50) / (9.84)	Benetti Shipyard / Benetti/Zuretti/Natucci / Viareggio/Italy/1997	2 x Turbo charged / 1573hp / Deutz SBV 6M628 diesels	Featured in The Superyachts, Volume 12 / Lloyd's ✠100A1, ✠LMC
MARIDOME ex-Stefaren	Twin Screw / Motor Yacht / Steel	54.00 / 46.50	(177.17) / (152.55)	11.80 / 2.80	(38.71) / (9.19)	Brooke Yachts International / Diana Yacht Design/Bannenberg / Lowestoft/UK/1989	2 x 16 cylinder / 1550hp / Caterpillar 3516 diesels	Featured in The Superyachts, Volume 3 / Lloyd's ✠100A1, ✠LMC
SHENANDOAH OF SARK	Auxiliary Three Masted / Gaff Schooner / Steel/Teak	54.00 / 30.48	(177.17) / (100.00)	8.60 / 4.70	(28.22) / (15.42)	Townsend & Downey / Ferris/Francis & Francis/Disdale / Shooters Island/USA/1902	2 x Lugger diesels	Featured in The Superyachts, Volume 7 / Rebuilt at McMullen & Wing, Auckland, NZ in 1996
PERFECT PRESCRIPTION	Twin Screw / Motor Yacht / Steel/Aluminium/Composite	54.00	(177.17)	10.00 / 3.00	(32.80) / (9.84)	Oceanfast / Tim Heywood / Fremantle/Australia/2003	2 x 2330hp / MTU	
ITASCA	Single Screw / Motor Yacht / Steel	53.98 / 48.98	(177.10) / (160.60)	10.00 / 4.69	(32.81) / (15.39)	J & K Smits Scheepswerven / Smits/Bell Davis / Kinderdijk/The Netherlands 1961/1980	2 x 9 cylinder / 2500hp / MAN diesels	Lloyd's ✠100A1, ✠LMC. Converted from tug in 1980. Refitted 1994
KATHARINE ex-Seahawk	Twin Screw / Motor Yacht / Aluminium	53.96 / 47.44	(177.00) / (155.62)	9.45 / 2.23	(31.00) / (7.33)	Trinity Yachts / Trinity/Claudette Bonville/Trinity / New Orleans/USA/2001	2 x 12 cylinder / 2735hp / MTU/DDEC 12V4000 diesels	
ADAMAS II ex-Azzam	Twin Screw / Motor Yacht / Steel	53.95 / 46.50	(176.99) / (152.55)	9.25 / 2.47	(30.34) / (8.10)	Dauphin Offshore Engineering / Kenton Marine Pte Ltd / Singapore/1987	2 x 16 cylinder / 1950hp / MTU diesels	Owned by the Sheikh of Abu Dhabi. Lloyd's ✠100A1, ✠LMC
BLUE NARWHAL ex-Mau Mau V	Twin Screw / Motor Yacht / Steel	53.95 / 42.90	(176.99) / (140.75)	9.10 / 4.00	(29.85) / (13.12)	Fratelli Benetti / Benetti/Dell'Anna/Mongiadino / Viareggio/Italy/1984	2 x 12 cylinder / 2991 hp / MAK diesels	Lengthened by Palmer Johnson in 1993/94
ADEL XII ex-Malahne, ex-Narcissus ex-Lev III, ex-Malahne	Twin Screw / Motor Yacht / Steel	53.94 / 45.70	(176.97) / (150.00)	7.92 / 3.96	(26.00) / (13.00)	Camper & Nicholsons / CE Nicholson / Southampton/UK/1937	2 x 12 cylinder / 740hp / MTU diesels	Substantial modifications made to bow, stern and superstructure during a rebuild by Campanella in 1983
BAKHSHISH ex-Little Sis, ex-Merlin ex-Kremlin Princess ex-Oceana	Twin Screw / Motor Yacht / Aluminium/Composite	53.50 / 46.00	(175.53) / (150.92)	10.00 / 2.34	(32.81) / (7.68)	Oceanfast Pty Ltd / Curran/Bannenberg / Perth/Australia/1994	2 x 16 cylinder / 2435hp / MTU 396TE84 diesels	Featured in The Superyachts, Volume 8
PETARA	Twin Screw / Motor Yacht / Steel/Aluminium	53.50 / 48.30	(175.53) / (158.46)	9.30 / 2.80	(30.51) / (9.18)	Proteksan-Turquoise / Dubois/Donald Starkey Designs / Tuzla/Turkey/2002	2 x 12 cylinder / 1500hp / Caterpillar 3512	
SANSSOUCI STAR	Twin Screw / Motor Yacht / Steel	53.50 / 46.83	(175.53) / 153.65	7.70 / 2.60	(25.26) / (8.53)	Husum Shipyard / Husum Shipyard / Husum/Germany/1982	2 x 12 cylinder / 1380hp / MTU 396 TC82 diesels	Germanischer Lloyd classified
KISSES	Twin Screw / Motor Yacht / Aluminium	53.34 / 46.40	(175.00) / (152.21)	9.80 / 3.03	(32.15) / (9.68)	Feadship – De Vries Scheepsbouw / De Voogt/De Voogt/Larson / Aalsmeer/The Netherlands/2000	2 x 12 cylinder / 1360hp / Caterpillar 3512E diesels	Lloyd's ✠100A1, SSC, Yacht(P) mono G6, ✠LMC / Featured in The Superyachts, Volume 14
LADY FIESTA ex-Princess Lauren, ex-Lady Azteca, ex-Azteca II ex-New Santa Mary	Twin Screw / Motor Yacht / Steel	53.31 / 48.64	(174.91) / (159.57)	8.20 / 4.00	(26.90) / (13.12)	CRN Ancona / CRN/Francis & Francis/Zuretti / Ancona/Italy/1984	2 x 8 cylinder / 2200hp / Deutz diesels	Refit undertaken by CUV/Mobilart during 1988-90 / Featured in The Superyachts, Volume 4
INDISCRETION ex-Texas	Twin Screw / Motor Yacht / Steel/Aluminium	53.04	(174.00)	9.33 / 2.93	(30.60) / (9.60)	Sensation Yachts / John Overing/François Zuretti / Auckland/New Zealand	2 x 2200hp / Caterpillar 3516b diesels	
ATMOSPHERE	Auxiliary Twin Screw / Ketch / Steel/Aluminium	53.00 / 44.54	(173.88) / (144.11)	11.41 8.30/3.90	(37.43) 27.23/12.79	Perini Navi / Perini Navi/Perini Navi/Perini Navi / Viareggio/Italy/2000	2 x 12 cylinder / 1257hp / Deutz TBD616 diesels	ABS ✠A1 Yachting Services, AMS, ABCU / Featured in The Superyachts, Volume 14 / MCA Code

Name	Type / Construction	LOA m / LWL m	LOA ft / LWL ft	Beam m / Draft m	Beam ft / Draft ft	Builder / Designer	Engines	Notes
INDEPENDENCE	Auxiliary Twin Screw Ketch Steel/Aluminium	53.00 44.08	(173.88) (144.62)	11.41 3.83	(37.43) (12.57)	Perini Navi Perini Navi/Perini Navi/Perini Navi Viareggio/Italy/1998	2 x 12 cylinder 1256hp Deutz TBD6 diesels	Featured in The Superyachts, Volume 12 ABS ✠A1 Yachting Service, AMS
SALPERTON	Auxiliary Ketch Alloy/Aluminium	53.00 44.60	(173.88) (146.31)	10.40 4.60	(34.12) (15.01)	Alloy Yachts International Dubois/Dubois/Alloy Yachts Auckland/New Zealand/2002	1 x 12 cylinder 1350hp Caterpillar 3412E diesels	ABS ✠AMS, A1 Yachting Services, MCA Code Featured in The Superyachts, Volume 16
GALU	Twin Screw Motor Yacht Steel	52.90 44.80	(173.56) (146.99)	9.42 2.74	(30.90) (8.99)	Fratelli Benetti Benetti/Bannenberg Viareggio/Italy/1977	2 x 12 cylinder 1600hp MAK diesels	Featured in The Superyachts, Volume 1 Bureau Veritas 13/3E ✠Yacht, ✠MOT Refitted in 1986
CHIMON ex-Camargo V ex-Running Eagle ex-Huong Giang, ex-Jagusy ex-Maid Marion	Twin Screw Motor Yacht Steel	52.79 49.37	(173.20) (162.00)	8.07 3.35	(26.50) (11.00)	Camper & Nicholsons CE Nicholson Southampton/UK/1938	2 x 8 cylinder 510hp MAN diesels	
PASSION ex-Destiny Langkawi ex-Destiny	Twin Screw Motor Yacht Steel/Aluminium	52.73 47.55	(173.00) (156.00)	9.09 3.19	(29.83) (10.46)	AB Nya Oskarshamn Varv Diana Yacht Design/Disdale Oskarshamn/Sweden/1988/refit 2003	2 x 16 cylinder 1550hp Caterpillar diesels	Featured in The Superyachts, Volume 2 Major refits 1999 and 2001 Det Norske Veritas ✠1A1, ✠MV
ZINAT AL BIHAAR	Auxiliary Twin Screw Three Masted Lateen Rig Schooner	52.60 40.10	(172.57) (131.56)	9.57 3.80	(31.39) (12.46)	Oman Royal Yacht Squadron Colin Mudie & Three Quays Oman/1988	2 x 700hp diesels Driving Electric Motors	Omani Royal Yacht Lloyd's ✠100A1, ✠LMC
NATALINA B ex-Europa Sun	Twin Screw Motor Yacht Steel	52.47 46.50	(172.16) (152.55)	8.90 2.50	(29.19) (8.20)	Picchiotti Picchiotti Viareggio/Italy/1985	2 x 12 cylinder 1202hp MTU diesels	Featured in The Superyachts, Volume 1. Lloyd's ✠100A1, ✠LMC
BIG EAGLE ex-Papa's Place ex-Lady Angela ex-Gran Mudder	Twin Screw Motor Yacht Steel	52.42	(172.00)	7.92 2.74	(26.00) (9.00)	Mei Shipyard Mei/Georgio Vafiadis/Susan Puleo Mei/Japan/1980	2 x 16 cylinder 900hp Caterpillar 16V92 diesels	Lengthened by 19ft by Bradford Marine in 1991 New engines installed in 1988
TAIPAN ex-Pearl Star, ex-North Star ex-Awal	Twin Screw Motor Yacht Steel	52.42 40.22	(172.00) (131.96)	8.35 2.01	(27.40) (6.59)	CRN CRN/Kevin Calhoun/Merritt-Knowles Ancona/Italy/1980	2 x 8 cylinder 1220hp 78-ESL-8 Mirrlees Blackstone diesels	Major refit and lengthened in 1998 Lloyd's ✠100A1, ✠LMC Featured in The Superyachts, Volume 13
SQUALL	Auxiliary Ketch Aluminium	52.34 44.33	(171.72) (145.43)	10.35 5.01	(33.96) (16.43)	Perini Navi Perini Navi/Dubois Naval Architects Viareggio/Italy/2002	1 x 12 cylinder 1400hp Caterpillar 3412E	Lloyd's ✠100A1, AMS, ABS, MCA Code Ocean Yacht Systems rigging
DARNICE III	Twin Screw Motor Yacht Steel	52.30 45.50	(171.59) (149.28)	9.14 3.09	(30.00) (10.16)	Fratelli Benetti Benetti/Carugati-Serena Viareggio/Italy/1986	2 x 16 cylinder 1250hp Caterpillar diesels	Featured in The Superyachts, Volume 2
LIBERTY	Auxiliary Twin Screw Ketch Steel/Aluminium	52.28 43.90	(171.52) (144.03)	11.41 3.79	(37.43) (12.43)	Perini Navi Perini Navi Viareggio/Italy/1997	2 x 12 cylinder 1256hp Deutz TBD6 diesels	Featured in The Superyachts, Volume 11
SEA JEWEL	Twin Screw Motor Yacht Steel/Aluminium	52.12 48.00	(171.00) (157.48)	10.30 3.50	(33.79) (11.48)	Abeking & Rasmussen Espen Øino/Sturchio Lemwerder/Germany/1997	2 x 16 cylinder 1900hp Caterpillar 3516 DI-TA diesels	Lloyd's ✠100A1, SSC, ✠LMC MCA Code
ABU AL ABYAD	Twin Screw Motor Yacht Steel	52.09 46.23	(170.89) (151.67)	9.11 4.67	(29.88) (15.33)	Feadship – Van Lent & Zonen BV De Voogt Kaag/The Netherlands/1980	2 x 16 cylinder 1141hp Caterpillar 399PCTA diesels	Lloyd's ✠100A1, ✠LMC
FLEURTJE ex-Argonaftis ex-Carita	Auxiliary Twin Screw Three Mast Schooner Steel	52.06 37.05	(170.80) (121.56)	8.57 4.78	(28.12) (15.68)	NV Amsterdamsche Scheepswerft G de Vries Lentsch/Robert Clarke Jr Amsterdam/The Netherlands/1960	2 x 12 cylinder 623hp Caterpillar diesels	Lloyd's ✠100A1, ✠LMC Refitted at Pendennis Shipyard 1995
AIRWAVES	Twin Screw Motor Yacht Steel/Aluminium	52.00 48.00	(170.60) (157.49)	10.30 3.50	(33.79) (11.48)	Abeking & Rasmussen Espen Øino/Sturchio Lemwerder/Germany/2000	2 x 16 cylinder 3746hp Caterpillar 3516 DI-TA diesels	
ALFA	Twin Screw Motor Yacht Steel	52.00 43.60	(170.60) (143.04)	9.40 2.96	(30.84) (9.71)	Benetti Shipyard Benetti/Zuretti/Natucci Viareggio/Italy/2001	2 x 12 cylinder 1575hp Caterpillar 3512B diesels	Featured in The Superyachts, Volume 15
BATTERED BULL	Twin Screw Motor Yacht Steel	52.00 45.00	(170.60) (147.64)	9.30 2.74	(30.51) (8.98)	Feadship – Van Lent & Zonen BV De Voogt/De Voogt Kaag/The Netherlands/1995	2 x 12 cylinder 1430hp Caterpillar 3512DI-TA diesels	

YACHT'S NAME ex-name(s)	DIMENSIONS LOA/LOA including spars / Length water line m (ft)	Beam (Maximum) / Draught m (ft)	PROPULSION TYPE CONSTRUCTION	BUILDER NAVAL ARCHITECT/STYLIST/ INTERIOR DESIGNER WHERE/YEAR	ENGINES Number & Cylinders Horse Power Maker/Type	REMARKS
GEORGINA	52.00 (170.60) / 46.50 (152.55)	9.00 (29.52) / 3.10 (10.17)	Twin Screw Motor Yacht Steel/Aluminium	Amels Schelde Amels/Terence Disdale Vlissingen/The Netherlands/2003	2 x 12 cylinder 2400hp Cummins KTA 38 M2	Lloyds ✠100A1
TIGRE D'OR	52.00 (170.60) / 46.50 (152.57)	9.00 (29.50) / 3.10 (10.17)	Twin Screw Motor Yacht Steel	Amels Makkum Amels/Disdale/Disdale Makkum/The Netherlands/1999	2 x 6 cylinder 1200hp Cummins KTA 38 M2 diesels	Lloyd's ✠100A1,SSC Yacht(P), Momo G6, ✠ LMC Featured in The Superyachts, Volume 14
KISS THE SKY ex-Toinie	52.00 (170.60) / 46.50 (152.57)	9.00 (29.50) / 3.10 (10.17)	Twin Screw Motor Yacht Steel/Aluminium	Amels Makkum Amels/Disdale/Disdale Makkum/The Netherlands/2001	2 x 12 cylinder 1200hp Cummins KTA 38 M2 diesels	
RASSELAS	52.00 (170.60) / 45.00 (147.70)	9.30 (30.60) / 3.10 (10.20)	Twin Screw Motor Yacht Steel	Feadship – De Vries Scheepsbouw De Voogt/De Voogt/Munford Aalsmeer/The Netherlands/1994	2 x 12 cylinder 1298hp Caterpillar 3512DI-TA diesels	Catalytic exhaust cleaners fitted to generators. Lloyd's ✠100A1 Featured in The Superyachts, Volume 9
SEA SHAW II	52.00 (170.60) / 46.28 (151.83)	9.40 (30.83) / 3.13 (10.26)	Twin Screw Motor Yacht Composite/Steel	Yantai Raffles Shipyard/Cheoy Lee Shipyard Mulder Design/Dee Robinson Kowloon/Hong Kong/2003	2 x 16 cylinder 1796hp MTU 12V4000M60	
SOLEMATES	52.00 (170.60) / 46.70 (153.22)	9.80 (32.15) / 3.10 (10.17)	Twin Screw Motor Yacht Steel	Feadship – De Vries Scheepsbouw De Voogt/The 'A' Group/Winch Aalsmeer/The Netherlands/1998	2 x 16 cylinder 1901hp Caterpillar 3516B DI-TA diesels	Featured in The Superyachts, Volume 13
RIO RITA	51.99 (170.58) / 46.51 (152.59)	9.08 (29.78) / 2.84 (9.33)	Twin Screw Motor Yacht Steel	Feadship-De Vries Scheepsbouw Diana Yacht Design/Disdale Aalsmeer/The Netherlands/1984	2 x 12 cylinder 1080hp Caterpillar 3512 DI-TA diesels	Lloyd's ✠100A1, ✠LMC
SUNRISE ex-Acclaim	51.93 (170.37) /	9.90 (32.47) / 3.36 (11.02)	Twin Screw Motor Yacht Steel/Aluminium	Oceanco The 'A' Group/The 'A' Group Dreumel/The Netherlands/1999	2 x 12 cylinder 1714hp MTU 396 TE 74 diesels	
TOMMY	51.82 (170.00) / 46.00 (150.93)	8.82 (28.94) / 2.70 (8.86)	Twin Screw Motor Yacht Steel	Benetti Shipyard Benetti/Benetti/Disdale Viareggio/Italy/1995	2 x 16 cylinder 3046hp Deutz TBD604B diesels	ABS ✠A1 Yachting Service Featured in The Superyachts, Volume 10
MADIZ ex-Hinestia ex-President Roberts ex-Hinestia ex-Rhouma, ex-Osprey ex-Rhouma, ex-Triton	51.81 (170.00) / 47.61 (156.21)	6.83 (22.41) / 3.35 (11.00)	Auxiliary Twin Screw Schooner Steel	Ailsa Shipbuilding Co GL Watson & Co Troon/UK/1902	2 x 650hp Maybach/Mercedes diesels	
XASTERIA	51.80 (170.00) / 44.00 (144.60)	10.80 (35.50) / 8.20 (26.10)	Auxiliary Twin Screw Ketch Steel/Aluminium	Perini Navi Perini Navi/Perini Navi/Perini Navi Viareggio/Italy/1995	2 x 6 cylinder 980hp Deutz-MWM TBD604 diesels	Featured in The Superyachts, Volume 9
GALLANT LADY	51.50 (168.97) / 43.90 (144.03)	9.58 (31.43) / 2.70 (8.85)	Twin Screw Motor Yacht Steel/Aluminium	Feadship – De Vries Scheepsbouw De Voogt/Paola Smith Aalsmeer/The Netherlands/1995	2 x 8 cylinder 973hp Caterpillar 3508 DI-TA diesels	Featured in The Superyachts, Volume 10
JAMAICA BAY ex-Intrepid II, ex-Mylin III ex-Leocric III	51.25 (168.14) / 45.50 (149.27)	9.10 (29.86) / 3.00 (9.84)	Twin Screw Motor Yacht Steel	Fr Schweers Fr Schweers/Disdale Bardenfleth/West Germany/1987	2 x 12 cylinder 1414hp Caterpillar diesels	Featured in The Superyachts, Volume 1 Lloyd's ✠100A1, ✠LMC. Refitted 1999 at Astilleros de Mallorca with interior design by Buytendijk and furniture from de Ruiter
PATAGONIA ex-Robur IV ex-Southern Breeze	51.23 (168.08) / 48.80 (160.11)	8.65 (28.41) / 3.40 (11.15)	Twin Screw Motor Yacht Steel	GB Zigler Zigler/Bannenberg Louisiana/USA/1964	2 x 1800hp Fairbanks Morse diesels	Featured in The Superyachts, Volume 4 Major refit undertaken and stern enclosure added at Palmer Johnson in 1994
ENTERPRISE V	51.20 (167.98) / 44.00 (144.36)	8.65 (28.38) / 2.97 (9.74)	Twin Screw Motor Yacht Steel/Aluminium	Feadship – Van Lent & Zonen BV De Voogt/Tanter/Brady Kaag/The Netherlands/1993	2 x 12 cylinder 1191hp Caterpillar 3512DI-TA diesels	Featured in The Superyachts, Volume 7

Name	Type / Construction	LOA / LWL (m)	(ft)	Beam / Draft (m)	(ft)	Builder / Designer / Year	Engine	Classification / Remarks
HAIDA ex-Ashtoreth, ex-Astarte, ex-Elda, ex-Haida	Twin Screw Motor Yacht / Steel	51.05 / 49.16	(167.50) (161.30)	7.62 / 3.13	(25.00) (10.30)	Bath Iron Works Corp / JH Wells / Bath/USA/1947	2 x 8 cylinder 1100hp Enterprise diesels	ABS ✠A1, ✠ AMS Yachting Service
DOUBLE HAVEN	Twin Screw Motor yacht / Steel	51.00 / 45.50	(167.33) (149.28)	9.30 / 3.45	(30.51) (11.31)	Feadship – De Vries Scheepsbouw / Gilgenast/Hein/De Voogt/Glade Johnson / Aalsmeer/The Netherlands/1993	2 x 12 cylinder 1430hp Caterpillar 3512DI-TA diesels	Featured in The Superyachts, Volume 8 / Lloyd's ✠100A1, ✠LMC
ICE BEAR ex-Royal Pacific, ex-Gallant Lady	Twin Screw Motor Yacht / Steel	50.90 / 44.00	(167.00) (144.36)	9.14 / 2.46	(30.00) (8.08)	Feadship – De Vries Scheepsbouw / De Voogt/Smith / Aalsmeer/The Netherlands/1988	2 x 12 cylinder 1191hp Caterpillar 3512DI-TA diesels	Featured in The Superyachts, Volume 8
ILLUSION ex-Pilar, ex-Le Pharaon	Twin Screw Motor Yacht / Steel	50.69 / 46.20	(166.13) (151.58)	9.15 / 2.89	(30.01) (9.33)	Feadship – Van Lent & Zonen BV / De Voogt / Kaag/The Netherlands/1983	2 x 16 cylinder 1141hp Caterpillar 399PCTA diesels	Lloyd's ✠100A1, ✠LMC
KALINGA	Twin Screw Motor Yacht / Steel	50.69 / 46.20	(166.13) (151.58)	8.81 / 2.99	(28.90) (9.83)	Feadship – Van Lent & Zonen BV / De Voogt / Kaag/The Netherlands/1982	2 x 6 cylinder 1141hp Caterpillar 399PCTA diesels	Lloyd's ✠100A1, ✠LMC. Refitted at Vitters Shipyard in 1996
BORKUMRIFF IV	Auxiliary Schooner / Aluminium	50.58 / 35.80	(165.92) (117.44)	9.20 / 4.30	(30.18) (14.11)	Royal Huisman Shipyard / Dijkstra/Alden/Munford / Vollenhove/The Netherlands/2002	1 x cylinder 1072hp MTU 12V 2000 M70 diesel	Lloyds certificate for pleasure craft / Featured in The Superyachts, Volume 16.
LAZY Z ex-Lady S, ex-Accolade	Twin Screw Motor Yacht / Steel/Aluminium	50.55	(165.84)	9.45 / 3.10	(31.00) (10.17)	Oceanco / Richard Hein/The 'A' Group / Dreumel/The Netherlands/1997	2 x 12 cylinder 1714hp MTU 396TE 74 diesels	
FANTASIA ex-Marcalan IV, ex-Aleanna	Twin Screw Motor Yacht / Steel	50.46 / 44.10	(165.55) (144.69)	9.29 / 4.19	(30.50) (13.75)	Codecasa / Codecasa/Manfredi & Sforzi/Cerruti / Viareggio/Italy/1986	2 x 8 cylinder 1090hp MAN diesels	ABS classified. Refitted 1993
BLUE MOON	Twin Screw Motor Yacht / Aluminium	50.28	(165.00)	9.45 / 2.43	(31.00) (8.00)	Feadship – Van Lent & Zonen / De Voogt/Don Starkey / Kaag/The Netherlands/2000	2 x 12 cylinder 1500hp Caterpillar 3512B diesels	Lloyd's ✠100A1 / MCA Code
YANBU ex-Pollyanna, ex-Aleta II, ex-Corfu, ex-Calypso, ex-Seapine, ex-Yankee	Twin Screw Motor Yacht / Steel	50.26 / 45.71	(164.89) (149.96)	7.92 / 3.35	(26.00) (11.00)	Bath Iron Works Corp / Henry J Gielow / Bath/USA/1931	2 x 16 cylinder 800hp GM diesels	Lloyd's ✠100A1, ✠LMC
DEERRAMA ex-Yanka, ex-Myrna, ex-Donapila II	Twin Screw Motor Yacht / Steel	50.11 / 44.53	(164.41) (146.10)	7.47 / 5.20	(24.50) (17.06)	Arsenal do Alfeite / D'Almeida Araujo / Alfeite/Spain/1968	2 x 12 cylinder 2350hp Mercedes-Benz diesels	Lloyd's ✠100A1, ✠LMC
BLUE SHADOW C ex-New Horizon C, ex-New Horizon III, ex-Blue Horizon III, ex-Astromar II, ex-Katy II, ex-Blue Shadow	Twin Screw Motor Yacht / Steel	50.02 / 44.86	(164.11) (147.17)	8.33 / 2.50	(27.33) (8.20)	Cantiere Navale Apuania SA / Cantiere Navale Apuania SA / Marina di Carrara/Italy/1964	2 x 12 cylinder 1350hp MTU diesels	Underwent major refit in 1985 at Fr. Lürssen Werft, Bremen / Lloyd's ✠100A1, ✠LMC
AURORA ex-Felicita West	Auxiliary Twin Screw Ketch / Steel/Aluminium	50.00 / 40.33	(164.05) (132.30)	10.27 / 3.39&8.39	(33.69) (11.12/27.52)	Perini Navi / Perini Navi/Perini Navi / Viareggio/Italy/2000	2 x 12 cylinders 965hp Deutz TBD616 V12 diesels	
ALEXANDRA ex-Golden Bay VI	Twin Screw Motor Yacht / Steel/Aluminium	50.00	(164.05)	9.40 / 3.40	(30.84) (11.15)	Benetti Shipyard / Benetti/Stefano Natucci/Disdale/Alan Jones / Viareggio/Italy/2002	2 x 12 cylinder 2262hp MTU 12V 396TE94 diesels	Featured in The Superyachts, Volume 16
GOLDEN CELL	Twin Screw Motor Yacht / Steel	50.00 / 42.00	(164.05) (137.79)	9.00 / 2.20	(29.52) (7.22)	Benetti Shipyard / Benetti/Benetti/Zuretti / Viareggio/Italy/1996	2 x 12 cylinder 2260hp MTU 396TE94 diesels	ABS ✠A1 Yachting Service
KERMIT	Twin Screw Motor Yacht / Steel/Aluminium	50.00 / 44.50	(164.00) (146.00)	9.00 / 3.00	(29.52) (9.84)	Amels Holland BV / Amels/Disdale/Disdale / Makkum/Holland/2001	2 x 12 cylinder 1,199hp Cummins	Lloyd's ✠100A1, SSC Yacht Mono, G6, LMS, UMS / Featured in The Superyachts, Volume 15 / MCA Code
LADY M ex-Lady Marina	Twin Screw Motor Yacht / Steel/Aluminium	50.00 / 45.00	(164.05) (147.64)	9.35 / 2.90	(30.68) (9.51)	Hakvoort Shipyard / Diana Yacht Design/Starkey/Starkey / Monnickendam/The Netherlands/1993	2 x 12 cylinder 1379hp Caterpillar 3512DI-TA diesels	Featured in The Superyachts, Volume 8 / Lloyd's ✠100A1, ✠LMC

YACHT'S NAME ex-name(s)	PROPULSION TYPE / CONSTRUCTION	DIMENSIONS LOA/LOA including spars / Length water line m (ft)	Beam (Maximum) / Draught m (ft)	BUILDER / NAVAL ARCHITECT/STYLIST/ INTERIOR DESIGNER / WHERE/YEAR	ENGINES Number & Cylinders / Horse Power / Maker/Type	REMARKS
MOSAIQUE	Twin Screw / Motor Yacht / Steel/Aluminium	50.00 / 44.55 (164.05) / (146.16)	9.30 / 2.75 (30.51) / (9.02)	Proteksan/Turquoise Yacht Construction / Dubois/Dubois/Starkey & Ferrand / Tuzla/Turkey/2001	2 x 8 cylinder / 1100hp / Caterpillar 3508 diesels	ABS✠A1-AMS / Featured in The Superyachts, Volume 15 / MCA Code
THE PEARL ex-Princess of Adriatic ex-Empress Subaru ex-New Santa Maria ex-Santa Maria	Twin Screw / Motor Yacht / Steel	50.00 / 39.31 (164.05) / (128.96)	7.74 / 2.59 (25.39) / (8.49)	CRN / CRN/CRN/Mantovani / Ancona/Italy/1979	2 x 16 cylinder / 2000hp / Deutz diesels	Total refit including entirely new superstructure, bow and stern in 2000
SOUNDS OF PACIFIC	Twin Screw / Motor Yacht / Steel/Aluminium	50.00 / (164.05)	9.02 / 2.32 (29.60) / (7.60)	Sensation Yachts / Sensation Yachts/François Zuretti / Auckland/New Zealand/2002	2 x 1500 / Caterpillar 3516b diesels	
AURORA B	Twin Screw / Motor Yacht / Steel	49.99 / 43.50 (164.01) / (142.72)	9.50 / 3.20 (31.16) / (10.50)	Feadship—De Vries Scheepsbouw / De Voogt/De Voogt/Munford / Aalsmeer/The Netherlands/1992	2 x 16 cylinder / 1430hp / Caterpillar 3516DI-TA diesels	
IROQUOIS	Twin Screw / Motor Yacht / Steel	49.98 / 43.65 (164.00) / (143.21)	9.10 / 2.95 (29.86) / (9.68)	Feadship—De Vries Scheepsbouw / De Voogt/De Voogt/Glade Johnson / Aalsmeer/The Netherlands/1998	2 x 12 cylinder / 1379hp / Caterpillar 3512BDI-TA diesels	
THUNDER GULCH ex-Louise	Twin Screw / Motor Yacht / Steel	49.98 / (164.00)	9.00 / 3.10 (34.24) / (10.17)	Amels / Amels/Disdale/Disdale / Makkum/The Netherlands/1999	2 x 12 cylinder / 1199hp / Cummins KTA-38-M2 diesels	Lloyd's ✠100A1, ✠LMC, UMS / MCA Code
TEDDY ex-Tigre d'Os ex-Tigre d'Or	Twin Screw / Motor Yacht / Steel/Aluminium	49.98 / (164.00)	9.00 / 3.00 (29.53) / (9.84)	Amels / Amels/Disdale/Disdale / Makkum/The Netherlands/1997	2 x 12 cylinder / 1199hp / Cummins KTA-38-M2 diesels	Lloyd's ✠100A1, ✠LMC, UMS / Featured in The Superyachts, Volume 11 / MCA Code
TAIBA V ex-Golden Bay	Twin Screw / Motor Yacht / Steel	49.95 / 42.00 (163.86) / (137.79)	9.00 / 2.50 (29.52) / (8.20)	Benetti Shipyard / Benetti/Benetti/Zuretti / Viareggio/Italy/1997	2 x 12 cylinder / 2262hp / MTU 396TE94 diesels	ABS✠A1 Yachting Service / Featured in The Superyachts, Volume 11
LIONHEART	Twin Screw / Motor Yacht / Steel/Aluminium	49.95 / 42.00 (163.86) / (137.80)	9.00 / 2.85 (29.52) / (9.35)	Benetti Shipyard / Benetti/Natucci/Natucci / Viareggio/Italy/1999	2 x 12 cylinder / 2262hp / MTU 396TE94 diesels	Featured in The Superyachts, Volume 14
MARACUNDA	Twin Screw / Motor Yacht / Steel/Aluminium	49.95 / 45.10 (163.86) / (147.97)	9.20 / 4.30 (30.18) / (14.11)	CRN / CRN/CRN/Pinto / Ancona/Italy/1990	2 x 9 cylinder / 2450hp / Deutz MWM BV9M628 diesels	Featured in The Superyachts, Volume 5 / Lloyd's ✠100A1, ✠LMC
QUEEN M	Twin Screw / Motor Yacht / Steel	49.95 / 47.53 (163.86) / (155.92)	9.00 / 2.77 (29.53) / (9.09)	Benetti Shipyard / Benetti/Natucci/Disdale / Viareggio/Italy/1998	2 x 12 cylinder / 2262hp / MTU 396TE94 diesels	Featured in The Superyachts, Volume 13
SAHAB IV	Twin Screw / Motor Yacht / Steel/Aluminium	49.95 / 43.80 (163.86) / (143.70)	9.20 / 2.55 (30.18) / (8.37)	CRN / CRN/Disdale/Disdale / Ancona/Italy/1997	2 x 12 cylinder / 2068hp / Deutz TBD620 diesels	Lloyd's ✠100A1, ✠LMC / Featured in The Superyachts, Volume 11
INVADER	Twin Screw / Motor Yacht / Steel/Aluminium	49.90 / 42.95 (163.72) / (140.90)	9.50 / 3.10 (31.17) / (10.17)	Codecasa Shipyards / Codecasa/Della Role/Godfrey Associates / Viareggio/Italy/1999	2 x 16 cylinder / 2200hp / Caterpillar 3516B diesels	Featured in The Superyachts, Volume 14
LADY ANN MAGEE	Twin Screw / Motor Yacht / Steel/Aluminium	49.90 / 41.70 (163.72) / (136.82)	9.50 / 3.10 (31.17) / (10.17)	Codecasa / Della Role / Viareggio/Italy/2001	2 x 16 cylinder / 2200hp / Caterpillar 3516 B	Lloyd's 100✠A1 SSC, ✠LMC, MCA Code / Featured in The Superyachts, Volume 16
LA NATURALLE DEE ex-Turquoise ex-Turquoise C	Twin Screw / Motor Yacht / Steel	49.90 / 44.60 (163.72) / (146.33)	8.80 / 2.18 (28.87) / (7.15)	Turquoise Yacht Construction / Dubois/Dubois/Starkey / Tuzla/Turkey/1994	2 x 12 cylinder / 764hp / Caterpillar 3412DI-TA diesels	ABS✠A1, ✠ AMS Yachting Service / Featured in The Superyachts, Volume 8
MARIU	Twin Screw / Motor Yacht / Steel/Aluminium	49.90 / 41.70 (163.71) / (136.81)	9.50 / 5.10 (31.16) / (16.73)	Codecasa / Ortelli/Della Role / Viareggio/Italy/2003	2 x 16 cylinder / 4400hp / Caterpillar 3516B	Lloyds ✠100 A 1 ✠LMC, MCA Code

Name	Type / Material	LOA/LWL (m)	(feet)	Beam/Draft (m)	(feet)	Builder / Designer / Location / Year	Engines	Classification / Notes
MONEIKOS	Twin Screw Motor Yacht Steel	49.90 41.70	(163.72) (136.82)	9.50 3.10	(31.17) (10.17)	Codecasa / Della Role / Viareggio/Italy/2000	2 x 16 cylinder 2200hp Caterpillar 3516 B	ABS ✠A1-AMS, MCA Code
MULTIPLE	Twin Screw Motor Yacht Steel/Aluminium	49.90 44.00	(163.71) (144.4)	9.50 2.70	(31.16) (8.85)	Benetti Shipyard / Jon Bannenberg Ltd / Viareggio/Italy/2002	2 x 16 cylinder 7400hp MTU 16v 4000 M90	
IS... A ROSE	Auxiliary Twin Screw Ketch Steel/Aluminium	49.80 41.38	(163.39) (135.74)	10.27 8.39/3.99	(33.69) (27.52/11.12)	Perini Navi / Perini Navi / Viareggio/Italy/2002	2 x 12 cylinder 979hp Deutz TBD616 V12 diesels	ABS ✠A1-AMS, MCA Code
PERSEUS	Auxiliary Twin Screw Ketch Steel/Aluminium	49.80 41.38	(163.39) (135.74)	10.27 8.39/3.99	(33.69) (27.52/11.12)	Perini Navi / Perini Navi / Viareggio/Italy/2001	2 x 12 cylinder 979hp Deutz TBD616 V12 diesels	
PHRYNE	Auxiliary Twin Screw Ketch Steel/Aluminium	49.80	(163.39)	10.27	(33.69)	Perini Navi / Perini Navi/Perini Navi / Viareggio/Italy/1999	2 x 8 cylinder 980hp Deutz diesels	Featured in The Superyachts, Volume 13
PRINCESS VALENTINA ex-Indian Achiever ex-Achiever	Twin Screw Motor Yacht Steel/Aluminium	49.80 44.30	(163.39) (145.35)	9.20 2.80	(30.18) (9.87)	Oceanco / Gilgenast/Gilgenast/Starkey / Monnickendam/The Netherlands/1993	2 x 12 cylinder 1530hp MTU 396TE74 diesels	ABS ✠A1, AMS, ABCU Yachting Service Featured in The Superyachts, Volume 7
THUNDER	Triple Water Jet Motor Yacht Composite	49.80 39.00	(163.39) (127.95)	8.00 1.50	(26.25) (4.92)	Oceanfast Pty Ltd / Curran/Bannenberg / Perth/Australia/1998	2 x 16 cylinder 2682hp MTU 16V 396.84SE diesels & 1 x Textron TF40 gas turbine	Featured in The Superyachts, Volume 13
PESTIFER	Twin Screw Motor Yacht Steel/Aluminium	49.75	(163.22)	9.30 3.00	(30.51) (9.84)	CRN Shipyards / Studio Scanu/Zuretti / Ancona/Italy/1998	2 x 16 cylinder 2000hp Caterpillar 3516 diesels	Featured in The Superyachts, Volume 13
TE MANU ex-Andale	Twin Screw Motor Yacht Steel	49.65	(162.92)	9.50 3.10	(31.16) (10.17)	Codecasa / Codecasa/Dellarole / Viareggio/Italy/1998	2 x 18 cylinder 2200hp Caterpillar 3516B diesels	Lloyd's ✠100A1, SSC Yachts Featured in The Superyachts, Volume 13
AWAY S	Twin Screw Motor Yacht Steel/Aluminium	49.60 42.00	(162.73) (137.80)	9.30 2.68	(30.50) (8.79)	Codecasa / Codecasa/Manfredi & Sforzi/Castellini / Viareggio/Italy/1991	2 x 6 cylinder 1875hp Wärtsilä Nohab diesels	Featured in The Superyachts, Volume 5 Lloyd's ✠100A1, ✠LMC Fitted with Renk Tacke TNT Drives
BABOON	Auxilliary Three Masted Schooner Steel	49.50/62.00 43.00	(162.38/203.42) (141.08)	8.50 4.20	(27.88) (13.78)	Tradewind Cruises/Feab. Skarhamn / Tradewind Cruises/Arredamenti/d'Andons / Skärhamn/Marstrand/Sweden/1990	1 x 16 cylinder 2000hp Caterpillar diesel	DNV 1A1, ✠MV
FRANCINE ex-Sahab III	Twin Screw Motor Yacht Steel	49.50 35.70	(162.38) (117.13)	7.77 2.00	(25.50) (6.58)	Benetti Shipyard / Nicholson/Harvey/Disdale / Viareggio/Italy/1989	2 x 12 cylinder 1609hp Deutz MWM TB604B diesels	Refitted and extended with naval architecture by Tom Fexas in 1999. ABS ✠A1 AMS Yachting Service
PRINCESS MARLA ex-Flying Eagle ex-White Rabbit	Twin Screw Motor Yacht Steel	49.50 44.00	(162.38) (144.40)	9.30 3.20	(30.60) (10.60)	Feadship – De Vries Scheepsbouw / De Voogt/Winch / Aalsmeer/The Netherlands/1995	2 x 16 cylinder 2839hp Caterpillar 3516DI-TA diesels	Featured in The Superyachts, Volume 9 Refitted in 1999 with design by Andrew Winch Designs
RIMA'S II ex-Rima	Twin Screw Motor Yacht Steel	49.50 37.60	(162.38) (123.36)	8.80 2.15	(28.87) (7.05)	Benetti Shipyard / Benetti/Disdale / Viareggio/Italy/1987	2 x 16 cylinder 3480hp MTU 396TB94 diesels	ABS classified
SUSSURRO	Triple Waterjet Motor Yacht Aluminium/Carbon Fibre	49.50 39.70	(162.38) (130.25)	8.40 2.03	(27.56) (6.66)	Feadship – De Vries Scheepsbouw / De Voogt/Shead/Disdale / Aalsmeer/The Netherlands/1998	2 x 12 cylinder 3442hp Paxman 12VP185 diesels & 2 x 4250hp Textron Lycoming TF40 gas turbines	2 x Lips LJ-95DL steerable & 1 x Lips LJ-110DL fixed waterjet units. Featured in The Superyachts, Volume 13
MYSTIQUE	Triple Waterjet Motor Yacht Aluminium/GRP	49.47 39.31	(162.31) (129.00)	9.30 1.50	(30.50) (4.92)	Oceanfast Pty Ltd / Curran/Bannenburg / Perth/Australia/1989	2 x 16 cylinder TB 94 1 x 12 cylinder TB 93 MTU diesels	Featured in The Superyachts, Volume 2
AQUARIUS W ex-Black Douglas ex-Te Quest	Auxiliary Three Mast Schooner Iron/Aluminium	49.41/53.30	(162.11/174.80)	9.80 3.80	(32.15) (12.46)	Bath Iron Works / Henry J Gielow / Bath/USA/1930	2 x 350hp Volvo diesels	Featured in The Superyachts, Volume 2 Refitted in 1983 by Abeking & Rasmussen with interior by John Munford
MICHAELA ROSE	Twin Screw Motor Yacht Steel	49.25 43.52	(161.57) (142.78)	8.72 2.89	(28.60) (9.48)	Fr Schweers / Schweers / Bardenfleth/Germany/1984	2 x 6 cylinder 1037hp Deutz MWM diesels	Lloyd's ✠100A1, ✠LMC

YACHT'S NAME ex-name(s)	PROPULSION TYPE CONSTRUCTION	DIMENSIONS LOA/LOA including spars Length water line m (ft)	Beam (Maximum) Draught m (ft)	BUILDER NAVAL ARCHITECT/STYLIST/ INTERIOR DESIGNER WHERE/YEAR	ENGINES Number & Cylinders Horse Power Maker/Type	REMARKS
NAFISA ex-Princess Kelly, ex-Brave Goose, ex-Edenforth	Twin Screw Motor Yacht Steel	49.25 43.52	(161.57) (142.78)	8.71 2.90	(28.57) (10.33)	Fr Schweers Schweers Bardenfleth/Germany/1986	2 x 6 cylinder 1037hp Deutz diesels	Lloyd's ✠100A1, ✠ LMC Featured in The Superyachts, Volume 4
LADY ELLEN	Auxiliary Three Mast Schooner Steel/Teak	49.20 36.00	(161.40) (118.11)	7.84 3.90	(25.72) (12.80)	Tradewind Cruises/Kockums Lars Johansen Shipping Skårhamn/Malmo/Sweden/1981	1 x 8 cylinder 385hp Iveco 8280SRM diesel	Det Norske Veritas ✠1A1, ✠ MV.
BERMIE	Twin Screw Motor Yacht Steel/Aluminium	49.00 43.56	(160.77) (142.89)	9.60 2.85	(31.49) (9.35)	Oceanco/CMN Oceanco/Andrew Winch Design Cherbourg/France/2001	2 x 12 cylinder 1650hp Caterpillar 3512B-TA diesels	Bureau Veritas 13/3E✠ Special Service Charter Yacht Featured in The Superyachts, Volume 15
BLUE GOLD ex-White Gull	Auxiliary Twin Screw Staysail Schooner Steel	49.00 36.00	160.77 (118.12)	9.00 4.15	(29.52) (13.61)	Fratelli Benetti Laurent Giles Varazze/Italy/1986	2 x 12 cylinders 1040hp Caterpillar diesels	Rebuilt and refitted in 1988 Bureau Veritas 1 3/3E, ✠Yacht, ✠MOT
BRAVEHEART ex-Jefferson Beach	Twin Water Jet Motor Yacht Steel/Aluminium	49.00 41.37	(160.76) (135.90)	8.60 2.74	(28.22) (8.99)	Oskarshamns Varv AB Beeldsnijder/Beeldsnijder Oskarshamn/Sweden/1989	2 x 12 cylinder 1630hp MTU 396TB diesels	Featured in The Superyachts, Volume 5 Refits in 1997 and 1999
ELEONORA	Auxiliary Single Screw Gaff Schooner Steel	49.00 29.30	(160.76) (96.13)	8.20 5.28	(26.90) (17.32)	Van der Graaf Ship Design/Herreshoff Giessendam/The Netherlands/2002	1 x 460hp Baudouin 6R124SR	Bureau Veritas 13/3E, ✠CY, MACH Featured in The Superyachts, Volume 16
EVVIVA	Twin Screw Motor Yacht GRP Composite	49.00	(160.76)	9.14 2.43	(30.00) (8.00)	Admiral Marine Garden/Starkey/Starkey Port Townsend//USA/1993	2 x 16 cylinder 3460hp MTU 396TB94 diesels	Featured in The Superyachts, Volume 8
EL CHRIS ex-Lina III	Twin Screw Motor Yacht Wood/Aluminium	48.85	(160.25)	7.00 3.67	(22.97) (12.04)	Lürssen Werft Lürssen/Sandy C Bremen/Germany/1960	2 x Deutz 1400hp diesels	Bureau Veritas 12-4 3/3 Yacht. Lengthened by 4 metres in 1997
GALLANT LADY	Twin Screw Motor Yacht Aluminium/Composite	48.80 40.20	(160.11) (131.89)	8.80 2.08	(28.87) (6.83)	Delta Marine Sharp/Las Olas Design/Glade Johnson Seattle/USA/2000	2 x 8 cylinder 1100hp Caterpillar 3508 B diesels	Featured in The Superyachts, Volume 14
TELEOST ex-Ulysses	Twin Screw Motor Yacht Steel/Aluminium	48.80 42.30	(160.11) (138.78)	8.90 2.75	(29.20) (9.02)	Feadship – Van Lent & Zonen BV De Voogt/John Munford Kaag/The Netherlands/1998	2 x 8 cylinder 918hp Caterpillar 3508 DI-TA diesels	Featured in The Superyachts, Volume 16
SHANDOR ex-The Griff, ex-Louisianna ex-Margaux Rose	Single Screw Motor Yacht Steel	48.80 43.22	(160.11) (141.79)	9.10 2.70	(29.85) (8.85)	Fr Schweers Gilgenast/Munford Bardenfleth/Germany/1988	1 x 8 cylinder 2300hp Krupp MAK diesel	Lloyd's ✠100A1, ✠ LMC Refitted and lengthened in 1994 by Abeking & Rasmussen Featured in The Superyachts, Volume 2
IMAN ex-Dragomar	Twin Screw Motor Yacht Steel	48.76	(160.00)	8.83 2.28	(29.00) (7.50)	Dragomar SPA Coluccia/Fexas/Zampetti Italy/1994	2 x 16 cylinder 2600hp Deutz 604BV diesels	
HALAS ex-Water Witch ex-Reshid Pasha	Twin Screw Motor Yacht Steel	48.76	(160.00)	7.90 2.40	(25.92) (7.87)	Fairfield Shipping Co Fairfield Shipping Co Glasgow/UK/1914	2 x 12 cylinder 503hp Caterpillar diesels	Built as Bosphorus passenger ferry. Converted in Istanbul to yacht in 1985
RENALO	Twin Screw Motor Yacht Steel	48.70 41.70	(159.77) (136.81)	9.50 2.30	(31.17) (7.55)	Codecasa Codecasa/Della Role Viareggio/Italy/1997	2 x 12 cylinder 2285hp MTU 396TE94 diesels	Lloyd's ✠100A1, ✠LMC
GEORGIA	Auxiliary Centreboard Sloop Aluminium	48.60 41.00	(159.46) (134.50)	10.10 3.66/7.31	(33.13) (11.8/23.9)	Alloy Yachts International Studio Scanu & Dalrymple-Smith/Glade Johnson Auckland/New Zealand/2000	1 x 8 cylinder 1000hp Caterpillar 3508 B diesel	Lloyd's ✠100A1, SSC MCA Code Featured in The Superyachts, Volume 14
LAND'S END ex-Fantasia ex-New Horizon IV ex-Anemos I	Twin Screw Motor Yacht Steel	48.55 43.61	(159.28) (143.07)	8.75 2.86	(28.70) (9.33)	Botje Ensing & Co Botje Ensing Groningen/The Netherlands/1965	2 x 7 cylinder 1020hp MAN diesels	Jon Bannenberg redesigned crew and guest cabins Featured in The Superyachts, Volume 3 Lloyd's ✠100A1, ✠LMC

Name	Type	Length m	Length ft	Beam/Draft m	Beam/Draft ft	Builder / Designer / Build	Engines	Notes
CHRISTINA I ex-Zurga	Twin Screw Motor Yacht Steel	48.51 43.61	(159.16) (143.07)	8.76 2.84	(28.75) (9.33)	Botje Ensing & Co Botje Ensing Groningen/The Netherlands/1961	2 x 7 cylinder 1020hp MAN diesels	Rebuilt and modernised 1984
BELLISSIMA C ex-Bellissima ex-Dora H	Twin Screw Motor Yacht Steel	48.50 44.05	(159.13) (144.53)	8.64 2.40	(28.35) (7.89)	Anastassiades & Tsortanides Diana Yacht Design/1988 Perama/Greece/1973	2 x 12 cylinder 1050hp MTU diesels	Lloyd's ✠100A1, ✠LMC. Refitted during 1988/1989 Featured in The Superyachts, Volume 3
THALIA	Auxiliary Ketch Aluminium	48.42 37.60	(158.86) (123.36)	9.70 4.10	(31.82) (13.45)	Vitters Shipyard BV Holland/Meurer Zwartsluis/The Netherlands/1994	1 x 8 cylinder 1000hp Caterpillar 3508 DI-TA diesel	Featured in The Superyachts, Volume 8
CORELIA	Auxiliary Centreboard Ketch Steel/Aluminium	48.28 37.79	(158.40) (124.00)	9.14 3.44	(30.00) (11.30)	Perini Navi Perini Navi/Perini Navi Viareggio/Italy/1992	2 x MTU 739hp	
MORNING GLORY	Auxiliary Centreboard Ketch Steel/Aluminium	48.28 37.79	(158.40) (124.00)	9.14 3.44	(30.00) (11.30)	Perini Navi Perini Navi/Perini Navi Viareggio/Italy/1992	2 x MTU 739hp	
KATRION	Twin Screw Motor Yacht Steel/Aluminium	48.20 41.75	(158.10) (136.97)	8.68 2.90	(28.48) (9.51)	Feadship – De Vries Scheepsbouw De Voogt/De Voogt/Munford Aalsmeer/The Netherlands/1997	2 x 12 cylinder 918hp Caterpillar 3508 DI-TA diesels	Featured in The Superyachts, Volume 11 Lloyd's ✠100A1, ✠LMC
KANALOA ex-Pegaso of the Cayman Islands	Twin Screw Motor Yacht Steel	48.20 42.30	(158.14) (138.78)	9.08 2.40	(29.80) (7.87)	CRN CRN/Scanu/Zuretti Ancona/Italy/1996	2 x 12 cylinder 2100hp Deutz MWM TBD 620 diesels	Featured in The Superyachts, Volume 10 Lloyd's ✠100A1, ✠LMC
LADY GEORGINA ex-Klementine ex-Katalina	Twin Screw Motor Yacht Steel	48.19 42.70	(158.10) (140.09)	8.69 2.89	(28.51) (9.48)	Amels Makkum BV Diana Yacht Design Makkum/The Netherlands/1982	2 x 6 cylinder 910hp Deutz diesels	Lloyd's ✠100A1, ✠LMC
LEGACY	Auxiliary Twin Screw Ketch Steel/Aluminium	48.15 38.57	(158.00) (126.52)	9.20 7.71/3.38	(30.18) (25.29/11.09)	Perini Navi Perini Navi/Perini Navi/Perini Navi Viareggio/Italy/1995	2 x 12 cylinder 750hp MTU 183 12V diesels	
MI GAEA ex-Blue Moon C ex-Mi Gaea	Twin Screw Motor Yacht Steel/Aluminium	48.15 42.10	(158.00) (138.12)	8.75 2.95	(28.70) (9.70)	Feadship – De Vries Scheepsbouw De Voogt/Starkey Aalsmeer/The Netherlands/1990	2 x 12 cylinder 913hp Caterpillar 3512 DI-TA diesels	Featured in The Superyachts, Volume 4 Lloyd's ✠100A1, ✠LMC
ASEAN LADY	Twin Screw Motor Yacht GRP	48.00 44.51	(157.48) (146.04)	8.20	(27.00)	Sterling Yacht & Shipbuilders (Formerly Nishi Dockyards) Ise City/Japan/1983	2 x 12 cylinder 1055hp Caterpillar 3512 DI-TA diesels	
ATTESSA ex-Impromptu Atlanta	Twin Screw Motor Yacht Steel	48.00 39.15	(157.48) (128.45)	8.18 2.62	(26.83) (8.59)	Feadship – Van Lent & Zonen De Voogt/De Voogt/Chase Kaag/The Netherlands/1988	2 x 16 cylinder 730hp GM92TA diesels	Featured in The Superyachts, Volume 2 Lengthened by 11.5m and refitted with interior design by Glade Johnson in 1999
WEDGE ONE ex-Daria	Twin Screw Motor Yacht Steel	47.85 43.30	(157.00) (142.06)	8.65 2.87	(28.42) (9.42)	Feadship – De Vries Scheepsbouw De Voogt/Barnard Aalsmeer/The Netherlands/1980	2 x 16 cylinder 1141hp Caterpillar 399PCTA diesels	
GULNEV	Twin Screw Motor Yacht Steel	47.78	(156.75)	8.10	(26.58)	Fratelli Benetti Benetti/Benetti/Benetti Viareggio/Italy/1970	2 x 8 cylinder 640hp MAN diesels	Bureau Veritas 13/3E, ✠Yacht, ✠MOT
BLOWZY	Triple Water Jet Motor Yacht Aluminium	47.64 40.90	(156.30) (134.17)	8.50 2.00	(27.88) (6.56)	Diaship/Heesen Shipyards Mulder/Mulder/Diaship Oss/The Netherlands/1998	2 x 16 cylinder 3699hp MTU4000 TE90 diesels 1 x Lycoming TF 40 gas turbine	
MONITOR ex-Legend of Tintagel, ex-Lady in Red, ex-Parts V	Twin Screw Motor Yacht Aluminium	47.60	(156.20)	8.53 2.74	(28.00) (8.99)	Picchiotti SpA Arthur De Fever/Murray & Assoc 1982	2 x 12 cylinder 850hp	Lloyd's ✠100A1, ✠LMC Lengthened and refitted in 1999 at Colonna, Virginia Featured in The Superyachts, Volume 2
NENINKA ex-Azzurra	Twin Screw Motor Yacht Steel	47.58	(156.10)	9.20 2.40	(30.18) (7.87)	CRN CRN/Gilgenast/Paola D Smith Ancona/Italy/1988	2 x 12 cylinder 500hp MTU 396TB93 diesels	Featured in The Superyachts, Volume 2
ARIA	Twin Screw Motor Yacht Aluminium	47.50 39.80	(156.00) (130.50)	9.02 2.13	(29.59) (7.00)	Sensation Yachts Ray Harvey/Donald Starkey/Sensation Auckland/New Zealand/2000	2 x 16 cylinder 2650hp Caterpillar 3516 diesels	MCA Code Featured in The Superyachts, Volume 15

YACHT'S NAME ex-name(s)	PROPULSION TYPE / CONSTRUCTION	DIMENSIONS LOA/LOA including spars / Length water line m (ft)	Beam (Maximum) / Draught m (ft)	BUILDER / NAVAL ARCHITECT/STYLIST/ INTERIOR DESIGNER / WHERE/YEAR	ENGINES Number & Cylinders / Horse Power / Maker/Type	REMARKS
ANSON BELL	Twin Screw Motor Yacht Aluminium	47.55 40.30 (156.00) (132.20)	8.65 4.50 (28.38) (14.76)	Palmer Johnson Vripack International/Sparkman & Stephens Wisconsin/USA/2002	2 x 8 cylinder 2000hp Caterpillar 3508B DI-TA diesels	Lloyds ✠100A1, ✠LMC, MCA Code
THEMIS ex-Allegra	Twin Screw Motor Yacht Aluminium	47.54 (156.00)	8.53 2.13 (28.00) (7.00)	Trinity Yachts Trinity/Paragon Design/ Robinson & Sabates New Orleans/USA/1998	2 x 8 cylinder 1191hp Caterpillar 3512B diesels	ABS ✠A1 AMS Yachting Service
CHARLY COPPERS	Twin Screw Motor Yacht Steel/Aluminium	47.50 40.70 (155.84) (133.50)	9.50 2.30 (31.16) (7.55)	Codecasa Codecasa/Codecasa/Della Role Viareggio/Italy/1996	2 x 12 cylinder 2285hp MTU 396TE94 diesels	Lloyd's ✠100A1, ✠LMC Featured in The Superyachts, Volume 10
D'NATALIN II ex-Excellence II	Twin Screw Motor Yacht Steel	47.50 42.00 (155.10) (137.10)	8.90 2.90 (29.20) (9.51)	Feadship – Van Lent & Zonen BV De Voogt/Sam Sorgiovanni Kaag/The Netherlands/1999	2 x 8 cylinder 2250hp Caterpillar 3508B DI-TA diesels	
TATASU	Twin Screw Motor Yacht Steel/Aluminium	47.50 (155.84)	8.60 2.80 (28.21) (9.18)	Feadship – Van Lent & Zonen BV De Voogt/Tanter/Larvor Kaag/The Netherlands/1994	2 x 12 cylinder 12V 149TA DDEC Detroit diesels	
HYPERION	Sloop Aluminium	47.42 38.80 (155.58) (127.30)	9.56 4.80 (31.36) (15.75)	Royal Huisman Shipyard German Frers/Beeldsnijder Vollenhove/The Netherlands/1998	2 x 12 cylinder 1100hp MTU DDC 2000 diesels	Lloyd's hull certificate Featured in The Superyachts, Volume 13
MITSEAAH	Auxiliary Sloop Alustar	47.40 42.50 (155.8) (139.43)	10.20 7.00/2.00 (33.5) (22.96/6.56)	Pendennis Shipyard Pedrick/Leibowitz & Pritchard Falmouth/UK/2003	2 x 12 cylinder 3500hp Paxman 12vp	ABS classification
VA BENE ex-Petara ex-Anthea PA	Twin Screw Motor Yacht Steel/Aluminium	47.40 42.00 (155.51) (137.80)	9.10 2.75 (29.85) (9.02)	Euroship Kees Cornelissen Richard Hein TAG Waaldijk/The Netherlands/1992	2 x 12 cylinder 1750hp Caterpillar 3512DI-TA diesels	Featured in The Superyachts, Volume 8 Lloyd's ✠100A1, ✠LMC
VAVA	Twin Screw Motor Yacht Steel/Aluminium	47.30 (155.18)	8.70 2.70 (28.54) (8.86)	Feadship – Van Lent & Zonen De Voogt/De Nijs Kaag/The Netherlands/1996	2 x 12 cylinder 1191hp Caterpillar 3512 DI-TA diesels	
INSPIRATION ex-Bubba Too	Twin Screw Motor Yacht Aluminium	47.26 41.18 (155.06) (135.10)	8.53 2.15 (28.00) (7.06)	Broward Marine Broward/Broward/Marc-Michaels Fort Lauderdale/USA/1994	2 x 16 cylinder 2400hp Detroit/Allison 16V-149 DDEC	
LIQUIDITY	Twin Screw Motor Yacht GRP	47.24 42.98 (155.00) (141.00)	8.53 2.32 (28.00) (7.60)	Christensen Shipyard Christensen Vancouver/Canada/2001	2 x 16 cylinder 1820hp Detroit diesels	ABS AMS, ✠100A1 MCA Code
ORIENTAL HONOUR	Twin Screw Motor Yacht GRP	47.24 42.98 (155.00) (141.00)	8.53 2.32 (28.00) (7.60)	Christensen Shipyard Christensen Vancouver/Canada/2002	2 x 12 cylinder 2200hp MTU T396 TE 84 diesels	ABS, AMS ✠100A1. MCA Code
SILVER LINING	Twin Screw Motor Yacht GRP	47.24 42.98 (155.00) (141.00)	8.38 2.13 (27.50) (7.00)	Christensen Motor Yacht Corporation Christensen/Glade Johnson Vancouver/USA/1997	2 x 12 cylinder 1948hp Deutz 604BV12 diesels	
KALIZMA ex-Odysseia ex-Cortynia, ex-Minona	Triple Screw Motor Yacht Steel	47.20/50.30 37.50 (154.86/165.03) (123.03)	6.40 2.89 (21.00) (9.50)	Ramage & Ferguson GL Watson Leith/UK/1906	1 x 12 cylinder 550hp MAN & 2 x 6 cylinder 250hp Mercedes diesels	Rebuilt and modernised 1955 and restored to original hull lines in 1991. Featured in The Superyachts, Volume 5
ANDROMEDA LA DEA	Auxiliary Twin Screw Ketch Steel/Aluminium	47.00 34.69 (154.20) (113.82)	9.20 3.37 (30.18) (11.06)	Perini Navi Perini Navi/Perini Navi/Perini Navi Viareggio/Italy/1990	2 x 12 cylinder 600hp MTU diesels	Featured in The Superyachts, Volume 4
EDGEWATER FORTUNE	Twin Screw Motor Yacht Wood/Aluminum	46.93 40.84 (154.00) (134.00)	8.53 2.74 (28.00) (9.00)	Victoria Machinery HR Johansen (refit) Victoria/British Colombia/1954	2 x 12 cylinder 1265hp Cleveland GM12	Canadian Navy minesweeper converted in 1969 in New Westminster
SCHEHERAZADE	Auxiliary Ketch Composite	46.93 (154.00)	8.71 (28.57)	Hodgdon Yachts Bruce King/Andrew Winch Maine/USA/2003		

Name	Type / Construction	LOA m (ft)	LWL m (ft)	Beam m (ft)	Draft m (ft)	Builder / Designer / Year	Engines	Notes
ROXANA	Twin Screw Motor Yacht / GRP	46.93 (154.00)	41.45 (136.00)	9.14 (30.00)	2.13 (7.00)	Admiral Marine/Glenn Bauer / Donald Starkey Designs / Port Townsend/USA/1997	2 x 12 cylinder 1650hp Caterpillar 3512B diesels	Featured in The Superyachts, Volume 13
MIKADO	Auxiliary Twin Screw Ketch / Aluminium	46.93 (154.00)	38.04 (126.00)	9.30 (30.51)	3.23 (10.50)	Hitachi Zosen / Garden/Francis & Francis / Kanagawa/Japan/1987	2 x 16 cylinder 486hp Detroit 92NA diesels	Featured in The Superyachts, Volume 6. Lengthened and refitted by Camper & Nicholsons 1992
HUD HUD ex-Yemoja	Twin Screw Motor Yacht / Steel/Aluminium	46.90 (153.86)	42.00 (137.80)	8.60 (28.21)	2.75 (9.02)	Feadship – Van Lent & Zonen BV / De Voogt/De Voogt/Lanvor / Kaag/The Netherlands/1994	2 x 8 cylinder 918hp Caterpillar 3508 DI-TA diesels	Lloyd's ✠100A1, ✠LMC
CHARADE	Twin Screw Motor Yacht / Steel	46.88 (153.81)	41.84 (137.27)	8.51 (27.11)	2.93 (9.61)	Feadship – De Vries Scheepsbouw / De Voogt/De Voogt/McMillan / Aalsmeer/The Netherlands/1990	2 x 8 cylinder 918hp Caterpillar 3508 DI-TA diesels	Featured in The Superyachts, Volume 4
CHEROSA	Twin Screw Motor Yacht / Steel/Aluminium	46.80 (153.54)	42.06 (138.00)	8.50 (28.00)	2.70 (9.00)	Swiftships Inc / Boland/Chase/Franzen & Associates / Louisiana/USA/1999	2 x 12 cylinder 2250hp MTU 12V396TE94 diesels	Featured in The Superyachts, Volume 13. ABS, ✠A1 Yachting Service, AMS
ELPAGA ex-Alpega, ex-Aresa ex-Mohameda Ecoblanca ex-Alpega	Twin Screw Motor Yacht / Steel	46.72 (153.28)	40.83 (133.95)	9.51 (31.20)	4.20 (13.77)	Campanella Cantieri Navali Boretti / Boretti/de Jorio / Savona/Italy/1975	2 x 6 cylinder 870hp Deutz MWM diesels	Lloyd's ✠100A1, ✠LMC. Rebuilt 1977 and 1982
DAYBREAK ex-Quintessence	Twin Screw Motor Yacht / Steel/Aluminium	46.70 (153.21)	40.20 (131.89)	8.65 (28.38)	2.75 (9.02)	Feadship – Van Lent & Zonen / De Voogt/De Voogt/Lanvor / Kaag/The Netherlands/1997	2 x 12 cylinder 918hp Caterpillar 3508DI-TA diesels	Featured in The Superyachts, Volume 11
MADIBLUE ex-Parts VI	Triple Water Jet Motor Yacht / Aluminium	46.66 (153.08)	37.47 (122.93)	8.36 (27.42)	1.12 (3.66)	Oceanfast Pty Ltd / Curran/Bannenberg/Bannenberg / Perth/Australia/1986	2 x 1960hp & 1 x 1305hp MTU diesels	Featured in The Superyachts, Volume 1
CHARISMA ex-Sea Kingdom ex-Sea Amenity ex-Enterprise IV	Twin Screw Motor Yacht / Steel	46.63 (153.00)		8.40 (27.56)	2.60 (8.53)	Feadship – Van Lent & Zonen / De Voogt/De Voogt/Melse / Kaag/The Netherlands/1985	2 x 12 cylinder 800hp GM 149 diesels	Refitted in 2000
DETROIT EAGLE	Twin Screw Motor Yacht / Aluminium	46.60 (152.89)	39.57 (129.83)	8.80 (28.87)	2.00 (6.56)	Feadship – De Vries Scheepsbouw / De Voogt/De Voogt/Munford / Aalsmeer/The Netherlands/2000	2 x 16 cylinder 3650hp MTU DDC 4000 diesels & 1 x Honeywell TF50 gas turbine	Water jet propulsion
LION WIND ex-Mi Alicia, ex-Azteca	Twin Screw Motor Yacht / Aluminium	46.60 (152.89)	39.65 (130.09)	8.40 (27.56)	2.55 (8.36)	Feadship/De Vries Scheepsbouw / De Voogt/Bannenberg/Bannenberg / Aalsmeer/The Netherlands/1983	2 x 16 cylinder 2706hp MTU diesels	Lloyd's ✠100A1, ✠LMC. Featured in The Superyachts Volume 4
PARAISO	Twin Screw Motor Yacht / Aluminium	46.60 (152.89)	39.65 (130.09)	8.40 (27.56)	2.55 (8.36)	Feadship – Van Lent & Zonen / De Voogt/Bannenberg/Bannenberg / Kaag/The Netherlands/1983	2 x 16 cylinder 2706hp MTU diesels	Lloyd's ✠100A1, ✠LMC
SHERGAR	Triple Water Jet Motor Yacht / Steel	46.60 (152.89)		7.45 (24.44)	2.00 (6.56)	Lürssen Werft / Lürssen/Gilgenast / Bremen/Germany/1983	2 x 1480hp 12V 396T883-MTU diesels & 2 x 6100hp Allison Gas Turbines	Owned by the Aga Khan
GENESIS	Twin Screw Motor Yacht / Aluminium	46.50 (152.56)	39.00 (127.94)	9.00 (29.52)	2.20 (7.22)	North American Yachts & Shipbuilding / Sergio Cutolo/Luiz de Basto/Ralph Lauren / Livorno/Italy/2002	2 x 12 cylinder 2250hp Caterpillar 3512 diesels	ABS, MCA Code
PIROPO IV	Auxiliary Twin Screw Ketch / Steel/Aluminium	46.50 (152.56)	34.96 (113.82)	9.20 (30.19)	3.32 (10.89)	Perini Navi / Perini Navi/Perini Navi / Viareggio/Italy/1991	2 x 12 cylinder 600hp MTU 183TC91 diesels	ABS classified
QUINTESSA ex-Anastasia Ve	Twin Screw Motor Yacht / Steel	46.50 (152.56)	42.00 (137.80)	8.59 (28.20)	3.09 (10.23)	Feadship – Van Lent & Zonen / De Voogt/De Voogt/Sturchio / Kaag/The Netherlands/1989	2 x 16 cylinder 1572hp Caterpillar 3516DI-TA diesels	Lloyd's ✠100A1, ✠LMC
TAMSEN ex-Liberty	Auxiliary Twin Screw Ketch / Steel/Aluminium	46.50 (152.56)	34.96 (113.82)	9.20 (30.19)	3.32 (10.89)	Perini Navi / Perini Navi/Perini Navi/Perini Navi / Viareggio/Italy/1991	2 x 12 cylinder 600hp MTU 183TC91 diesels	ABS classified
KWIKUMAT ex-Limelight ex-Confidante	Twin Screw Motor Yacht / Steel/Aluminium	46.45 (152.40)	41.35 (135.66)	8.18 (26.83)	2.73 (8.95)	Feadship – Van Lent & Zonen / De Voogt/De Voogt/P Tanter / Kaag/The Netherlands/1987	2 x 8 cylinder 1000hp Caterpillar diesels	Lengthened in 1992 and interior refitted to the design of Paola D Smith

Yacht's name / ex-name(s)	Propulsion Type / Construction	LOA/LOA incl. spars / LWL — m (ft)	Beam (Max) / Draught — m (ft)	Builder / Naval Architect/Stylist/Interior Designer / Where/Year	Engines — Number & Cylinders / Horse Power / Maker/Type	Remarks
CHANTAL MA VIE, ex-Atlantique, ex-Nordic Prince	Twin Screw Motor Yacht, Steel	46.32 (152.00)	7.40 (24.27) / 2.60 (8.53)	Nylen / Nylen/Krogen/Benskey / Fort Lauderdale/USA/1984	2 x 6 cylinder 365 hp Caterpillar diesels	Lengthened in 1995
MONTIGNE, ex-Monteath, ex-Paminusch	Twin Screw Motor Yacht, Steel	46.32 / 39.30 (152.00)/(128.94)	8.40 (27.56) / 2.90 (9.51)	Feadship—De Vries Scheepsbouw / De Voogt/Glade Johnson/Tanter / Aalsmeer/The Netherlands/1986	2 x 12 cylinder 913 hp Caterpillar 3512DI-TA diesels	Lloyd's ✠100A1, ✠LMC. Lengthened in 1998
TM BLUE ONE	Twin Screw Motor Yacht, Steel	46.32 / 37.70 (152.00)/(123.60)	9.20 (30.25) / 2.40 (7.75)	Picchiotti SpA / Gilgenas/Marino / Viareggio/Italy/1988	2 x 12 cylinder 1250hp Caterpillar 3412TA diesels	Featured in The Superyachts, Volume 3. Refitted 1995
WINDROSE	Auxiliary Schooner, Aluminium	46.32 / 29.30 (152.00)/(96.12)	8.00 (24.24) / 4.30 (14.10)	Holland Jachtbouw / Dijkstra & Partners / Zaandam/Holland/2001	1 x cylinder 425hp Lugger diesel	Featured in The Superyachts, Volume 16
ONTARIO, ex-Maalana, ex-Falco	Twin Screw Motor Yacht, Steel	46.30 / 40.80 (151.91)/(133.86)	9.60 (31.50) / 2.60 (8.53)	Lürssen Werft / Lürssen/MPS Design/Sylvestrin / Bremen/Germany/1988	2 x 8 cylinder 855hp Caterpillar 34508DI-TA diesels	Featured in The Superyachts, Volume 6
SHANTI, ex-Shireen, ex-El Bravo	Twin Screw Motor Yacht, Steel	46.26 / 41.08 (151.80)/(134.80)	8.38 (27.50) / 2.71 (8.90)	Campanella / Navigator / Savona/Italy/1981	2 x 6 cylinder 1320hp Nohab Polar diesels	Lloyd's ✠100A1, ✠LMC. Refitted 1993
SALLY ANN	Twin Screw Motor Yacht, GRP	46.23 / 41.15 (151.66)/(135.00)	9.32 (30.58) / 2.56 (8.41)	Delta Marine / Delta/Delta/Hoeferlin / Seattle/USA/1996	2 x 12 cylinder 855hp Caterpillar 3508TA diesels	Featured in The Superyachts, Volume 11
OCEAN STAR, ex-Fath Al Khair	Twin Screw Motor Yacht, Steel	46.20 / 38.73 (151.58)/(127.06)	6.72 (22.05) / 3.98 (13.06)	CRN / CRN/Dilday / Ancona/Italy/1978	2 x 16 cylinder 1355hp GM149TI diesels	Lloyd's ✠100A1, ✠LMC
WHITE KNIGHT, ex-White Night of Araby, ex-Night, ex-Sociego	Twin Screw Motor Yachts, Steel	46.20 / 41.74 (151.55)/(136.92)	7.20 (23.62) / 2.40 (7.87)	CRN / Astillero Navale Argentina/Jorge Chediek / Ancona/Italy/1985	2 x cylinders 1300hp GM Detroit diesels	Refitted at Cormoran Ltd, Greece in 2000 with styling by Aldo Viani and interior designer by Katia Corfini
TURMOIL	Twin Screw Motor Yacht, Aluminium	46.19 / 41.75 (151.54)/(136.97)	8.81 (28.90) / 2.74 (9.00)	Palmer Johnson Incorporated / Vripack Yachting/Van der Meulen / Sturgeon Bay/USA/1996	2 x 8 cylinder 820hp Caterpillar 3508DI-TA diesels	Featured in The Superyachts, Volume 10
FLAMINGO DAZE	Motor Yacht	46.12 (151.31)	8.84 (29.00)	Hakvoort / Vripack/Clade Johnson Design, Inc / The Netherlands/2003	2 x 1920hp	
AFFINITY	Twin Screw Motor Yacht, GRP	46.02 / 41.15 (150.99)/(135.00)	9.58 (31.42) / 2.21 (7.25)	Delta Marine / Delta/Holland/Ardeo Design / Seattle/USA/1999	2 x 8 cylinder 1000hp Caterpillar 3508TA diesels	
THE HIGHLANDER	Twin Screw Motor Yacht, Steel	46.02 / 39.70 (150.99)/(130.25)	8.59 (28.17) / 2.97 (9.75)	Feadship—De Vries Scheepsbouw / De Voogt/Bannenberg/Bannenberg / Aalsmeer/The Netherlands/1986	2 x 16 cylinder 1060hp Detroit diesels	
ADELA	Auxiliary Schooner, Steel	46.00/55.10 / 30.20 (150.91/180.77)/(99.09)	7.90 (25.92) / 4.80 (15.75)	Pendennis Shipyard / Dijkstra/Leroy / Falmouth/UK/1995	1 x 6 cylinder 640hp Lugger 6170A diesel	Featured in The Superyachts, Volume 9. Lengthened by 3.6m at Pendennis Shipyard in 2000
MAUPITI	Twin Screw Motor Yacht, Steel	46.00 / 42.00 (150.90)/(137.80)	9.00 (29.52) / 3.40 (11.15)	Amels Holland BV / Amels/Disdale/Marino / Makkum/The Netherlands/1993	3 x 8 cylinder 745hp Caterpillar 3508DI-TA diesels	Lloyd's ✠100Al, ✠LMC, UMS. Exploration Yacht. diesel Electric Propulsion
MYSTERE, ex-Australian Enterprise	Twin Screw Motor Yacht, Aluminium	46.00 / 35.00 (150.90)/(114.83)	9.00 (29.52) / 2.40 (7.87)	Lloyd's Ships / Lloyd's Ships / Bulimba/Australia/1987	2 x 12 cylinder 1500hp MTU 396TB83 diesels	Lloyd's ✠100A1, ✠LMC. Carries a submarine. Fourth deck, built from carbon fibre, added in 1995
SHAMWARI	Twin Screw Motor Yacht, Steel	46.00 (150.90)	8.82 (28.93) / 2.02 (6.63)	Benetti Shipyard / Benetti/Natucci/Zuretti / Viareggio/Italy/1991	2 x 12 cylinder 2000hp MTU 396TB93 diesels	Featured in The Superyachts, Volume 5

Name	Type / Construction	LOA / LWL (m)	LOA / LWL (ft)	Beam / Draft (m)	Beam / Draft (ft)	Builder / Designer / Place / Year	Engines	Notes
NORTHERN LIGHT	Twin Screw Motor Yacht	46.00	(150.90)	8.80 / 2.95	(28.87) / (9.67)	Feadship – De Vries Scheepsbouw De Voogt/De Voogt/Munford The Netherlands/2001	2 x 8 cylinder 1014hp Caterpillar 3508B DI-TA diesels	Lloyd's ✠100A1, SSC Yacht G6, ✠LMC MCA Code Featured in The Superyachts, Volume 16
PARIS ex-Paminusch	Twin Screw Motor Yacht Steel	45.99 / 41.78	(150.89) / (137.08)	8.32 / 2.68	(27.29) / (8.79)	Feadship – De Vries Scheepsbouw De Voogt/De Voogt/De Fever Aalsmeer/The Netherlands/1982	2 x 12 cylinder 862hp Caterpillar 398PC-TA diesels	Lloyd's ✠100A1, ✠LMC
FORTUNATE SUN ex-Dream ex-Samantha Lin	Twin Screw Motor Yacht Steel	45.97 / 39.80	(150.81) / (130.57)	9.40 / 2.67	(30.84) / (8.76)	Tacoma Shipbuilding, Inc. Gilgenast/Teague/Carson Tacoma/USA/1992	2 x 8 cylinder 775hp Caterpillar 3508 diesels	ABS ✠A1, Circle E, AMS, ABCU
SUNRISE ex-Xasteria	Auxiliary Twin Screw Ketch Steel	45.88 / 34.75	(150.50) / (114.00)	9.21 / 6.16	(30.20) / (20.20)	Perini Navi Perini Navi/Perini Navi Viareggio/Italy/1990	2 x 12 cylinder 600hp MTU diesels	Featured in The Superyachts, Volume 9
NO ESCAPE ex-Flying Dutchman	Twin Screw Motor Yacht Aluminium	45.86 / 39.20	(150.46) / (128.62)	8.50 / 2.50	(27.89) / (8.20)	Diaship/Heesen Shipyards Diaship Design Team Oss/The Netherlands/1999	2 x 16 cylinder 3482hp MTU 396TB94 diesels	ABS ✠A1 Yachting Service, AMS. Featured in The Superyachts, Volume 13
AMORAZUR II ex-La Baroness	Twin Screw Motor Yacht Aluminium	45.75	(150.10)	8.23 / 1.83	(27.00) / (6.00)	Palmer Johnson Incorporated Palmer Johnson/Tom Fexas/Knack Sturgeon Bay/USA/1994	2 x 12 cylinder 1900hp Deutz TBD604 diesels	Interior refit by Terence Disdale Design/1999
ETOILE DU NORD ex-Havre du Grace	Twin Screw Motor Yacht Steel	45.75	(150.10)	7.52 / 3.90	(24.67) / (12.80)	Auroux Auroux Arcachon/France/1968	2 x 12 cylinder 725hp Baudoin DVX diesels	Built as a pilot vessel and converted to superyacht standards in 1990 in Barcelona. Bureau Veritas Class 1 3/3E
IONIAN PRINCESS	Twin Screw Motor Yacht Composite	45.72	(150.00)	8.40 / 2.16	(27.55) / (7.08)	Christensen/Palmer Johnson Palmer Johnson/Pavlik Design Savannah/USA/2003	2 x 16 cylinder 2040hp MTU 396TE84 diesels	ABS
ISTRANKA ex-Princess Haifa ex-Istranka, ex-Kraljevica	Twin Screw Motor Yacht Steel	45.72 / 42.36	(150.00) / (139.00)	7.59 / 2.64	(24.93) / (8.69)	Brodogradiliste Shipyard Brodogradiliste Rijeka/Yugoslavia/1959	2 x 12 cylinder 1120hp Maybach diesels	Formerly Presidential Yacht of President Tito of Yugoslavia. Rebuilt 2000 by Valdettaro Shipyard
LADY LINDA ex-Bellini	Twin Screw Motor Yacht Aluminium	45.72 / 40.54	(150.00) / (132.99)	8.53 / 2.13	(28.00) / (7.00)	Trinity Yachts Trinity Yachts/Paragon/Robinson New Orleans/USA/1999	2 x 12 cylinder 2250hp Caterpillar 3512 B diesels	Featured in The Superyachts, Volume 14
MATANTHAR ex-Carmac VII	Twin Screw Motor Yacht Steel/Aluminium	45.72 / 41.52	(150.00) / (136.23)	8.60 / 2.72	(28.22) / (8.92)	Feadship – Van Lent & Zonen De Voogt/De Voogt/Chan Kaag/The Netherlands/1991	2 x 16 cylinder 930hp Detroit 149N diesels	Featured in The Superyachts, Volume 5
MYSTIC	Twin Screw Motor Yacht Composite	45.72 / 41.33	(150.00) / (135.59)	8.53 / 2.32	(27.98) / (7.61)	Christensen Shipyards Christensen Shipyards Vancouver/Canada/2002	2 x V8 1820hp MTU/DDC V8 4000	
NOBLE HOUSE ex-Princess Marla ex-Victory Lane	Twin Screw Motor Yacht Aluminium	45.72	(150.00)	8.53 / 2.13	(27.98) / (7.00)	Trinity Yachts Trinity/Paragon/Robinson New Orleans/USA/1998	2 x 16 cylinder 1800hp DDC/MTU 16V2000 diesels	Featured in The Superyachts, Volume 12
NOVA SPIRIT	Twin Screw Motor Yacht Aluminium	45.72	(150.00)	9.14 / 2.13	(30.00) / (7.00)	Trinity Yachts Trinity/Paragon/Robinson New Orleans/USA/1999	2 x 8 cylinder 2250hp Caterpillar 3508B diesels	ABS, A1 yachting Service, AMS
VICTORS CHOICE	Twin Screw Motor Yacht GRP	45.72 / 42.06	(150.00) / (138.00)	8.38 / 2.08	(27.50) / (6.83)	Christensen Motor Yacht Corporation Christensen/Yamkasikom Vancouver/USA/1997	2 x 12 cylinder 2040hp MTU 396TE84 diesels	
PERFECT PERSUASION ex-Perfect Prescription	Twin Screw Motor Yacht Composite	45.70 / 40.87	(149.93) / (134.09)	8.10 / 2.32	(26.57) / (7.61)	Oceanfast Pty Ltd Curran/Starkey/Starkey Perth/Australia/1997	2 x 12 cylinder 3147hp Paxman 185 diesels	DNV ✠1A1, LCRO, Yacht EO Featured in The Superyachts, Volume 11
FULMARA ex-Paget, ex-Niki I ex-Luisa II, ex-Carmac III ex-Leonore, ex-Janidore	Twin Screw Motor Yacht Steel	45.69	(149.92)	7.47 / 3.20	(24.50) / (10.50)	Defoe Boat & Motor Works John H Wells Bay City/USA/1930	2 x 8 cylinder 650hp Caterpillar diesels	Rebuilt and lengthened by 4.26m in 1965/1966 and subsequently rebuilt in 1976 and 1991
ANEMOS ex-Eros, ex-Eros II, ex-Dolly	Twin Screw Motor Yacht Steel	45.62 / 41.72	(149.70) / (136.90)	7.58 / 2.56	(24.90) / (8.40)	Ishikawajima-Harima Shipyard IHS/Bannenberg/Bannenberg Tokyo/Japan/1969	2 x 16 cylinder 540hp GM diesels	

YACHT'S NAME ex-name(s)	PROPULSION TYPE / CONSTRUCTION	DIMENSIONS LOA/LOA including spars / Length water line m (ft)	Beam (Maximum) / Draught m (ft)	BUILDER / NAVAL ARCHITECT/STYLIST/ INTERIOR DESIGNER / WHERE/YEAR	ENGINES Number & Cylinders / Horse Power / Maker/Type	REMARKS
ILONA	Twin Screw Motor Yacht / Aluminium/Composite	45.60 40.6 (149.61) (133.21)	9.5 2.7 (31.17) (8.86)	Pendennis Shipyard / Dubois/Redman Whiteley/Nicholsons / Falmouth/UK/1999	2 x 8 cylinder / 960hp / Caterpillar 3508 diesels	DNV, ✠A1, LC RO, Yacht EO / Featured in The Superyachts, Volume 13
NORTHWIND II ex-Chambel IV	Twin Screw Motor Yacht / Steel	45.59 41.10 (149.58) (135.00)	7.22 2.68 (23.69) (8.79)	Camper & Nicholsons Ltd / Nicholson/Nicholson/Nicholson / Gosport/UK/1966	2 x 6 cylinder / 600hp / MAN G6V 23.5/33M diesels	Lloyd's ✠100A1, ✠LMC
APPLAUSE	Twin Screw Motor Yacht / Aluminium	45.55 38.67 (149.45) (126.87)	8.92 1.76 (29.30) (5.50)	Oceanco / The 'A' Group/The 'A' Group / Dreumel/The Netherlands/1994	2 x 16 cylinder / 3045hp / MTU 396TE94 diesels	ABS ✠A1, AMS Yachting Service / Featured in The Superyachts, Volume 9
MAYAN QUEEN ex-Kisses ex-Alfa Alfa III	Twin Screw Motor Yacht / Steel	45.55 39.90 (149.45) (130.91)	8.18 2.64 (26.10) (8.66)	Feadship – Van Lent & Zonen / De Voogt/De Voogt/Knack / Kaag/The Netherlands/1990	2 x 6 cylinder / 770hp / Detroit diesels	Lloyd's ✠100A1, ✠LMC
TERANCAR NADINE ex-Terancar Nitani	Twin Screw Motor Yacht / Steel	45.52 41.10 (149.35) (134.85)	7.86 2.70 (25.79) (8.86)	Camper & Nicholson Ltd / Nicholson/Nicholson/Pomodoro & Fontana / Gosport/UK/1967	2 x 6 cylinder / 600hp / MAN G6V23.5/33M diesels	Lloyd's ✠100A1, ✠LMC / Featured in The Superyachts, Volume 12
BIG D ex-Idolwood II, ex-Katamarino ex-Calliope	Twin Screw Motor Yacht / Steel	45.30 39.50 (148.62) (129.59)	9.00 2.70 (29.52) (8.85)	Hitachi Zosen / Hargrave/Hargrave/Tanter / Tokyo/Japan/1986	2 x 12 cylinder / 1050hp / Caterpillar 3612 diesels	
ALL SEVEN ex-Abdulaziz ex-Aziz I	Twin Screw Motor Yacht / Steel	45.25 38.92 (148.46) (130.65)	8.40 2.20 (27.56) (7.22)	CRN / CRN/CRN/Garzouzi / Ancona/Italy/1987	2 x 8 cylinder / 2200hp / Deutz MWM5BV8M628 diesels	Lloyd's ✠100A1, ✠LMC
TUGATSU ex-September Blue	Twin Screw Motor Yacht / Steel	45.20 (148.29)	8.18 2.56 (26.84) (8.40)	Feadship – Van Lent & Zonen / De Voogt/Starkey / Kaag/The Netherlands/1989	2 x 16 cylinder / 770hp / Detroit 92TA diesels	Featured in The Superyachts, Volume 3 & Volume 10 / Rebuild 1995 by Lürssen Werft with new interior by Bannenberg / and lengthened to incorporate a diving room and stern cockpit
MORE	Twin Screw Motor Yacht / Composite	45.00 37.90 (147.64) (124.34)	9.26 2.72 (30.83) (8.92)	Benetti Shipyard / Benetti/Stefano Righini/François Zuretti / Viareggio/Italy/2002	2 x 16 cylinder / 1325hp / Caterpillar 3508 B	Lloyds ✠100A1 SSC G6 Yacht, / ✠LMC, MCA Code
PATRICIA	Twin Screw Motor Yacht / Composite	45.00 37.90 (147.64) (124.34)	9.26 2.72 (30.83) (8.92)	Benetti Shipyard / Benetti/Stefano Righini/François Zuretti / Viareggio/Italy/2002	2 x 16 cylinder / 1325hp / Caterpillar 3508 B	Lloyds ✠100A1 SSC G6 Yacht, ✠LMC, MCA Code / Featured in The Superyachts, Volume 16
AL MAHBOBA ex-Taiba IV, ex-Big R ex-Jardell II	Twin Screw Motor Yacht / Steel	45.00 39.66 (147.64) (130.12)	8.41 2.79 (27.59) (9.15)	Feadship – De Vries Scheepsbouw / De Voogt/De Voogt / Aalsmeer/The Netherlands/1970	2 x 900hp / GM diesels	
JOALMI	Twin Screw Motor Yacht / Steel	45.00 37.60 (147.64) (123.36)	8.82 2.02 (28.93) (6.63)	Benetti Shipyard / Benetti/Disdale / Viareggio/Italy/1992	2 x 12 cylinder / 2040hp / MTU 396TE84 diesels	Featured in The Superyachts, Volume 6
MOECCA	Twin Water jet Catamaran Motor Yacht / Aluminium/Composite	45.00 34.60 (147.64) (113.52)	13.00 1.80 (42.65) (5.90)	Oceanfast Pty Ltd / Curran/Bannenberg/Bannenberg / Perth/Australia/1992	2 x 16 cylinder / 2584hp / MTU 396TB94 diesels	Featured in The Superyachts, Volume 6
NUFFER ex-Princess Magna ex-Sea Sedan	Twin Screw Motor Yacht / Steel	45.00 37.60 (147.64) (123.36)	8.80 2.15 (28.87) (7.05)	Benetti Shipyard / Benetti/Natucci/Longari / Viareggio/Italy/1988	2 x 12 cylinder / 1958hp / Deutz MWM TBD604B diesels	Refitted in 1993 to designs by Terence Disdale. ABS classified
SECRET LOVE	Auxiliary Ketch / Steel	45.00 35.60 (147.64) (116.79)	8.90 4.38/7.70 (29.19) (14.37)/(25.26)	Jongert BV / Jongert/André Hoek / Medemblik/The Netherlands/2003	1 x 12 cylinder / 714hp / MTU 12V	Lloyds ✠100A1, ✠LMC
ZEUS	Auxiliary Twin Screw Sloop / Wood	45.00 36.50 (147.64) (119.76)	7.40 3.80 (24.28) (12.47)	Robertson / Pedrick Yacht Designs/Thompson / Fort Lauderdale/USA/1993	2 x 8 cylinder / 680hp / MAN D2848LX diesels	
LADY PITA ex-Bengal I ex-Sterling Lady	Twin Screw Motor Yacht / GRP	44.96 36.90 (147.51) (121.10)	8.10 2.40 (26.50) (7.90)	Sterling Yacht and Shipbuilders / Bannenberg/Bannenberg/Pavlik / Ise/Japan/1986	2 x 12 cylinder / 1300hp / Caterpillar diesels	Refitted in 1999 to designs by Pavlik Design Team

Name (ex-names)	Type / Construction	LOA / LWL (m)	LOA / LWL (ft)	Beam / Draft (m)	Beam / Draft (ft)	Builder / Designer / Location / Year	Engines	Classification / Notes
RUSALKA, ex-BBC Challenge	Twin Screw Motor Yacht / GRP	44.96 / 36.90	(147.51) / (121.10)	8.10 / 2.40	(26.50) / (7.90)	Sterling Yacht and Shipbuilders / Bannenberg/Jojima / Ise/Japan/1986	2 x 16 cylinder 1340hp Mitsubishi diesels	
MAHA, ex-Matahari, ex-Maha Al Mojil, ex-Al Mojil 5, ex-Bernadette, ex-Cibeles V, ex-Zimba, ex-Halimede, ex-Mimosan, ex-Bymar, ex-Paridot	Twin Screw Motor Yacht / Steel	44.83 / 40.71	(147.09) / (133.56)	7.04 / 2.89	(23.09) / (9.48)	Defoe Boat and Motor Works / Cox and Stevens / Bay City/USA/1938	2 x 8 cylinder 500hp Caterpillar diesels	
AL FAHEDI	Twin Screw Motor Yacht / Aluminium	44.82 / 40.00	(147.05) / (131.24)	8.00 / 1.80	(26.25) / (5.90)	Baglietto / Baglietto/Zuccon / Varazze/Italy/1986	2 x 16 cylinder 1958hp MTU diesels	Lloyd's ✠100A1, ✠LMC
FORTUNA, ex-Contico of Cayman, ex-Contico	Twin Screw Motor Yacht / Steel	44.80 / 39.31	(147.00) / (128.98)	9.14 / 2.74	(30.00) / (9.00)	Keith Marine / Fryco/Rezende / Florida/USA/1992	2 x 8 cylinder 850hp Caterpillar 3508 diesels	Featured in The Superyachts, Volume 7. Complete refit 1999 with Donald Starkey Design and Nicholson Interiors
GRAN FINALE	Twin Screw Motor Yacht / GRP	44.80 / 39.02	(147.00) / (128.00)	8.69 / 2.06	(28.50) / (6.75)	Delta Marine / Delta Marine/Espinosa/QB Designs / Seattle/USA/2001	2 x 12 cylinder 2400hp Caterpillar 3512 diesels	Featured in The Superyachts, Volume 16
MARATANI X	Twin Screw Motor Yacht / Aluminium	44.80	(147.00)	8.84 / 2.10	(29.00) / (6.88)	Sensation Yachts / Phil Curran/Evan K Marshall / Auckland/New Zealand/2003	2 x 1500hp Caterpillar 3516B	
TAJIN, ex-Nassa Too	Twin Screw Motor Yacht / FRP/Composite	44.80 / 37.18	(147.00) / (122.00)	8.53 / 1.98	(28.00) / (6.50)	Trident Shipworks Inc / Trident/Cutolo/Espinosa / Tampa/USA/2000	2 x 16 cylinder 3050hp MTU 16V 396TE94 diesels	ABS Classification
ZEIN, ex-Angela, ex-Daska, ex-Deo Juvante II, ex-Arion, ex-Rion, ex-Monica	Twin Screw Motor Yacht / Steel	44.80	(147.00)	7.01 / 2.98	(23.00) / (9.80)	Camper & Nicholson / Nicholson/Nicholson/Nicholson / Southampton/UK/1928	2 x 400hp Deutz diesels	Rebuilt in 1966
LADY CHRISTINA OF MERSEYSIDE, ex-Lady Lola, ex-Ambrosia	Twin Screw Motor Yacht / Steel/Aluminium	44.76 / 38.20	(146.85) / (125.33)	8.82 / 3.09	(28.94) / (10.13)	Benetti Shipyard / Benetti/Natucci/Zuretti / Viareggio/Italy/1994	2 x 16 cylinder 2184hp Deutz NWN TBD	ABS ✠A1 AMS. Featured in The Superyachts, Volume 9
TIMONEER II	Auxiliary Ketch / Aluminium	44.75 / 34.51	(146.82) / (113.23)	9.42 / 4.26	(35.89) / (13.98)	Vitters Shipyard / Dubois/Munford/Halstead / Zwartsluis/The Netherlands/2001	1 x 12 cylinder 825hp Caterpillar 3412 diesel	ABS ✠A1. MCA Code
CLELIA, ex-Klelia I, ex-Klelia, ex-Elda, ex-Allebo II, ex-Xinatra	Twin Screw Motor Yacht / Steel	44.74 / 41.02	(146.79) / (134.59)	6.52 / 2.50	(21.39) / (8.20)	NV Scheepswerft Kersholt / Beck / Groningen/The Netherlands/1957	2 x 6 cylinder 200hp GM diesels	Lloyd's ✠100A1, ✠LMC
MARI CHA III	Auxiliary Ketch / Carbon-fibre Composite	44.70 / 38.10	(146.64) / (125.00)	9.14 / 4.50	(30.00) / (14.76)	Sensation Yachts / Briand/Munford / Auckland/New Zealand/1997	1 x 8 cylinder 430hp Caterpillar diesel	Hull built by Marten Marine Industries. Featured in The Superyachts, Volume 12
ANTARCTICA, ex-Enchanter, ex-Turki, ex-Chantal II, ex-Westlake III	Twin Screw Motor Yacht / Steel/Aluminium	44.68 / 39.13	(146.59) / (128.38)	8.02 / 2.92	(26.31) / (9.60)	Feadship – Van Lent & Zonen / De Voogt/De Voogt / Kaag/The Netherlands/1966	2 x 8 cylinder 620hp Deutz diesels	Lloyd's ✠100A1, ✠LMC. Refitted at Perini Navi 2000
CAMPBELL BAY	Twin Screw Motor Yacht / Steel/Aluminium	44.60 / 30.25	(146.30) / (99.23)	8.80 / 3.00	(28.87) / (9.84)	Hakvoort Shipyard / Diana Yacht Design/Buytendijk/Winch / Monnickendam/The Netherlands/2002	2 x 8 cylinder 1828hp Caterpillar 3508 diesels	Featured in The Superyachts, Volume 16
BALAJU	Twin Screw Motor Yacht / Composite	44.50 / 37.40	(145.98) / (122.69)	8.20 / 1.86	(26.90) / (6.10)	Intermarine SpA / Studio Zuretti / La Spezia/Italy/2002	2 x 8 cylinder 1300hp Caterpillar 3508B diesels	Featured in The Superyachts, Volume 16
GRAY MIST III	Twin Screw Motor Yacht / Aluminium	44.50	(146.00)	8.23 / 2.44	(27.00) / (8.00)	Breaux's Bay Craft / Breaux's Bay Craft/Borland/Marchetti / Louisiana/USA/1998	2 x 12 cylinder 1540hp Caterpillar 3512 diesels	Featured in The Superyachts, Volume 12
NO LO SE, ex-Shark, ex-Still-Shark, ex-Shark	Twin Screw Motor Yacht / Steel	44.50 / 38.30	(145.98) / (125.66)	7.25 / 2.90	(23.78) / (9.51)	Abeking & Rasmussen / JFH Roget / Lemwerder/Germany/1971	2 x 6 cylinder Caterpillar diesels	Lloyd's ✠100A1, ✠LMC. Lengthening, extension of superstructure, and complete interior refit at Astilleros de Mallorca in 2001. Interior designer Felix Buytendijk.

YACHT'S NAME ex-name(s)	PROPULSION TYPE CONSTRUCTION	DIMENSIONS LOA/LOA including spars Length water line m (ft)	Beam (Maximum) Draught m (ft)	BUILDER NAVAL ARCHITECT/STYLIST/ INTERIOR DESIGNER WHERE/YEAR	ENGINES Number & Cylinders Horse Power Maker/Type	REMARKS
LADY VICTORIA ex-Khalidia ex-Tracinda Jean, ex-Ultima ex-Kara Kara, ex-Ariane III	Twin Screw Motor Yacht Steel	44.37 39.95 (145.58) (131.07)	7.53 2.62 (24.70) (8.60)	Atlantic Shipbuilding Co Kervarec Newport/UK/1962	2 x 12 cylinder 650hp Baudouin diesels	Refitted at Watershed International Shipyard 1999
CURT-C ex-Netanya V ex-Eastwind	Twin Screw Motor Yacht Aluminium	44.20 38.90 (145.00) (127.62)	7.71 2.40 (25.30) (7.87)	NQEA Australia Pty Ltd Hargrave Cairns/Australia/1989	2 x 12 cylinder 1500hp diesels	Lengthened by 12ft and refitted in 1996 by Dudley Dawson, Palmer Johnson and Glade Johnson. Lloyd's ✠100A1, ✠LMC
PRIMADONNA	Twin Screw Motor Yacht Composite	44.20 (145.00)	8.36 2.06 (27.42) (6.75)	Christensen Shipyard Christensen/Christensen/Smith Vancouver/USA/2002	2 x 8 cylinder 1820hp DDC/MTU diesels	ABS ✠A1, AMS, MCA Code Featured in The Superyachts, Volume 16
LADY M ex-Raven	Twin Screw Motor Yacht Composite	44.20 38.92 (145.00) (127.66)	8.54 2.16 (28.00) (7.08)	Intermarine Savannah Intermarine/Hansen/Cross-Buchanan Savannah/USA/2001	2 x 12 cylinder 4500hp Caterpillar 3512 diesels	
ARTFUL DODGER ex-L'Aquasition	Twin Water Jet Motor Yacht Aluminium	44.19 (144.99)	8.20 2.28 (26.90) (7.5)	Diaship/Heesen Shipyards Gilgenast/Smith Oss/The Netherlands/1990	2 x 16 cylinder 2610 hp MTU 396TB93 diesels	Featured in The Superyachts, Volume 4 Refitted in 1999
IRISH ROVER ex-Aussie Rules ex-Cakewalk, ex-Fiffanella	Twin Screw Motor Yacht Steel	44.10 (144.68)	7.93 2.41 (26.01) (7.91)	Feadship – Van Lent & Zonen De Voogt/De Voogt/Puleo Kaag/The Netherlands/1987	2 x 8 cylinder 786hp Caterpillar 3508DI-TA diesels	Featured in The Superyachts, Volume 3 Lengthened by 12ft in 1995
SEA SHAW	Twin Screw Motor Yacht GRP	44.10 37.40 (144.68) (122.70)	8.80 2.00 (28.87) (6.56)	Cheoy Lee Shipyards Mulder/Mulder/In-Design Hong Kong/1995	2 x 12 cylinder 1980hp MTU 396TE84 diesels	Featured in The Superyachts, Volume 10
FORTUNATE SUN ex-Cristal A ex-Sea Jewel	Twin Screw Motor Yacht Steel	44.00 38.10 (144.36) (125.00)	8.20 2.96 (26.90) (9.71)	Feadship – De Vries Scheepsbouw De Voogt/Disdale/Disdale Aalsmeer/The Netherlands/1987	2 x 8 cylinder 786hp Caterpillar 3508DI-TA diesels	Lloyd's ✠100A1, ✠LMC
JAMEEL ex-Eastern Star ex-Jameel	Twin Screw Motor Yacht Steel	44.00 37.64 (144.36) (123.50)	7.76 2.31 (25.46) (7.58)	CRN CRN/Dilday Ancona/Italy/1985	2 x 12 cylinder 2058hp MTU 652TB61 diesels	Owned by Sheik Khalid Bin Ahmed Al Khalifa Lloyd's ✠100A1, ✠LMC
NEW MASTER ex-Master II	Twin Screw Motor Yacht Aluminium	44.00 (144.36)	8.80 2.60 (28.87) (8.53)	Baglietto Shipyard SpA Studio Ruggiero/Studio Ruggiero Varazze/Italy/2001	2 x 16 cylinder 2450hp MWM620 TBD 16V diesels	RINA, ✠A1.1'Y'
RHAPSODY	Twin Screw Motor Yacht Steel/Aluminium	44.00 37.50 (144.36) (123.04)	8.80 2.80 (28.87) (9.19)	Hakvoort Shipyard Diana Yacht Design/DYD/Buytendijk Monnickendam/The Netherlands/2000	2 x 8 cylinder 940hp Caterpillar 3508 diesels	
SANDRA ex-Xanthia B, ex-Rora V	Twin Screw Motor Yacht Steel	44.00 38.80 (144.36) (127.30)	8.40 2.90 (27.56) (9.51)	Feadship – De Vries Scheepsbouw De Voogt/De Voogt/Munford Aalsmeer/The Netherlands/1994	2 x 8 cylinder 786hp Caterpillar 3508DI-TA diesels	Lloyd's ✠100A1, ✠LMC Featured in The Superyachts Volume 8
SOUTHERLY	Twin Screw Motor Yacht Steel	44.00 39.10 (144.36) (128.28)	9.00 2.75 (29.52) (9.02)	Picchiotti De Fever/Rybar Viareggio/Italy/1982	2 x 12 cylinder 900hp Caterpillar diesels	
STARSHIP ex-Grand Eagle ex-Almaviva, ex-Le Soleil II ex-Luisamar	Twin Water Jet Motor Yacht Aluminium	43.95 (144.20)	8.23 2.10 (27.00) (6.89)	Van Mill Beeldsnijder/Procase Hardinxvelt/The Netherlands/1988	2 x 16 cylinder 2520hp MTU 396TB84 diesels	
ULTIMATE	Twin Screw Motor Yacht Aluminium	43.70 (143.37)	8.85 2.25 (29.03) (7.38)	Oceanco The 'A' Group/Starkey/Starkey Dreumel/The Netherlands/1996	2 x 12 cylinder 2285hp MTU 396TE94 diesels	Featured in The Superyachts, Volume 10
NEW CENTURY ex-Headlines II	Twin Screw Motor Yacht Aluminium	43.65 38.14 (143.19) (125.13)	8.50 2.50 (27.88) (8.20)	Diaship/Heesen Shipyards Diaship/Art-Line Oss/The Netherlands/1997	2 x 16 cylinder 2980hp MTU 396TE94 diesels	ABS ✠A1, AMS Yachting Service Featured in The Superyachts, Volume 12

Name	Type / Material	Length m	Length ft	Beam / Draft m	Beam / Draft ft	Builder / Designer / Place / Year	Engine	Classification / Notes
SYL	Auxiliary Sloop / Aluminium	43.64 / 37.87	(143.16) / (124.23)	9.01 / 2.00	(29.56) / (6.56)	Barcos Deportivos / German Frers/BD design / Tarragona/Spain/2002	1 x 12 cylinder 738hp MTU 12V TE62 diesel	
ATTESSA ex-Yecats	Twin Screw Motor Yacht / Steel/Aluminium	43.62/47.55	(143.11/156.0)	8.24 / 2.59	(27.00) / (8.50)	Kong & Halvorsen / De Fever/Glade Johnson / Hong Kong/1985	2 x 12 cylinder 1165hp Caterpillar 3012 diesels	Rebuilt in San Diego in 1991
ANATOLIA	Twin Screw Motor Yacht / Steel/Wood/Aluminium/Composite	43.60 / 34.50	(143.03) / (113.18)	7.00 / 2.4	(22.96) / (7.87)	Turquoise Yacht Construction / Kalaycioglu/Kalaycioglu/Redman Whiteley / Tuzla/Turkey/2001	2 x 6 cylinder 480hp Caterpillar 3406C diesels	Lloyd's Hull Certificate / Featured in The Superyachts, Volume 15
FRANCESCA PETRARCA ex-Raphaelo ex-Taitu	Auxiliary Three Mast Schooner / Wood	43.60 / 36.00	(143.03) / (118.12)	8.50 / 3.65	(27.89) / (11.97)	Fratelli Benetti / Benetti/Boretti / Viareggio/Italy/1939	2 x 12 cylinder 450hp Caterpillar 3406E diesels	Rebuilt at Valdettaro Shipyard 1971
LADY DUVERA	Twin Screw Motor Yacht	43.60 / 37.50	(143.03) / (123.00)	8.80 / 2.80	(28.83) / (9.17)	Hakvoort Shipyard / Diana Yacht Design/DYD/Buytendijk / Monnickendam/The Netherlands/2001	2 x 8 cylinder 914hp Caterpillar 3508DI-TA diesels	Lloyds ✠100A1, SSC Mono G6, ✠LMC
LORD JIM ex-Joanna Alexandra ex-Lady Duvera II	Twin Screw Motor Yacht / Steel/Aluminium	43.60 / 37.50	(143.05) / (123.04)	8.80 / 2.90	(28.87) / (9.51)	Hakvoort Shipyard / Diana Yacht Design/Buytendijk / Monnickendam/The Netherlands/1991	2 x 8 cylinder 786hp Caterpillar 3508DI-TA diesels	Lloyd's ✠100A1, C / Featured in The Superyachts, Volume 6
MARJORIE MORNINGSTAR ex-Lindeza ex-Shalimar	Twin Screw Motor Yacht / Composite	43.60	(143.05)	7.90	(25.91)	Sterling Yacht & Shipbuilders / Sterling/Bannenberg / Ise/Japan/1986	2 x 12 cylinder 1010hp Mitsubishi diesels	Rebuilt in 1991 with interior design by Susan Puleo
SEA FALCON	Twin Screw Motor Yacht / Aluminium	43.60 / 40.23	(143.05) / (132.00)	7.47 / 1.83	(24.60) / (6.00)	Angus Yachts / Edwards/Edwards / Alabama/USA/1990	2 x 12 cylinder 1250hp MTU 331TI diesels	
JANET	Twin Screw Motor Yacht / Composite	43.59 / 36.96	(143.00) / (121.25)	8.68 / 2.06	(28.50) / (6.75)	Trident Shipworks / Paragon/Milton Klein / Tampa/USA/1997	2 x 16 cylinder 3000hp MTU 396TE94 diesels	
JULIET B	Auxiliary Ketch / Aluminium	43.58 / 35.21	(142.99) / (115.51)	9.00 / 4.58	(29.53) / (15.00)	Royal Huisman Shipyard / Holland/Holland/Beeldsnijder / Vollenhove/The Netherlands/1992	1 x 12 cylinder 780hp MTU 183TE92 diesel	Featured in The Superyachts, Volume 7
OCTOPUSSY	Triple Water Jet Motor Yacht / Aluminium	43.58 / 32.95	(142.98) / (108.10)	7.95 / 1.40	(26.08) / (4.59)	Diaship/Heesen Shipyards / Mulder/Gilgenast/Art Line/The 'A' Group / Oss/The Netherlands/1988	3 x 16 cylinder 3500hp MTU 396TB94 diesels	When first launched Octopussy held the record as the world's fastest yacht, achieving a top speed of 53.7 knots. Refitted and lengthened by 11ft in 1996 / Featured in The Superyachts, Volume 2
RADIAL ex-Alphee ex-Beluga	Twin Screw Motor Yacht / Steel	43.50 / 38.30	(142.72) / (125.66)	8.10 / 3.00	(26.57) / (9.84)	Astilleros Zamacona SA / Myers-Coty / Bilbao/Spain/1985	2 x 12 cylinder 1148hp Caterpillar diesels	Lloyd's ✠100A1, ✠LMC
ENTERPRISE ex-Felicitam	Auxiliary Centreboard Ketch / Steel/Aluminium	43.40 / 32.30	(142.39) / (105.99)	8.80 / 6.00/2.50	(28.87) / (19.68/8.20)	Perini Navi / Perini Navi/Perini Navi / Viareggio/Italy/1988	2 x 12 cylinder 464hp MTU 183TA61 diesels	
PAZ ex-Andromeda	Auxiliary Centreboard Ketch / Steel/Aluminium	43.40 / 32.30	(142.39) / (105.99)	8.80 / 6.00/2.50	(28.87) / (19.68/8.20)	Perini Navi / Perini Navi/Perini Navi/Perini Navi / Viareggio/Italy/1987	2 x 12 cylinder 464hp MTU 183TA61 diesels	Featured in The Superyachts, Volume 1
SLIPSTREAM	Twin Screw Motor Yacht / Composite	43.30 / 37.30	(142.06) / (122.37)	8.54 / 2.07	(28.02) / (6.79)	David Warren Yachts / Dubois/Dubois/Sorgiovanni / Kincumber/NSW/Australia/2000	2 x 12 cylinder 1350hp Caterpillar 3412E DI-TA diesels	ABS ✠A1 Yachting Service AMS / Featured in The Superyachts, Volume 15 / MCA Code
XARIFA ex-Capitone, ex-Radiant ex-Georgette, ex-Xarifa	Auxiliary Three Mast Schooner / Steel	43.30 / 36.20	(142.06) / (118.77)	8.60 / 4.60	(28.21) / (15.09)	Samuel White / J M Soper & Son / Cowes/UK/1927	1 x 6 cylinder 230hp Deutz diesel	Rebuilt in 1954 & 1970
NAMOH ex-Soldier of Fortune	Twin Screw Motor Yacht / GRP	43.28	(142.00)	8.41 / 2.10	(27.60) / (6.90)	Christensen Motor Yacht Corporation / Ward Setzer/Paragon Design/Robinson / Vancouver/USA/1995	2 x 12 cylinder 1948hp Deutz TBD604BV diesels	Featured in The Superyachts, Volume 10
AZURE LEISURE ex-Paraffin	Twin Screw Motor Yacht / Aluminium	43.28	(142.00)	7.60 / 1.80	(24.93) / (5.90)	Palmer Johnson Incorporated / Palmer Johnson/Fexas/Disdale / Sturgeon Bay/USA/1997	2 x 12 cylinder 1800hp Detroit 149 DDEC diesels	ABS ✠A1 Yachting Service AMS / Featured in The Superyachts, Volume 11

YACHT'S NAME ex-name(s)	PROPULSION TYPE / CONSTRUCTION	LOA/LOA incl. spars, Length water line m	(ft)	Beam (Maximum) / Draught m	(ft)	BUILDER / NAVAL ARCHITECT/STYLIST/ INTERIOR DESIGNER / WHERE/YEAR	ENGINES Number & Cylinders / Horse Power / Maker/Type	REMARKS
LAMBDA MAR	Triple Water Jet / Motor Yacht / Aluminium	43.26 35.70	(141.90) (117.10)	8.30 1.60	(27.20) (5.20)	Marinteknik Verkstads / Mulder/Mulder/Smith / Oregrund/Sweden/1994	2 x MTU 16V396TE94 3050hp diesels & 1 x Textron Lycoming TF-40 4056hp Gas Turbine	Det Norske Veritas Class Contemplated
NORTHERN CROSS	Twin Water Jet / Motor Yacht / Aluminium	43.25	(141.90)	7.98 1.50	(26.18) (4.92)	Marinteknik Verkstads AB / Marinteknik/Hinders / Oregrund/Sweden/1991	2 x 12 cylinder 1750hp Caterpillar 3512 diesels	Det Norske Veritas ✠A1 Marine Jet Power J650R water jets
COCOA BEAN	Twin Screw / Motor Yacht / Aluminium	43.24 38.06	(141.86) (125.00)	8.53 2.98	(28.00) (9.80)	Broward Marine / Broward/Rose / Fort Lauderdale/USA/1996	2 x 16 cylinder 2400hp Detroit DDEC diesels	ABS classified
RAMSES ex-Khalifah ex-My Gail II	Twin Screw / Motor Yacht / Steel	43.15 36.90	(141.57) (121.06)	7.80 2.80	(25.59) (9.19)	Feadship – De Vries Scheepsbouw / De Voogt/Bannenberg / Aalsmeer/The Netherlands/1981	2 x 12 cylinder 948hp Caterpillar D398PCTA diesels	Exterior restyling and interior refit by Howard and Horsfield 1996. Lloyd's ✠100A1, ✠LMC
HARBOUR MOON ex-Honey Money ex-Youngblood	Twin Screw / Motor Yacht / Aluminium	43.14 39.14	(141.54) (125.13)	8.50 2.50	(27.88) (8.20)	Diaship/Heesen Shipyards / Diaship/Diaship / Oss/The Netherlands/1996	2 x 16 cylinder 2954hp MTU 396TE94 diesels	ABS ✠A1, Yachting Service, AMS Featured in The Superyachts, Volume 10 Full refit completed 1999. Interior designed by Don Starkey
ALBACORA OF TORTOLA	Twin Screw / Motor Yacht / Steel	43.01	(141.11)	6.70 3.70	(21.98) (12.14)	NV Wilton Fijenoord / NVWF / Schiedam/The Netherlands/1948	2 x 6 cylinder 210hp Stork Werkspoor 4TS6 diesels	Converted to a yacht by CRN in 1969 Refitted in 1999 Featured in The Superyachts, Volume 3
INDEPENDENT OF LONDON	Twin Screw / Motor Yacht / Aluminium	43.00 37.79	(141.08) (124.00)	7.46 2.89	(24.50) (9.50)	Cantiere Navale Nicolini / Cantiere Navale Nicolini/Tagliavini / Ancona/Italy/1995	2 x 16 cylinder 2600hp MTU 396TB93 diesels	Lloyd's ✠100A1, ✠LMC
KAHALANI ex-Sea Sedan II	Twin Screw / Motor Yacht / Steel	43.00	(141.08)	8.40 2.90	(27.56) (9.51)	Feadship – De Vries Scheepsbouw / De Voogt/Disdale / Aalsmeer/The Netherlands/1993	2 x 8 cylinder 786hp Caterpillar 3508DI-TA diesels	Featured in The Superyachts, Volume 7 Lloyd's ✠100A1, ✠LMC
LADY IN BLUE ex-Charlie's Angels ex-Idyll ex-Giamin	Twin Screw / Motor Yacht / Steel	43.00	(141.08)	7.27 4.00	(23.85) (13.12)	Fratelli Benetti / Benetti / Viareggio/Italy/1981	2 x 8 cylinder 750hp Caterpillar diesels	Bureau Veritas 13/3E ✠Yacht, ✠MOT. Refitted in 1992 and again in 1998 Featured in The Superyachts, Volume 6
LADY SHERIDAN ex-L'Elegance, ex-Mia Elise ex-Easy to Love IV	Twin Screw / Motor Yacht / Steel	43.00	(141.08)	8.25 2.85	(27.07) (9.35)	Feadship – Van Lent & Zonen / De Voogt/De Voogt/Guillard / Kaag/The Netherlands/1988	2 x 16 cylinder 730hp Detroit 92TA diesels	
MAGNIFICA	Twin Screw / Motor Yacht / Steel/Aluminium	43.00 37.70	(141.08) (123.67)	8.40 4.50	(27.55) (14.76)	CRN-Ferretti Group / CRN/Nuvolari-Lenard/Nuvolari-Lenard / Ancona/Italy/2001	2 x 12 cylinder 1950hp Caterpillar 3512 diesels	
ONLY YOU I ex-Lady Suffolk II	Twin Screw / Motor Yacht / Steel	43.00 39.02	(141.08) (128.02)	7.96 2.42	(26.11) (7.94)	Brooke Yachts International / Scanu/Disdale/Disdale / Lowestoft/UK/1992	2 x 12 cylinder 940hp Deutz MWM TBD234 diesels	Lloyd's ✠100A1, ✠LMC Featured in The Superyachts, Volume 8
UNIWEST ex-Bernie ex-Aliosha VII of Rurik	Twin Screw / Motor Yacht / GRP	43.00 38.28	(141.08) (125.60)	9.20 2.80	(30.19) (9.19)	Siar & Moschini SpA / Siar & Moschini / Fano/Italy/1991	2 x 16 cylinder 1360hp Caterpillar 3512TA diesel	
ZACA A TE MOANA	Auxiliary Gaff Schooner / Steel	43.00	(141.08)	7.20 4.28	(23.62) (14.04)	De Amstel Shipyard / Olivier F Van Meer / Ouderkerk/The Netherlands/1992	1 x 6 cylinder 300hp Lugger	Refitted 2002
MIA ELISE	Twin Screw / Motor Yacht / Steel	42.98	(141.00)	8.38	(27.50)	Trinity Yachts / Dee Robinson / New Orleans/USA/2001	2 x 16 cylinder 1800hp MTU/DDEC 16V2000 diesels	
WALKABOUT ex-Big Bad John	Twin Screw / Motor Yacht / GRP	42.98	(141.00)	8.53 1.98	(28.00) (6.50)	Christensen Shipyard / Christensen/KC Designs / Vancouver/Canada/1999	2 x 16 cylinder 2000hp Detroit diesels	ABS ✠A1, AMS MCA Code
AFRICAN QUEEN	Auxiliary Sloop / Aluminium	42.90 35.20	(140.75) (115.48)	8.77 4.10	(28.77) (13.45)	Vitters Shipyard / Dubois/Dubois/Redman Whiteley / Zwartsluis/The Netherlands/2001	1 x 12 cylinder 850hp MTU 12V183 TE72 diesel	ABS ✠, AMS A1 Yachting Service Featured in The Superyachts, Volume 16

Name	Type / Construction	LOA / LWL (m)	(ft)	Beam / Draft (m)	(ft)	Builder / Designer / Location / Year	Engines	Classification / Notes
LADY ANGELA, ex-Avante Dos, ex-Imperator, ex-Les Amis, ex-Pilgrim, ex-Lady Alicia	Twin Screw Motor Yacht, Steel	42.90 / 37.30	(140.75) (122.38)	8.00 / 2.00	(26.24) (6.56)	Hall Russell, Rhodes/Rhodes/Puleo, Aberdeen/UK/1964	2 x 8 cylinder, 650hp, Caterpillar diesels	
WHIRLAWAY	Auxiliary Sloop, Aluminium	42.90 / 35.20	(140.75) (115.50)	8.80 / 4.80/7.00	(28.87) (15.7/23.0)	Vitters Shipyard, Dubois/Dubois/Redman Whiteley, Zwartsluis/The Netherlands/2002	1 x 12 cylinder, 818hp, MTU 12V 183TE72 diesels	Lloyd's ✠100A1, ✠LMC
TYNDAREO, ex-Varmar	Twin Screw Motor Yacht, Steel	42.82 / 35.95	(140.49) (117.95)	7.74 / 1.31	(25.39) (4.30)	CRN, CRN/Bannenberg/Hicks, Ancona/Italy/1982	2 x 6 cylinder, 1590hp, Deutz SBV6M628 diesels	
ROYAL EAGLE, ex-Pegaso, ex-Ginny Lou ex-Grand Bleu of the Cayman Island	Twin Screw Motor Yacht, Steel	42.75 / 37.75	(140.26) (123.85)	8.50 / 2.50	(27.89) (8.20)	Cantiere Picchiotti SpA, Picchiotti/Picchiotti/Dilday, La Spezia/Italy/1990	2 x 6 cylinder, 800hp, Deutz diesels	Lloyd's ✠100A1, ✠LMC, Featured in The Superyachts, Volume 4
RENEGADE	Twin Screw Motor Yacht, Aluminium	42.70 / 39.50	(140.00) (116.57)	8.80 / 2.80	(28.87) (9.19)	Lloyds Ship, Brisbane, Allan Dowd/Bernie Cohen, Brisbane/Australia/1992	2 x 16 cylinder, 3,600hp, MTU 396 TB94	DNV ✠1A1 R280, Light Craft FLC, Refitted 1997/1999
ALEXANDRA K, ex-Anastasia Th	Twin Screw Motor Yacht, Steel	42.70 / 36.81	(140.09) (120.77)	7.56 / 2.13	(24.80) (6.99)	CRN, CRN, Ancona/Italy/1981	2 x 16 cylinder, Klockner-Humboldt diesels	Lloyd's ✠100A1, ✠LMC
FIESTA 23	Twin Screw Motor Yacht, Aluminium	42.70 / 35.50	(140.09) (116.47)	8.90 / 2.00	(29.20) (6.56)	Lloyd's Ships, Lloyd's Ships/Cohen, Bulimba/Australia/1987	2 x 16 cylinder, 2900hp, MTU 396TB94 diesels	DNV ✠1A1 Light Craft, ✠NK NS* NMS*
ISLAND BREEZE II, ex-Blue Legend	Triple Screw Motor Yacht, Aluminium	42.70	(140.09)	7.80 / 2.00	(18.57) (6.56)	Mefasa, Shead/Echenique, Aviles/Spain/1992	1 x Gas Turbine, 2 x MTU diesels	
APHRODITE 2	Twin Screw Motor Yacht, Aluminium	42.67 / 35.81	(140.00) (117.49)	9.26 / 4.30	(30.38) (14.11)	Vitters Shipyard, Hoek Design/Hoek Design, Zwartsluis/The Netherlands/1999	2 x 12 cylinder, 940hp, TTU 183TE93 diesels	
MAGNIFICO III	Twin Screw Motor Yacht, GRP	42.67 / 38.71	(140.00) (120.00)	8.23 / 2.05	(27.00) (6.75)	Christensen Motor Yacht Corporation, Apollonio/Roberts, Vancouver/USA/1991	2 x 16 cylinder, 1400hp, Detroit V92TI DDEC diesels	
TEXAS, ex-Permaisuri	Twin Screw Motor Yacht, Steel	42.67 / 34.83	(140.00) (114.27)	7.32 / 2.65	(24.01) (8.69)	Proteksan AS, Idronautica Costaguta, Tuzla/Turkey/1984	2 x 12 cylinder, 520hp, Caterpillar diesels	Lloyd's ✠100A1, ✠LMC, Lengthened and refitted to design of John Cotte at Sensation Yachts 2001
WESTSHIP LADY	Twin Screw Motor Yacht, Aluminium	42.67 / 37.49	(140.00) (123.00)	8.53 / 1.83	(28.00) (6.00)	Trident Shipworks, Sarin/Carr/Yacht Design Associates, Tampa/USA/2000	2 x 12 cylinders, 2285hp, MTU 12V396 TE94	
MARTHA ANN, ex-Westship One	Twin Screw Motor Yacht, Aluminium	42.67 / 37.49	(140.00) (123.00)	8.53 / 1.83	(28.00) (6.00)	Westship World Yachts, Sarin/Carr/Yacht Design Associates, Miami/USA/2001	2 x 12 cylinders, 2285hp, MTU 12V396 TE94	
HELOVAL	Twin Screw Motor Yacht, Steel/Aluminium	42.62 / 37.00	(139.82) (121.39)	8.60 / 2.70	(28.21) (8.85)	CMN Cherbourg, Stirling Design/Breteche, Cherbourg/France/2002	2 x V8, 2400hp, Caterpillar 3508B	
ANDIAMO	Twin Screw Motor Yacht, Steel/Aluminium	42.56 / 38.10	(139.61) (125.00)	8.60 / 2.70	(28.22) (8.86)	Feadship/Royal Van Lent, DeVoogt/Sharp Design/Glade Johnson, Kaag/The Netherlands/2002	2 x 12 cylinder, 720hp, Caterpillar 3412E DI-TA diesels	
BLUE CRYSTAL	Twin Water Jet Motor Yacht, Aluminium	42.50 / 34.10	(139.44) (111.88)	7.98 / 1.50	(26.18) (4.92)	Marinteknik Verkstads AB, Marinteknik/Kavli, Oregrund/Sweden/1991	2 x 12 cylinder, 1609hp, Deutz MWM TBD604B diesels	DNV 1A1, EO, Light Craft
CAMELEON B	Twin Screw Motor Yacht, Alloy	42.50	(139.44)	8.51 / 1.80	(27.92) (5.91)	Proteksan/Cuttolo, Caliari, Tuzla/Turkey/2002	2 x 12 cylinder, 2385hp, MTU 12V396	
REBECCA	Auxiliary Ketch, Aluminium	42.40 / 33.00	(139.10) (108.27)	8.70 / 4.50	(28.54) (14.76)	Pendennis Shipyard, G Frers/Black, Falmouth/UK/1998	1 x 12 cylinder, 535hp, MTU 12V 183 TE61 diesel	ABS ✠A1, AMS Yachting Service, Featured in The Superyachts, Volume 13

YACHT'S NAME ex-name(s)	PROPULSION TYPE CONSTRUCTION	DIMENSIONS LOA/LOA including spars Length water line m (ft)		Beam (Maximum) Draught m (ft)		BUILDER NAVAL ARCHITECT/STYLIST/ INTERIOR DESIGNER WHERE/YEAR	ENGINES Number & Cylinders Horse Power Maker/Type	REMARKS
EQUINOCCIO ex-Aspiration	Twin Screw Motor Yacht Steel/Aluminium	42.37	(139.02)	9.00 2.10	(29.52) (6.90)	Oceanco The 'A' Group Dreumel/The Netherlands/1998	2 x 12 cylinder 2285hp MTU 396TE 94 diesels	
AMERICA	Auxiliary Schooner Composite	42.36 28.95	(139.00) (95.00)	7.62 3.04	(25.00) (10.00)	Scarano Boat Building Scarano Albany/USA/1995	2 x 200hp John Deere 6068TFM	Modern replica of the original America's Cup winning schooner. ABS
CYCLOS III	Auxiliary Ketch Aluminium	42.36 34.80	(139.00) (114.17)	8.85 4.88	(29.03) (160.01)	Royal Huisman Shipyard Holland/Holland/Winch Vollenhove/The Netherlands/1990	1 x 8 cylinder 878hp MTU 396TB63 diesel	Featured in The Superyachts, Volume 13
FRIDAY STAR ex-Vendredi 13	Auxiliary Three Mast Schooner Aluminium	42.36	(139.00)	5.88	(19.30)	Dick Carter France/1972	1 x 300hp diesel	Extended from the original length of 39m
CANICA	Auxiliary Sloop Composite	42.35 35.75	(138.94) (117.29)	8.34 3.50/5.90	(27.36) (11.48/19.35)	Baltic Yachts Judel/Vrolijk/John Munford Design Newport/USA/2003	12 cylinder 1000hp Caterpillar 3412 Ditta	
MASQUERADE OF SOLE ex-Limitless, ex-Circus II	Twin Screw Motor Yacht Steel	42.35 38.03	(138.95) (124.78)	8.08 2.41	(26.51) (7.91)	Feadship – De Vries Scheepsbouw De Voogt/De Voogt/Puleo Aalsmeer/The Netherlands/1983	2 x 8 cylinder 634hp Caterpillar 379PCTA diesels	
DREAM SEEKER ex-Bridlewood	Twin Screw Motor Yacht Steel	42.31 38.03	(138.81) (124.78)	8.13 2.41	(26.67) (7.91)	Feadship – Van Lent & Zonen De Voogt/De Voogt Kaag/The Netherlands/1984	2 x 12 cylinder 1181hp Caterpillar 3512DI-TA diesels	
MEA CULPA	Motor Yacht Composite	42.31	(138.81)	8.23 1.83	(27.00) (6.00)	McMullen & Wing Jack W Sarin/Marnell Corrao Assoc New Zealand/2003	2 x 2735bhp MTU 4000 diesels	MCA Code
DOUCE FRANCE	Auxiliary Twin Screw Catamaran Schooner Aluminium	42.20 38.25	(138.45) (125.49)	15.40 2.50	(50.52) (8.20)	Alumarine/CNC2 Peteghem & Lauriot-Prevost/Bonadei Nantes/France/1998	2 x 290hp Nanni diesels	
LIBRA Y ex-Solitaire of the Isles	Twin Screw Motor Yacht Steel	42.11 32.39	(138.16) (106.27)	7.55 2.50	(24.77) (8.20)	Cantieri Picchiotti SpA Shead/Bannenberg/Bannenberg Viareggio/Italy/1977	2 x 12 cylinder 1650hp MTU diesels	Extended by 3.5m in 1994
BLUE HAREM ex-Lady Christine	Twin Screw Motor Yacht Aluminium	42.10 33.38	(138.12) (109.51)	7.60 2.00	(24.93) (6.56)	Diaship/Heesen Shipyards Diaship/Mulder/Diaship Oss/The Netherlands/1994	2 x 12 cylinder 2040hp MTU 396TE94 diesels	Lengthened by 3m 1997
O'PARI	Twin Screw Motor Yacht GRP	42.10 35.70	(138.12) (117.12)	8.20 2.45	(26.90) (8.04)	Intermarine SpA Intermarine SpA/Vafiadis Sarzana/Italy/1997	2 x 12 cylinder 2285hp MTU 396TE94 diesels	ABS ✠A1, ✠AMS Yachting Service Featured in The Superyachts, Volume 11
ISTROS ex-Andros ex-Istros	Twin Screw Motor Yacht Steel	42.09 39.34	(138.09) (129.07)	6.89 2.83	(22.60) (9.28)	NV Amsterdamsche Scheepswerft De Vries Lentsch Jr. Amsterdam/The Netherlands/1954	2 x 6 cylinder 570hp Crossley diesels	Lloyd's ✠100A1, ✠LMC
FORTY LOVE	Twin Screw Motor Yacht Composite/Aluminium	42.07	(138.00)	7.62 1.92	(25.00) (6.29)	West Coast Custom Yachts Jack Sarin/Brilliant Yachts 2002	2 x 1350hp Caterpillar 3412	ABS, MCA Code
HIS GRACE	Twin Screw Motor Yacht GRP/Composite	42.06 35.05	(137.99) (115.00)	7.92 2.13	(26.00) (7.00)	Westport Shipyard Sarin/Caliari Westport/USA/1989	2 x 12 cylinder 1958hp MWM-Deutz 604B diesels	Refitted and extended in 1999
OUR WAY	Twin Screw Motor Yacht Steel	42.02	(137.86)	8.38 2.20	(27.50) (7.50)	Palmer Johnson Incorporated Palmer Johnson Sturgeon Bay/USA/1998	2 x 12 cylinder 720hp Caterpillar 3412C diesels	
ACAJOU	Twin Screw Motor Yacht Wood	42.00 38.34	(137.80) (125.79)	7.80 2.10	(25.59) (6.89)	Chantiers Navals de L'Esterel Mauric/Bannenberg/Bannenberg Cannes/France/1984	2 x 16 cylinder 7340hp MTU diesels	Featured in The Superyachts, Volume 1

Name	Type / Construction	Length (m)/(ft)	Beam/Draft (m)/(ft)	Builder / Designer / Location/Year	Engines	Classification / Notes
L'ALDEBARAN	Twin Screw Motor Yacht Steel/Aluminium	42.00 / 36.00 (137.80)/(118.11)	8.50 / 2.70 (27.88)/(8.10)	Codecasa Bacigalupo/Cerruti Viareggio/Italy/2002	2 x 8 cylinder 2600hp Caterpillar 3508B	LRS ✠100 A1 ✠LMC, MCA Code, R.I.N.A.
ALOUETTE ex-Diana I	Twin Screw Motor Yacht Steel	42.00 (137.80)	7.30 / 2.40 (23.95)/(7.87)	Fratelli Benetti Benetti Viareggio/Italy/1972	2 x 12 cylinder 825hp MTU diesels	
TRINITY II ex-Elenesse II ex-Antares I	Twin Screw Motor Yacht Steel	42.00 / 35.00 (137.80)/(114.83)	8.30 / 2.50 (27.23)/(8.20)	Mondomarine Mondomarine/Sivell-Muller/Jacobs Gallo d'Alba/Italy/1991	2 x 12 cylinder 1050hp Caterpillar diesels	Extended by 3m in 2000
FAIR LADY	Twin Screw Motor Yacht Steel	42.00 (137.80)	6.50 / 3.05 (21.32)/(10.00)	Camper & Nicholsons CE Nicholson/CE Nicholson/CE Nicholson Southampton/UK/1928	2 x Deutz 275hp diesels	Refitted in 1984 and 1996 Featured in The Superyachts, Volume 1
PASSE PARTOUT	Auxiliary Ketch Steel/Aluminium	42.00 / 31.00 (137.80)/(101.71)	8.50 / 2.70/5.00 (27.88)/(8.85/16.4)	Jongert Castro/Sijm Medemblik/The Netherlands/2000	1 x 12 cylinder 1071hp MTU diesel	Lloyd's ✠100A1
SHEERGOLD ex-Seratina ex-Sheergold	Twin Screw Motor Yacht Steel/Aluminium	42.00 / 36.50 (137.80)/(119.76)	8.00 / 2.50 (26.25)/(8.20)	Amels Diana Yacht Design/Bannenberg Makkum/The Netherlands/1987	2 x 8 cylinder 786hp Caterpillar 3508DI-TA diesels	Lloyd's ✠100A1, ✠LMC Featured in The Superyachts, Volume 3
TRANQUILLITY ex-Jamaica Bay	Twin Screw Motor Yacht Steel/Aluminium	42.00 / 36.50 (137.80)/(119.75)	8.00 / 2.60 (26.25)/(8.53)	Amels Diana Yacht Design/Buytendijk Makkum/The Netherlands/1984	2 x 12 cylinder 862hp Caterpillar D398PCTA diesels	Lloyd's ✠100A1, ✠LMC Refitted in 1999
BELESBAT QUEEN ex-Galaxy Star	Twin Screw Motor Yacht Steel	41.87 / 36.46 (137.37)/(119.62)	7.30 / 2.00 (23.95)/(6.56)	Proteksan Proteksan Tuzla/Turkey/1986	2 x 12 cylinder 854hp Detroit diesel diesels	Lloyd's ✠100A1, ✠LMC
CELESTIAL ex-Trelawney, ex-Arbitrage ex-Chambel	Twin Screw Motor Yacht Steel	41.80 / 37.00 (137.14)/(121.39)	7.00 / 1.90 (22.96)/(6.23)	De Beer Philip Rhodes Zaandam/The Netherlands/1963	2 x 12 cylinder 600hp Baudouin diesels	
CHRISTIANNE B	Auxiliary Twin Screw Ketch Steel	41.80 / 33.28 (137.14)/(109.20)	7.65 / 2.50/5.80 (25.10)/(8.20/19.02)	Ortona Navi/Perini Navi Perini Navi Viareggio/Italy/1986	2 x 12 cylinder 420hp MTU Mercedes diesels	Featured in The Superyachts, Volume 3 Refitted in 1999
FARIBANA	Twin Screw Motor Yacht Steel	41.75 / 36.98 (137.00)/(121.33)	8.28 / 2.95 (27.17)/(9.58)	Feadship – De Vries Scheepsbouw De Voogt/Disdale Aalsmeer/The Netherlands/1989	2 x 8 cylinder 786hp Caterpillar 3508DI-TA diesels	Lloyd's ✠100A1, ✠LMC Featured in The Superyachts, Volume 3
LADYSHIP	Twin Screw Motor Yacht Aluminium	41.75 (137.00)	7.80 / 2.40 (25.59)/((7.87)	Diaship/Heesen Shipyards Mulder Design/Diaship Design Team Oss/The Netherlands/1993	2 x 12 cylinder 2560hp MTU 396 TB94 diesels	ABS ✠A1 AMS Yachting Service
KING K ex-King ex-Carmac VI	Twin Screw Motor Yacht Steel	41.70 / 37.45 (136.82)/(122.87)	8.00 / 2.51 (26.25)/(8.25)	Feadship – Van Lent & Zonen De Voogt/De Voogt/De Voogt Kaag/The Netherlands/1981	2 x 12 cylinder 675hp GM 149 diesels	Featured in The Superyachts, Volume 6 Major refit in 1998
STARFORD ex-Americana ex-Liberty, ex-Campana ex-Dixonia, ex-Acania	Twin Screw Motor Yacht Steel	41.70 / 40.80 (136.82)/(133.86)	7.10 / 3.10 (23.29)/(10.17)	Consolidated John H Wells USA/1930	2 x 6 cylinder 500hp GM diesels	Rebuilt in 1986
ST JEAN ex-Number One	Auxiliary Ketch Steel/Aluminium	41.60 / 28.40 (136.48)/(93.17)	7.88 / 4.85/2.65 (25.85)/(15.91/8.69)	Jachtwerf Jongert Tony Castro/Peter Sijm Medemblik/The Netherlands/1999	1 x 12 cylinder 534hp MTU 12V 183 TE61 diesel	Lloyd's ✠100A1 Featured in The Superyachts, Volume 13
ANNA CHRISTINA	Auxiliary Ketch Steel/Aluminium	41.55 / 28.40 (136.32)/(93.18)	7.88 / 4.50/2.30 (25.85)/(14.76/7.55)	Jachtwerf Jongert Tony Castro/Peter Sijm Medemblik/The Netherlands/2000	1 x 8 cylinder 714hp MTU 8V diesels	
ISLANDIA	Auxiliary Ketch Steel/Aluminium	41.55 / 28.40 (136.32)/(93.18)	7.88 / 3.70/6.80 (25.85)/(12.10/22.30)	Jachtwerf Jongert Tony Castro/Peter Sijm Medemblik/The Netherlands/2001	1 x 8 cylinder 714hp MTU 8V diesels	Lloyd's ✠100A1
D'ANGLETERRE II ex-Irina M ex-Argolyme	Twin Screw Motor Yacht Aluminium	41.50 / 35.10 (136.15)/(115.16)	7.31 / 2.20 (23.98)/(7.22)	WA Souter & Son Shead/Mechiche Cowes/UK/1987	2 x 12 cylinder 1110hp Deutz 12M816 CR diesels	Bureau Veritas I3/3 E Yacht Refit by Codecasa Due, Viareggio 1995 to designs of Don Shead Featured in The Superyachts Volume 6

YACHT'S NAME ex-name(s)	PROPULSION TYPE CONSTRUCTION	DIMENSIONS LOA/LOA including spars Length water line m / (ft)	Beam (Maximum) Draught m / (ft)	BUILDER NAVAL ARCHITECT/STYLIST/ INTERIOR DESIGNER WHERE/YEAR	ENGINES Number & Cylinders Horse Power Maker/Type	REMARKS
FORTUNA	Triple Water Jet Motor Yacht Aluminium/Composite	41.50 (136.16) 37.00 (121.39)	9.20 (30.18) 1.50 (4.92)	FN San Fernando Blount/Spadolini/Dell'Anna Bazan/Spain/2000	3 x Allison Gas Turbines 2 x MAN diesels	CODOG propulsion system. The world's fastest superyacht with speeds in excess of 65 knots. Spanish Royal Yacht. Featured in The Superyachts, Volume 14
O'REA ex-Joy Star ex-Joy	Twin Screw Motor Yacht Steel	41.50 (136.15) 33.61 (110.27)	7.32 (24.02) 2.01 (6.59)	Cantiere Navale Fano Idronautica Costaguta Fano/Italy/1984	2 x 8 cylinder 565hp Caterpillar diesels	Lengthened and refitted to the design of Studiovafiadis in 1999
LADY JENN	Twin Screw Motor Yacht Aluminium	41.45 (136.00) 36.51 (119.08)	7.93 (26.04) 1.86 (6.11)	Palmer Johnson Incorporated Tom Fexas Yacht Design Sturgeon Bay/USA/1994	2 x 16 cylinder 1040hp Detroit diesels	Featured in The Superyachts, Volume 8
ALEJANDRA	Auxiliary Ketch Aluminium	41.15 (135.00) 30.48 (100.00)	8.04 (26.40) 3.85 (12.63)	Mefasa Shipyard King/King/King Aviles/Spain/1992	1 x 8 cylinder 650hp MAN 2842LE diesel	Featured in The Superyachts, Volume 7
CAMBRIA	Auxiliary Sloop Mahogany/steel frames	41.15 (135.00) 23.80 (78.08)	6.10 (20.01) 4.25 (13.94)	William Fife & Sons William Fife Fairlie/UK/1928	1 x 300hp Cummins	Refitted in 1995 by Norman Wright Shipwrights Featured in The Superyachts, Volume 15
ATLANTICA	Twin Screw Motor Yacht Cored GRP	41.10 (135.00) 37.00 (121.39)	8.38 (27.50) 2.05 (6.58)	Christensen Shipyard Christensen/Christen/Starkey Vancouver/Canada/2000	2 x 16 cylinder 1800hp DDC/MTU 16V2000 diesels	ABS AMS, ✠A1 MCA Code Featured in The Superyachts, Volume 14
RICK'S CARLTON	Twin Screw Motor Yacht Cored GRP	41.10 (135.00) 37.00 (121.39)	8.53 (28.00) 2.14 (7.00)	Christensen Shipyard Christensen/Christensen/Starkey Vancouver/Canada/1998	2 x 16 cylinder 1800hp DDC/MTU 16V2000 diesels	
ATLANTIC GOOSE ex-Brave Goose	Twin Screw Motor Yacht Steel	41.03 (134.61) 35.86 (117.65)	7.62 (25.00) 2.59 (8.50)	Tough Shipyards Tough Teddington/UK/1987	2 x 8 cylinder 520hp Kelvin diesels	Lloyd's ✠100A1, ✠LMC Featured in The Superyachts, Volume 1
L'ESCAPADE OF LONDON ex-Valerie ex-J Olives	Twin Screw Motor Yacht GRP	41.00 (134.52)	9.20 (30.18) 2.80 (9.18)	Siar-Moschini Bacigalupo/Leusch Fano/Italy/1988	2 x 12 cylinder 1280hp Caterpillar diesels	Refitted in 1999
MIRABELLA III	Auxiliary Sloop Composite	41.00 (134.52) 36.00 (118.12)	9.00 (29.53) 3.80 (12.46)	Concorde Yachts Farr/Koskenkyla Chonburi/Thailand/1995	1 x 6 cylinder 500hp Lugger diesel	
SOPHIE BLUE	Twin Screw Motor Yacht Steel	41.00 (134.52)	8.60 (28.21) 2.30 (7.54)	CBI Navi CBI Navi/Luca Dini Design Viareggio/Italy/1998	2 x 12 cylinder 1800hp Caterpillar 3512 diesels	RINA ✠100A1 MCA Code
HARLEQUIN	Auxiliary Sloop Aluminium	40.90 (134.19) 34.00 (111.53)	8.70 (28.54) 4.60 (15.09)	Alloy Yachts International Dubois/Dubois/Redman Whiteley Dixon Auckland/New Zealand/2002	1 x 6 cylinder 800hp Caterpillar 3406 diesel	ABS ✠AMS A1 Yachting Service
MAXIME Z ex-Cleopatra ex-L'Aprilia	Twin Screw Motor Yacht Steel	40.90 (134.19) 36.05 (118.28)	7.16 (23.49) 2.19 (7.18)	Astilleros de Mallorca Camper & Nicholson Palma de Mallorca/Spain/1977	2 x 12 cylinder 1200hp Baz Arl diesels	Featured in The Superyachts, Volume 3
NOURAH OF RIYAD ex-Nourah II	Twin Screw Motor Yacht Steel	40.90 (134.19) 36.92 (121.13)	8.40 (25.56) 2.10 (6.89)	CRN CRN/Cichero/Garzouzi Ancona/Italy/1987	2 x 16 cylinder 3480hp MTU 396TB94 diesels	Lloyd's ✠100A1, ✠LMC
TE VEGA ex-Etak ex-Vega	Auxiliary Schooner Steel	40.90 (134.19) 30.48 (100.00)	8.53 (28.00) 4.88 (16.01)	Fr Krupp Germania Werft Cox & Stevens/Giorgetti & Magrini Kiel/Germany/1930/La Spezia/1997	1 x 6 cylinder 750hp MTU diesel	Complete restoration in 1997 by Cantieri Beconcini, Italy. Featured in The Superyachts, Volume 11
XENIA	Twin Screw Motor Yacht Steel	40.90 (134.19) 33.50 (109.10)	8.00 (26.30) 1.80 (5.11)	Lürssen Werft Beiderbeck/Schnaase Bremen/Germany/1995	2 x 16 cylinder 3433hp MTU 396TB94 diesels	Featured in The Superyachts, Volume 9
CLOUD NINE	Twin Screw Motor Yacht Composite	40.84 (134.00) 37.79 (124.00)	8.35 (27.39) 2.10 (6.88)	Sovereign Setzer Design Group Richmond/Canada/2003	2 x 16 cylinder	

Name	Type / Construction	LOA / LWL (m)	LOA / LWL (ft)	Beam / Draft (m)	Beam / Draft (ft)	Builder / Designer / Location / Year	Engines	Classification / Notes
AETEA	Twin Screw Motor Yacht Steel	40.81 36.53	(133.90) (119.85)	7.85 2.50	(25.75) (8.20)	Cantieri Picchioti SpA De Fever Viareggio/Italy/1981	2 x 12 cylinder 1735hp MTU diesels	Lloyd's ✠100A1, ✠LMC
BENEDETTA 2	Twin Screw Motor Yacht Aluminium	40.80 35.65	(133.86) (116.97)	8.00 2.55	(26.25) (8.37)	Baglietto Ruggiero/Ruggiero/Ruggiero Varazze/Italy/1999	2 x 16 cylinder 1502hp Deutz MWM620TBD16V diesels	RINA ✠A1.1Y' Featured in The Superyachts, Volume 14
BLUE ICE	Twin Screw Motor Yacht Aluminium	40.80 35.50	(133.86) (116.48)	8.20 1.52	(26.90) (4.99)	Baglietto Rodriquez Engineering/Studio Cerri & Assoc. Varazze/Italy/1999	2 x 12 cylinder 2774hp MTU 4000 M90 diesels	ABS ✠100A1
EL SHUJAH ex-Albecaro II	Twin Screw Motor Yacht Steel	40.80 35.70	(133.86) (117.13)	7.60 2.90	(24.93) (9.51)	Kersholt Beck Groningen/Netherlands/1963	2 x 8 cylinder 590hp MAN diesels	
SURAMA C	Auxiliary Twin Screw Ketch Aluminium	40.68 30.09	(133.46) (98.72)	8.82 2.70	(28.94) (8.86)	Royal Huisman Shipyard Hood/Winch Vollenhove/The Netherlands/1997	2 x 6 cylinder 570hp MTU-Mercedes Benz diesels	Featured in The Superyachts, Volume 12
DHAFIR	Twin Screw Motor Yacht Steel	40.56 36.05	(133.08) (118.28)	7.50 2.04	(24.61) (6.69)	Feadship – Van Lent & Zonen De Voogt/De Voogt Kaag/The Netherlands/1980	2 x 12 cylinder 1570hp MTU diesels	Lloyd's ✠100A1, ✠LMC
ALLIANCE	Twin Screw Motor Yacht GRP	40.53 36.11	(133.00) (118.50)	7.92 2.40	(26.00) (8.00)	Delta Marine Schubert/Lehrer Seattle/USA/1989	2 x 8 cylinder 705hp Caterpillar 3508 TA diesels	Lengthened by Delta Marine in 1994 to include a bathing platform and fishing cockpit
UTHINGO ex-Candida A	Twin Screw Motor Yacht Steel	40.53 38.50	(133.00) (126.31)	6.40 3.04	(21.00) (9.97)	Lawley & Son Lawley Massachusetts/USA/1930	2 x 8 cylinder 680hp GM diesels	Featured in The Superyachts, Volume 4
CORSTA V	Auxiliary Twin Screw Sloop Aluminium	40.50 32.40	(132.88) (106.30)	8.96 3.00	(29.39) (9.84)	Sterling Yachts Lavranos & Associates/Puleo Capetown/South Africa/1994	2 x 8 cylinder 890hp Cummins diesels	
TWIRLYBIRD	Auxiliary Ketch Aluminium	40.45 32.50	(132.71) (106.63)	9.20 4.00	(30.18) (13.12)	Lürssen Werft Holland/Freivokh Bremen/Germany/1993	1 x 12 cylinder 750hp MTU 183TE62 diesel	Featured in The Superyachts, Volume 8
THETIS	Auxiliary Twin Screw Ketch Steel/Aluminium	40.40 32.12	(132.53) (105.38)	8.00 6.46/3.53	(26.24) 21.19/11.58	Perini Navi Perini Navi Viareggio/Italy/2001	2 x 8 cylinder 469hp MTU 8VTE62 diesels	ABS ✠A1 Yachting Service, AMS Featured in The Superyachts, Volume 15 MCA Code
KOKOMO	Auxiliary Sloop Aluminium	40.38 33.47	(132.51) (109.80)	8.70 4.16	(28.50) (13.64)	Alloy Yachts Dubois/Dubois/Redman Whiteley Auckland/New Zealand/2000	1 x 10 cylinder 985hp MTU 12V 183TE92 diesel	ABS ✠A1 Yachting Service Featured in The Superyachts, Volume 15
BE MINE	Twin Screw Motor Yacht Aluminium	40.35 35.10	(132.39) (115.20)	8.00 1.85	(26.24) (6.06)	Lürssen Werft Lürssen/Beiderbeck Design/Dell'Anna Bremen/Germany/1991	2 x 12 cylinder 1041hp Caterpillar 3508DI-TA diesels	Featured in The Superyachts, Volume 5 Lloyd's ✠100A1, ✠LMC
ARGENTUM	Twin Screw Motor Yacht Aluminium	40.30 35.70	(132.22) (117.13)	7.60 1.90	(24.93) (6.23)	Benetti Shipyard Nicholson/Harvey/Zuretti Viareggio/Italy/1991	2 x 12 cylinder 2180hp MTU 396TB93 diesels	ABS ✠A1, AMS Yachting Service
BLYSS ex-Sanctuary ex-Iliki V	Twin Screw Motor Yacht Steel	40.30 35.30	(132.22) (115.81)	8.50 2.25	(27.88) (7.38)	Codecasa Codecasa/Della Role Viareggio/Italy/1994	2 x 12 cylinder 2284hp MTU 396TE94 diesels	Lloyd's ✠100A1, ✠LMC
DORITA ex-Marina II, ex-Marina ex-Grey Mist	Twin Screw Motor Yacht Steel	40.30 35.60	(132.22) (116.80)	5.90 2.50	(19.35) (8.20)	Camper & Nicholsons CE Nicholson/CE Nicholson/CE Nicholson Gosport/UK/1920/Rebuild/1964	2 x 8 cylinder 250hp MWM diesels	
OPAL C	Twin Water Jet Motor Yacht Aluminium/Composite	40.30 33.70	(132.22) (110.57)	8.00 1.30	(26.25) (4.26)	Oceanfast Pty Ltd Curran/Bannenberg Perth/Australia/1990	2 x 16 cylinder 3500hp MTU TB94 diesels	Featured in The Superyachts, Volume 3
ANAKENA	Auxiliary Twin Screw Ketch Aluminium	40.23 30.09	(132.00) (98.72)	8.82 2.70	(28.94) (8.86)	Royal Huisman Shipyard Hood/Hood/Munford Vollenhove/The Netherlands/1996	2 x 6 cylinder 570hp MTU/Mercedes Benz diesels	Featured in The Superyachts, Volume 10

YACHT'S NAME ex-name(s)	PROPULSION TYPE CONSTRUCTION	DIMENSIONS LOA/LOA including spars Length water line m (ft)	Beam (Maximum) Draught m (ft)	BUILDER NAVAL ARCHITECT/STYLIST/ INTERIOR DESIGNER WHERE/YEAR	ENGINES Number & Cylinders Horse Power Maker/Type	REMARKS
HALCYON ex-Synthesis, ex-Spellbound ex-Big Eagle II	Twin Screw Motor Yacht Steel	40.23 (132.00)	7.92 2.44 (26.00)(8.00)	Feadship – De Vries Scheepsbouw De Voogt/De Voogt Aalsmeer/The Netherlands/1982	2 x 8 cylinder 573hp Caterpillar 379PCTA diesels	
SANDRA LYNN ex-Katharine	Twin Screw Motor Yacht FRP/Composite	40.23 (132.00)	8.53 1.83 (28.00)(6.00)	Trident Shipworks Inc Trident/Cutolo/Carr/Dalton Tampa/USA/1999	2 x 12 cylinder 720hp Caterpillar 3412DI-TA diesels	
MIRAGE ex-El Corsario	Triple Water Jet Motor Yacht Aluminium	40.23 33.60 (132.00)(110.24)	7.90 1.50 (25.92)(4.92)	Diaship/Heesen Shipyards Mulder/Mulder/Art Line Oss/The Netherlands/1991	3 x 16 cylinder 3500hp MTU 396TB94 diesels	Sistership to Octopussy
NORWEGIAN QUEEN	Twin Screw Motor Yacht FRP/Composite	40.23 (132.00)	8.22 1.83 (27.00)(6.00)	Trident Shipworks Inc Trident/Sarin/Carr/Yacht Design Associates Tampa/USA/2000	2 x MTU diesels	
PRINCESS K ex-La Bella, ex-Headlines ex-Whirlwind II	Twin Screw Motor Yacht Aluminium	40.23 (132.00)	8.50 2.25 (27.89)(7.38)	Diaship/Heesen Shipyards Diaship Design Team/Art Line/TAG Oss/The Netherlands/1993	2 x 12 cylinder 2250hp MTU 396TE94 diesels	Featured in The Superyachts, Volume 7 ABS ✠A1 AMS, Yachting Service
LIFE'S FINEST II ex-Aquasition ex-Life's Finest	Twin Screw Motor Yacht FRP	40.23 (132.00)	7.93 1.96 (26.00)(6.42)	Northcoast Yachts Robin Rose Tacoma/USA/2001	2 x 16 cylinder 2400hp Detroit 149TA diesels	
MASHALACK ex-Lady Victoria ex-Ark Royal ex-Bluejacket of Hamble	Twin Screw Motor Yacht Teak/Steel Frames	40.20 35.70 (131.89)(117.13)	7.60 2.40 (24.93)(7.87)	Tough Tough Bros Teddington/UK/1979	2 x 8 cylinder 230hp Gardner diesels	Restyled in 1988 by Glade Johnson interior design
HEMISPHERE	Sloop Catamaran Cored FRP Composite	40.23 37.23 (131.56)(122.13)	15.61 2.4 (51.21)(7.87)	Blubay Yachts Blubay Yachts/Blubay Yachts Cannes/France/2003	2 x 6 cylinder 450hp Caterpillar 3126b diesels	
BLUE BELLE ex-New York Lady	Twin Screw Motor Yachts Aluminium	40.10 33.80 (131.56)(110.88)	8.20 1.95 (26.90)(6.40)	Mondomarine SYDAC/Isabelle Blanchère/Cor D Rover Savona/Italy/2002	2 x 12 cylinder 2285hp MTU 12V 396TE94 diesels	
LADY SANDALS ex-Lady Kathryn ex-Ms Barbara Anne ex-Gallant Lady	Twin Screw Motor Yacht Steel	40.07 (131.47)	7.26 2.36 (23.82)(7.74)	Feadship – De Vries Scheepsbouw De Voogt Aalsmeer/The Netherlands/1985	2 x 12 cylinder 1191hp Caterpillar D3512DI-TA diesels	
A KHALIQ	Twin Screw Motor Yacht Aluminium	40.00 (131.24)	8.50 2.20 (27.88)(7.21)	Heesen Shipyards Omega Architets/Diaship Design Oss/The Netherlands/2002	2 x MTU 12V4000M90	
ASK ex-Cosmopolitan Lady	Twin Water Jet Motor Yacht Aluminium	40.00 35.50 (131.24)(116.47)	7.98 1.40 (26.18)(4.59)	Mariteknik Verkstads AB Mariteknik-Kavli/Finne & Co Oregrund/Sweden/1989	2 x 12 cylinder 1200hp MTU diesels	DNV ✠A1 Fitted with 2 x Marine Jet Power water jets Featured in The Superyachts, Volume 4 Major interior and exterior re-design by Howard &Horsfield in 1997
BIG EAGLE II ex-Enterprise ex-Alma	Twin Screw Motor Yacht Steel	40.00 35.10 (131.24)(115.16)	7.90 2.40 (25.91)(7.87)	Feadship – De Vries Scheepsbouw De Voogt Aalsmeer/The Netherlands/1980	2 x GM 675hp diesels	
BORKUMRIFF	Schooner Aluminium	40.00 30.00 (131.23)(98.42)	8.67 4.00 (28.46)(13.12)	Royal Huisman Shipyard Lunstroo/John Munford Vollenhove/The Netherlands/1997	1 x 650hp MTU 12V183TE62	
CECILE MARIE	Auxiliary Sloop Aluminium	39.92 28.00 (130.97)(91.85)	7.95 3.82 (26.08)(12.53)	Royal Huisman Shipyard Bruce King Design/King/Dick Young Design Vollenhove/The Netherlands/2002	1 x 8 cylinder 640hp MTU 8V 2000 M70 diesel	Lloyds ✠100A1, SSC G6 Mono Yacht, ✠LMC, UMS, MCA Code
CLIPPER 40	Twin Screw Motor Yacht Steel	40.00 (131.24)	6.49 2.30 (21.30)(7.54)	Universal Yachts Universal Chonburi/Thailand/1992	2 x 6 cylinder 620hp Caterpillar diesels	

Name	Type / Construction	LOA / LWL (m)	(ft)	Beam / Draft (m)	(ft)	Builder / Designer / Location / Year	Engines	Notes
CV-9 OF CAYMAN	Twin Screw Motor Yacht GRP	40.00 / 36.28	(131.24) (119.00)	7.93 / 2.29	(26.00) (7.51)	Delta Marine / Delta/Delta/Glade Johnson Design / Seattle/USA/1995	2 x 16 cylinder 775hp Caterpillar 3508 diesel	Featured in The Superyachts, Volume 9
LADY ANNE	Twin Screw Motor Yacht Steel	40.00 / 36.00	(131.24) (118.11)	8.00 / 2.00	(26.24) (6.60)	CRN Shipyard / CRN/Franchini/Franchini / Ancona/Italy/1994	2 x 16 cylinder 2504hp	Featured in The Superyachts, Volume 9
LETHANTIA ex-Borkumriff III	Auxiliary Schooner Aluminium	40.00 / 30.00	(131.24) (98.43)	8.65 / 4.00	(28.38) (13.12)	Royal Huisman Shipyard / Lunstroo Custom Design/Lunstroo/Munford / Vollenhove/The Netherlands/1993	1 x 12 cylinder 650hp MTU 12V183 diesel	Featured in The Superyachts, Volume 8
MIRABELLA	Auxiliary Sloop Composite	40.00 / 36.00	(131.24) (118.12)	9.00 / 3.80	(29.53) (12.46)	Concorde Yachts / Farr/Koskenkyla/Frost Associates / Chonburi/Thailand/1991	1 x 6 cylinder 470hp Lugger L614A Turbo diesel	Featured in The Superyachts, Volume 5
NAWAL J ex-Libra Star	Twin Screw Motor Yacht Steel/Aluminium	40.00	(131.24)	7.90 / 2.60	(25.91) (8.53)	Benetti Shipyard / Benetti/Disdale / Viarregio/Italy/1994	2 x 12 cylinder 2040hp MTU 369 TE 84 diesels	Featured in The Superyachts, Volume 8
PHILANDERER	Auxiliary Sloop Composite	40.00 / 35.50	(131.24) (116.47)	9.50 / 3.90	(31.16) (12.79)	Concorde Yachts / Farr/Koskenkyla/Frost Associates / Chonburi/Thailand/1993	1 x 6 cylinder 470hp Lugger L614A Turbo diesel	Refitted in 1996
PHILOSOPHY ex-Philante, ex-Philante IX	Twin Screw Motor Yacht Aluminium	40.00 / 33.00	(131.24) (108.25)	7.80 / 2.00	(25.59) (6.56)	Brooke Yachts International / Shead/Shead/Twigg / Lowestoft/UK/1991	2 x 8 cylinder 1332hp MTU 396TE84 diesels	Lloyd's ✠100A1, ✠LMC / Featured in The Superyachts, Volume 5
PRINCIPESSA VAIVIA ex-Marisa	Auxiliary Centreboard Ketch Steel/Aluminium	40.00 / 31.85	(131.24) (104.50)	8.23 6.37/3.44	(27.00) (20.90/11.28)	Perini Navi / Perini Navi / Viareggio/Italy/1990	2 x 402hp Caterpillar diesels	
SOLAIA	Twin Screw Motor Yacht Steel/Aluminium	40.00 / 36.40	(131.24) (119.42)	8.60 / 2.70	(28.21) (8.85)	Hakvoort Shipyard / Diana Yacht Design/Felix Buytendijk / Monnickendam/The Netherlands/2001	2 x 12 cylinder 720hp Caterpillar 3412C DI-TA diesels	Lloyd's ✠100A1, SSC Yacht G6, ✠LMC / Featured in The Superyachts, Volume 15
SEAFLOWER	Twin Screw Motor Yacht Steel/Aluminium	40.00 / 34.60	(131.42) (113.51)	8.95 / 2.75	(29.36) (9.02)	Feadship/Royal Van Lent / De Voogt/Lanvor / Kaag/The Netherlands/2002	2 x 12 cylinder 1248hp Caterpillar 3412E DI-TA diesels	Lloyds 100A1, SSC G6 Yacht, ✠LMC
COUNTACH	Twin Screw Motor Yacht GRP	39.93 / 34.75	(131.00) (114.00)	7.92 / 1.98	(26.00) (6.50)	Northcoast Yachts / Sarin/Henderson/Pokela/GTH Design / Tacoma/USA/1995	2 x 16 cylinder 2400hp Detroit 149TIB diesels	
INEVITABLE	Twin Screw Motor Yacht Aluminium	39.93	(131.00)	7.35	(28.00)	Palmer Johnson / Vripack/Boon/Palmer Johnson / Sturgeon Bay/USA/2000	2 x 12 cylinder 1700hp Caterpillar 3412 TA diesels	
CARMEN FONTANA	Twin Screw Motor Yacht Steel	39.90 / 37.00	(130.91) (121.39)	7.40 / 2.50	(24.27) (8.20)	Marine Industrial Technologies / Malliris / Piraeus/Greece/1992	2 x 12 cylinder 2714hp Deutz MWM diesels	
CARMEN SERENA	Twin Screw Motor Yacht Steel	39.90 / 37.00	(130.91) (121.39)	7.40 / 2.50	(24.27) (8.20)	Marine Industrial Technologies / Malliris / Piraeus/Greece/1993	2 x 12 cylinder 2714hp Deutz MWM diesels	
MAVERICK ex-Polar Bear, ex-Ice Bear	Twin Screw Motor Yacht Carbon fibre	39.90 / 37.49	(130.91) (123.00)	7.90 / 1.98	(25.91) (6.50)	Sterling / Susan Puleo / Ise/Japan/1988	2 x 8 cylinder 890hp MTU diesels	Lengthened in 1991
PUTERI SABAH II ex-Puteri Berjaya, ex-Lac III	Twin Screw Motor Yacht Steel	39.89 / 35.92	(130.88) (117.85)	7.80 / 2.22	(25.59) (7.28)	Maritime de Axpe SA / De Fever / Bilbao/Spain/1976	2 x 12 cylinder 725hp Caterpillar diesels	Lloyd's ✠100A1, ✠LMC
AL FARAH ex-Hannibal, ex-Lac II	Twin Screw Motor Yacht Steel	39.87 / 35.73	(130.83) (117.25)	7.80 / 2.88	(25.58) (8.16)	Feadship – De Vries Scheepsbouw / De Voogt/De Fever/Tanter / Aalsmeer/The Netherlands/1975	2 x 12 cylinder 735hp Caterpillar D348PCTA diesels	Libyan State Yacht
JANGADA IV	Twin Screw Motor Yacht Steel	39.80 / 34.00	(130.00) (111.55)	8.30 / 2.45	(27.23) (8.04)	Diaship/Heesen Shipyards / Diaship Design Team / Oss/The Netherlands/2001	2 x 12 cylinder 825hp Caterpillar 3412 CDI-TTA	

YACHT'S NAME / ex-name(s)	PROPULSION TYPE / CONSTRUCTION	LOA/LOA including spars / Length water line (m / ft)	Beam (Maximum) / Draught (m / ft)	BUILDER / NAVAL ARCHITECT/STYLIST/ INTERIOR DESIGNER / WHERE/YEAR	ENGINES Number & Cylinders / Horse Power / Maker/Type	REMARKS
PARI ex-Alshain	Twin Screw Motor Yacht / Steel	39.80 (130.58) 32.50 (106.63)	7.20 (23.62) 1.80 (5.90)	Tuzla/Cantiere Navale dell'Argentario Richard Davies/Ruggiero Porto Santo Stefano/Italy/1989	2 x 12 cylinder 1440hp MAND 2842LE	ABS✠A100
MONTE CARLO ex-Sea Pumpkin ex-Princess Marla ex-Princess Tina	Twin Screw Motor Yacht / Aluminium	39.77 (130.48) 34.69 (113.83)	8.00 (26.25) 2.21 (7.25)	Amels/Hakvoort Diana Yacht Design/Buytendijk The Netherlands/1988	2 x 12 cylinder 1960hp MTU 396TB93 diesel	Built to ABS Rules for Aluminium Yachts
VICTORIA OF STRATHEARN	Auxiliary Ketch / Aluminium	39.75 (130.41) 29.80 (97.77)	7.70 (25.26) 3.9 (12.79)	Alloy Yachts Langan Design/Andrew Winch Design Auckland/New Zealand/2001	1 X 12 cylinder 748hp MTU 12V 183 TE62	ABS A1✠ Yacht Service Featured in The Superyachts, Volume 15 MCA Code
ALITHIA ex-Triwac	Auxiliary Sloop / Alustar	39.62 (130.00)	8.38 (27.49) 4.00 (13.12)	Abeking & Rasmussen Tripp/Andrew Winch Design Lemwerder/Germany/2001	1 x 6 cylinder 543hp MTU 6R 183TE93 diesel	Featured in The Superyachts, Volume 16
ALTEZA	Twin Screw Motor Yacht / GRP	39.62 (130.00) 35.66 (117.00)	8.23 (27.00) 2.05 (6.75)	Christensen Motor Yacht Corporation Howard Apollonio/Puleo Vancouver/USA/1992	2 x 16 cylinder 1400hp Detroit V92TI-DDEC diesels	
CHARISMA ex-Allegra ex-Victory Lane	Twin Screw Motor Yacht / GRP	39.62 (130.00)	7.32 (24.00) 1.98 (6.60)	Hatteras Yachts Hatteras/Hargrave/Robinson High Point/USA/1995	2 x 16 cylinder 2500hp Detroit 149DDEC diesels	Featured in The Superyachts, Volume 9
INEKE IV ex-Hakim	Twin Screw Motor Yacht / Aluminium	39.62 (130.00) 35.00 (114.83)	8.50 (27.89) 2.50 (8.20)	Lloyd's Ships Lloyd's Ships/Curran Bulimba/Australia/1989	2 x 12 cylinder 1750hp Caterpillar 3512TA diesels	Featured in The Superyachts, Volume 6
LT SEA	Twin Screw Motor Yacht / FRP/Airex	39.62 (130.00) 34.65 (113.66)	8.23 (27.00) 1.83 (6.00)	Westport Shipyard Garden/Marshall/Pacific Custom Interiors Westport/USA/2000	2 x 12 cylinder 2735hp MTU/DDC4000 diesels	
MAGIC	Twin Screw Motor Yacht / FRP	39.62 (130.00) 36.88 (121.00)	8.23 (27.00) 2.07 (6.79)	Northern Marine Setzer/Ardeo Design/Setzer Seattle/USA/2003	2 x 12 cylinder 3700hp Detroit 2000 DDEC diesels	
PEGASUS	Triple Screw Motor Yacht / Aluminium	39.62 (130.00) 35.36 (116.00)	8.28 (27.17) 1.98 (6.50)	Broward Marine Broward/Hermanson & Bey Fort Lauderdale/USA/1991	3 x 16 cylinder 1450hp Detroit 92TA DDEC diesels	ABS✠A1 AMS Yachting Service Featured in The Superyachts, Volume 5
REJOYCE II	Twin Screw Motor Yacht / FRP/Airex	39.62 (130.00) 34.65 (113.66)	8.23 (27.00) 1.83 (6.00)	Westport Shipyard Garden/Marshall/Pacific Custom Interiors Westport/USA/2001	2 x 12 cylinder 2735hp MTU/DDC 4000 diesels	
ROYAL OAK	Twin Screw Motor Yacht / GRP	39.62 (130.00) 35.66 (117.00)	8.08 (26.51) 2.05 (6.75)	Christensen Motor Yacht Corporation Apollonio/Roberts Vancouver/USA/1989	2 x 12 cylinder 1150hp Mitsubishi diesels	
SACAJAWEA ex-Bellini ex-Daybreak	Twin Screw Motor Yacht / GRP	39.62 (130.00)	7.32 (24.00) 1.98 (6.60)	Hatteras Yachts Hatteras/Hargrave/Robinson High Point/USA/1994	2 x 16 cylinder 2400hp Detroit 149DDEC diesels	
SERENGETI	Twin Screw Motor Yacht / Composite	39.62 (130.00) 34.69 (113.81)	8.23 (27.00) 1.83 (6.00)	Westport Shipyard Garden/Greg Marshall/Pacific Custom Westport/USA/2002	2 x 12 cylinder 2735hp MTU/DDC 12V 4000	
SKYETYME ex-Bonheur II	Twin Screw Motor Yacht / GRP	39.62 (130.00) 35.66 (117.00)	8.23 (27.00) 2.05 (6.75)	Christensen Motor Yacht Corporation Apollonio/Glade Johnson Vancouver/USA/1990	2 x 12 cylinder 1080hp Detroit V92 diesels	Featured in The Superyachts, Volume 4
SOJOURN	Twin Screw Motor Yacht / FRP	39.62 (130.00)	7.93 (26.00) 1.83 (6.00)	Gambol Industries Sarin/Renee Brown/Sarin Long Beach/USA/1999	3 x 12 cylinder 1350hp Caterpillar 3412 diesels	
DETROIT EAGLE ex-Gallant Lady	Twin Screw Motor Yacht / Aluminium	39.60 (129.93)	8.00 (26.25) 1.88 (6.17)	Feadship – De Vries Scheepsbouw De Voogt/De Voogt/Smith Aalsmeer/The Netherlands/1992	2 x 16 cylinder 1400hp Detroit 92TADDEC diesels	Featured in The Superyachts, Volume 6

Name	Type	Length (m)	Length (ft)	Beam/Draft (m)	Builder / Designer / Place / Year	Engines	Notes
ELIKI ex-Christina II ex-Triaina	Twin Screw Motor Yacht Steel	39.60 35.50	(129.93) (116.47)	7.90 2.80	Boije Ensing Boije Ensing Groningen/The Netherlands/1960	2 x 5 cylinder 350hp B&W Alpha diesels	Rebuilt 1985
LES GIRLS DELFINO ex-Delfino II	Twin Screw Motor Yacht Steel	39.60 37.30	(129.93) (122.38)	7.30 3.00	Axpe De Fever/Puleo Bilbao/Spain/1971	2 x 6 cylinder 425hp Caterpillar diesels	
LEOCRIE II ex-Maria del Mar	Twin Screw Motor Yacht Steel	39.60	(129.93)	7.52 3.75	CRN CRN/Dilday Ancona/Italy/1985	2 x 12 cylinder 770hp GM 149 diesels	Bureau Veritas I3/3E, ⚓Yacht, ⚓MOT
ENDEAVOUR	Auxiliary Sloop Steel	39.56 26.88	(129.97) (88.19)	6.78 4.76	Camper & Nicholson Nicholson/Dijkstra Gosport/UK/1934	1 x 6 cylinder 352hp Caterpillar 3506 diesel	Featured in The Superyachts, Volume 3. Tommy Sopwith's original 1934 America's Cup challenger. Rebuilt in 1989 by Royal Huisman Shipyard with interiors by John Munford
CHARISMA A ex-Suvretta II	Twin Screw Motor Yacht Steel	39.55 35.83	(129.75) (117.55)	7.33 2.34	Clelands Shipbuilding Co Clelands Wallsend-on-Tyne/UK/1967	2 x 8 cylinder 495hp Rolls Royce D68TM diesels	
ATLANTICA SECONDA ex-Tanit, ex-Paminusch ex-Duni, ex-Galu	Twin Screw Motor Yacht Steel	39.50 33.20	(129.59) (108.92)	7.40 3.00	Fratelli Benetti Benetti/Benetti Viareggio/Italy/1971	2 x 12 cylinder 1000hp Caterpillar diesels	
SILVER SHALIS	Triple Water Jet Motor Yacht Aluminium	39.50 34.45	(129.59) (113.03)	7.90 1.80	Abeking & Rasmussen Diana Yacht Design/Buytendijk Lemwerder/Germany/1987	3 x 16 cylinder 3480hp MTU diesels	3 x KaMeWa Water jets
STILVI	Twin Screw Motor Yacht Steel	39.43 34.58	(129.36) (113.45)	6.92 2.07	Camper & Nicholson Ltd C&N/Bannenberg Southampton/UK/1974	2 x 12 cylinder 1215hp MTU diesels	Lloyd's ⚓100A1, ⚓LMC
LADY HALIMA	Twin Screw Motor Yacht Steel/Aluminium	39.40 34.00	(129.27) (111.55)	8.32 2.45	Diaship/Heesen Shipyards Diaship Design Team/Paola Smith Oss/The Netherlands/2001	2 x 12 cylinder 825hp Caterpillar 3412 CDI-TTA	Featured in The Superyachts, Volume 15
CHRISTINE ex-Sounds of Pacific	Twin Water Jet Motor Yacht Aluminium	39.32 31.40	(129.00) (103.02)	7.50 1.32	Oceanfast Pty Ltd Curran/Bannenberg Perth/Australia/1991	2 x 16 cylinder 2250hp Deutz diesels	Lengthened during refit at Sensation Yachts 2002. Naval architecture by Phil Curren. Interior designer Sensation Yachts.
BELGRAVIA ex-Hormoz	Twin Screw Motor Yacht Steel	39.35 34.45	(129.10) (113.02)	7.50 3.20	Astilleros Armon Madarro Navia/Spain/1978	2 x 16 cylinder 1676hp Caterpillar D398 diesels	Lloyd's ⚓100A1, ⚓LMC
MYSTIC W ex-Moldavia ex-Aliosha VI	Twin Screw Motor Yacht Steel	39.35 34.52	(129.10) (113.26)	7.53 2.95	Astilleros Armon Madarro Navia/Spain/1981/refitted 2002	2 x 12 cylinder 850hp Caterpillar diesels	Lloyd's ⚓100A1, ⚓LMC Total rebuild designed by Studio Scanu in 2001
RED SAPPHIRE	Twin Screw Motor Yacht Aluminium	39.10	(128.28)	7.98 3.90	Diaship/Heesen Shipyards Diaship Design Team Oss/The Netherlands/1999	2 x 16 cylinder 3699 hp MTU 4000TE90diesels	ABS ⚓A1, AMS Yachting Service. Sportfishing yacht. Featured in The Superyachts, Volume 13
TULLY	Twin Screw Motor Yacht Steel/Aluminium	39.10 34.46	(128.28) (113.06)	8.29 2.31	Benetti Shipyard Benetti/Natuci/Natuci Viareggio/Italy/1993	2 x 12 cylinder 2400hp MTU 396TB93 diesels	
LIBERTY GB ex-Irina	Twin Screw Motor Yacht Steel/Aluminium	39.05	(128.12)	8.70 2.75	Feadship – Van Lent & Zonen BV De Voogt/Larvor Kaag/The Netherlands/1997	2 x 12 cylinder 632hp Caterpillar 3412DI-TA diesels	
QUETZAL SPIRIT ex-If Only ex-Walanka	Twin Screw Motor Yacht Steel	39.04 33.73	(128.09) (110.67)	7.10 2.44	Van de Werf/Van Lent & Zonen BV Roger Deest Kaag/The Netherlands/1974	2 x 8 cylinder 690hp MTU diesels	
INEVITABLE	Twin Screw Motor Yacht Aluminium	39.02 35.00	(128.00) (114.82)	8.5 2.2	Palmer Johnson Vripack/Palmer Johnson Patrick Knowles Design Sturgeon Bay, USA/2001	2 x 12 cylinder 825hp Caterpillar 3412CTA diesels	Lloyd's ⚓100A1 Yacht, ⚓LMC
AQUARIUS L ex-Al Madina	Twin Screw Motor Yacht Steel	39.01 31.80	(128.00) (104.33)	6.70 1.80	CRN CRN Ancona/Italy/1976	2 x 8 cylinder 795hp Deutz BF 16M716	Lloyds

YACHT'S NAME ex-name(s)	PROPULSION TYPE CONSTRUCTION	DIMENSIONS LOA/LOA including spars Length water line m (ft)	Beam (Maximum) Draught m (ft)	BUILDER NAVAL ARCHITECT/STYLIST/ INTERIOR DESIGNER WHERE/YEAR	ENGINES Number & Cylinders Horse Power Maker/Type	REMARKS
MOONMAIDEN II ex-Yildiz 10	Twin Screw Motor Yacht Steel	39.01 (128.00)	7.01 (23.00) 2.59 (8.50)	Beykoz Shipyard Beykoz Istanbul/Turkey/1975	2 x 12 cylinder 600hp Deutz diesels	Featured in The Superyachts Volume 4
LADY VAL	Twin Screw Motor Yacht FRP	39.01 (128.00)	7.93 (26.00) 1.96 (6.42)	Northcoast Yachts Robin Rose Tacoma/USA/2001	2 x 12 cylinder 1450hp Caterpillar 3412 diesels	
CATALONIAN ex-Extasea A	Twin Screw Motor Yacht Aluminium	39.00 (127.94) 32.88 (106.89)	7.60 (24.93) 3.80 (12.47)	Diaship/Heesen Shipyards Mulder/Mulder/Art Line Oss/The Netherland/1986	2 x 16 cylinder 1600hp Deutz BAM816C-R diesels	
MAMAMOUCHI	Auxiliary Sloop Aluminium	39.00 (127.94) 31.59 (103.64)	8.96 (29.40) 3.45 (11.32)	Pendennis Shipyard Dubois/Dubois/Redman Whiteley Falmouth/UK/1996	1 x 12 cylinder 527hp MTU 183TE61 diesel	Featured in The Superyachts Volume 10
VINIDREA II	Motor Yacht Alloy	39.00 (127.94) 32.70 (107.28)	8.31 (27.26) 1.85 (6.06)	Cuttolo Caliari Tuzla/2002	2 x 12 cylinders 2385hp MTU 12V396	
VELSHEDA	Auxiliary Sloop Steel Composite	39.00 (127.94) 25.30 (83.00)	6.40 (20.99) 4.60 (15.09)	Camper & Nicholsons/SYS CE Nicholson/Dijkstra/Munford Gosport/UK/1933/Southampton/UK/1997	1 x 6 cylinder 415hp MTU 6R183TE72 diesel	Converted J-Class racing yacht rebuilt by Southampton Yacht Services in 1997
CYRANO DE BERGERAC	Auxiliary Twin Screw Ketch Aluminium	38.86 (127.49) 31.07 (101.94)	8.71 (28.58) 3.35 (10.99)	Camper & Nicholsons Humphreys/Munford Gosport/UK/1993	2 x 6 cylinder 520hp Caterpillar 3406B diesels	Featured in The Superyachts, Volume 7
BLACKSHEEP	Twin Water Jet Motor Yacht Cored Composite	38.71 (127.00) 32.00 (105.00)	7.31 (24.00) 1.21 (4.00)	Trident Shipworks Inc Cutola/Wesley Carr/Savio Interiors Tampa/USA/1998	2 x 16 cylinder 3048hp MTU 396TE94 diesels	Featured in The Superyachts, Volume 12
EXCELLENCE	Twin Screw Cockpit Motor Yacht Steel	38.71 (127.00)	8.12 (26.67) 2.33 (7.67)	Feadship—Van Lent & Zonen BV De Voogt/Glade Johnson Kaag/The Netherlands/1986	2 x 16 cylinder 1300hp Detroit diesels	
SAYONARA ALPHA ex-Talofa IV ex-Sayonara	Auxiliary Twin Screw Ketch Aluminium	38.71 (127.00)	7.00 (22.97) 4.27 (14.00)	Chantier Navale Lorient CNL Lorient/France/1968	2 x 6 cylinder 200hp GM diesels	Rebuilt and lengthened in 1991
ALTA ex-Talon ex-Ginmylou	Twin Screw Motor Yacht Steel	38.70 (126.95) 32.50 (106.63)	7.65 (25.09) 2.15 (7.05)	Cantiere Picchiotti SpA Picchiotti/Dilday Viareggio/Italy/1987	2 x 12 cylinder 624hp Caterpillar diesels	Lloyd's ✠100A1, ✠LMC Featured in The Superyachts, Volume 3
MARIA CHRISTINA ex-Aleta ex-Felicita	Auxiliary Centreboard Ketch Steel/Aluminium	38.70 (126.97) 30.69 (100.70)	7.60 (24.93) 2.98 (9.80)	Perini Navi Perini Navi/Perini Navi/Perini Navi Viareggio/Italy/1984	2 x GM Type 861 diesels	
HEMILEA ex-Auriga ex-Elsewhere	Twin Screw Motor Yacht Aluminium	38.60 (126.65) 31.50 (103.35)	7.40 (24.28) 2.30 (7.55)	Baglietto Shipyard SpA Baglietto/Baglietto/Cichero Varazze/Italy/1992	2 x 12 cylinder 2285hp MTU 396TE94 diesels	ABS ✠ A1 Yachting sevice, AMS
ORION ex-Vira ex-Dianne ex-Pays-de-France	Auxiliary Twin Screw Two Masted Schooner Steel Composite	38.60 (126.64) 27.40 (89.89)	7.30 (23.95) 4.10 (13.45)	Camper & Nicholsons Charles E Nicholson Gosport/UK/1910	2 x 6 cylinder 230hp Caterpillar diesels	Rebuilt 1978-90 at Valdettaro Shipyard. Featured in The Superyachts Volume 3
SWEET PEA ex-Battered Bull ex-Dale R II, ex-Sylvana	Twin Screw Motor Yacht Aluminium	38.59 (126.28) 33.14 (108.73)	7.00 (22.97) 1.90 (6.25)	Abeking & Rasmussen A&R/Fexas/Saifuku Lemwerder/Germany/1985	2 x 12 cylinder 1500hp MTU 396TB93 diesels	Featured in The Superyachts Volume 3
DIONE STAR ex-Colombaio Star	Auxiliary Ketch Steel	38.50 (126.28) 32.50 (106.60)	8.10 (26.58) 3.50 (11.48)	Sheepswerft Friesland Diana Yacht Design Lemmer/The Netherlands/1991	1 x 12 cylinder MAN diesel	Lloyd's ✠100A1
INTUITION LADY ex-Deneb Star C	Twin Screw Motor Yacht Steel	38.50 (126.28)	7.20 (23.62) 3.30 (10.82)	Fratelli Benetti Benetti/Benetti/Benetti Viareggio/Italy/1978	2 x 8 cylinder 695hp MTU diesels	Featured in The Superyachts Volume 2

Name	Type / Construction	Length (m)	Length (ft)	Beam/Draft (m)	Beam/Draft (ft)	Builder / Designer / Location / Year	Engines	Notes
JASALI ex-Colombaio Sun	Auxiliary Ketch / Steel	38.50 / 32.50	(126.28) / (106.60)	8.10 / 3.50	(26.58) / (11.48)	Sheepswerft Friesland / Diana Yacht Design / Lemmer/The Netherlands/1991	1 x 12 cylinder MAN diesel	Refitted in 1994/1995, Lloyd's ✠100A1
LIFE OF RILEY ex-P'Zazz	Twin Screw Motor Yacht / GRP	38.50 / 34.30	(126.28) / (110.56)	7.92 / 2.43	(26.00) / (8.00)	Delta Marine / Schubert & Minor/Glade Johnson / Seattle/USA/1989	2 x 8 cylinder 705hp Caterpillar 3508TA diesels	Featured in The Superyachts Volume 3, Rebuild and complete refit at Delta Marine 2001
OKTANA	Twin Screw Motor Yacht / Steel/Aluminium	38.50 / 32.54	(126.28) / (106.90)	7.48 / 2.57	(24.60) / (8.50)	Codecasa / Codecasa/Manfredi & Sforzi/Laws / Viareggio/Italy/1995	2 x 12 cylinder 2100hp MTU 396TE94 diesels	Lloyd's ✠100A1, ✠LMC, Featured in The Superyachts, Volume 9
TIME	Twin Water Jet Motor Yacht / Aluminium	38.50 / 33.70	(126.28) / (112.50)	8.25 / 1.50	(27.07) / (4.92)	Palmer Johnson Incorporated / Fexas/Attwood / Sturgeon Bay/USA/1987	2 x 12 cylinder 2570hp MTU diesels	Featured in The Superyachts Volume 1
ANDREA		38.40	(126.00)	8.53	(28.00)	Delta Marine / Michael Kirschtein / Seattle/USA/2003		
BIG EASY ex-Algorithm	Twin Screw Motor Yacht / Aluminium	38.40	(126.00)	7.77 / 1.88	(25.50) / (6.00)	Trinity Yachts / Trinity Yachts/Dee Robinson / New Orleans/USA/2001	2 x 12 cylinder 1350hp Caterpillar 3412 diesels	
EMANUEL ex-Bravo Papa	Twin Screw Motor Yacht / Steel	38.40 / 33.70	(126.00) / (110.56)	7.50 / 2.20	(24.60) / (7.21)	Cantiere Navale Nicolini / Zampetti/Nicolini/Celi / Ancona/Italy/1992	2 x 16 cylinder 1962hp MTU diesels	
EMERALD ISLE	Twin Screw Motor Yacht / GRP	38.40	(126.00)	8.11 / 2.13	(26.60) / (7.00)	Christensen Motor Yacht Works / Apollonio/Johnson/Puleo / Vancouver/Canada/1992	2 x 12 cylinder 730hp Detroit 92TA diesels	
GLORIA	Auxiliary Schooner / Steel	38.40 / 24.00	(126.00) / (78.74)	6.90 / 4.20	(22.64) / (13.78)	Jachtwerf Jongert / Beeldsnijder/Belsnijder/Lowland / Medemblik/The Netherlands/1986	1 x 6 cylinder 406hp Caterpillar 3406 diesel	Featured in The Superyachts, Volume 2
LADY ALLISON ex-Virginian, ex-Highlander ex-Sharon S, ex-Claybeth	Twin Screw Motor Yacht / Steel	38.40 / 34.84	(126.00) / (114.33)	7.75 / 2.44	(25.42) / (8.00)	Feadship – Van Lent & Zonen / De Voogt/von Thaden / Kaag/The Netherlands/1978	2 x 6 cylinder 573hp Caterpillar D379PCTA diesels	
MARLENA	Twin Screw Motor Yacht / Aluminium	38.40	(126.00)	8.20 / 1.80	(27.00) / (5.91)	Trinity Yachts / Sharp Design/Trinity Yachts/Dee Robinson / New Orleans/USA/1998	2 x 12 cylinder 3500hp Paxman 12V185 diesels	ABS✠A1 Yachting Service. Sport fishing yacht
PARLAY	Auxiliary Ketch / Aluminium	38.40 / 30.50	(126.10) / (100.00)	8.40 / 6.30	(27.70) / (20.80)	Ortona Navi / JG Alden/JG Alden / Italy/1991	1 x 12 cylinder 425hp Caterpillar diesel	
SARITA C ex-Sarita U, ex-Virginia Alpha ex-Bagheera, ex-Idell V	Twin Screw Motor Yacht / Steel	38.40 / 34.40	(126.00) / (112.87)	7.20 / 3.25	(23.62) / (10.66)	CRN / CRN/Dilday / Ancona/Italy/1969	3 x 18 cylinder 1250hp CRM 18D/S2 diesels	
SINBAD	Twin Screw Motor Yacht / Composite	38.40 / 35.66	(126.00) / (117.00)	8.53 / 3.04	(28.00) / (10.00)	Delta Marine / Delta/Espinosa/Duet Design / Seattle/USA/2002	2 x 8 cylinder 1550hp Caterpillar 3508B	ABS
SIS W	Twin Screw Motor Yacht / Aluminium	38.40 / 34.02	(126.00) / (111.61)	8.11 / 1.82	(26.61) / (6.00)	Burger Boat Company / Owners/Joanne Walgreen/Douglas Richey / Manitowac/Wisconsin/2003	2 x 8 cylinder 1300hp Caterpillar 3508-D	ABS certified
IL CIGNO ex-Al Haja ex-Princess Kim	Twin Screw Motor Yacht / Steel	38.36 / 32.68	(125.85) / (107.22)	7.54 / 2.25	(24.73) / (7.38)	Cantiere Navale Nicolini / CNN / Ancona/Italy/1985	2 x 16 cylinder 2105hp MTU diesels	Lloyd's ✠100A1, ✠LMC, Featured in The Superyachts, Volume 5
CHEETAH MOON ex-Le Marriah, ex-Luwima ex-Luwima K	Twin Screw Motor Yacht / Steel	38.36 / 32.68	(125.85) / (107.22)	7.54 / 2.20	(24.73) / (7.22)	Cantiere Navale Nicolini / CNN / Ancona/Italy/1986	2 x 16 cylinder 2105hp MTU diesels	Lloyd's ✠100A1, ✠LMC, Refitted 1993 & 2002
SHALIMAR II	Twin Screw Motor Yacht / Steel	38.35 / 33.58	(125.83) / (110.17)	7.80 / 2.25	(25.59) / (7.38)	Feadship – Van Lent & Zonen / De Voogt/De Voogt/De Voogt / Kaag/The Netherlands/1974	2 x 8 cylinder 760hp Caterpillar diesels	

YACHT'S NAME ex-name(s)	PROPULSION TYPE / CONSTRUCTION	DIMENSIONS LOA/LOA including spars / Length water line m (ft)	Beam (Maximum) / Draught m (ft)	BUILDER / NAVAL ARCHITECT/STYLIST/ INTERIOR DESIGNER WHERE/YEAR	ENGINES Number & Cylinders / Horse Power / Maker/Type	REMARKS
OBSESSIONS	Twin Screw / Motor Yacht / Aluminium	38.34 / 30.50 (125.77)/(100.07)	7.98 / 2.10 (26.18)/(6.89)	Diaship/Heesen Shipyards / Diaship/Mulder/Diaship / Oss/The Netherlands/1996	2 x 16 cylinder / 3500hp / MTU 396TB94 diesels	ABS ✠A1 AMS Yachting Service Sport fishing styled yacht
PEGASUS III ex-Al Mubarakiah ex-Pegasus III ex-Pegasus	Twin Screw / Motor Yacht / Mahogany/Teak	38.30 / 35.00 (125.66)/(114.83)	7.10 / 1.80 (23.29)/(5.90)	Krogerwerft / Krogerwerft/Bannenberg/Bannenberg / Rendsburg/West Germany/1973	2 x 20 cylinder / 3530hp / MTU diesels	
HETAIROS	Auxiliary Centreboard / Ketch / Wood/West System	38.25 / 30.50 (125.50)/(100.00)	8.46 / 3.00/8.70 (27.80)/(9.84/28.54)	Abeking & Rasmussen / King/King/Winch / Lemwerder/Germany/1993	1 x 12 cylinder / 985hp / MTU 183TE92 diesel	Featured in The Superyachts, Volume 9
SANTA CRUZ TRES	Twin Screw / Motor Yacht / Steel	38.25 / 35.10 (125.50)/(115.14)	7.20 / 3.00 (23.62)/(9.80)	CRN / CRN / Ancona/Italy/1979	2 x 12 cylinder / 812hp / GM diesels	Lloyd's ✠100A1, ✠LMC. Rebuilt and extended at Watershed International/1999. Dowland Naval Architects/Michael Kirchstein Designs
WHISPERS ex-Longitude Zero ex-Moura	Triple Screw / Motor Yacht / Wood	38.20 / 32.65 (125.33)/(107.12)	8.40 / 2.30 (27.56)/(7.54)	Cantieri di Pisa / Cantieri di Pisa / Pisa/Italy/1984	3 x 12 cylinder / 1745hp / MTU 12V 396 TB 93 diesels	
DEJANEIRA	Twin Screw / Motor Yacht / Steel	38.12 / 34.77 (125.07)/(114.08)	6.34 / 2.74 (20.80)/(9.00)	Vosper Ltd / Vosper / Portsmouth/UK/1951	2 x 6 cylinder / 350hp / Caterpillar diesels	Lloyd's ✠100A1, ✠LMC
ACHILLES II	Twin Screw / Motor Yacht / Aluminium	38.10 (125.00)	8.10 / 2.02 (26.57)/(6.63)	Lloyd's Ships / Hargrave / Bulimba/Australia/1988	2 x 12 cylinder / Caterpillar diesels	
CENTURION ex-Taurus	Twin Screw / Motor Yacht / GRP	38.10 / 33.30 (125.00)/(109.25)	8.50 / 3.00 (27.88)/(9.84)	Delta Marine / Delta / Seattle/USA/1991	2 x 8 cylinder / 1070hp / Caterpillar diesels	Rebuilt in 1998
IL DOGE ex-Mariya Uno	Auxiliary Centreboard / Cutter / Steel/GRP	38.10 / 28.45 (125.00)/(93.34)	7.77 / 6.60/2.40 (23.95)/(21.65/7.87)	CCYD Srl / Holland/Holland/Spadolini / Venice/Italy/1990	2 x 6 cylinder / 404hp / Caterpillar diesels	Lloyd's ✠100A1, ✠LMC. 556 m² sail area. Refit and stern lengthened 1994 Featured in The Superyachts, Volume 4
JAGUAR	Twin Screw / Motor Yacht	38.10 (125.00)	7.80 / 3.40 (25.59)/(11.15)	Shipyard Haak / Shipyard Haak / Zaandam/The Netherlands/1998	2 x 730hp / Caterpillar	
JANET	Twin Screw / Motor Yacht / FRP	38.10 / 32.60 (125.00)/(106.92)	7.62 / 1.83 (25.00)/(6.00)	Cheoy Lee Shipyards / Mulder/Mulder/Savio / Hong Kong/2002	2 x 12 cylinder / 2250hp / Caterpillar 3512B diesels	
MILK AND HONEY	Twin Screw / Motor Yacht / Aluminium	38.10 / 34.10 (125.00)/(111.88)	7.92 / 2.01 (29.00)/(6.59)	Palmer Johnson / Vripack/Murray & Assoc / Wisconsin/USA/2002	2 x 16 cylinder / 2800bhp / DDEC 16V2000	Lloyds ✠100 A1 SSC, G6 Yacht, ✠LMC, MCA Code
MIMI ex-Kakapo Ex-Arara III	Twin Screw / Motor Yacht / Aluminium	38.10 / 35.10 (125.00)/(115.16)	7.60 / 2.00 (24.93)/(6.56)	Burger Boat Company / Hargrave / Manitowoc/USA/1977	2 x 12 cylinder / 725hp / Caterpillar diesels	
KAORI ex-Mandalay	Auxiliary Twin Screw / Schooner / Aluminium	38.10 / 32.77 (125.00)/(107.50)	8.59 / 3.28/5.49 (28.17)/(10.76/18.01)	Palmer Johnson Incorporated / Paine/Plachter / Sturgeon Bay/USA/1992	2 x 6 cylinder / 312hp / Caterpillar 3406TA diesels	Sail area 659m²
LADINA ex-White Rabbit A	Twin Screw / Motor Yacht / Steel	38.10 / 33.20 (125.00)/(108.91)	8.00 / 2.76 (26.25)/(9.05)	Feadship – De Vries Scheepsbouw / De Voogt / Aalsmeer/The Netherlands/1989	2 x 8 cylinder / 775hp / Caterpillar 3508DI-TA diesels	
SALAMAT ex-Alexandra	Triple Screw / Cockpit Motor Yacht / GRP	38.10 / 33.83 (125.00)/(111.00)	7.25 / 1.98 (23.78)/(6.50)	Hatteras Yachts / Hatteras/Hargrave/Fashions United / High Point/USA/1992	3 x 16 cylinder / 1345hp / Detroit 92TADDEC diesels	Featured in The Superyachts, Volume 6
SENSEI ex-Devil Queller	Twin Screw / Motor Yacht / GRP	38.10 / 33.80 (125.00)/(111.00)	8.20 / 2.10 (27.00)/(7.00)	Admiral Marine / Glade Johnson/Jonathan Barnett / Osaka/Japan/1991	2 x 12 cylinder / 2000hp / Mitsubishi diesels	Rebuilt and lengthened 3.66m (12ft) by Admiral Marine Works, with exterior re-design and interiors by JQB in 1995. Featured in The Superyachts, Volume 10

Name	Type / Construction	LOA / LWL (m)	(ft)	Beam / Draft (m)	(ft)	Builder / Designer / Place / Year	Engines	Notes
SHOW TIME ex-Nenika, ex-Kallista	Twin Screw Motor Yacht Aluminium	38.10 / 33.79	(125.00) (110.86)	7.31 / 1.86	(24.00) (6.00)	Broward Marine, Broward/Broward/Puleo, Fort Lauderdale/USA/1989	2 x 16 cylinder 1350hp Detroit 92TA diesels	Featured in The Superyachts, Volume 5
SUNCHASER Ex-Fifty One	Twin Screw Motor Yacht GRP	38.10 / 34.14	(125.00) (112.00)	8.08 / 2.05	(26.50) (6.75)	Christensen Motor Yacht Corporation, Howard Apollonio/Pagani, Vancouver/USA/1991	2 x 12 cylinder 860hp Caterpillar 3412TA diesels	Featured in The Superyachts, Volume 7
AIGLON	Auxiliary Two Masted Schooner Aluminium	38.00 / 29.60	(124.67) (97.11)	7.60 / 2.60	(24.93) (8.53)	Abeking & Rasmussen, Andre Mauris, Lemwerder/West Germany/1970	2 x 6 cylinder 340hp Caterpillar diesels	
BLUEMAR II	Twin Screw Motor Yacht Steel	38.00 / 33.51	(124.68) (109.95)	7.01 / 2.34	(23.00) (7.67)	Feadship – Van Lent & Zonen BV, Navigator/Picant, Kaag/The Netherlands/1976	2 x 16 cylinder 2200hp MTU diesels	Lloyd's ✠100A1, ✠LMC
FADLALLAH	Twin Screw Motor Yacht Aluminium	38.00 / 34.80	(124.67) (114.17)	8.50 / 2.00	(27.89) (6.56)	Sensation Yachts, Sharp/Sensation/Sensation, Auckland/New Zealand/1995	2 x 12 cylinder 1014hp Caterpillar 3412 diesels	Featured in The Superyachts, Volume 10
INCA ROSE	Twin Screw Motor Yacht Steel/Aluminium	38.00 / 33.80	(124.67) (110.89)	7.00 / 2.50	(10.28) (8.20)	Ocean Pacifico Incorporated, Diana Yacht Design/de la Vega, Subic Bay/Philippines/1998	2 x 6 cylinder 611hp Caterpillar 3412 DI-TA diesels	
LIGAYA	Twin Screw Motor Yacht Steel/Aluminium	38.00 / 33.80	(124.67) (110.89)	7.00 / 2.50	(10.28) (8.20)	Ocean Pacifico Incorporated, Diana Yacht Design/Peter Cannon, Subic Bay/Philippines/1998	2 x 6 cylinder 611hp Caterpillar 3412 DI-TA diesels	
MAYAN QUEEN ex-Lady Alice, ex-Excalibur ex-Lady Alice	Twin Screw Motor Yacht Aluminium	38.00 / 33.00	(124.67) (108.24)	8.00 / 1.80	(26.25) (5.90)	Hakvoort Shipyard, Diana Yacht Design/Wade, Monnickendam/The Netherlands/1986	2 x 6 cylinder 1555hp MTU diesels	Built to ABS Rules for Aluminium Yachts Featured in The Superyachts Volume 4
MUMU	Auxiliary Sloop Advanced Composite	38.00 / 33.70	(124.66) (110.55)	8.90 / 3.50	(29.20) (11.48)	RB Dereli, Philippe Briand/Eva Cadio/Act Studio, Turkey/2002	1 x 6 cylinder 550hp Caterpillar 3406E diesel	
SIDARTA 1	Twin Screw Motor Yacht Steel	38.00 / 33.57	(124.67) (110.14)	7.50 / 3.30	(24.60) (10.83)	Scheepswerf Haak BV, Haak, Zaandam/The Netherlands/1987	2 x 12 cylinder 913hp Caterpillar 3512DI-TA diesels	Lloyd's ✠100A1, ✠LMC
ORION	Twin Screw Motor Yacht Steel	37.94 / 32.33	(124.50) (106.08)	7.70 / 2.34	(25.25) (7.67)	Feadship – Van Lent & Zonen BV, De Voogt/De Voogt, Kaag/The Netherlands/1984	2 x 12 cylinder 633hp Caterpillar 3412PCTA diesels	
MONACO ex-Matanthar ex-Arkan	Twin Screw Motor Yacht Steel	37.90 / 33.30	(124.34) (109.25)	7.05 / 3.09	(23.13) (10.13)	Feadship – Van Lent & Zonen, De Voogt/Tanter/Disdale, Kaag/The Netherlands/1981	2 x 12 cylinder 933hp Caterpillar D348PCTA diesels	Refitted, lengthened & new stern added in 1992 by Pendennis Shipyard. Lloyd's ✠100A1, ✠LMC
AERIE	Twin Screw Motor Yacht GRP	37.80 / 33.84	(124.02) (111.00)	7.87 / 1.83	(25.83) (6.00)	Delta Marine, Delta/Delta/Jonathan Quinn Barnett, Seattle/USA/2001	2 cylinder 1800hp DDC/MTU 2000 diesels	
ANJILIS	TwinScrew Motor Yacht	37.80	(124.00)	7.93	(26.00)	Trinity Yachts, Dee Robinson, New Orleans/USA/2002	2 x 16 cylinder 1800hp MTU/DDEC 16V2000 diesels	
ANTONISA	Auxiliary Sloop Wood/Epoxy	37.80 / 27.40	(124.02) (89.90)	7.80 3.00/8.10	(25.59) (9.84/28.58)	Hodgdon Yachts, Bruce King Yacht Design, Maine/USA/1999	1 x 6 cylinder 535hp Lugger 6140 diesel	
CARDIGRAE VI	Twin Screw Motor Yacht Steel	37.80 / 34.40	(124.02) (112.86)	6.40 / 2.50	(20.99) (8.20)	Camper & Nicholson, C & N, Southampton/UK/1962	2 x 8 cylinder 350hp Crossley diesels	Rebuilt 1979 and 1992
FREEDOM OF ADA ex-Freedom	Auxiliary Twin Screw Ketch Aluminium	37.80 / 30.41	(124.02) (99.80)	7.92 3.05/5.89	(26.00) (10.00/19.30)	Cantiere Picchiotti SpA, Sparkman & Stephens, Viareggio/Italy/1986	2 x 6 cylinder 402hp Caterpillar 3406TA diesels	
GALE WINDS ex-Ste Iill	Twin Screw Motor Yacht GRP	37.80 / 33.83	(124.00) (111.00)	7.86 / 1.86	(25.80) (6.10)	Delta Marine, Delta/Delta/Jonathan Quinn Barnett, Seattle/USA/1997	2 x 16 cylinder 1450hp Detroit 92TA diesels	Featured in The Superyachts, Volume 12

YACHT'S NAME ex-name(s)	PROPULSION TYPE / CONSTRUCTION	DIMENSIONS LOA/LOA including spars / Length water line m (ft)		Beam (Maximum) / Draught m (ft)		BUILDER / NAVAL ARCHITECT/STYLIST/ INTERIOR DESIGNER / WHERE/YEAR	ENGINES Number & Cylinders / Horse Power / Maker/Type	REMARKS
JAMI	Twin Screw Motor Yacht GRP	37.80 37.80	(124.00) (111.00)	7.86 1.83	(25.80) (6.00)	Delta Marine Delta/Delta/A la Mer & Piquette Seattle/USA/1998	2 x 16 cylinder 1450hp Detroit 16V92TAC diesels	
LADY LINDA	Twin Screw Motor Yacht GRP	37.80 37.80	(124.00) (111.00)	7.86 1.83	(25.80) (6.00)	Delta Marine Delta/Delta/Claudette Bonville Seattle/USA/1999	2 x 16 cylinder 1800hp Detroit diesels	
MIMI ex-Scott Free	Twin Screw Motor Yacht GRP	37.80 33.83	(124.00) (111.00)	7.62 1.83	(25.00) (6.00)	Delta Marine Delta Design Group/Delta Seattle/USA/1997	2 x 16 cylinder 1450hp Detroit 92TA diesels	
MURPHY'S LAW ex-Janet	Twin Screw Motor Yacht Aluminium	37.80 29.57	(124.00) (97.00)	6.71 1.83	(22.03) (6.00)	Broward Marine Inc Broward Fort Lauderdale/USA/1987	2 x 16 cylinder 1350hp GM 16V92 DDEC diesels	Lengthened by 2.74m (9ft) in 1992
WEHR NUTS	Twin Screw Motor Yacht GRP	37.80 33.83	(124.00) (111.00)	8.37 2.13	(27.50) (7.00)	Christensen Shipyard Christensen/Robin Rose Vancouver/Canada/1998	2 x 16 cylinder 1800hp Detroit 2000V16 diesels	ABS ✠A1 AMS Yachting Service. Raised pilothouse
ALUMERCIA	Twin Screw Motor Yacht Aluminium	37.69 33.50	(123.66) (109.90)	8.40 2.40	(27.55) (8.00)	Heesen Shipyards Vripack/Omega/Omega Oss/The Netherlands/2001	2 x 6 cylinder 480hp Caterpillar 3406E DI-TA diesels	Featured in The Superyachts, Volume 15 Fitted with twin Schottel STP 200 rotating drives
SEABIRD ex-Destiny	Twin Screw Motor Yacht Aluminium	37.69 33.33	(123.66) (109.33)	6.70 1.83	(22.00) (6.00)	Broward Marine Inc Broward/Denison Fort Lauderdale/USA/1989	2 x 16 cylinder 1350hp Detroit 92TA diesels	Featured in The Superyachts, Volume 4
ATHINA ex-Annabelle	Twin Screw Motor Yacht GRP	37.60	(123.36)	7.20 2.70	(23.62) (8.85)	Fratelli Benetti Benetti Viareggio/Italy/1982	2 x 6 cylinder 650hp MTU diesels	
ROMINTA	Twin Screw Motor Yacht Aluminium	37.60 30.50	(123.36) (100.07)	7.40 1.20	(24.28) (3.94)	Baglietto Shipyard SpA Baglietto/Baglietto/Bruno & Agamemnone Varazze/Italy/1990	2 x 12 cylinder 2557hp MTU 396TB94 diesels	Lloyd's ✠100A1, ✠LMC
GALILEO	Auxiliary Ketch Aluminium	37.58 29.26	(123.30) (96.00)	7.95 3.50	(26.08) (11.48)	Palmer Johnson Incorporated Sparkman & Stephens/Munford Sturgeon Bay/USA/1989	1 x 12 cylinder 530hp MTU 183TC91 diesel	
MAYSYLPH	Auxiliary Ketch Aluminium	37.57 29.26	(123.27) (96.00)	8.08 3.66	(26.50) (12.00)	Palmer Johnson Incorporated Sparkman & Stephens/Munford Sturgeon Bay/USA/1990	1 x 12 cylinder 530hp MTU 183TE91 diesel	497m² sail area. Hood spars
BLACKHAWK IV	Twin Screw Motor Yacht Steel	37.55 34.40	(123.20) (112.86)	7.10 2.40	(23.29) (7.87)	Feadship – De Vries Scheepsbouw HW De Voogt Aalsmeer/The Netherlands/1971	2 x 12 cylinder 920hp Caterpillar 348TA diesels	
ALTHEA	Auxiliary Twin Screw Schooner Steel	37.50 23.70	(123.03) (77.75)	7.62 3.22	(25.00) (10.56)	Kanelos Bros Shipyard Moschonas/Winch Piraeus/Greece/1993	2 x 6 cylinder 520hp MAN diesels	Featured in The Superyachts, Volume 7
AMPHORA ex-Meltemi, ex-Braemar ex-Clorinde, ex-Braemar	Twin Screw Motor Yacht Steel/Aluminium	37.50 36.00	(123.03) (118.11)	5.60 2.40	(18.37) (8.87)	Samuel White Samuel White Cowes/UK/1931	2 x 6 cylinder 326hp DAF Turbo diesels	Rebuilt in 1984
BEAUGESTE ex-Beaupré	Auxiliary Twin Screw Sloop Aluminium	37.50 27.65	(123.03) (90.72)	7.95 3.90	(26.08) (12.79)	Brooke Yachts International Holland/Langevin/Bannenberg Lowestoft/UK/1989	2 x 6 cylinder 408hp MAN D2866LE diesels	Lloyd's ✠100A1, ✠LMC Featured in The Superyachts, Volume 4
CAPRICE ex-Orange Lady	Twin Screw Motor Yacht Aluminium	37.50 33.05	(123.03) (108.44)	8.00 1.50	(26.02) (4.92)	Oceanco-Hakvoort Shipyard BV Gilgenast/Gieso/Starkey/TAG Monnickendam/The Netherlands/1992	2 x 8 cylinder 1315hp Deutz TBD604 diesels	ABS ✠A1 AMS Yachting Service Featured in The Superyachts, Volume 8
INTRINSIC	TwinScrew Motor Yacht GRP	37.50 33.84	(123.03) (111.00)	7.62 1.83	(25.00) (6.00)	Delta Marine Intrinsic Design/Ardeo Design/Delta Seattle/USA/2002	2 x 12 cylinder 1400hp Caterpillar 3412B diesels	

Name	Type / Construction	LOA / LWL (m)	(ft)	Beam / Draft (m)	(ft)	Builder / Designer / Location / Year	Engines	Remarks
MERCEDES	Twin Screw / Motor Yacht / FRP Composites	37.50 / 31.67	(123.03) / (103.90)	8.23 / 1.78	(27.00) / (5.84)	Oceanfast Pty Ltd / Curran/Bannenberg / Perth/Australia/1996	2 x 8 cylinder / 1500hp / MTU 396TE94 diesels	Featured in The Superyachts, Volume 10
MY LITTLE STAR ex-LS Two	Twin Screw / Motor Yacht / Aluminium	37.50 / 32.00	(123.03) / (104.99)	7.49 / 2.35	(24.57) / (7.71)	Codecasa / Codecasa/Manfredi & Sforzi / Viareggio/Italy/1994	2 x 12 cylinder / 1860hp / MTU 396TE94 diesels	Lloyd's ✠100A1, ✠LMC
TOI ET MOI	Twin Screw / Motor Yacht / Steel	37.50 / 32.50	(123.03) / (106.63)	7.65 / 2.40	(25.09) / (7.87)	Cantiere Picchiotti SpA / Picchiotti / Viareggio/Italy/1988	2 x 12 cylinder / 624hp / Caterpillar diesels	Lloyd's ✠100A1, ✠LMC
CAROLINIAN ex-Lady Carolina ex-Granada City, ex-Cacique	Twin Screw / Motor Yacht / Steel	37.49 / 33.38	(123.00) / (109.51)	7.20 / 2.28	(23.62) / (7.48)	Feadship – Van Lent & Zonen / De Voogt / Kaag/The Netherlands/1982	2 x 12 cylinder / 625hp / Caterpillar D3412TA diesels	
LADY FLORENCE	Twin Screw / Motor Yacht / GRP	37.49	(123.00)	7.92 / 1.22	(26.00) / (4.00)	Trident Shipworks Inc. / Trident/Wesley Carr/Dawn Moffit / Tampa/USA/1998	2 x Detroit diesels	
NARANA ex-Moura	Triple Screw / Motor Yacht / Wood	37.42 / 31.66	(122.77) / (103.87)	8.42 / 1.32	(27.62) / (4.33)	Cantieri di Pisa / Cantieri di Pisa / Pisa/Italy/1985	3 x 12 cylinder / 1542hp / MTU diesels	Lloyd's ✠100A1, ✠LMC
SARIYAH	Auxiliary Ketch / Aluminium	37.40/42.60 / 28.95	(122.70/139.77) / (95.00)	8.38 / 3.35	(27.50) / (11.00)	Sensation Yachts / Sparkman & Stephens/Munford / Auckland/New Zealand/1994	1 x 12 cylinder / 578hp / MTU 183TE 91 diesel	Featured in The Superyachts, Volume 8
TARAMBER	Auxiliary Ketch / Aluminium	37.38 / 28.60	(122.64) / (93.83)	8.20 / 3.50	(26.92) / (11.50)	Pendennis Shipyard / Dubois/Disdale / Falmouth/UK/1991	1 x 12 cylinder / 543hp / MTU 183TE93 diesel	Featured in The Superyachts, Volume 6 / Refitted in 1995 and 1998
LA VENETIA ex-Iliad, ex-Bluet ex-Ajhory, ex-Masand	Twin Screw / Motor Yacht / Steel	37.34	(122.51)	7.36 / 3.00	(24.15) / (9.84)	Fratelli Benetti / Benetti / Viareggio/Italy/1975	2 x 16 cylinder / 624hp / GM 7 1N diesels	Total refit including engine rebuild in 1992
ATLANTIDE ex-Caleta	Twin Screw / Motor Yacht / Steel/Aluminium/Wood	37.30 / 34.80	(122.38) / (114.18)	5.45 / 2.73	(17.88) / (8.96)	Philip & Son / Alfred Mylne / Dartmouth/UK/1930	2 x 8 cylinder / 230hp / Gardner 8L3B diesels	Lloyd's ✠100A1. Rebuilt 1999 by Manoel Island Yacht Yard, Malta and Camper & Nicholsons, Gosport, with interior design by Ken Freivokh / Featured in The Superyachts, Volume 13
CROCE DEL SUD ex-Croix du Sud	Auxiliary Three Masted Schooner	37.30 / 28.00	(122.38) / (91.86)	6.80 / 4.30	(22.31) / (14.10)	Martinolich / Martinolich / Lussinpiccolo/Italy/1931	2 x 6 cylinder / 293hp / Volvo Penta diesels	
AQUAJOY	Twin Screw / Motor Yacht / Aluminium	37.20 / 31.40	(122.05) / (103.02)	7.40 / 1.50	(24.27) / (4.92)	Codecasa / Codecasa/Dellarole/Dellarole / Viareggio/Italy/1992	2 x 8 cylinder / 2500hp / Gardner 8L3B-230 HP diesels	Lloyd's ✠100A1, ✠LMC
SILVERADO	Twin Screw / Motor Yacht / GRP	37.20	(122.05)	7.80 / 2.60	(25.59) / (8.53)	Willard / Willard / Costa Mesa/USA/1974	2 x 16 cylinder / 970hp / Caterpillar diesels	
VAINQUEUR ex-Aquel II	Auxiliary Twin Screw / Cutter / Aluminium	37.20 / 29.90	(122.05) / (98.10)	7.60 / 5.86/2.74	(24.93) / (19.23/8.99)	Sensation Yachts / Dubois/Milhous/Meavers / Auckland/New Zealand/1987	2 x 375hp / MAN diesels	Featured in The Superyachts, Volume 1
INTENT	Twin Screw / Motor Yacht / GRP	37.19 / 33.22	(122.00) / (109.00)	7.86 / 1.83	(25.80) / (6.00)	Delta Marine / Delta Design Group/Delta Design Group / Seattle/USA/1997	2 x 12 cylinder / 1800hp / Detroit 71TA diesels	
LADY GRACE MARIE	Twin Screw / Motor Yacht / Aluminium	37.19 / 32.57	(122.00) / (106.83)	8.08 / 1.98	(26.50) / (6.50)	Burger Boat Company / O'Keeffe/Burger/Dee Robinson/Owner / Manitowoc/USA/2002	2 x 12 cylinder / 2735hp / DDC/MTU 12V 4000 diesels	
LOUISE G ex-Louise	Twin Screw / Motor Yacht / GRP	37.19 / 33.22	(122.00) / (109.00)	7.86 / 1.83	(25.80) / (6.00)	Delta Marine / Delta Design Group/Delta/Merritt-Knowles / Seattle/USA/1997	2 x 12 cylinder / 1800hp / Detroit 71TA diesels	
MARINER III ex-Sueja III ex-Golden Scimitar	Twin Screw / Motor Yacht / Steel	37.19	(122.00)	6.10 / 2.59	(20.00) / (8.50)	Winslow Marine Rail & Shipbuilding Co / Geary / Winslow/USA/1926	2 x 12 cylinder / 480hp / Detroit 71N diesels	Refitted in 1988
ATLANTA	Auxiliary Sloop / Aluminium	37.00 / 30.30	(121.00) / (99.41)	8.29 / 3.23	(27.20) / (10.60)	Alloy Yachts International / Dubois/Dubois/Glade Johnson / Auckland/New Zealand/1995	1 x 6 cylinder / 550hp / Lugger diesel	Featured in The Superyachts, Volume 10

YACHT'S NAME ex-name(s)	PROPULSION TYPE / CONSTRUCTION	DIMENSIONS LOA/LOA including spars, Length water line m (ft)	Beam (Maximum) / Draught m (ft)	BUILDER / NAVAL ARCHITECT/STYLIST/ INTERIOR DESIGNER / WHERE/YEAR	ENGINES Number & Cylinders / Horse Power / Maker/Type	REMARKS
CARLOTTA	Auxiliary Centreboard Ketch / Steel/Aluminium	37.00 / 30.39 (121.39 / 99.70)	7.30 / 3.05 (23.95 / 10.00)	Perini Navi / Perini Navi/Perini Navi / Viareggio/Italy/1992	1 x 6 cylinder 612hp Volvo Penta diesel	
CRYSTAL	Twin Screw Motor Yacht / Steel	37.00 / 33.80 (121.39 / 110.89)	7.90 / 2.00 (25.91 / 6.56)	San Pedro BW / Sarin/David/Peacock / San Pedro USA/1987	2 x 12 cylinder 1600hp Caterpillar diesels	
GIPSY GIRL III ex-Carolina	Twin Screw Motor Yacht / Aluminium	37.00 / 32.73 (121.38 / 107.38)	7.60 / 1.70 (24.93 / 5.58)	Palmer Johnson Incorporated / Tom Fexas/Palmer Johnson / Sturgeon Bay/USA/1995	2 x 16 cylinder 1400hp Detroit 92TA DDDEC diesels	
MAALANA STAR ex-Maal Star ex-Longitudine Zero	Twin Screw Motor Yacht / Aluminium	37.00 (121.39)	7.30 / 1.40 (23.95 / 4.59)	Technomarine / Technomarine/Righini / Viareggio/Italy/1987	2 x 12 cylinder 2610hp MTU 396TB94 diesels	
NORTHERN SPIRIT ex-Salperton	Auxiliary Ketch / Steel/Aluminium	37.00 (121.39)	7.60 / 3.13 (24.93 / 10.27)	Perini Navi / Perini Navi/Perini Navi / Viareggio/Italy/1996	1 x 6 cylinder 480hp Volvo diesel	
OUR BLUE DREAM	Auxiliary Sloop / Aluminium	37.00 / 30.45 (121.39 / 100.00)	8.38 / 3.75 (27.49 / 12.30)	Camper & Nicholsons (Yachts) Ltd / Dubois/Dubois/Redman Whiteley Design / Gosport/UK/1999	1 x 8 cylinder 540hp Caterpillar 3408TA diesel	ABS ✠A1, Yachting Service Featured in The Superyachts, Volume 14 MCA Code
LES CENTURIONS	Twin Screw Motor Yacht / Wood	36.90 (121.06)	6.30 / 1.90 (20.67 / 6.23)	Picchiotti / Pichiotti / Viareggio/Italy/1955	2 x 12 cylinder 535hp Fiat Carraro diesels	
MONTREVEL	Twin Screw Motor Yacht / Steel/Aluminium	36.90 (121.06)	7.00 / 1.85 (22.96 / 6.07)	Forges de l'Ouest, France / Refit: Studio Cervi Parma / St Nazaire/France/1958	2 x 340hp Caterpillar 3196-660 DI-TA	RINA ✠100A1 Rebuilt 2001 by Orlando Fratelli, Savona, Italy
SYLVIA	Auxiliary Twin Screw Ketch / Wood Composite	36.90/43.45 / 28.20 (121.06/142.55 / 92.52)	7.35 / 4.00 (24.11 / 13.12)	Camper & Nicholsons / CE Nicholson / Gosport/UK/1925	2 x 6 cylinder 103hp Gardner diesels	Rebuilt in 1991
TOPSY ex-Leander ex-Alliance	Twin Screw Motor Yacht / Aluminium	36.90 / 31.40 (121.06 / 103.02)	7.60 / 1.80 (24.93 / 5.90)	Denison / Langlois/Bursack Designs / Dania/USA/1986	2 x 12 cylinder 1530hp MTU diesels	Lengthened by 5.18m in 1989
DARDANELLA	Twin Screw Motor Yacht / Aluminium	36.88 / 33.22 (121.00 / 108.99)	8.18 / 2.44 (26.84 / 8.00)	Vitters Shipyard / Vripack/Vripack / Zwartsluis/The Netherlands/1997	2 x 6 cylinder 400hp Caterpillar 3406 diesels	
FREESIA	Twin Screw Motor Yacht / Aluminium	36.88 / 33.22 (121.00 / 108.99)	8.18 / 2.44 (26.84 / 8.00)	Hakvoort Shipyard / Vripack/JJ Van der Meulen / Monnickendam/The Netherlands/1997	2 x 8 cylinder 480hp Caterpillar 3408 diesels	
FULL BLOOM ex-Sea Quest	Twin Screw Motor Yacht / FRP/Composite	36.88 (121.00)	7.92 / 1.89 (26.00 / 6.20)	Trident Shipworks Inc. / Trident/Donald Starkey / Tampa/USA/1999	2 x 16 cylinder 1800hp MTU/DDC 2000 diesels	
LA BELLA II ex-Teeth	Triple Water Jet Motor Yacht / GRP	36.88 / 29.60 (121.00 / 97.12)	7.15 / 1.43 (23.46 / 4.69)	Diaship/Heesen Shipyards / Mulder/Mulder/Art-Line / Oss/The Netherlands/1995	2 x 16 cylinder 3,500hp 396TB94 & 1 x 12 cylinder 2330hp 396TB94 MTU diesels	Featured in The Superyachts, Volume 9
MAGIC ONE ex-Bonita	Triple Water Jet Motor Yacht / GRP	36.88 / 29.60 (121.00 / 97.12)	7.15 / 1.43 (23.46 / 4.69)	Diaship/Heesen Shipyards / Mulder/Mulder/Art-Line / Oss/The Netherlands/1995	2 x 16 cylinder 3,500hp 396TB94 & 1 x 12 cylinder 2330hp 396TB94 MTU diesels	Featured in The Superyachts, Volume 9
TITSA ex-Moneikos II ex-El Dato II	Twin Screw Motor Yacht / Aluminium	36.88 / 33.20 (121.00 / 108.92)	7.60 / 2.10 (24.93 / 6.89)	Diaship/Heesen Shipyards / Mulder/Diaship/Versilmarine / Oss/The Netherlands/1992	2 x 16 cylinder 2600hp Deutz SBA16M816 diesels	ABS classified
MY WEIGH	Twin Screw Motor Yacht / Aluminium	36.88 / 36.74 (121.00 / 120.54)	7.56 / 2.01 (24.81 / 6.60)	Palmer Johnson / Fexas/Fexas/Palmer Johnson / Sturgeon Bay/USA/2000	2 x 16 cylinder 1800hp MTU/DDC 2000 diesels	
NECTAR OF THE GODS	Twin Screw Motor Yacht / FRP	36.88 / 32.92 (121.00 / 108.00)	7.62 / 1.98 (25.00 / 6.50)	Crescent Custom Yachts / Sarin/Sarin/Scales / Vancouver/Canada/2000	2 x 16 cylinder 1800 hp MTU/DDC 2000 diesels	Featured in The Superyachts, Volume 14

Name	Type / Construction	LOA / LWL (m)	LOA / LWL (ft)	Beam / Draft (m)	Beam / Draft (ft)	Builder / Designer / Location / Year	Engines	Notes
QUEEN OF DIAMONDS ex-Limit Bid II, ex-Bugler ex-Cassiar, ex-Spellbound ex-Gillian, ex-Intent	Twin Screw Motor Yacht Steel	36.81 33.50	(120.77) (109.91)	7.08 2.03	(23.22) (6.66)	Feadship – Van Lent & Zonen De Voogt/De Voogt/Robin Rose & Associates Kaag/The Netherlands/1970	2 x 12 cylinder 920hp Caterpillar D348TA diesels	Full renovation in 1995
LE MONTRACHET ex-Magic One, ex-Bandia Mara, ex-Starlite	Twin Screw Motor Yacht Aluminium	36.80 32.28	(120.75) (105.92)	7.31 1.83	(24.00) (6.00)	Broward Marine Inc Broward Fort Lauderdale/USA/1986	2 x 16 cylinder 1350hp Detroit-92 TAM diesels	
BUCKPASSER	Twin Screw Motor Yacht Aluminium	36.75 32.38	(120.58) (106.25)	7.75 2.13	(25.42) (7.00)	Hitachi Zosen Corp. Hargrave Kanagawa/Japan/1986	2 x 12 cylinder 565hp Caterpillar diesels	
BIG CITY ex-Airwaves ex-Alexis	Twin Screw Motor Yacht Aluminium	36.74	(120.54)	7.79 1.98	(25.55) (6.50)	Palmer Johnson Vripack/Tom Fexas/Palmer Johnson Sturgeon Bay/USA/1999	2 x 16 cylinder 3600hp Detroit MTU 16V2000diesels	
BLUE ATTRACTION ex-Lady Duvera	Twin Screw Motor Yacht Steel	36.70	(120.41)	7.00 2.60	(22.96) (8.53)	Amels BV Diana Yacht Design/Hedvall Makkum/The Netherlands/1983	2 x 12 cylinder 431hp Caterpillar 3412DI-TA diesels	Lloyd's ✠100A1, ✠LMC Refitted and extended by Lürssen Werft in 1995 Featured in The Superyachts, Volume 3
OLYMPOS N ex-Beatriz of Bolivia ex-Isabella ex-Beatriz of Bolivia	Twin Screw Motor Yacht Steel	36.70 32.90	(120.41) (107.94)	6.10 2.20	(20.01) (7.21)	Camper & Nicholsons C & N Southampton/UK/1963	2 x 12 cylinder 540hp Caterpillar diesels	Rebuilt in 1985 with interior design by Jansen of Paris
MORGAN STAR ex-Mylin II ex-Tropic C	Twin Screw Cockpit Motor Yacht Aluminium	36.65 31.40	(120.23) (103.02)	7.35 2.10	(24.11) (6.89)	Diaship/Heesen Shipyards Mulder/Art Line Oss/The Netherlands/1986	2 x 12 cylinder 1600hp DeutzBA16M16C-R diesels	Featured in The Superyachts, Volume 1
BAH! HUMBUG	Twin Screw Motor Yacht GRP	36.60	(120.00)	7.92 1.83	(26.00) (6.00)	Christensen Motor Yacht Corporation Howard Apollonio/Roberts & Sherman Vancouver/USA/1991	2 x 16 cylinder 1040hp Detroit 92TA diesels	
BON BON	Twin Screw Motor Yacht GRP	36.60	(120.00)	7.42 1.83	(24.33) (6.00)	Flagship Marine Corporation Flagship/Overing Naples/USA/1994	2 x 12 cylinder 1080hp Detroit 92TA diesels	
CACIQUE ex-Liquidity	Twin Screw Motor Yacht GRP	36.60	(120.00)	7.92 2.07	(26.00) (6.80)	Christensen Motor Yacht Corporation Owners Vancouver/USA/1995	2 x 8 cylinder 1296hp Deutz 604B diesels	
CHAIRMAN	Twin Screw Motor Yacht FPR	36.60 33.53	(120.00) (110.00)	7.62 1.86	(25.00) (6.16)	Sovereign Yachts Setzer/Patrick Knowles Design Richmond/Canada/2001	2 x 16 cylinders 1800hp MTU/DDC 2000 diesels	
PATTI LOU ex-Crescent Lady	Twin Screw Motor Yacht	36.60	(120.00)	7.62 1.98	(25.00) (6.50)	Crecent Custom Yachts Jack Sarin/Robin Rose/Jack Sarin Vancouver/Canada/2002	2 x 16 cylinder 1800 hp MTU/DDC 2000 diesels	
EMA STAR ex-Emanuel	Twin Screw Motor Yacht Aluminium	36.60	(120.00)	6.70 2.30	(22.00) (7.55)	Lloyd's Ships Lloyd's Ships Bulimba/Australia/1984	2 x 8 cylinder 1150hp MTU 396TB83 diesels	
EMERALD K	Twin Screw Motor Yacht Steel	36.60 32.00	(120.00) (105.00)	7.36 2.33	(24.02) (7.08)	Feadship – De Vries Scheepsbouw De Voogt Aalsmeer/The Netherlands/1974	2 x 6 cylinder 480hp Caterpillar D346PCTA diesels	
ESCAPE	Twin Screw Motor Yacht Steel	36.60	(120.00)	7.32 2.13	(24.00) (7.00)	Crescent Custom Yachts Sarin/Scales Canada/1999	2 x 16 cylinder 1800hp MTU/DDC 2000 diesels	
INDIAN PRINCESS ex-La Bonne Vie	Twin Screw Motor Yacht Aluminium	36.60 32.28	(120.00) (105.92)	6.70 1.83	(22.00) (6.00)	Broward Marine Inc Broward Fort Lauderdale/USA/1989	3 x 12 cylinder 1000hp Caterpillar 3412TA diesels	
LADY NICOLE ex-Yahala ex-Lady Suffolk	Twin Screw Motor Yacht Steel	36.60	(120.00)	7.20 1.80	(23.62) (5.90)	Nicolini Nicolini Ancona/Italy/1983	2 x 16 cylinder 2160hp MTU diesels	
MELRENI	Twin Screw Motor Yacht FRP	36.60	(120.00)	7.62 2.13	(25.00) (7.00)	Sovereign Yachts Sarin/Sarin Richmond/Canada/2000	2 x 16 cylinder 1800hp MTU/DDC 2000 diesels	
PICANTE	Twin Screw Motor Yacht GRP	36.60 32.61	(120.00) (107.00)	7.92 2.05	(26.00) (6.66)	Christensen Motor Yacht Corporation Howard Apollonio/Roberts & Bennett Vancouver/USA/1989	2 x 16 cylinder 1400hp Detroit V92DDEC diesels	

YACHT'S NAME ex-name(s)	PROPULSION TYPE CONSTRUCTION	DIMENSIONS LOA/LOA including spars / Length water line m (ft)	Beam (Maximum) / Draught m (ft)	BUILDER NAVAL ARCHITECT/STYLIST/INTERIOR DESIGNER WHERE/YEAR	ENGINES Number & Cylinders Horse Power Maker/Type	REMARKS
RAMPAGER OF MONACO ex-Propo, ex-Criniera d'Oro ex-Blue Oliver	Twin Screw Motor Yacht Steel	36.60 (120.00) 32.30 (105.97)	6.10 (20.01) 2.50 (8.20)	Globe Camper & Nicholsons Capetown/South Africa/1966	2 x 16 cylinder 457hp GM diesels	Rebuilt 1976 & 1988
REEF CHIEF	Twin Screw Motor Yacht Aluminium	36.60 (120.00) 32.20 (105.65)	8.50 (27.89) 2.40 (7.87)	Lloyd's Ships Curran Bulimba/Australia/1989	2 x 12 cylinder 1750hp Caterpillar 3512TA diesels	Lloyd's ✠100A1, ✠LMC
SEAHAWK ex-Status Quo	Twin Screw Motor Yacht Aluminium	36.60 (120.00) 32.00 (105.00)	7.01 (23.00) 1.83 (6.00)	Broward Marine Inc Broward Yacht Interiors Fort Lauderdale/USA/1991	2 x 16 cylinder 1400hp Detroit 92TA diesels	
MY CHELLE ex-Sovereign Lady	Twin Screw Motor Yacht FRP	36.60 (120.00) 33.53 (110.00)	7.62 (25.00) 1.83 (6.00)	Sovereign Yachts Sarin/Sarin/Sarin Richmond/Canada/1999	2 x 16 cylinder 1800hp MTU/DDC 2000 diesels	
VALKYRIE	Twin Screw Motor Yacht FRP	36.60 (120.00) 35.06 (115.00)	7.62 (25.00) 1.98 (6.50)	Crecent Custom Yachts Jack Sarin/Robin Rose/Jack Sarin Richmond/Canada/2001	2 x 16 cylinder 1800hp MTU/DDC 2000 diesels	
DONNA C III	Twin Screw Motor Yacht GRP	36.58 (120.00)	7.62 (25.00) 2.13 (7.00)	Sovereign Yachts Sarin/Sarin Richmond/Canada/1999	2 x 16 cylinder 1800hp MTU/DDC 2000 diesels	
MISS EVIE ex-Sea Crest	Twin Screw Motor Yacht Steel	36.58 (120.00)	7.01 (23.00) 2.59 (8.50)	Hall Russell Co Ltd Hall Russell Aberdeen/UK/1963	2 x 8 cylinder 320hp Kelvin (Bergius) diesels	Featured in The Superyachts, Volume 5 Major refit 1998
JOZAMAR	Twin Screw Motor Yacht Aluminium	36.57 (119.96)	7.14 (23.42) 2.39 (7.84)	Tecnomarine Righini Viareggio/Italy/1995	2 x 16 cylinder 2600hp MTU 396TB93 diesels	
KALAMOUN	Twin Water Jet Motor Yacht Aluminium	36.54 (119.89) 32.14 (105.45)	7.00 (22.97) 2.10 (6.89)	Lürssen Werft Lürssen Bremen/Germany/1986	2 x 16 cylinder 2950hp MTU 396TB94 diesels	
CORONA DEL MAR	Twin Water Jet Motor Yacht Aluminium	36.53 (119.85) 27.90 (91.54)	7.40 (24.27) 1.60 (5.24)	Mefasa Shipyard Shead San Juan de Nieva/Spain/1992	2 x 16 cylinder 3627hp MTU 538TB93 diesels	Fitted with 2 x KaMeWa S62/80S water jets. 44-knot maximum speed
CANDIDA ex-Norlanda ex-Candida	Auxiliary Yawl Steel Composite	36.50 (119.75) 24.20 (79.40)	6.20 (20.34) 3.40 (11.15)	Camper & Nicholsons CE Nicholson Gosport/UK/1928	1 x 250hp Mercedes diesel	Converted to cutter in 1987, to ketch in 1938 and yawl in 1991. Rebuilt in 1991/2
TOSCA III ex-Centenarian	Auxiliary Sloop Steel/Aluminium	36.50 (119.75) 32.40 (106.29)	8.70 (28.54) 3.60 (11.81)	Yacht Building Management Stawinski/Cockram Gdansk/Poland/1993	2 x Iveco diesels 440hp	
DUKE TOWN	Twin Screw Motor Yacht Aluminium	36.50 (119.75)	8.32 (27.50) 2.75 (8.04)	Diaship/Heesen Shipyards Diaship Design Team Oss/The Netherlands/2001	2 x 12 cylinder 2285hp MTU 12V396TE94	Featured in The Superyachts, Volume 16
JAGARE	Auxiliary Ketch Aluminium	36.50 (119.75) 29.30 (96.13)	8.10 (26.58) 3.50 (11.48)	Abeking & Rasmussen W de Vries Lentsch Lemwerder/Germany/1981	1 x 6 cylinder 600hp MWM TBD604L6 diesel	Lloyd's ✠100A1, ✠LMC
NAHEMA	Twin Screw Motor Yacht Steel	36.50 (119.75)	7.50 (24.60) 2.40 (7.87)	Unale Bannenberg/Bannenberg Valencia/Spain/1982	2 x 16 cylinder 1060hp GM diesels	
SECRET LOVE ex-Amour Secret	Twin Screw Motor Yacht Steel	36.50 (119.75) 31.00 (101.71)	7.70 (25.26) 2.65 (8.69)	Amels/Hakvoort Amels/Struik & Hamerslag Makkum/The Netherlands/1990	2 x 12 cylinder 680hp Caterpillar 3412DI-TA diesels	Featured in The Superyachts Volume 4 Lloyd's ✠100A1, ✠LMC
WHITE HEAVEN	Twin Screw Motor Yacht Steel/Aluminium	36.50 (119.75) 31.50 (103.33)	8.00 (26.24) 4.50 (14.76)	Moonen Shipyards Jochim Kinder s'Hertogenbosch/The netherlands/2000	2 x 12 cylinder 685hp Caterpillar 3412DI-TA diesels	

Name	Type / Construction	Length m (ft)	Beam/Draft m (ft)	Builder / Designer	Engines	Notes
OUR TOY	Twin Screw / Motor Yacht / Steel	36.45 (119.59) / 31.40 (103.02)	8.00 (26.25) / 2.10 (6.89)	Feadship – Van Lent & Zonen BV / De Voogt/Chan / Kaag/The Netherlands/1991	2 x 12 cylinder 502hp MTU 183TC61 diesels	
SHAMROCK V ex-Quadrifoglio ex-Sea Song ex-Shamrock V	Auxiliary Sloop / Steel/Composite	36.42 (119.48) / 24.71 (81.06)	6.00 (19.68) / 4.87 (15.97)	Camper & Nicholsons / CE Nicholson / Gosport/UK/1930	2 x 6 cylinder 181hp GM diesels	Converted J-class racing yacht. Rebuilt 1980. Complete rebuild at Pendennis Shipyard 1999/2001. Naval architect/Interior design/ Gerard Dijkstra & Partners. Featured in The Superyachts, Volume 15
DAEDALUS ex-The A and Eagle ex-Big Eagle	Twin Screw / Motor Yacht / Steel	36.40 (119.42) / 33.60 (110.24)	6.90 (22.63) / 1.70 (5.57)	Abeking & Rasmussen / Rhodes / Lemwerder/West Germany/1966	2 x 6 cylinder 460hp Caterpillar diesels	
PARADIS ex-Marcalan III	Twin Screw / Motor Yacht / Wood	36.40 (119.42)	7.90 (25.91) / 1.35 (4.43)	Canados / Canados / Ostia/Italy/1984	2 x 12 cylinder 1680hp MTU diesels	
MAGISTRAL ex-Orejona	Auxiliary Twin Screw / Schooner / Steel	36.30 (119.07) / 25.50 (82.67)	8.00 (26.24) / 3.50 (11.48)	Cammenga Shipyard / De Vries Lentsch / Wormerveer/The Netherlands/1972	2 x 12 cylinder 600hp MWM diesels	Refitted at Astilleros Belliure, Spain 1987. Lloyd's ✠100A1, ✠LMC. Featured in The Superyachts, Volume 5. Lengthened & refitted at JFA Shipyard, France 2001
DENITTA II	Twin Screw / Motor Yacht / Aluminium	36.20 (118.77) / 29.60 (97.11)	7.21 (23.65) / 2.30 (7.55)	Baglietto Shipyard SpA / Baglietto/Cichero / Varazze/Italy/1990	2 x 12 cylinder 1920hp MTU 396TB93 diesels	Featured in The Superyachts, Volume 4. Lloyd's ✠100A1, ✠LMC
LADY F ex-Nastasha	Twin Screw / Motor Yacht / Aluminium	36.20 (118.77) / 29.60 (97.11)	7.21 (23.65) / 1.25 (4.10)	Baglietto Shipyard SpA / Baglietto/Acchiapati / Varazze/Italy/1989	2 x 12 cylinder 1920hp MTU 396TB93 diesels	
OLNICO ex-Wilelka ex-Cacouna	Twin Screw / Motor Yacht / Steel	36.20 (118.77) / 33.10 (108.60)	6.20 (20.34) / 2.30 (7.54)	Camper & Nicholsons / CE Nicholson/CE Nicholson / Gosport/UK/1932	2 x 6 cylinder 440hp MAN diesels	
PACHA III ex-Briseis, ex-Priamar ex-Cardigrae V, ex-Arlette II	Twin Screw / Motor Yacht / Steel	36.20 (118.77) / 31.90 (104.66)	5.60 (18.37) / 2.50 (8.20)	Camper & Nicholsons / CE Nicholson/J Grange / Southampton/UK/1936	2 x Caterpillar diesels	
SOVEREIGN	Auxiliary Sloop / Aluminium	36.20 (118.77) / 29.41 (96.49)	8.24 (27.00) / 3.33 (10.11)	Alloy Yachts / Dubois/Dubois/Whiteley / Auckland/New Zealand/1995	1 x 6 cylinder 570hp Lugger diesel	Featured in The Superyachts, Volume 9
VANLIS	Twin Screw / Motor Yacht / Aluminium	36.20 (118.77) / 29.60 (97.11)	7.21 (23.65) / 2.30 (7.55)	Baglietto Shipyard SpA / Baglietto/Acchiapati / Varazze/Italy/1990	2 x 12 cylinder 2557hp MTU 396TB94 diesels	
CAMELOT ex-Thor III ex-Fox II	Twin Screw / Motor Yacht / Aluminium	36.13 (118.54) / 31.60 (103.67)	7.19 (23.59) / 2.13 (6.99)	Royal Huisman Shipyard / De Vries Lentsch / Vollenhove/The Netherlands/1983	2 x 8 cylinder 1072hp MTU diesels	Lloyd's ✠100A1, ✠LMC
ESCAPE	Twin Screw / Motor Yacht / GRP	36.12 (118.50) / 32.80 (107.60)	8.11 (26.60) / 2.44 (8.00)	Trident Shipworks Inc. / Hargrave/Dean / Tampa/USA/1998	2 x 6 cylinder 706hp Caterpillar 3508 diesels	ABS ✠A1, AMS Yachting Service
KAYANA ex-Toby's Toy ex-Janette	Twin Screw / Motor Yacht / Aluminium	36.10 (118.44)	6.90 (22.63) / 1.80 (5.90)	Perry / Bannenberg/Williamson / Strood/UK/1978	2 x 16 cylinder 1224hp Deutz-MWM diesels	Rebuilt 1990
INTRIGUES ex-Frances Lady ex-Mes Amis	Twin Screw / Motor Yacht / Wood	36.05 (118.28)	7.80 (25.59) / 6.80 (22.31)	Esterel Shipyard / Mauric/Caliari/Smith / Cannes/France/1984	2 x 16 cylinder 2380hp MTU 396TB93 diesels	Lengthened by 2.0m and refitted in 1996
MY WAY ex-Ilona	Twin Screw / Motor Yacht / Aluminium	36.04 (118.25) / 31.00 (101.71)	7.35 (24.12) / 3.91 (12.83)	NQEA Australia Pty Ltd / Hargrave / Cairns/Australia/1986	2 x 12 cylinder 624hp Caterpillar 3412 diesels	Lengthened by 3.3m (11ft) in 1993
ANTIPODEAN	Twin Water Jet / Motor Yacht / Aluminium	36.00 (118.12) / 30.60 (100.40)	7.40 (24.28) / 1.00 (3.28)	Oceanfast Pty Ltd / Curran/Bannenberg / Perth/Australia/1988	2 x 12 cylinder 1960hp MTU 396TB93 diesels	
BLUE MERIDIAN ex-Santa Cruz III	Twin Screw / Motor Yacht / Steel	36.00 (118.12)	7.10 (23.29) / 3.55 (11.65)	CRN / CRN/Dilday / Ancona/Italy/1975	2 x 12 cylinder 770hp GM 149 diesels	Featured in The Superyachts, Volume 2

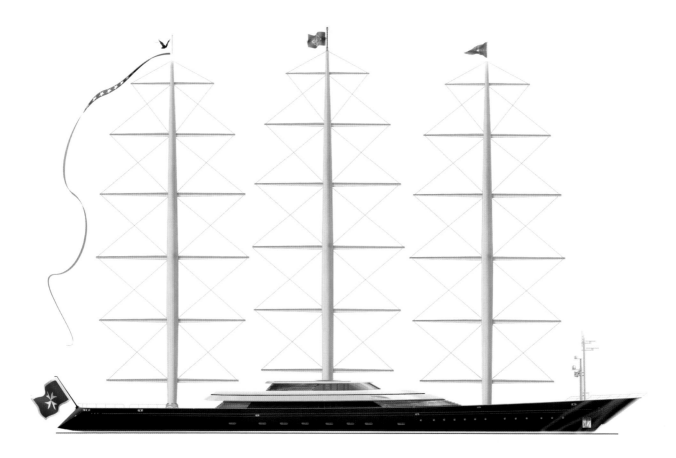

The 286 foot Clipper "Maltese Falcon"
The world's largest-ever privately-owned sailing yacht.

Perini Navi engineering and build.
Gerry Dijkstra Dynarig development.
Ken Freivokh Design external and internal styling.

KEN FREIVOKH DESIGN
ARCHITECTS AND YACHT DESIGNERS - WWW.FREIVOKH.COM

The Directory

*A Two-part Who's Who of Designers,
Management Companies, Builders' Marketing Agents,
Charter Agents, Superyacht Services, Builders and Brokers*

THE DIRECTORY — PART I

Superyacht Companies Listed by Category

BUILDERS OF SUPERYACHTS AND SUPERYACHT REPAIR YARDS

Abeking & Rasmussen
Alloy Yachts International
Amels Holland
Azimut-Benetti
Cantieri Navali Baglietto
Blohm + Voss
Blubay Yachts
Burger Boat Company
Camper & Nicholsons Yachting
CBI Navi
Cheoy Lee Shipyards
Christensen Shipyards
Christensen Yachts
Cielo Terra Mare
CMN
Cantieri Navali Ugo Codecasa
Codecasadue
Construction Navale Bordeaux
Crescent Custom Yachts
CRN Ancona – Ferretti Group
Delta Marine
Derecktor Shipyards
Devonport Yachts
De Vries Scheepsbouw
Fairlie Restorations
Feadship Papendrecht
Ferretti Customline
Hakvoort Shipyard
HDW-Nobiskrug
Heesen Shipyards
Heli dd
Hodgdon Yachts
Intermarine SpA
IZAR

Jongert
Kusch Yacht Agentur
Lürssen Werft
Marten Yachts
McMullen & Wing
Merrill-Stevens Dry Dock
Moonen Shipyards
Oceanco
Oceanfast
Offshore Nautical
Palmer Johnson Yachts
Palmer Johnson Savannah
Pendennis Shipyard
Perini Navi
Picchiotti
Platypus Marine
Rivolta Marine
RMK Marine
Royal Denship
Royal Huisman Shipyard
Royal Van Lent Shipyard
Rybovich Spencer
Sensation New Zealand
Southampton Yacht Services
Sovereign Yachts (Canada)
Trinity Yachts
Turquoise Yacht Construction
Vikal International
Vitters Shipyard
Vosper Thorneycroft
Wally
Warren Yachts
Westport Shipyard
Westship World Yachts

INDEPENDENT NAVAL ARCHITECTS

The 'A' Group Monte Carlo
Acubens
Andrawis Yachts & MDI
Apollonio Naval Architecture
Axis Group Yacht Design
Beiderbeck Designs
Donald L Blount and Associates
Philippe Briand
Tony Castro
Cor D Rover Design
Curran Design, Marine Consultants
Butch Dalrymple-Smith
De Voogt Naval Architects
Diana Yacht Design International
Gerard Dijkstra & Partners
Dixon Yacht Design
Dowland Naval Architects
Dubois Naval Architects
Tom Fexas Yacht Design
Fontaine Design Group
Francisdesign
Germán Frers
FRYCO
Hargrave Yacht Design & Engineering
Hoek Design Naval Architects
Ron Holland Design

JLS Design
Bruce King Yacht Design
Langan Design Associates
Luiz de Basto Design
Mulder Design
Nuvolari-Lenard
Offshore Nautical
Espen Øino Naval Architects
Oliver Design
PB Design – Pieter Beeldsnijder
Pedrick Yacht Design
Michael Peters Yacht Design
Rivolta Marine
Rogers Yacht Design
Jack W Sarin Naval Architects
Setzer Design Group
Sparkman & Stephens
Studio Scanu
Three Quays Marine Services
Tradewind Cruises
JJ Van Nus Yacht BV Holland
Van Peteghem Lauriot Prevost
Victory Design
Vripack Yachting International
Warwick Yacht Design
Hugh Welbourn Design

EXTERIOR STYLISTS AND/OR INTERIOR DESIGNERS

The 'A' Group Monte Carlo
Acubens
Andrawis Yachts & MDI
Apollonio Naval Architecture
Ardeo Design
Joseph Artese Design
Art-Line
Jon Bannenberg
Jonathan Quinn Barnett
Beiderbeck Designs
Donald L Blount and Associates
Blubay Yachts
Philippe Briand
Felix Buytendijk Yacht Design
Carr Design
Tony Castro
Bernie Cohen Design
Cor D Rover Design
Design Q
Design Unlimited
De Voogt Naval Architects
Diana Yacht Design International
Gerard Dijkstra & Partners
Terence Disdale Design
Dixon Yacht Design
Dowland Naval Architects
DSG Associates
Dubois Naval Architects
Juan Carlos Espinosa
Tom Fexas Yacht Design
Francisdesign
Ken Freivokh Design
FRYCO
Guido de Groot Design
Ray Harvey Design
Tim Heywood Designs
Ron Holland Design
H2, Howard & Horsfield
JLS Design
Glade Johnson Design
Kitty van der Kamp Design
Kirschstein Designs
Patrick Knowles Design
Kusch Yacht Agentur
Lars Modin

Michael Leach Design
Liebowitz & Pritchard
Luiz de Basto Design
Evan K Marshall
Mulder Design
John Munford Design
Pauline Nunns Associates
Nuvolari-Lenard
Oceanco
Offshore Nautical
Espen Øino Naval Architects
Oliver Design
Pacific Custom Interiors
PB Design – Pieter Beeldsnijder
Pedrick Yacht Design
Michael Peters Yacht Design
Pokela Design
Puléo Inc International Design
Redman Whiteley Dixon
Reymond Langton Design
Rivolta Marine
Dee Robinson Interiors
Robin M Rose & Associates
Jack W Sarin Naval Architects
Tim Saunders Design
Birgit Schnaase Interior Design
SETE Yachts
Setzer Design Group
Paola D Smith & Associates
Sam Sorgiovanni Designs
Tommaso Spadolini
Sparkman & Stephens
Donald Starkey Designs
Studio Scanu
Studiovafiadis
Tradewind Cruises
JJ Van Nus Yacht BV Holland
Victory Design
Vripack – Yachting International
Warwick Yacht Design
Andrew Winch Designs
Winston Green Design
Dick Young Designs
Zuretti

BUILDERS' MARKETING AGENTS & BUILDERS COOPERATIVES

Amels – Nigel Burgess
Blue Trend
Burger Yacht Sales
Nigel Burgess
Cheoy Lee Shipyards North America
Feadship America
Feadship France
Feadship Holland
Heliyachts International
Jongert International

Med-Sale UK
Oceanfast
Perini Navi USA
Royal Denship of America
Simpson Marine
SKG Yachts
Tiemann Yachts
Westport Yacht Sales
Westship

THE SUPERYACHTS 322 THE DIRECTORY

YACHT MANAGEMENT AGENCIES

Bartram & Brakenhoff of Florida
BCR Yachts
Nigel Burgess
Camper & Nicholsons International
Cavendish White
Jens Cornelsen
Emerald Yacht & Ship
Fraser Yachts Worldwide
Hill Robinson
Ron Holland Design
Peter Insull's Yacht Marketing
Koch, Newton & Partners
Malcolm J Horsley International
The Marblehead Company
Mega Yachts

Moncada di Paterno
Moran Yacht and Ship
Navigator
Northrop & Johnson
Rigo Yachts International
The Sacks Group
Safehaven International
Bob Saxon Associates
Claude Schmitt Organisation
SETE Yachts
Simpson Marine
Thirty Seven South
Titan, Hyde & Torrance
Tradewind Cruises
Yachting Partners International

YACHT BROKERS

Ardell Yacht & Ship Brokers
Bartram & Brakenhoff of Florida
BCR Yachts
Blue Trend
Broward Yacht Sales
Luke Brown & Associates
Burger Yacht Sales
Nigel Burgess
Camper & Nicholsons International
Cavendish White
Cheoy Lee Shipyards North America
William Collier
Crestar Yachts
Dahm International
Dubois Yachts
Edmiston & Company
Emerald Yacht & Ship
Fraser Yachts Worldwide
Fredericks/Power & Sail
Heliyachts International
Peter Insull's Yacht Marketing
Koch, Newton & Partners
Malcom J Horsley International
Med-Sale UK

Mega Yachts
Merrill-Stevens Yacht Sales
Moncada di Paterno
Moran Yacht and Ship
Navigator
Northrop & Johnson
Rex Yacht Sales
Rigo Yachts International
Rybovich Spencer
The Sacks Group
Claude Schmitt Organisation
Silver Yachts
Simpson Marine
Sparkman & Stephens
Superyachts International
Thirty Seven South
Titan, Hyde & Torrance
JJ Van Nus Yacht BV Holland
Vripack Yachting International
Waite & Morrow Associates
Webster Associates
Westport Yacht Sales
Woods & Oviatt
Yachting Partners International

CHARTER AGENCIES

Ardell Yacht & Ship Brokers
Bartram & Brakenhoff of Florida
BCR Yachts
Blue Trend
Broward Yacht Sales
Luke Brown & Associates
Nigel Burgess
Camper & Nicholsons International
Cavendish White
Crestar Yachts
Dahm International
Dubois Yachts
Edmiston & Company
Emerald Yacht & Ship
Fraser Yachts Worldwide
Peter Insull's Yacht Marketing
Lynn Jachney Charters
Koch, Newton & Partners
Liveras Yachts
Malcolm J Horsley International

Mega Yachts
Moncada di Paterno
Moran Yacht and Ship
Navigator
Northrop & Johnson
Rigo Yachts International
RNR Yacht Charters
The Sacks Group
Bob Saxon Associates
Claude Schmitt Organisation
SETE Yachts
Silver Yachts
Simpson Marine
Sparkman & Stephens
Superyachts International
Thirty Seven South
Titan, Hyde & Torrance
Webster Associates
Yachting Partners International

YACHT EQUIPMENT MANUFACTURERS

Alaska Diesel Electric
Atlas Energy Systems
Baccarat
B&G
Carbospars
Caterpillar
Cramm Ingenieurs & Handelsburo
Doyle Sailmakers
Freeman Marine Equipment
Halyard (M & I)
Heinen & Hopman Engineering
H & M Electronic Systems
Intelect Integrated Electronics
International Paint/Akzo Nobel
Interlux Yacht Finishes
Koopnautic Holland
Linn Products
Marten Spars
MTU Friedrichshafen
Muir Winches & Windlasses

Naiad Marine
Nirvana Spars
North Superyacht Group
Novurania
Ocean Yacht Systems UK
Piening-Propeller
Reckmann Yacht Equipment
Rolla SP Propellers
Rondal
Sea Recovery
Sikkens Yachtpaints
Simrad
SP Systems
Sterling Lacquer Manufacturing Co
Summit Furniture
Teignbridge Propellers
US Paint/NOF Europe
Vacuum Systems Australia
Vosper Thornycroft Marine Products
Westerbeke Corporation

SUPERYACHT SERVICES

Act Studio
Alliance Marine Risk Managers
Amico & Co
Bachmann Marine Services
Burger Marine Services
Camper & Nicholsons International
The Crew Network – Worldwide
Dahm International
Dockwise Yacht Transport
Fairmont Insurance Services Group
Adrian J Fisher
Fraser Yachts Worldwide
Fraser Yacht Insurance Services
Fredericks/Power & Sail
Gerard's, Service en Mer
Grant & Horton
Harris Grant Associates
Ray Harvey Design
Heliyachts International
Hill Dickinson
Hunt, Deltel & Co
Peter Insull's Yacht Marketing
Marelux
Maritime Research Institute Netherlands
MCA
MCN International

Ocean Yacht Systems UK
Offshore Nautical
Pantaenius
Patton Marine
Pensum (Cayman Islands)
Pinmar
Platypus Marine
Port de Plaisance de la Rochelle
RMK Marine
Rybovich Spencer
Safehaven International
Sarnia Yachts
SETE Yachts
Simpson Marine
Southampton Yacht Services
Southern Spars
St Katherine Haven
SP Technologies
Sundeck
Tahiti Ocean
Thirty Seven South
Tilse Industrie und Schiffstechnik
Vins Sans Frontieres Group
Woods Marine Management
Wolfson Unit
Yacht Fuel Services

SPECIALIST YACHT INTERIOR MANUFACTURERS

Fairlie Restorations
Loher Raumexclusiv
Metrica Interior
Nicholson Interiors
Novulari-Lenard
Oldenburger Mobelwerkstätten
Pacific Custom Interiors

Rivolta Marine
Sinnex Steinheimer Innenausbau
Silver Lining Workshops
Southampton Yacht Services
Struik & Hamerslag International

The right people
worldwide

SALE & PURCHASE
YACHT MANAGEMENT
CREW SELECTION
CHARTER MANAGEMENT
CHARTER
NEW CONSTRUCTION

CAMPER & NICHOLSONS
INTERNATIONAL

YACHTING SINCE 1782

A Subsidiary of **RODRIGUEZ** GROUP
A publicly traded company listed on the Paris Stock Exchange

www.cnconnect.com

THE DIRECTORY – PART 2
Contact Information

TELEPHONE NUMBERS

Please note that telephone numbers are written in *International Notation*, with the national code number prefixed with a '+'. To call *foreign* numbers you must first dial your own country's *International Access Code* – i.e. **00** if you are in the UK, or **011** if you are in the USA – and omit any number within brackets. If the number is within your own country you should omit the number prefixed with a '+' and include the bracketed numbers.
E-mail (Em) addresses may be printed on two lines in *The Directory* but when used they should always be typed without breaks.

The 'A' Group Monte Carlo Interior Design,
Gildo Pastor Center,
7 rue du Gabian,
MC 98000,
Monaco.
Tel:+377 93.10.02.80
Fax:+377 92.05.27.20
Em: jpf@theagroup-mc.com
A full-service interior design, exterior design and refit company. Offers clients full assistance from beginning until delivery using the latest high technology computerised network.
NA, D.

Abeking & Rasmussen Schiffs und Yachtwerft,
An der Fähre 2,
27809 Lemwerder,
Germany.
Tel:+49 (0)421-6733531
Fax:+49 (0)421-6733115
Em: yacht@abeking.com
A long-established yard providing design, engineering and construction, as well as repair and retro-fitting of high quality motor and sailing yachts of up to 80m, built from steel, stainless steel, aluminium, and wood.
B.

Act Studio,
Istanbul Mercan,
Ihlamur Sok 14,
Tuzla, 81700 Istanbul,
Turkey.
Tel:+90 (0)532 597-6124
Fax:+90 216 395-4001
Em: actstudio@turk.net
An interior design and project management team located in Tuzla, the centre of the expanding Turkish superyacht industry.
YS.

Acubens SL,
C/Diego Ayllon No 1,
28043 Madrid, Spain.
Tel:+34 (0)917.59.68.06
Fax:+34 (0)913.00.55.72
Em: acubens@telegonica.net
Founded in 1991 and managed by the naval architect Inigo Echenique. Acubens is specialised in the complete design of motor and sailing yachts from high speed yachts to tall ships.
NA, D.

Alaska Diesel Electric,
PO Box 70543,
4420 14th Avenue NW,
Seattle, Washington
98107-0543, USA.
Tel:+1 206 789-3880
Fax:+1 206 782-5455
Em: ade@northern-lights.com
Maker of Northern Lights marine generator sets, (4.5-520kW), and Lugger marine diesels (70-900hp). Specialising in challenging custom diesel applications on the world's finest yachts.
YEM.

Alliance Marine Risk Managers Inc,
1400 Old Country Road,
Suite 307, Westbury,
New York 11590, USA.
Tel:+1 516 333-7000
Fax:+1 516 333-9529
Also:
Alliance Marine Risk Managers Inc,
901 SE 17th Street,
Suite 209, Fort Lauderdale,
Florida 33316, USA.
Tel:+1 954 522-7755
Fax:+1 954 522-7765
Em: AMRM-FL@worldnet.att.net
International yacht insurance broker.
YS.

Alloy Yachts International Ltd,
1 Selwood Road,
Henderson,
Auckland,
New Zealand.
Tel:+64 9-838-7350
Fax:+64 9-838-7393
Em: mailbox@alloyyachts.co.nz
Builder of luxury power and sailing yachts from 30m to 60m in aluminium.
B.

Amels Holland BV,
Strandweg 6,
PO Box 1,
8754 ZN Makkum,
The Netherlands.
Tel:+31 (0)515-334334
Fax:+31 (0)515-232719
Em: info@amels-holland.com
Specialists in the new construction and refit/repair of superyachts. Makkum features a 120m (394ft) covered drydock. Schelde features two fully covered drydocks, 145m (476ft) and 200m (656ft). First class quality is standard at both facilities.
B.
Also:
**Amels –
Nigel Burgess Inc,**
801 Seabreeze Boulevard,
Bahia Mar Yachting Center,
Fort Lauderdale,
Florida 33316,
USA.
Tel:+1 954 525-1090
Fax:+1 954 525-0297
Em: ftlaud@amels.nigelburgess.com
Marketing arm of Amels shipyard in conjunction with Nigel Burgess Ltd.
BMA.

Amico & Co,
Via dei Pescatori,
16128 Genova, Italy.
Tel:+39 010-2470067
Fax:+39 010-2470552
Em: amico.yard@amico.it
Refit and repair of yachts from 20m to 70m. Top quality painting. Facilities include a new 520-tonne travelift in addition to the 300-tonne lift, 15,000m² open areas, concrete and fabric paint sheds, covered areas, covered dry-dock up to 70m.
YS.

Andrawis Yachts & Marine Design International,
3821 NE 12 Terrace, Pompano Beach, Florida 33064, USA.
Tel:+1 954 785-6893
Tel:+1 954 785-0233
Em: phil8ships@aol.com
Specialising in yacht designing, exterior styling, interior design, naval architecture and retrofit. Construction management. High speed monohulls or displacement design in aluminium/GRP/steel.
D, NA.

Apollonio Naval Architecture,
PMB 514, 1225 East Sunset Drive, Bellingham, Washington 98226, USA.
Tel:+1 360 733-6859
Fax:+1 360 715-9474
Em: hapollo@az.com
Naval architects and marine engineers. Leading edge yacht and commercial craft design, engineering, styling and space planning for a wide range of unique and advanced vessels, including catamarans and SWATHS.
D, NA.

Ardell Yacht & Ship Brokers,
1550 SE 17th Street,
Fort Lauderdale,
Florida 33316, USA.
Tel:+1 954 525-7637
Fax:+1 954 527-1292
Em: yachts @ardell-fl.com
Also:
Ardell Yacht & Ship Brokers,
2101 West Coast Highway,
Newport Beach,
California 92663, USA.
Tel:+1 949 642-5735
Fax:+1 949 642-9880
Em:yachts@ardell-ca.com
Specialises in the brokerage and charter of large power and sailing yachts.
BR, C.

Ardeo Design Inc,
755 Winslow way E. Suite 301, Bainbridge Island, Washington 98110, USA.
Tel:+1 206 855-9027
Fax:+1 206 855-9028
Em: scott@ardeodesign.com
Ardeo is the Latin word for passion, which describes the design team's commitment to excellence. This extends from the smallest detail to the most important element of a yacht's design: the client.
D.

Joseph Artese Design,
16003 34th Avenue NE,
Seattle,
Washington 98155,
USA.
Tel:+1 206 365-4326
Fax:+1 206 365-7009
Em: artesedesign@attbi.com
Internationally respected for creative, functional, award-winning interior design and exterior styling of sail and power yachts, custom and production, ranging from traditional to contemporary. 25 years experience.
D.

Art-Line,
Hulkesteinseweg 35,
6812 DB Arnhem,
The Netherlands.
Tel:+31 (0)26-4436703
Fax:+31 (0)26-4459182
Em: artline1@chello.nl
Interior architects specialised in designing custom build yacht interiors and cruise-ship interior concepts. Innovative spatial designs and 15 years experience in lightweight interior construction.
D.

Atlas Energy Systems,
5101 NW 21st Avenue,
Suite 520,
Fort Lauderdale,
Florida 33309, USA.
Tel:+1 954 735-6767
Fax:+1 954 735-7676
Em: mikep@atlasenergysystems.com
Leading manufacturer of marine frequency and power conversion equipment and electrical switchboards.
YEM.

Axis Group Yacht Design Inc,
Via Paola Savi 319,
55049 Viareggio (LU),
Italy.
Tel:+39 0584-389631
Fax:+39 0584-399014
Em: axisgyd@aol.com
Axis Group Yacht Design is a naval architecture company specialised in megayachts, from concept design to the entire engineering.
NA.

Azimut-Benetti SpA,
Via Martin Luther King, 9-11,
10051 Avigliana,
Torino, Italy.
Tel:+39 0119-3161
Fax:+39 0119-316688
B.
Also:
Azimut-Benetti SpA
Via Michele Coppino 441
55049 Viareggio
Lucca,
Italy.
Tel: +39 0584-3801
Fax: +39 0584-3801500
B.

B&G,
Premier Way, Abbey Park,
Romsey SO51 9AQ,
United Kingdom.
Tel:+44 (0)1794 518448
Fax:+44 (0)1794 518077
Em: sales@BandG.com
Yacht instrument manufacturer with global coverage.
YEM.

Baccarat,
30 Bis rue de Paradis,
75010 Paris, France.
Tel:+33 (0)1.40.22.11.52
Fax:+33 (0)1.42.46.97.08
Em: charles.gaschignard@baccarat.fr
Manufacturer of fine crystal.
YEM.

Bachmann Marine Services Ltd,
PO Box 175, Frances House,
Sir William Place, St Peter Port, Guernsey GY1 4HQ,
Channel Islands.
Tel:+44 (0)1481 723-573
Fax:+44 (0)1481 711-353
Em: jamesa@bachmanngroup.com
Bachmann provides an unrivalled service to yacht owners and their agents in all matters relating to registration, corporate ownership, insurance, satcom billing, bunkering and VAT advice.
YS.

Cantieri Navali Baglietto SpA,
Viale S Bartolomeo, 414,
19138 La Spezia, Italy.
Tel:+39 0187-59831
Fax+39 0187-564765
Em: baglietto@baglietto.com
Builder of motor yachts up to 150m in length.
B.

Jon Bannenberg Ltd,
6 Burnsall Street,
London SW3 3ST,
United Kingdom.
Tel:+44 (0)20 7352-4851
Fax:+44 (0)20 7352-8444
Em: yachts@bannenberg.com
Internationally known exterior styling and interior design company.
D.

Jonathan Quinn Barnett Ltd,
116 Vine Street,Seattle,
Washington 98121, USA.
Tel:+1 206 322-2152
Fax:+1 206 322-2153
Em: info@jqbltd.com
Specialises in the interior and exterior design of motor and sailing yachts. Services include project management for new construction and refits.
D.

Bartram & Brakenhoff LLC,
2 Marina Plaza,
Goat Island, Newport,
Rhode Island 02840, USA.
Tel:+1 401 846-7355
Fax:+1 401 847-6329
Em: florida@bartbrak.com
Also:

Bartram & Brakenhoff of Florida,
304 SE 20th Street,
Fort Lauderdale,
Florida 33316,
USA.
Tel:+1 954 779-7377
Fax:+1 954 522-9425
Em: florida@bartbrak.com
Professional and personalised
service with integrity since
1967. Specialising in sales,
charter, new construction
and charter marketing of high
quality power and sailing
yachts throughout the world.
BR, C, YMA.

BCR Yachts,
14 bis boulevard d'Aguillon,
06600 Antibes,
France.
Tel:+33 (0)4.93.34.92.45
Fax:+33 (0)4.93.34.84.25
Em: info@bcryachts.com
BR, C, YMA.

Beiderbeck Designs,
Gerhard-Rohlfs-Strasse 81,
28757 Bremen,
Germany.
Tel:+49 (0)421-662353
Fax+49 (0)421-662425
*Em: yacht@
beiderbeckdesigns.de*
NA, D.

Benetti,
Via M Coppino 104,
55049 Viareggio,
Italy.
Tel:+39 0584-3821
Fax:+39 0584-396232
Em: info@benettiyachts.it
Custom yacht builder from
30m to 45m in composite
and in steel and aluminium
from 50m to 70m plus.
B.

Blohm + Voss GmbH,
Postfach 10 07 20,
Dept SC,
20005 Hamburg,
Germany.
Tel:+49 (0)40-31191301
Fax:+49 (0)40-31193338
*Em: engelskirchen@
blohmvoss.thyssen.com*
Specialises in large yachts
up to 180m.
B.

**Donald L Blount
and Associates Inc,**
1316 Yacht Drive,
Suite 305,
Chesapeake,
Virginia 23320,
USA.
Tel:+1 757 545-3700
Fax:+1 757 545-8227
Em: dlba@dlba-inc.com
Designers of innovative
custom motor yachts.
Our distinctive designs
have yielded motor
yachts with superior
ride quality, acoustically
quiet interiors, and
stringent speed/range
requirements. Past
designs include *Fortuna*
and *Destriero*.
NA, D.

Blubay Yachts SA,
130, rue d'Antibes,
06400 Cannes,
France
Tel:+33 (0)4.97.06.20.20
Fax:+33 (0)4.97.06 .54.97
Em: info@blubay.com
Blubay Yachts aims to open
up new horizons to
demanding enthusiasts by
creating a catamaran
concept that allies the most
up-to-date technologies of
a fast sailing yacht with
a streamlined design.
B, D.

Blue Trend,
Galerie du Port,
8 Bd d'Aguillon,
06600 Antibes, France.
Tel:+33 (0)6.09.06.91.13
Fax:+33 (0)4.93.34.99.11
Em: info@Blue-trend.com
Marketing agent for Guy
Couach Yachts.
BR, C, BMA.

Philippe Briand,
26 Rue Saint Sauveur,
17000 La Rochelle, France.
Tel:+33 (0)5.46.50.57.44
Fax:+33 (0)5.46.50.57.94
*Em: philippebriand@
compuserve.com*
Well-known in the field
of international racing,
this company is currently
concentrating on the design
of large luxury yachts.
NA, D.

Broward Yacht Sales,
1635 Miami Road,
Suite 1, Fort Lauderdale,
Florida 33316, USA.
Tel:+1 954 763-8201
Fax:+1 954 763-9079
Em: sales@browardyacht.com
*also: charters@
browardcharters.com*
Our professional and close
relationship with our clients
allow for our unique ability
to assist with the design,
construction, purchase, sales
or charter of world class
motor yachts.
BR, C.

Luke Brown & Associates,
1500 Cordova Road,
Suite 200,
Fort Lauderdale,
Florida 33316, USA.
Tel:+1 954 525-6617
Fax:+1 954 525-6626
Em: sales@lukebrown.com
BR, C.

Burger Boat Company,
1811 Spring Street,
Manitowoc,
Wisconsin 54220, USA.
Tel:+1 920 684-1600
Fax:+1 920 684-6555
*Em: davidross@
burgerboat.com*
140-year-old shipyard
specialising in custom
aluminium construction
ranging in length from
25.9m to 50.2m.
B.
Also:

Burger Yacht Sales,
17th Street Quay,
1535 SE 17th Street,
Suite 107, Fort Lauderdale,
Florida 33316, USA.
Tel:+1 954 463-1400
Fax:+1 954 463-3100
Em: bys@burgerboat.com
Brokerage division of
Burger Boat Company,
specialising in new
construction orders and the
sale of pre-owned yachts.
BR, BMA.
Also:
Burger Marine Services,
1535 SE 17th Street,
Suite 107, Fort Lauderdale,
Florida 33316, USA.
Tel:+1 954 463-8806
Fax:+1 954 463-8807
Em: BMS@burgerboat.com
Yacht refit, repair and service
division of Burger Boat
Company.
YS.

Nigel Burgess Ltd,
16/17 Pall Mall,
London SW1Y 5LU,
United Kingdom.
Tel:+44 (0)20 7766-4300
Fax:+44 (0)20 7766-4329
*Em: london@
nigelburgess.com*
Specialist in the sale,
purchase, charter,
management and new
construction of large motor
and sailing yachts
worldwide. Our reputation is
built on reliability,
confidentiality,
professionalism and trust.
Agent for Amels Holland.
BR, YMA, C, BMA.
Also:
Nigel Burgess,
Monte-Carlo Sun,
74 Boulevard d'Italie,
MC 98000, Monaco.
Tel:+377 97.97.81.21
Fax:+377 97.97.81.25
*Em: monaco@
nigelburgess.com*
BR, YMA, C, BMA.
Also:
Amels-Nigel Burgess Inc,
801 Seabreeze Boulevard,
Bahia Mar Yachting Center,
Fort Lauderdale,
Florida 33316, USA.
Tel:+1 954 525-1090
Fax:+1 954 525-0297
*Em: ftlaud@
amels.nigelburgess.com*
Specialist in the sale,
purchase, management and
charter of large motor and
sailing yachts worldwide.
Agent for Amels Holland.
BMA, BR, C.

**Felix Buytendijk Yacht
Design,**
Uiterdijk 13,
4011 ET Zoelen,
The Netherlands.
Tel:+31 (0)34-4682596
Fax:+31 (0)34-4682595
*Em: fbdesign@
worldonline.nl*
Interior and exterior styling
of sail and motor yachts.
D.

**Camper & Nicholsons
International,**
57,rue Grimaldi,
MC 98000 Monaco.
Tel:+377 97.97.77.00
Fax:+377 93.50.25.08
Em: info@mon.cnyachts.com
Head office of the
international chain of
Camper & Nicholsons
International yacht sales,
management and charter
brokerage offices. CNI's
global office network
delivers clients an unrivalled
range of services. CNI is a
full service company, with
the emphasis in the field
of larger yachts.
BR, YMA, C, YS.
Comprising:

**Camper & Nicholsons
International,**
25 Bruton Street,
London W1J 6QH,
United Kingdom.
Tel:+44 (0)20 7491-2950
Fax:+44 (0)20 7629-2068
Em: info@lon.cnyachts.com
BR, YMA, C, YS.
Also:
**Camper & Nicholsons
International,**
Port Camille Rayon,
06220 Golfe Juan,
France.
Tel:+33 (0)4.97.04.10.50
Fax:+33 (0)4.97.04.10.60
Em: info@can.cnyachts.com
BR, YMA, C, YS.
Also:
**Camper & Nicholsons
International,**
12 avenue de la Liberation,
06600 Antibes, France.
Tel:+33 (0)4.92.91.29.12
Fax:+33 (0)4.92.91.29.00
Em: info@ant.cnyachts.com
BR, YMA, C, YS.
Also:
**Camper & Nicholsons
International,**
Club de Mar,
07015 Palma de Mallorca,
Spain.
Tel:+34 971.40.33.11
Fax:+34 971.40.14.12
Em: info@cnipalma.com
BR, YMA, C, YS.
Also:
**Camper & Nicholsons
International,**
450 Royal Palm Way,
Palm Beach,
Florida 33480, USA.
Tel:+1 561 655-2121
Fax:+1 561 655-2202
Em: info@pal.cnyachts.com
BR, YMA, C, YS.
Also:
**Camper & Nicholsons
International,**
The Courts, 141 Alton Road,
Miami Beach,
Florida 33139, USA.
Tel:+1 305 604-9191
Fax:+1 305 604-9196
Em: info@mia.cnyachts.com
BR, YMA, C, YS.
Also:

**Camper & Nicholsons
International,**
Av San Jeronimo 273,
Local 21,Suite MX067-382,
Tizapan Pedregal San Angel,
CP 10908 Mexico, DF.
Tel:+52 5 281-4545
Fax:+52 5 281-5926
Em: al@mia.cnyachts.com
BR, YMA, C, YS.
**Camper & Nicholsons
International,**
801 Seabreeze Blvd,
Fort Lauderdale,
Florida 33316,
USA.
Tel:+1 954 524-4250
Fax:+1 954 524-4249
Em: info@ftl.cnyachts.com
Specialist in superyacht
brokerage, custom building
and the charter of motor
yachts of over 25m, and
sailing yachts over 21m,
in the Mediterranean,
Caribbean and worldwide.
BR, C, YMA, YS.

**Camper & Nicholsons
Yachting Ltd,**
The Green,
Mumby Road, Gosport,
Hampshire PO12 1AH,
United Kingdom.
Tel:+44 (0)23 9258-0221
Fax:+44 (0)23 9250-1882
Em: design@cnyachts.co.uk
Now part of Nautor Swan.
Camper & Nicholsons has
been buiding world class
yachts for over 200 years.
B.

Carbospars SL,
Avenida Son Noguera,
Solar A9,
Poligono Industrial
Son Noguera,
07620 Llucmajor,
Baleares, Spain.
Tel:+34 (9)71.66.92.29
Fax:+34 (9)71.66.43.27
*Em: carbospars@
compuserve.com*
Composite and carbon-fibre
specialist, offering custom
spars up to 60m in length,
general composite design
and repair, consultancy
and smart mast systems.
Designer and manufacturer
of the AeroRig® system.
Now based at Palma.
YEM.

Carr Design,
338 First Avenue North,
St Petersburg,
Florida 33701, USA.
Tel:+1 727 894-3660
Fax:+1 727 894-3666
Em: info@carr-design.com
Design, planning and
development for yacht
exterior design. Interior
architecture, and furniture
design. Distinctive design,
construction management
experience, and the finest
computer technology
come together to assure
design success.
D.

Tony Castro Ltd,
Rio House, 76 Satchell Lane,
Hamble, Southampton,
Hampshire SO31 4HL,
United Kingdom.
Tel:+44 (0)23 8045-4722
Fax:+44 (0)23 8045-6011
*Em: tonycastro@
tonycastro.co.uk*
Complete naval architecture,
styling, interior and
engineering service.
Power or sail. Full 2D/3D
CAD-equipped office,
tank or wind tunnel testing
arranged. Grand Prix
racing pedigree.
NA, D.

Caterpillar Inc,
Engine Division, N4-AC6110,
PO Box 610, Mossville,
Illinois 61552-0610, USA.
Tel:+1 309 578-6298
Fax:+1 309 578-2559
Em: cat_power@cat.com
Caterpillar offers 27 engine
models, 13 featuring
state-of-the-art electronic
engine control. Marine
propulsion engines are
rated 63-9,660 bhp, marine
generator sets 34-5200ekW;
and marine auxiliary engines
70-7200 bhp, all backed
and serviced by Cat.
YEM.

Cavendish White Ltd,
4 Bramber Court, Bramber
Road,London W14 9PW,
United Kingdom.
Tel:+44 (0)20 7381-7600
Fax:+44 (0)20 7381-7601
*Em:yachts@
cavendishwhite.com*
Yacht broker and charter
agent for yachts from 20m
and upwards. The company
specialises in high-level
personalised service.
YMA, BR, C.

CBI Navi SpA,
Via Giannessi-Via Pescatori,
55049 Viareggio, Lucca, Italy.
Tel:+39 0584-388192
Fax:+39 0584-388060
Em: info@cbinavi.com
Financial soundness,
quality, strength and design
are their creeds, supported
by a reliable and well-
established organisation,
in building seaworthy full
or semi-displacement
superyachts up to 55m in
steel and/or aluminium.
B.

Cheoy Lee Shipyards Ltd,
89 & 91 Hing Wah Street West,
Lai Chi Kok, Kowloon,
Hong Kong.
Tel:+852 2307-6333
Fax:+852 2307-5577
Em: info@cheoylee.com.
Builder of production,
pleasure craft up to 35m in
fibreglass and steel and
custom pleasure craft in
fibreglass, steel and
aluminium up to 60m.
B.
Also:

Cheoy Lee Shipyards North America Inc,
Bahia Mar Yachting Center,
801 Seabreeze Blvd,
Fort Lauderdale,
Florida 33316, USA.
Tel:+1 954 527-0999
Fax:+1 954 527-2887
Em: info@cheoyleena.com
BMA, BR.

Christensen Shipyards Ltd,
4400 SE Columbia Way,
Vancouver,
Washington 98661, USA.
Tel:+1 360 695-3238
Fax:+1 360 695-3252
*Em: info@
christensenyachts.com*
Builder of custom motor
yachts from 32m to 48m
in cored GRP composite
material. All Christensen
yachts are ocean-going
vessels built to ABS ✠A1-
AMS and MCA regulations in
a state-of-the-art shipyard.
B.
Also:
Christensen Yachts, Inc,
1000 Siminole Drive,
Suite 100,Fort Lauderdale,
Florida 33304, USA
Tel:+1 954 766-8888
Fax:+1 954 766-8889
B.

Cielo Terra Mare CTM Sas,
Via Coppino 84,
Viareggio 55049, Italy.
Tel:+39 0584-384515
Fax:+39 0584-384113
Em: info@falconyachts.com
Builders of Falcon range of
motor yachts in GRP from
24m up to 35m.
B.

CMN,
51 rue de la Bretonniere,
BP 539, 50105 Cherbourg,
Cedex, France.
Tel:+33 (0)2.33.88.30.20
Fax:+33 (0)2.33.88.31.98
B.

**Cantieri Navali
Ugo Codecasa,**
via Amendola,55049
Viareggio, Italy.
Tel:+39 0584-383221
Fax:+39 0584-383531
*Em: info@
codecasayachts.com*
Builds motor yachts up to
80m in steel and aluminium
alloy in three yards.
B.
Also:
Codecasadue SpA
Via Trieste, 3/7,
55049 Viareggio (LU), Italy.
Tel:+39 0584-383945
Fax:+39 0584-388076
*Em:codecasadue@
codecasayachts.com*
A family-owned company
specialising in building and
refitting custom yachts.
B.

Bernie Cohen Design Pty Ltd,
1 Musa Place, Aroona,
Queensland, Australia 4551.
Tel:+61 754-926-200
Fax:+61 754-926-229
Em: bernie@cohen.com.au
D.

William Collier & Co Ltd,
12 Falkner Street,
Liverpool, L8 7PZ
United Kingdom.
Tel:+44 (0)151 7076-490
Fax:+44 (0)151 7076-491
*Em: williamcollier@
compuserve.com*
Classic yacht specialist
offering restoration,
brokerage, research and
project management services.
BR.

**Construction
Navale Bordeaux,**
162 Quai de Brazza,
33100 Bordeaux,
France.
Tel:+33 (0)5.57.80.85.50
Fax:+33 (0)5.57.80.85.51
Em: cnb@cnb.fr
B.

Cor D Rover Design BV,
Toulouselaan 79,
3311 LT Dordrecht,
The Netherlands.
Tel:+31 (0)78-6133822
Fax:+31 (0)78-6390293
Em: cdrd@euronet.nl
A company specialising
in styling and naval
architecture of motor yachts.
D, NA.

Jens Cornelsen GmbH,
D-25348 Glückstadt,
Germany.
Tel:+49 (0)41-242495
Fax:+49 (0)41-245978
*Em: Jens_Cornelsen@
t-online.de*
Management of yachts
while under construction,
as well as in operation.
Several of our highly
admired projects have
been nominated and
selected for prestigious
awards by the
Superyacht Society
and other institutions.
YMA.

**Cramm Ingenieurs &
Handelsburo BV,**
Uranusweg 22, Postbus 510,
8901 BH Leeuwarden,
The Netherlands.
Tel:+31 (0)582-880700
Fax:+31 (0)582-880643
Em: sales@cramm.nl
Hydraulic engineers
concerned with the
largest yachts.
YEM.

Crescent Custom Yachts Inc,
11580 Mitchell Road,
Richmond,
British Columbia V6V 1T7,
Canada.
Tel:+1 604 301-3900
Fax:+1 604 301-3901
*Em: jhawkins@
crescentcustomyachts.com*
Specialises in the
construction of fully-
classed fibreglass motor
yachts. Crescent has built
its reputation on both
quality mechanical
applications and luxurious
interior custom woodwork
and finishing.
B.

Crestar Yachts Ltd,
Colette Court,
125 Sloane Street,
London SW1X 9AU,
United Kingdom.
Tel:+44 (0)20 7730-2299
Fax:+44 (0)20 7824-8691
*Em: charters@
crestaryachts.com*
Specialist in brokerage
and chartering of
substantial luxury yachts.
Charter fleet encompasses
the Mediterranean,
Caribbean, Pacific
and Indian Oceans.
BR, C.

**The Crew
Network Worldwide,**
1053 SE 17th Street Annex,
Fort Lauderdale,
Florida 33316,
USA.
Tel:+1 954 467-9777
Fax:+1 954 527-4083
*Em: info@
crewnetwork.com*
Antibes, France, Fort
Lauderdale, Florida,
USA, Palma De Mallorca,
Spain, Auckland, New
Zealand, Cebu City,
Philippines. Worldwide
professional crew placement
agency. Providing the
highest standards in
matching talented crew with
quality yachts worldwide.
Representing qualified
professionally trained
crew and satisfied
yacht captains/owners
& brokers worldwide.
YS.

**CRN Ancona –
Ferretti Group,**
Via Enrico Mattei 26,
60125 Ancona,
Italy.
Tel:+39 071-5011111
Fax:+39 071-200008
*Em: info@
crn-yacht.com*
CRN is a leading shipyard
in the construction and
refitting of luxury custom
motor yachts with 116
superyachts built during
its 40-year history.
Now headquaters of the
Superyachts Division of
the Ferretti Group.
B.

**Curran Design,
Marine Consultants,**
Lot 300, Sparks Road,
Henderson,
Western Australia 6166,
Australia.
Tel:+61 894-102-988
Fax:+61 894-102-553
*Em: curran@
curran.com.au*
Naval architect of
the extraordinary in
performance superyachts.
Award-winning superyachts
include *Perfect Prescription*,
Mercedes II, *Aussie Rules*
and *Thunder*.
NA.

Dahm International, SA,
Club de Mar s/n,
E-07015 Palma de Mallorca,
Spain.
Tel:+34 (9)71.40.44.12
Fax:+34 (9)71.40.23.27
*Em: info@
dahm-international.com*
New construction,
brokerage and charter of
the world's finest yachts.
Service and refit, mobile
yacht service, engineering
and design, berth, crew
and yacht management.
BR, C, YS.
Also:
Dahm International, SA,
Camino De La Escollera, 5
E-07012 Palma de Mallorca,
Spain.
Tel+34 (9)71.72.52.46
Fax:+34 (9)71.72.52.47
*Em: service@
dahm-international.com*
YS.
Also:
Dahm International, sarl,
Résidence du Port Vauban,
13, av du 11 Novembre,
06600 Antibes, France.
Tel:+33 (0)4 .93.34.51.20
Fax:+33 (0)4 .93.34.71.59
*Em: antibes@
dahm-international.com*
BR, C, YS.
Also:
Dahm International, SA,
Steinstrasse 30,
D-40210 Düsseldorf,
Germany.
Tel:+49 (0)211-3555444
Fax:+49 (0)211-3555499
*Em: charter@
dahm-international.com*
C.

**Butch Dalrymple-Smith,
Butchdesign sarl,**
Chantier Naval,
13600 La Ciotat, France.
Tel:+33 (0)4.42 98.09.18
Fax:+33 (0)4.42 98.09.19
*Em: mail@
butchdesign.com*
Design and engineering
of large sailing yachts.
Technical management
of refits and
classic restorations.
NA.

Delta Marine,
1608 South 96th Street,
Seattle,
Washington 98108,
USA.
Tel:+1 206 763-2383
Fax:+1 206 762-2627
Em: info@deltamarine.com
Specialist in large yacht
(32m to 61m) fibreglass
construction. Metal hull
construction capabilities.
Delta combines new
technologies and creative
ideas with proven building
techniques. All yachts are
custom designed, engineered
and constructed on-site.
B.

Derecktor Shipyards,
311 East Boston Post Road,
Mamaroneck,
New York 10543,
USA.
Tel:+1 914 698-5020
Fax:+1 914 698-6596
*Em: marketing@
derecktor.com*
High-quality custom
construction of large
yachts in aluminium,
steel or special composites,
as well as conversion
and repair with three
locations in New York,
Connecticut and Florida.
B.

Design Q Ltd,
60 Heming Road,
Redditch,
B98 0EA,
United Kingdom.
Tel:+44 (0)1527 501499
Fax:+44 (0)1527 515314
Em: mail@designq.co.uk
Specialists in marine,
automotive and aviation
styling and interior design.
Their experienced team
consists of 15 dedicated and
passionate people who are
able to deliver concept
designs, detailed
engineering
drawings and prototype/
evaluation models.
D.

Design Unlimited,
Lakeside Studio,
Carron Row Farm,
Segensworth Road,
Titchfield,
Fareham,
Hampshire PO15 5DZ,
United Kingdom.
Tel:+44 (0)1329 847712
Fax:+44 (0)1329 841068
*Em: info@
designunlimited.net*
Studio specialising in yacht
interior and exterior design
and styling. Offering fresh
inspiration to classical,
traditional and hi-tech
yacht design.
D.

Devonport Yachts,
Devonport Royal Dockyard,
Plymouth,
Devon PL1 4SG,
United Kingdom.
Tel:+44 (0)1752 323213
Fax:+44 (0)1752 324007
*Em: paul.mabbett@
devonport.co.uk*
Specialist in new construction,
refit and conversion of the
largest yachts in steel,
aluminium and composites.
Extensive facilities include
design capability, several
drydocks, engineering
workshops, building sheds
and alongside berths.
B.

De Voogt Naval Architects,
PO Box 5238,
2000 GE Haarlem,
The Netherlands.
Tel:+31 (0)23-5247000
Fax:+31 (0)23-5248639
*Em: info@
devoogtnavalarchitects.nl*
De Voogt is the Feadship
Naval Architect specialising
in high-quality yachts.
Feadship is a joint venture
of two families, De Vries
and Van Lent and they have
one goal to design and build
the most perfect custom-built
luxury yachts in the world.
NA, D.

De Vries Scheepsbouw,
PO Box 258,
Oosteinderweg 25,
1430 AG Aalsmeer,
The Netherlands.
Tel:+31 (0)297-388900
Fax:+31 (0)297-388901
*Em: henk3@
vriesyard.feadship.nl*
Member of the Feadship
group. Builder of high-
quality steel and aluminium
yachts of 30m to 90m LOA.
B.

**Diana Yacht Design
International BV,**
Engelandlaan 232,
2034 NH Haarlem,
The Netherlands.
Tel:+31 (0)23-5364464
Fax:+31 (0)23-5365504
*Em: info@
dianayachtdesign.com*
Leading designer of
high-quality ocean-going
displacement motor yachts,
sailing yachts and semi-
displacement yachts built
to the most demanding
standards of luxury and
technology.
NA, D.

Gerard Dijkstra & Partners,
Lutra Design Group, Naval
Architects and Marine
Engineers, Kruithuisstraat 21,
1018 WJ, Amsterdam,
The Netherlands.
Tel:+31 (0)20-6709533
Fax:+31 (0)20-6753118
Em: info@gdnp.nl
In addition to general
naval architecture,
specialises in quality
sailing yachts; combining
proven performance
with exceptional
classic appearance.
NA, D.

Terence Disdale Design Ltd,
31 The Green,
Richmond,
Surrey TW9 1LX,
United Kingdom.
Tel:+44 (0)20 8940-1452
Fax:+44 (0)20 8940-5964
*Em: terencedisdale@
terencedisdale.co.uk*
Specialist interior and exterior
design of yachts from 25m
LOA upwards.
D.

Dixon Yacht Design,
Greydowns,
School Rd,
Old Bursledon,
Southampton,
Hampshire SO31 8BX,
United Kingdom.
Tel:+44 (0)23 8040-5280
Fax:+44 (0)23 8040-6203
Em: Bill@
DixonYachtDesign.com
Specialises in sail and
power yachts covering
all aspects of design.
NA, D.

Dockwise Yacht Transport,
1535 SE 17th Street,
Fort Lauderdale,
Florida 33316,
USA.
Tel:+1 954 525-8707
Fax:+1 954 525-8711
Em: dyt@dytinc.com
Offers an extensive schedule
of sailings between US
and Mediterranean and
US and Pacific destinations,
providing float-on/float-off
transportion for superyachts
aboard its dockships.
YS.

Dowland Naval Architects,
7 Spruce Park,
Cumberland Road,
Bromley,
London BR2 0EH,
United Kingdom.
Tel:+44 (0)20 8289-0537
Fax:+44 (0)20 8249-7665
Em: post@dowland.com
Design, consultancy
and project management
services for large motor
yachts and specialist craft.
MCA compliance experts.
D, NA.

Doyle Sailmakers,
89 Front St,
Marblehead,
Massachusetts 01945,
USA.
Tel:+1 781 639-1490
Fax:+1 781 639-1497
Em: doyle@doylesails.com
Doyle Sailmakers with
34 lofts in 18 countries
offer a complete line
of products for all
your sailing needs.
YEM.

DSG Associates,
4511 DuBois Drive,
Vancouver,
Washington 98661,
USA.
Tel:+1 360 735-1638
Fax:+1 360 735-1637
Em: mtm@
dsgassociates.com
A marine industry consultancy
specialising in all phases of
yacht design and construction.
Additional capabilities include
research and development,
project management and
maritime arbitration.
D.

Dubois Naval Architects Ltd,
Beck Farm, Sowley,
Lymington, Hampshire SO41
5SR, United Kingdom.
Tel:+44 (0)1590 626-666
Fax:+44 (0)1590 626-696
Em: design@
duboisyachts.com
Specialises in large, fast
and innovative cruising
yachts both power and
sail, as well as Grand prix
racing yachts. Complete
design and styling service.
NA, D.
Also:

Dubois Yachts Ltd,
Beck Farm, Sowley,
Lymington,
Hampshire SO41 5SR,
United Kingdom.
Tel:+44 (0)1590 626-688
Fax:+44 (0)1590 626-696
Em: yachts@
duboisyachts.com
Specialises in the charter
and sale of Dubois
designed yachts.
BR, C.

**Edmiston & Company
Limited,**
62 St. James's Street,
London SW1A 1LY,
United Kingdom.
Tel:+44 (0)20 7495-5151
Fax:+44 (0)20 7495-5150
Em: london@
edmistoncompany.com
Also:

Edmiston & Company,
Le Panorama,
57 Rue Grimaldi,
MC 98000,
Monaco.
Tel:+377 93.30.54.44
Fax:+377 93.30.55.33
Em: mc@
edmistoncompany.com
Internationally known
superyacht brokers working
with the largest yachts.
BR, C.

Emerald Yacht & Ship,
900 W Marion Ave,
Punta Gorda,
Florida 33950, USA.
Tel:+1 941 639-6987
Fax:+1 941 639-9498
Em:11075.1261@
compuserve.com
BR, C, YMA

Juan Carlos Espinosa,
1320 S Federal Highway,
Suite 216, Stuart,
Florida 34994,
USA.
Tel:+1 561 287-4925
Fax:+1 561 287-4858
Em: info@espinosainc.com
Architectural interior
design firm specialising in
exterior styling, space
planning and world-class
interior design for custom
and production yachts.
Construction supervision
and refurbishing services
are also provided.
D.

Fairlie Restorations,
Unit 4, Port Hamble,
Hamble,
Hampshire SO31 4NN,
United Kingdom.
Tel:+44 (0)23 8045-6336
Fax:+44 (0)23 8045-6166
Em: info@
fairlierestorations.com
Small yard specialising in
authentic restoration and
refit of classic yachts up to
36.7m. New builds in
traditional or strip plank.
Resources include the
original drawings of William
Fife & Son, and a highly
experienced workforce.
B, YI.

**Fairmont Insurance
Services Group Ltd,**
33-34 Bury Street,
London EC3A 5AT,
United Kingdom.
Tel:+44 (0)20 7929-6880
Fax:+44 (0)20 7929-6889
Em: mike@
superyachtcover.com
Specialist yacht insurance
brokers protecting vessel,
liability and crew. Specialist
cover for crew medical
employer's liability.
YS.

Feadship Holland BV,
Zijlweg 148c,
PO Box 5238,
2000 GE Haarlem,
The Netherlands.
Tel:+31 (0)23-5247000
Fax:+31 (0)23-5248639
Em: info@feadship.nl
Feadship is a joint venture
of De Vries and Van Lent.
There are three yards:
Aalsmeer, Kaag Island and
in Papendrecht. They have
one goal: to build the most
perfect custom-built luxury
yachts in the world.
BMA.
Also:

Feadship Papendrecht,
Scheepvaartweg 11,
PO Box 1146,
3350 CC Papendrecht,
The Netherlands.
Tel:+31 (0)78-6150266
Fax:+31 (0)78-6411199
Em: shipyard@slob.demon.nl
B.
Also:

Feadship America Inc,
801 Seabreeze Blvd,
Bahia Mar, Fort Lauderdale,
Florida 33316, USA.
Tel:+1 954 761-1830
Fax:+1 954 761-3412
Em: feadship@ix.netcom.com
Also:

Feadship France,
7 bis avenue Paul Arene,
06600 Antibes, France.
Tel:+33 (0)4.93.34.28.77
Fax:+33 (0)4.93.34.71.60
Em: info@feadship.fr
BMA.

Ferretti Custom Line,
Ferretti Group,
Via Enrico Mattei 26,
60125 Ancona,
Italy.
Tel:+39 0715-011111
Fax:+39 0712-00008
Em: info@
customline-yacht.com
Located in Ancona, Custom
Line is a leading shipyard
specialising in the
construction of luxury
planing and semi-
displacement motor yachts
in composite from 25m
(94ft) up to 40m (130ft).
Together with CRN,
Custom Line is part of the
Superyachts Division of
the Ferretti Group.
B.

**Tom Fexas Yacht
Design Inc,**
1320 S Federal Highway,
Suite 104,
Stuart,
Florida 34994,
USA.
Tel:+1 561 287-6558
Fax:+1 561 287-6810
Em: info@tomfexas.com
Over 900 vessels from 9.1m
to 45.7m designed since
1966 are currently in use.
Power boat and yacht design
for craft of any size, type or
material. Sea-going planing
and semi-displacement
hulls are its speciality.
NA, D.

Adrian J Fisher,
Private Yacht Personnel
Consultant,
8 avenue Mirabeau,
06600 Antibes,
France.
Tel:+33 (0)4.93.42.42.92
Fax:+33 (0)4.93.34.65.23
Em: adrianfisher@riviera.fr
Individual, personal service
to owners, captains,
managers and crew for
worldwide crew recruitment.
YS.

Fontaine Design Group,
92 Maritime Drive,
Portsmouth,
RI 02871, USA.
Tel: +1 401 682-9101
Fax: +1 401 682-9102
Em: inquiries@
fontainedesigngoup.com
NA.

Francisdesign,
BP 072,
2960 Route des Cretes,
06902 Sophia Antipolis,
Cedex, France.
Tel:+33 (0)4.93.95.85.10
Fax:+33 (0)4.93.95.85.07
Em: francis@
francisdesign.com
Specialises in concept
design, naval architecture,
interior and exterior
design on high-quality
and innovative power
and sailing yachts.
NA, D.

Fraser Yachts Worldwide,
2, quai Antoine 1er,
Monte Carlo 98000, Monaco.
Tel:+377 93.10.04.50
Fax:+377 93.10.04.51
Em: salesmonaco@
fraseryachts.com
Fraser Yachts Worldwide is
an international team of
specialists dedicated to large
yacht services. Brokerage
purchase/sale/charter,
charter maketing,
new construction,
yacht management, crew
placement and insurance.
YMA, BR, C, YS.
Also:

Fraser Yachts Worldwide,
1800 SE 10th Ave. Suite 400,
Fort Lauderdale,
Florida 33316, USA.
Tel:+1 954 463-0600
Fax:+1 954 463-1053
Em: salesflorida@
fraseryachts.com
Also:

Fraser Yachts Worldwide,
2353 Shelter Island Drive,
San Diego,
California 92106, USA.
Tel:+1 619 225-0588
Fax:+1 619 225-1325
Em: isalessandiego@
fraseryachts.com
Also:

Fraser Yachts Worldwide,
3471 Via Lido, Suite 200
Newport Beach,
California 92663, USA.
Tel:+1 949 673-5252
Fax:+1 949 673-8795
Em: salesnewportbeach@
fraseryachts.com
Also:

Fraser Yachts Worldwide,
320 Harbor Drive, Sausalito,
California 94965, USA.
Tel:+1 415 332-5311
Fax:+1 415 332-7036
Em: infosanfrancisco@
fraseryachts.com
Also:

Fraser Yachts Worldwide,
1001 Fairview Ave North,
Ste 1300, Seattle,
Washington 98109, USA.
Tel:+1 206 382-9494
Fax:+1 206 382-9480
Em: infoseattle@
fraseryachts.com
Also:

Fraser Yachts Worldwide,
53, Makriyinni Street,
Athens, 157 72, Greece.
Tel: +30 210 77 05 865
Fax: +30 210 77 05 865
Em: infogreece@
fraseryachts.com
Also:

Fraser Yacht Management,
9, Avenue d'Ostende,
Monte Carlo 98000,
Monaco.
Tel:+377 93.10.04.80
Fax:+377 93.10.04.81
Em: yachtmanagement@
fraseryachts.com
Also:

Fraser Yacht Management,
1800 SE 10th Ave., Suite
400, Fort Lauderdale,
Florida 33316, USA.
Tel:+1 954 463-0640
Fax:+1 954 463-0766
Em: yachtmanagement@
fraseryachts.com
Also:

Fraser Charters, Inc,
2, quai Antoine 1er,
Monte Carlo 98000,
Monaco.
Tel:+377 93.10.04.60
Fax:+377 93.10.04.61
Em: chartermonaco@
fraseryachts.com
Also:

Fraser Yacht Charters,
1800 SE 10th Ave.,
Suite 400,
Fort Lauderdale,
FL 33316, USA.
Tel:+1 954 463-0600
Fax:+1 954 462-1028
Em: charterflorida@
fraseryachts.com
Also:

Fraser Charters Inc,
3471 Via Lido,
Suite 200,
Newport Beach,
California 92663, USA.
Tel:+1 949 675-6960
Fax:+1 949 673-8795
Em:charternewportbeach@
fraseryachts.com
Also:

Fraser Charters Inc,
2353 Shelter Island Drive,
San Diego,
California 92106, USA.
Tel:+1 619 523-8723
Fax:+1 619 523-8745
Em: chartersandiego@
fraseryachts.com
Also:

Fraser Charter Marketing,
2, quai Antoine 1er,
Monte Carlo 98000,
Monaco.
Tel:+377 93.10.04.90
Fax:+377 93.10.04.91
Em: chartermarketing@
fraseryachts.com
Also:

**Fraser Yacht Insurance
Services Inc,**
3471 Via Lido,
Suite 200,
Newport Beach,
California 92663, USA.
Tel:+1 949 675-5262
Fax:+1 949 673-8795
Em: insurance@
fraseryachts.com
YS.
Also:

Thirty Seven South,
15 Halsey Street,
Box 1874
Auckland,
New Zealand.
Tel: +64 9-302-0178
Fax: +64 9-307-0871
Em: infoauckland@
fraseryachts.com
B, C, YMA.

Fredericks/Power & Sail,
16 Rainbow Falls,
Irvine,
California 92612,
USA.
Tel:+1 949 854-2696
Fax:+1 949 854-4598
Em: fredericks.p-s@
att.net
Specialises in the brokerage
of yachts both power and sail
and project co-ordination
and management for new
yacht construction.
BR, YS.

**Freeman Marine
Equipment Inc,**
28336 Hunter
Creek Road,
Gold Beach,
Oregon 97444,
USA.
Tel:+1 541 247-7078
Fax:+1 541 247-2114
Em: info@
freemanmarine.com
Manufactures weathertight
and watertight single,
Dutch, French and
pantograph doors,
single and dual-axis
sliding doors, custom
and standard hatches,
windows and
portlights for the finest
yachts worldwide.
YEM.

Ken Freivokh Design,
Ash Studio,
Crocker Hill,
Fareham,
Hampshire PO17 5DP,
United Kingdom.
Tel:+44 (0)1329 832-514
Fax:+44 (0)1329 833-326
Em: all@freivokh.com
Styling and interior design
studio specialising in the
highest-quality motor and
sailing superyachts.
D.

Germán Frers,
Guido 1926-1 floor,
1119 Buenos Aires,
Argentina.
Tel:+54 11-4806-4806
Fax:+54 11-4801-0423
Em: gfrers@
germanfrers.net
Also:
Germán Frers,
Via S Paolo 1,
20121 Milan,
Italy.
Tel:+39 0286-465417
Fax:+39 0286-465464
Em: debFrers@
compuserve.com
Internationally-known
naval architectural practice,
fast expanding from racing
craft into the largest
cruising superyachts.
NA.

**FRYCO,
Edward D Fry,**
5420 Waddell Hollow Rd,
Franklin,
Tennessee 37064-9422,
USA.
Tel:+1 615 591-8455
Fax:+1 615 591-8454
Em: frycoyacht@aol.com
Turn-key approach saves
owner's time, by dealing
with one firm for all design
and contract management.
Specialises in yachts of 30m
to 100m diesel, gas/turbine,
including 50-knot air
cushion yachts.
NA, D.

Gerard's, Service en Mer,
Bahia Mar Yachting Center,
801 Seabreeze Boulevard,
Fort Lauderdale,
Florida 33316, USA.
Tel:+1 954 523-0465
Fax:+1 954 523-6156
Em: gerards@
mindspring.com
Established in 1997.
Gerard's has rapidly become
the source that owners,
designers, builders and crew
depend on for their outfitting
needs including china,
crystal, cutlery, fine linens
and speciality service items.
Recent projects include the
198ft Oceanco, *Pegasus*;
157ft CRN, *Kanaloa*; 150ft
Feadship *Charisma*; 173ft
Amels, *Kiss the Sky* and the
185ft Halter, *Pangea*.
YS.

Grant & Horton,
Marine Solicitors,
Lynher Building,
Queen Anne's Battery,
Plymouth, Devon PL4 0LP,
United Kingdom.
Tel:+44 (0)1752 265-265
Fax:+44 (0)1752 265-260
Em: grant&horton@
marine-law.co.uk
Also:
Grant & Horton,
Marine Solicitors,
Suites 6 & 7, Second Floor,
Canute Chambers,
Canute Road,
Southampton SO14 3AB,
United Kingdom.
Tel:+44 (0)23 8048-8727
Fax:+44 (0)23 8048-8728
A firm of marine lawyers
supplying legal advice to
the international marine
community with a specialist
superyacht department.
YS.

Guido de Groot Design,
Hogewoerd 122,
2311 HT Leiden,
The Netherlands.
Tel:+31 (0)71-5663040
Fax:+31 (0)71-5663039
Em: info@guidodegroot.com
Design team specialising in
the design of innovative
interiors and exteriors for
both luxury motor yachts
and sailing yachts.
D.

Hakvoort Shipyard,
Havenstraat 17-22,
1141 AX Monnickendam,
The Netherlands.
Tel:+31 (0)29-9651403
Fax:+31 (0)29-9651041
Em: sales@hakvoort.com
Hakvoort Shipyard specialises
in new construction and
refits of luxury yachts in
the range of 20m to 50m
in aluminium and steel.
B.

Halyard (M & I) Ltd,
Whaddon Business Park,
Southampton Road,
Whaddon,
Nr Salisbury,
Wiltshire SP5 3HF,
United Kingdom.
Tel:+44 (0)1722 710-922
Fax:+44 (0)1722 710-975
Em: techhelp@
halyard.eu.com
Halyard is Europe's
foremost designer
and manufacturer of
marine exhaust systems
for engines up to 1500kW.
The company produces
silencers, separators
and stainless exhaust
components for use on
superyachts worldwide.
YEM.

**Hargrave Yacht
Design and Engineering,**
901 SE 17 Street,
Suite 203,
Fort Lauderdale,
Florida 33316,
USA.
Tel:+1 954 463-0555
Fax:+1 954 463-8621
Em: mjoyce@
hargrave-usa.com
Designer of power
vessels ranging from
small craft to large
motor yachts and
commercial craft in
all materials.
NA.

**Harris Grant
Associates Ltd,**
16 Trinity Churchyard,
Guildford,
Surrey GU1 3RR,
United Kingdom.
Tel:+44 (0)1483 885-678
Fax:+44 (0)1483 885-677
Em: info@
harrisgrant.com
Acoustic and Design
Consultants specialising
in system design for
audio, video, climate,
communications and
networks, furniture and
hoists, and integrated
systems control. Also
architectural acoustics:
modelling and prediction,
room optimisation,
isolation, ambient
noise analysis.
YS

HDW-Nobiskrug,
Kielerstrasse 53,
D-24768 Rendsburg,
Germany.
Tel:+49 (0)433-120720
Fax:+49 (0)433-1207117
Em: hmk@
hdw-nobiskrug.de
A major shipyard specialising
in the new construction,
conversions and refit
of superyachts.
B.

Heesen Shipyards,
PO Box 8,
NL- 5340 AA Oss,
The Netherlands.
Tel:+31 (0)412-665544
Fax:+31 (0)412-665566
Em: info@
heesenshipyards.nl
Specialises in the
construction of fast,
semi-displacement and
displacement ocean-going,
custom-built aluminium
motor yachts up to 65m.
B.

**Heinen & Hopman
Engineering BV,**
Zuidwenk 45,
3751 CB Spakenburg,
The Netherlands.
Tel:+31 (0)33-2992500
Fax:+31 (0)33-2992599
Em: info@
heinenhopman.com
Technical advisor on and
manufacturer of, heating,
air-conditioning, mechanical
ventilation, sprinkler and
sanitary systems.
YEM.

Heliyachts International SA,
Via Motta 34, CH-6900
Lugano, Switzerland.
Tel:+41 91.924.9950
Fax:+41 91.924.99 51
Em: info@heliyachts.com
A Swiss/Croatian company
building high quality motor
and sailing yachts. Handles
yachts up to 50m and offers
complete services for repair
and refit. Registration,
financing and management
also available.
YS, BR, BMA.
Also:
Heli dd,
Sv. Polikarpa 8,
HR-52100 Pula,
Croatia.
Tel:+385 52 37.55.00
Fax:+385 52 37.55.10
Em: info@heliyachts.com
A Swiss/Croatian company
building high quality motor
and sailing yachts.
Handling yachts up
to 50m and offering
complete services
for repair, refit
and restoration.
B.

Tim Heywood Designs Ltd,
1E Olivers Wharf,
64 Wapping High Street,
London E1W 2PJ,
United Kingdom.
Tel:+44 (0)20 7481-8958
Fax:+44 (0)20 7481-4133
Em: tim@
timheywooddesigns.co.uk.
Specialising in the design
of high quality exteriors
and interiors of large
yachts. Designer of
the *Carinthia VII*,
launched 2002.
D.

Hill Dickinson,
Sun Court,
66/67 Cornhill,
London EC3V 3RN,
United Kingdom.
Tel:+44 (0)20 7695-1000
Fax:+44 (0)20 7695-1001
Em: AAllen@hilldicks.com
A service dedicated to yacht-
related commercial and
contractual matters: new
constructions, sale and
purchase, financing,
professional services, crew
employment and charter
parties; Codes of Practice,
VAT, registration, UK and
offshore incorporation.
YS.

Hill Robinson,
Residences du Port Vauban,
17 Avenue du 11 Novembre,
06600 Antibes, France.
Tel:+33 (0)4.92.90.59.59
Fax:+33 (0)4.92.90.59.60
Em: info@hillrobinson.com
We provide independent
and confidential operational,
financial and safety
management to owners,
captains and brokers of
large yachts. ISM certified
in 2001 by Lloyds Register,
we provide a simple,
flexible SMS.
YMA.

H & M Electronic Systems,
D 28790 Schwanewede,
Schützenplatz 9,
Germany.
Tel:+49 (0)421-661546
Fax:+49 (0)421-6530543
Em: Trempnau@t-online.de
YEM.

Hodgdon Yachts Inc,
14 School Street.
PO Box 505,
East Boothbay,
Maine 04544, USA.
Tel:+1 207 633-4194
Fax:+1 207 633-0539
Em: info@hodgdon
yachts.com
B.

**Hoek Design
Naval Architects bv,**
Grote Kerkstraat 23,
1135 BC Edam,
The Netherlands.
Tel:+31 (0)29-9372853
Fax:+31 (0)29-9371519
Em: info@hoekdesign.com
NA.

Ron Holland Design,
PO Box 23,
Kinsale,
County Cork,
Ireland.
Tel:+353 21-4774866
Fax:+353 21-4774808
Em: info
@ronhollanddesign.com
Designer of high-
performance sailing
and motor yachts.
NA, D, YMA.

H2, Howard & Horsfield,
9 Princeton Court,
53-55 Felsham Road,
Putney, London SW15 1AZ,
United Kingdom.
Tel:+44 (0)20 8788-5008
Fax:+44 (0)20 8788-8043
Em: info@h2yachtdesign.com
International superyacht
designer specialising in
high-quality interiors and
exterior styling of motor
yachts and sailing yachts.
D.

Hunt, Deltel & Co Ltd,
PO Box 14, Victoria, Mahe,
Seychelles.
Tel:+248 380300
Fax:+248 255367
Em: hundel@seychelles.net
Comprehensive yacht
support service. Member
of AYSS. Processing of
Charter Licences, cruising
permits, outer island calls
and clearance.
YS.

Peter Insull's Yacht Marketing,
Residences du Port Vauban,
19 Avenue du 11 Novembre,
Antibes 06600, France.
Tel:+33 (0)4.93.34.44.55
Fax:+33 (0)4.93.34.92.74
Em: info@insull.com
Specialists in the sale,
purchase and charter of large
motor yachts. Construction
consultancy, Management
and Crew Agency.
BR, YMA, YS, C.

**Intelect Integrated
Electronics,**
2500 NW 55th Court,
Suite 210,
Fort Lauderdale,
Florida 33309, USA.
Tel:+1 954 739-4449
Fax:+1 954 739-4342
Em: enquiries@
intelect-electronics.com
Intelect designs and installs
integrated electronic systems
exclusively for the
superyacht market. Designs
include A/V entertainment,
home theatre, satellite
television, touchscreen
control systems, computer
distribution, security
systems and display
technology.
YEM.

Intermarine SpA,
PO Box 185, 19038
Sarzana,
La Spezia, Italy.
Tel:+39 0187-617285
Fax:+39 0187-674249
Em: marketing@
intermarine.it
Designer and builder of FRP
megayachts. Availability of
moulds and projects in the
range 30m to 60m. One
MEGA 445 and one 118ft
are under construction.
B.

**International Paint/
Akzo Nobel,**
24-30 Canute Road,
Southampton,
Hampshire SO14 3PB,
United Kingdom.
Tel:+44 (0)23 8022-6722
Fax:+44 (0)23 8022-2090
*Em: drew.allen@
uk.akzonobel.com*
Marine paint manufacturer
with a global support
network. Guaranteed
specialised superyacht
paint system.
YEM.
Also:
Interlux Yacht Finishes,
2270 Morris Avenue,
Union,
NJ 07083,
USA.
Tel:+1 908 964-2353
Fax:+1 908 686-8545
YEM.

IZAR,
San Fernando Shipyard,
PO Box 18,
San Fernando,
Cadiz,
Spain.
Tel:+34 (9)56.59.98.97
Fax:+34 (9)56.59.98.98
Em:comercialsf@izar.es
IZAR, the ninth largest
shipbuilder in the world,
has facilities for building
yachts in composites, steel
or aluminium, up to
65m under cover and
up to 130m in covered
slipway. Built the 41m
motor yacht *Fortuna.*
With a top speed of 67
knots she is the fastest
megayacht in the world.
B.

Lynn Jachney Charters, Inc,
PO Box 302,
Marblehead,
Massachusetts 01945,
USA.
Tel:+1 781 639-0787
Fax:+1 781 639-0216
Em: ljc@boston.sisna.com
Experienced charter brokers
providing personalised,
outstanding private yacht
charters aboard motor yachts
and sailing yachts
worldwide.
C.

JLS Design,
Barrack Lane, Kinsale,
Co. Cork,
Ireland.
Tel:+353 21-4773377
Fax:+353 21-4773299
Em: info@jlsdesign.ie
Superyacht designers, naval
architects, exterior stylists and
structural engineers with
experience in large motor and
sailing yachts. sailing yachts.
NA, D.

**Glade Johnson
Design Bellevue WA,**
11820 Northup Way,
Suite 220,
Bellevue,
Washington 98005,
USA.
Tel:+1 425 827-1600
Fax:+1 425 827-2147
Em: gjdi@gjdi.net
Completed projects include:
51m *Double Haven,* 50m
Iroquois, 49m *Gallant Lady,*
48m *Georgia,* 48m *Attessa,*
47m *Silver Lining,* 44m
Montigne, 43m *Attessa,*
40m *CV-9,* 39.6m *Netanya
V,* 38m *Excellence,* 38m
Sen Sei, 37m *Atlanta* 36m
P'Zazz, 33.5m *Venturosa,*
33m *Onika,* 31.4m Hulls
Number 3 and Number 4,
and 31m *Shana II.*
D.

Jongert BV,
Industrieweg 6,
PO Box 116,
1670 AC Medemblik,
The Netherlands.
Tel:+31 (0)227-542544
Fax:+31 (0)227-541246
Em: info@jongert.nl
J Jongert and N H van der
Ree, builders of luxury
custom designed sailing and
motor superyachts,
renowned for innovative
design, outstanding quality
of construction and
excellent workmanship.
B.
Also:
Jongert International SAM
17 Boulevard Albert 1er,
MC-98000,
Monaco.
Tel:+377 93.50.25.86
Fax:+377 93.25.36.56
Em: info@jongert.mc
Sales office for the Dutch
shipyard Jongert.
BMA.

Kitty van der Kamp Design,
Hyacintenlaan 13,
6866 DV Heelsum,
The Netherlands.
Tel:+31 (0)317-350031
Fax:+31 (0)317-350145
Interior designer for *Honey
Money* and *Obsessions.*
D.

Bruce King Yacht Design,
PO Box 599,
Newcastle Square,
Newcastle,
Maine 04553,
USA.
Tel:+1 207 563-1186
Fax:+1 207 563-1189
*Em: kingydes@
lincoln.midcoast.com*
NA.

Kirschstein Designs, Ltd,
Lynton, Church Lane,
Peppard, Henley,
Oxon RG9 5JN,
United Kingdom.
Tel:+44 (0)1491 628-073
Fax:+44 (0)1491 628-087
*Em: mikekirschstein@
aol.com*
International superyacht
designer specialising in
interior design, exterior
styling and project
co-ordination of large
yacht new constructions
and refits combining
high-tech CAD design
with conventional
design methods.
D.

Patrick Knowles Design,
2030 Northeast 18th Street,
Fort Lauderdale,
Florida 33305,
USA.
Tel:+1 954 832-0108
Fax:+1 954 537-7766
*Em: pknowles@
PatrickKnowlesDesigns.com*
Yacht, residential and
executive aircraft interior
design. Acclaimed for
projects such as 40m Palmer
Johnson MY *Inevitable,*
37m Delta *Louise,* and
Taipan, a 52m Rybovich
Spencer refit and MY *Sir Jon,*
a 90ft Hatteras Sportfish.
D.

Koch, Newton & Partners,
Calle Porto Pi 4,
E-07015 Palma de Mallorca,
Spain.
Tel:+34 (0)971.70.04.45
Fax:+34 (0)971.70.05.51
Em: info@kochnewton.net
Also:
Koch, Newton & Partners,
1700 E Las Olas Boulevard,
Suite 100,
Fort Lauderdale,
Florida 33301,
USA.
Tel:+1 954 525-7080
Fax:+1 954 525-7095
Em: yachts@kochnewton.com
Internationally known, full
service yacht brokerage
team specialising in the sale
and charter of large motor
and sailing yachts. Offices
in Fort Lauderdale, Palma de
Mallorca and Singapore.
BR, C, YMA.

KoopNautic Holland bv,
Breukerweg 3A,
6411 RP Heerlen,
PO Box 140,
6430 AC Hoensbroek,
The Netherlands.
Tel:+31 (0)45-5447100
Fax:+31 (0)45-5742345
Em: sales@koopnautic.com
YEM.

**Kusch Yacht
Agentur GmbH,**
Ivo-Hauptmann-Ring 16,
22159 Hamburg,
Germany.
Tel:+49 (0)406-60786
Fax:+49 (0)406-683693
*Em: Kusch-Yacht@
t-online.de*
A major yacht design
and project management
company that has recently
acquired the Peters Shipyard.
B, D.

**Langan Design
Associates Inc,**
105 Spring Street,
Newport,
Rhode Island 02840,
USA.
Tel:+1 401 849-2249
Fax:+1 401 849-3288
*Em: info@
langandesign.com*
NA.

Lars Modin,
Strandgatan 5,
SE-185 32 Vaxholm,
Sweden.
Tel:+46 85-4133445
Fax:+46 85-4133446
*Em: Lars@
Modin-Design.com*
Highly qualified yacht
designer who has practised
as both captain and broker
to learn the demands from
crew, owners and industry.
D.

Michael Leach Design,
9a Great Minster Street,
Winchester,
Hampshire SO23 9HA,
United Kingdom.
Tel:+44 (0)1962 849737
Fax:+44 (0)1962 849717
*Em: michael.leach.design@
dial.pipex.com*
Professional consultants
for the exterior and interior
design of yachts 30m to
160m. Specialising in
listening to and reaching
our clients expectations.
D.

Liebowitz & Pritchard
Architects & Yacht
Designers,
13 Erisey Terrace
Falmouth,
Cornwall TR11 2AP,
United Kingdom.
Tel: +44 (0)7970 270500
Fax: +44 (0)1326 312653
Em: Rich@LParch.com
Firm specialises in yacht
planning, exterior design,
interior detailing and
decoration as well as
project supervision.
D.

Linn Products Ltd,
Floors Road, Waterfoot,
Glasgow G76 OEP,
United Kingdom.
Tel:+44 (0)1413 077777
Fax:+44 (0)1416 444262
Em: info@linnmarine.com
Linn manufactures and
supplies high-quality
integrated music and
cinema systems that are
proven at sea to deliver
uncompromised sound and
picture quality, and are
supported by an expert
worldwide service network.
YEM.

Liveras Yachts,
Rose de France,
17 Boulevard de Suisse,
9800 Monaco.
Tel:+377 97.97.45.10
Fax:+377 97.97.45.13
Em: info@liverasyachts.com
A charter company offering
the largest yachts.
C.

Loher Raumexclusiv GmbH,
Wallersdorfer Str 17,
94522 Haidlfing, Germany.
Tel:+49 (0)993-39100
Fax:+49 (0)993-3910280
Em: info@loher-rauexclusiv.de
Specialising in exclusive
interior finishes.
YI.

Luiz de Basto Design Inc,
444 Brickell Avenue,
Suite 928, Miami,
Florida 33131, USA.
Tel:+1 305 373-1500
Fax:+1 305 377-0900
Em: luizbasto@aol.com
Naval architects and interior
designers serving a global
clientele. A wide repertoire
of size and styling.
NA, D.

Lürssen Werft,
Friedrich-Klippert Strasse 1,
28759 Bremen, Germany.
Tel:+49 (0)421-6604166
Fax:+49 (0)421-6604170
Em: uy@lurssen.de
Specialises in construction,
repair and refitting of yachts
in steel, aluminium and
wood up to 120m. Has the
world's largest environment-
controlled paint shed.
B.

**Malcolm J Horsley
International,**
Résidence du Port Vauban,
1 Avenue de la Liberation,
06600 Antibes, France.
Tel:+33 (0)4.93.34.68.98
Fax:+33 (0)4.93.34.69.96
Em: info@mjhyachts.com
Specialist in the sale and
purchase of larger sailing
yachts, with a particular
knowledge of classics.
Offering a personalised
service covering all aspects
of yacht ownership.
BR, C, YMA.

The Marblehead Co Ltd,
6 Burnsall Street,
London, SW3 3ST,
United Kingdom.
Tel:+44 (0)20 7352-8437
Fax:+44 (0)20 7351-5373
*Em: dickie
@marblehead.co.uk*
ISM certified yacht
management company.
YMA.

Marelux SA,
55 Boulevard de la Petrusse,
L-2320 Luxembourg
Tel:+352 40 49 45
Fax:+352 40 49 46
Em:marelux@cmdnet.lu
YS.

**Maritime Research Institute
Netherlands,**
2 Haagsteeg,
PO Box 28,
6700 AA Wageningen,
The Netherlands.
Tel:+31 (031-7493911
Fax:+31 (0)31-7493245
Em: info@marin.nl
Specialists in hydrodynamic
research by means of
desk studies, simulations,
training, model and full-scale
testing, MARIN can advise
the maritime industry
worldwide. Software
development. Simulator
training for navigation.
YS.

Evan K Marshall,
Usonia IV,
4 Coral Row,
Plantation Wharf,
York Road,
London SW11 3UF,
United Kingdom.
Tel:+44 (0)20 7801-9244
Fax:+44 (0)20 7801-9245
Em: ekmu4@aol.com
D.

Marten Spars,
40 Ben Lomond Crescent,
Pakuranga, PO Box 38-484,
Auckland, New Zealand.
Tel:+64 9-576-3573
Fax:+64 9-576-2150
*Em: design@
marten-spars.co.nz*
Marten Spars has become
recognised as a world leader
in high tech composite
construction of carbon-fibre
masts and booms. The
international award winning
'Leisure furl' system offers
huge benefits to cruising
performance and efficiency.
YEM.
Also:
Marten Yachts,
26 Bowden Road,
Mt Wellington, Auckland,
New Zealand.
Tel:+64 9-573-2190
Fax:+64 9-573-2199
*Em: info@
martenyachts.co.nz*
A family-owned company
specialising in carbon-fibre
high performance
cruising yachts.
B.

MCA,
Spring Place,
105 Commercial Road,
Southampton,
Hampshire,
United Kingdom.
Tel:+44 (0)23 8032-9100
Fax:+44 (0)23 8032-9404
YS.

McMullen & Wing Ltd,
21 Gabador Place,
Mount Wellington,
PO Box 14-218,
Auckland 1006,
New Zealand.
Tel:+64 9-573-1405
Fax:+64 9-573-0393
Em: mcwing.boats@
xtra.co.nz
Building sailing and
motor yachts in steel,
aluminium and FRP
to 40m. Comprehensive
in-house marine skills
from joiner work to
electrical. Refit service
and painting on a 300-
tonne, covered 50m
slipway. Custom tenders
and RIBs built to order.
B.

MCN International Ltd,
Unit 10,
Shield Drive,
West Cross Centre,
Brentford,
Middlesex TW8 9EX,
United Kingdom.
Tel:+44 (0)20 8580-1001
Fax:+44 (0)20 8580-1002
Em: info@
mcninternational.com
An agency specialising
in the packing of luxury
interiors, fine arts and
antiques and their
forwarding by air,
sea or road. Project
warehousing available.
YS.

Med-Sale UK Ltd,
Universal Shipyard,
Crableck Lane,
Sarisbury Green,
Southampton,
Hampshire SO31 7ZN,
United Kingdom.
Tel:+44 (0)1489 565-555
Fax:+44 (0)1489 565-111
Em: sales@
medsale.net
Exclusive distributor
for Azimut.
BR, BMA.

Mega Yachts Ltd,
Suite 20,
Block 6,
Watergardens,
Gibraltar.
Tel:+350 41516
Fax:+350 47998
Em: mega_yachts@
yahoo.com
Offering individual
brokerage services
to the superyacht market
at very competitive
rates. Strictest
confidence maintained.
YMA, BR, C.

Merrill-Stevens Dry Dock,
1270 NW 11th Street,
Miami, Florida 33125, USA.
Tel:+1 305 324-5211
Fax:+1 305 326-8911
Em: msddmiami@aol.com
Provide labour and materials
for every aspect of
superyacht refit repair
and maintenance.
B.
Also:
Merrill-Stevens Yacht Sales,
1270 NW 11th Street,
Miami, Florida 33125, USA.
Tel:+1 305 547-2650
Fax:+1 305 547-2660
A division of Merrill-Stevens
Dry Dock Company.
BR.

Metrica Interior,
Bahnhofstrasse 73,
D-48308 Senden, Germany.
Tel:+49 (0)253-6330900
Fax:+49 (0)253-6330919
Em: info@metrica.de
YI.
Also:
Metrica Interior AG,
Marketing & Sales,
Terossenweg 17,
CH-Oberaggeri/ZG,
Switzerland.
Tel:+41 41.750.4475
Fax:+41 41.750.6270
YI.

Moncada di Paterno,
Ship & Yacht Broker SRL,
Via Montenapoleone 8,
20121 Milan, Italy.
Tel:+39 0276-004649
Fax:+39 0276-004904
BR, C, YMA.

Moonen Shipyards,
Graaf van Solmsweg 52,
5222 BP, 's-Hertogenbosch,
The Netherlands.
Tel:+31 (0)73-6210094
Fax:+31 (0)73-6219460
Em: info@moonen.com
Specialists in steel and
aluminium motor yachts
up to 36m.
B.

Moran Yacht & Ship Inc,
1300 SE 17th Street,
Suite 204, Fort Lauderdale,
Florida 33316, USA.
Tel:+1 954 768 0707
Fax:+1 954 768 0057
Em:gina@moranyachts.com
BR, C, YMA.

MTU Friedrichshafen GmbH,
Maybachplatz 1
88045 Friedrichshafen,
Germany.
Tel:+49 (0)7541-902159
Fax:+49 (0)7541-903918
Em: daniel.reinhardt@
mtu-online.com
MTU offers propulsion and
on-board power generation
systems with diesel engines
and gas turbines (80-
27,600kW), transmissions
and electronic monitoring
and control systems
for yachts.
YEM.

**Muir Winches
& Windlasses,**
100 Browns Road,
Kingston,
Tasmania 7050,
Australia.
Tel:+61 362-295-188
Fax:+61 362-297-030
Em: info@muir.com.au
Specialist design and
manufacturer of complete
anchoring systems for all
mega and superyachts up
to 120m or 10000kg lift,
including anchor winches,
windlasses, docking
capstans, deck equipment,
chain compressors and
stoppers, devil claw
assemblies, anchors, chain
and electric and hydraulic
control systems. Finished
in polished stainless steel,
chrome plated or
polished bronze.
YEM.

Mulder Design,
Benedeneind Zuidzijde
289B
3405 CK Benschop,
The Netherlands.
Tel:+31 (0)348-452925
Fax:+31 (0)348-452926
Em: info@
mulderdesign.nl
Specialises in design,
styling, naval architecture
and engineering of
high-quality fast motor
yachts and displacement
motor yachts.
NA, D.

John Munford Design,
Building 2,
Shamrock Quay,
Northam,
Southampton,
Hampshire SO14 5QL,
United Kingdom.
Tel:+44 (0)23 8063-0880
Fax:+44 (0)23 8033-2117
Em: design@j-m-d.co.uk
Internationally-known
interior design specialist
involved with the largest
projects. Very well-known
for classical design.
D.

Naiad Marine,
50 Parrott Drive,
Shelton,
Connecticut 06484,
USA.
Tel:+1 203 929-6355
Fax:+1 203 929-3594
Em: sales@naiad.com
Manufactures complete
line of roll stabilisers,
bowthrusters and
custom-engineered
integrated hydraulic
systems for yachts.
Worldwide technical
support including
Naiad Marine, Florida,
a dedicated service and
installation operation in
Fort Lauderdale.
YEM.

Navigator SAM,
14, Quai Antoine 1er,
Monte Carlo,
98000 Monaco.
Tel:+377 93.10.41.04
Fax:+377 93.30.26.51
Em: navigatorme@
monaco377.com
Navigator has been
a specialist in large
yachts since 1939.
BR, C, YMA.

Nicholson Interiors,
Unit 4, Imperial Park,
Empress Road,
St Denys,
Southampton,
Hampshire SO14 0JW,
United Kingdom.
Tel:+44 (0)23 8023-3722
Fax:+44 (0)23 8023-3994
Em: mail@
nicholsoninteriors.com
Internationally renowned
interior specialists for new
build and refit work. Market
leaders in light weight
innovation. High speed ferry
interiors with a track record
of 43 new builds to date.
YI.

Nirvana Spars BV,
Kanaalweg 4,
8356 VS Blokzijl,
The Netherlands.
Tel:+31 (0)52-7291555
Fax:+31 (0)52-7291777
Em: info@nirvana.spars@.nl
Manufacturers of aluminium
and carbon-fibre masts and
spars, in-boom furling
systems, standing and
running rigging.
YEM.

North Superyacht Group,
9 Fielder Drive,
Fareham,
Hampshire PO14 1JE,
United Kingdom.
Tel:+44 (0)1329 508-050
Fax:+44 (0)1329 220-442
Em: info@gb.northsails.com
Sailmaker with specialist
superyacht division,
providing the highest
level of technology in
sail design and custom
fabric production. Has
the most comprehensive
service network in the world.
YEM.

**Northrop & Johnson
Yacht-Ships, Inc,**
1901 SE 4th Ave,
Fort Lauderdale,
Florida 33316, USA.
Tel:+1 954 522-3344
Fax:+1 954 522-9500
info@njyachts.com
BR, C.
Also:
Northrop & Johnson,
5 Marina Plaza,
Newport,
Rhode Island 02840,
USA.
Tel:+1 401 849-0120
Fax:+1 401 849-0620
Em: yachts@nandj.com
Also:

**Northrop & Johnson
Yacht Charters,**
O Lee's Wharf,
Newport,
Rhode Island 02840, USA.
Tel:+1 401 848-5540
Fax:+1 401 848-0120
Em: njricharters@
edgenet.net
Also:
**Northrop & Johnson
(France),**
13 Rue Pasteur,
06400 Cannes, France.
Tel:+33 (0)4.93.94.20.08
Fax:+33 (0)4.93.94.42.29
Em: office@northrop.fr
Major US charter and
brokerage company with
offices throughout the USA.
BR, C, YMA.

Novurania,
2105 S US 1,
Vero Beach,
Florida 32962, USA.
Tel:+1 772 567-9200
Fax:+1 772 567-1056
Em: info@novurania.com
Builder of high quality
tenders, outboard, jet,
petrol and diesel
powered, from 3m
to 9m in length.
YEM.

**Pauline Nunns
Associates Ltd,**
Chartered Architect & Designer,
Efailrhyd,
Near Oswestry,
Shropshire SY10 0DU,
United Kingdom.
Tel:+44 (0)1691 791-394
Fax:+44 (0)1691 791-507
Internationally known office,
specialising in high-quality
classical superyacht
interiors. Provides a personal
service, for scheme designs,
full architectural detail
drawings, fabric and
furniture selection.
D.

Nuvolari-Lenard,
39a via Della Chiesa,
31020 Zerman,
Italy.
Tel:+39 041-457272
Fax:+39 041-457393
Em: nlyachts@mpbnet.it
Design and management
of construction of large
motor yachts. Naval
architects, external stylists
and interior designers.
Building supervision and
owner representative.
D, NA, YI.

Ocean Yacht Systems UK,
Ocean House
Aviation Park West,
Bournemouth
International Airport
Christchurch
Dorset, BH23 6NW,
United Kingdom.
Tel:+44 (0)1202 596600
Fax:+44 (0)1202 596670
Also:

**Ocean Yacht
Systems USA,**
300 Highpoint Avenue
Portsmouth,
Rhode Island 02840,
USA.
Tel:+1 401 682-2488
Fax:+1 401 682-2487
Em: mail@
oceanyachtsystems.co.uk
YEM, YS.

Oceanco
Gildo Pastor Center
7 rue du Gabian
98000 Monaco.
Tel:+377 93.10.02.81
Fax:+377 92.05.65.99
Em: oceanco@
oceanco.mc
Dutch shipyard specialising
in building custom
yachts from 50m (160ft)
and larger. Oceanco
Design, Management
and Marketing departments
are concentrated in
Monaco. Oceanco
manufacturing facilities
are based in Holland
(Alblasserdam Yachtbuilding
bv) and Germany (Kusch
Yachtbau GmbH).
B, D.

Oceanfast Pty Ltd,
18 Clarence Beach Road,
Henderson,
WA 6166,
Australia.
Tel:+61 894-949-999
Fax:+61 894-949-900
Em: boats@oceanfast.com.au
Oceanfast is a world
class Austrilian
superyacht builder,
offering its customers
exciting designs
and specialising in
manufacturing
excellence with
personal service.
Oceanfast employs
around 500 skilled
tradespeople and is
capable of building
in steel, aluminium and
composite materials.
B.
Also:
Oceanfast LLC,
1515 SE 17th St,
Suite 119 (The Quay),
Fort Lauderdale,
Florida 33316,
USA.
Tel:+1 954 610-2138
Fax:+1 954 581-7948
Em: oceanfastusa@
attglobal.net
Builder of technically
advanced motor yachts.
Capable of building in
steel, aluminium and
composite fibreglass or
combinations thereof.
BMA.

Offshore Nautical Ltd,
La Collette,
Le Quai D'Avergne,
St Helier, Jersey JE2 3NX,
United Kingdom.
Tel:+44 (0)1534 514444
Fax:+44 (0)1534 514445
Em:info@
offshore-nautical.com
Specialists in the design and
construction of innovative and
exclusive Superyachts. Our
unique in-house skills and
facilities ensure synergy of
quality and service from
conceptual designs to
fleet management.
D, B, NA,YS.

Espen Øino Naval Architects,
10 Avenue de la Libération,
06600 Antibes. France
Tel:+33 (0)4.92.91.07.77
Fax:+33 (0)4.92.91.07.18
Em: mail@espenoino.com
Creative naval architecture
practice specialising in power
craft. Fully-qualified staff
undertake all aspects of the
design process from feasibility
studies through project
definition to detailed design.
Fully CAD equipped.
NA, D.

**Oldenburger
Mobelwerkstätten,**
Sanderstrasse 21,
D-49413 Dinklage,
Germany.
Tel:+49 (0)444-3972135
Fax:+49 (0)444-3972 275
Em: cad@oldenburger.com
Yacht interior manufacturers.
YI.

Oliver Design S.L.,
Estrada Diliz 33,
48990 GETXO,
Vizcaya, Spain.
Tel:+34 (9)44.91.40.54
Fax:+34 (9)44.60.82.05
Em: oliver@oliverdesign.es
D, NA.

Pacific Custom Interiors Inc,
2742 Alki Avenue SW,
Suite 200, Seattle,
Washington 98116, USA.
Tel:+1 206 938-8700
Fax:+1 206 938-8707
Em: pcinteriors@uswest.net
Designer of elegant yacht
interiors, specialising in
fabricating fine upholstery
and hand-crafted interiors.
D, YI.

Palmer Johnson Yachts Inc.,
61 Michigan Street,
PO Box 109,
Sturgeon Bay,
Wisconsin 54235, USA.
Tel:+1 920 743-4412
Fax:+1 920 743-3381
Em: info@
palmerjohnson.com
Builder of top-quality
custom yachts, both sail
and power, in aluminium.
B.
Also:

**Palmer Johnson
Savannah Inc,**
3124 River Drive,
Savannah,
Georgia 31404,
USA.
Tel:+1 912 352-4956
Fax:+1 912 352-0593
Em: haberli@
pjsavannah.com
Specialising in refit, repair and
conversion of superyachts.
B.

**Pantaenius GmbH
& Co KG**
Cremon 32,
20457 Hamburg,
Germany.
Tel:+49 (0)40-370910
Fax:+49 (0)40-37091109
Em: info@pantaenius.com
Also:
Pantaenius,
34 Quai Jean-Charles Rey,
MC 98000,
Monaco.
Tel:+377 97.98.43.43
Fax:+377 97.98.43.40
Em: info@
monaco.pantaenius.com
Also:
Pantaenius UK Ltd,
Marine Building,
Victoria Wharf,
Plymouth,
Devon PL4 0RF,
United Kingdom.
Tel:+44 (0)1752 223-656
Fax:+44 (0)1752 223-637
Em: info@pantaenius.co.uk
Pantaenius is one of
Europe's largest yacht
insurance brokers, offering
a complete insurance
advisory service from
project concept,
through building to
worldwide cruising.
YS.

Patton Marine Inc,
Surveyors & Consultants,
PO Box 451135,
Miami,
Florida 33245, USA.
Tel:+1 305 854 -3821
Fax:+1 305 854 -3855
Em: Pattonmare@aol.com
An eight-man survey team,
with worldwide service
since 1981. Specialising
in purchase, insurance and
damage surveys of any size
and type of yacht. New build
specification review and
construction management.
YS.

**PB Design –
Pieter Beeldsnijder,**
Voorhaven 20-22,
1135 BR Edam,
The Netherlands.
Tel:+31 (0)299-372739
Fax:+31 (0)299-371591
Em: Beeldsnijder@
pbdesign-edam.nl
Specialises in the design of
large power and sail yachts
using CAD/CAM, and of
complete building and
rebuilding projects.
NA, D.

Pedrick Yacht Designs Inc,
Three Ann St,
Newport,
Rhode Island 02840, USA.
Tel:+1 401 846-8481
Fax:+1 401 846-0657
Em: pedrickyacht@
compuserve.com
America's Cup technology
applied to superyacht
cruising. Comprehensive
design skills, carefully
integrating high-tech
engineering and performance
with beauty, comfort and
elegance. Current projects
constructed of advanced
composites, as well as
cold-moulded wood, steel
and aluminium.
NA, D.

Pendennis Shipyard,
The Docks,
Falmouth,
Cornwall TR11 4NR,
United Kingdom.
Tel:+44 (0)1326 211-344
Fax:+44 (0)1326 319-253
Em: info@pendennis.com
Specialises in the new-build
and refit of custom sail and
motor yachts from 25m to 70m,
in steel, aluminium, wood
and high-tech composites.
B.

**Pensum Ltd,
(Cayman Islands),**
Cayman Business Park,
A7, PO Box 10024 APO,
Grand Cayman,
Cayman Islands.
Tel:+1345 945-1830
Fax:+1345 945-1835
Em: pensum@candw.ky
Cayman Islands Yacht
Registration including
vessels under construction,
registration of mortgages,
financial administration.
Corporate and Mutual
Fund services.
YS.

Perini Navi SpA,
Via Coppino 114,
50049 Viareggio,
Lucca, Italy.
Tel:+39 0584-4241
Fax:+39 0584-424200
Em: info@perininavi.it
Founded by Fabio Perini.
Perini Navi focuses on the
engineering and
construction of highly
automated blue-water
sailing yachts.
B.
Also:
Perini Navi USA,
One Maritime Drive,
Portsmouth,
RI 02871, USA.
Tel:+1 401 683-5600
Fax:+1 401 683-5611
BMA.

**Michael Peters
Yacht Design,**
47 South Palm Avenue,
Suite 202, Sarasota,
Florida 34236, USA.
Tel:+1 941 955-5460
Fax:+1 941 957-3151
Em: info@mpyd.net
A full-service yacht design
resource, providing exterior
styling and detailing,
interior layout, hull design
and propulsion and
structural engineering.
D, NA.

Picchiotti SpA,
Darsena Italia 42,
55049 Viareggio, Italy.
Tel:+39 0584-4241
Fax:+39 0584-424343
Em: info@periniavi.it
This famous yard with three
centuries of tradition and
history has been owned by
Perini Navi since 1989. It
now includes the mast
division of Perini Navi
sailing yachts, and
specialises in repair and
refit work both for motor
and sailing yachts.
B.

Piening-Propeller,
Otto Piening GmbH,
Am Altendeich 83,
D-25348 Glückstadt,
Germany.
Tel:+49 (0)412-4916812
Fax:+49 (0)412-43716
Em: pein@
piening-propeller.de
Piening Propeller supplies
complete propulsion
systems for superyachts
and high speed yachts
with various types
of propellers from
500mm upwards, paying
special attention to
maximum efficiency.
YEM.

Pinmar SA,
Contramuella Mollet 6,
07012 Palma de Mallorca,
Spain.
Tel:+34 (0)971.71.37.44
Fax:+34 (0)971.71.81.43
Em: pinmar@pinmar.com
One of the largest yacht
painting companies in
the world, with 30 years
experience in painting
superyachts in covered
facilities in Palma
and Barcelona. Distributors
of all major paints and
marine supplies.
YS.

Platypus Marine, Inc.,
102 North Cedar Street,
Port Angeles, WA 98363
USA.
Tel: +1 360 417-0709
Fax: +1 360 417-0729
Em: info@
platypusmarine.com
Full service yacht centre
specialising in yacht
construction and refit.
B, YS.

Pokela Design,
2907 Harborview Drive,
Suite P, Gig Harbor,
Washington 98335, USA.
Tel:+1 253 853-4240
Fax:+1 253 853-4230
Em: pokeladesign@
compuserve.com
International yacht styling
and interior design of power
and sailing yachts. New
construction or renovations.
D.

**Port de Plaisance
de la Rochelle,**
Capitainerie du Port des
Minimes, Mole Central,
17000 La Rochelle,
France.
Tel:+33 (0)5.46.44.41.20
Fax:+33 (0)5.46.44.36.49
Em: port.lr@wanadoo.fr
Yacht harbour, newly
refurbished to accommodate
large yachts. Well situated in
the centre of town with all
technical services on site.
YS.

**Puléo Inc
International Design,**
733 West Las Olas Blvd,
Fort Lauderdale,
Florida 33312, USA.
Tel:+1 954 522-0173
Fax:+1 954 761-3216
Em: slpuleo@aol.com
Specialists in renovations
and new construction with
exceptional space planning.
Original architectural
designs and thorough
experience in yacht projects
internationally. Project
problem solving a speciality.
D.

**Reckmann Yacht
Equipment GmbH,**
Siemensstrasse 37/39,
25462 Rellingen, Germany.
Tel:+49 (0)4101-38490
Fax:+49 (0)4101-384950
Em: info@reckmann.com
Products include high-tech
hydraulic, electric and
manual reefing systems for
yacht sails, carbon-fibre
furling sections, masts,
hydraulic pump systems and
associated accessories.
YEM.

Redman Whiteley Dixon,
Old Electric Light Station,
Beaulieu, Brockenhurst,
Hampshire,
United Kingdom.
Tel:+44 (0)1590 611-300
Fax:+44 (0)1590 611-301
Em: studio@rwd.co.uk
By blending together
backgrounds from the classical
and contemporary yacht
design business, Redman
Whiteley Dixon provides
world-class personalised
yacht interiors and exteriors.
D.

Rex Yacht Sales,
2152 SE 17th St,
Suite 202, Fort Lauderdale,
Florida 33316, USA.
Tel:+1 954 463-8810
Fax:+1 954 462-3640
Em: rex@rexyachts.com
BR.

**Reymond Langton Design
Limited,**
Raleigh House,
No 2 Richmond Hill,
Richmond,
Surrey TW10 6QX,
United Kingdom.
Tel:+44 (0)20 8332-7789
Fax:+44 (0)20 8332-6890
Em: yachtdesigns@aol.com
An international design
studio, focusing on the
conception, exterior/
interior styling, and
decoration of the
world's finest sailing
and motor yachts.
D.

Rigo Yachts International,
Via Pindaro, 50/9,
00125 Rome, Italy.
Tel: +39 06- 5090222
Fax: +39 06 50917530
Em: rigoyachts@tin.it
Over 20 years of experience
in the yachting field. Sale,
purchase, management and
very active in crewed charter
business with some
interesting Central Agencies
for charter and sale.
C, BR, YMA.

Rivolta Marine,
1741 Main Street,
Suite 201, Sarasota,
Florida 34236, USA.
Tel:+1 941 954-0355
Fax:+1 941 954-0111
Em: rrivolta@gte.net
Full-service marine design,
engineering and build firm
specialising in the union of
modern technology with
traditional craftsmanship,
blending American
engineering with
European design in
yachts from 9m to 30m.
B, D, NA, YI.

Dee Robinson Interiors Inc,
2755 East Oakland Park Blvd,
Suite 301, Fort Lauderdale,
Florida 33306, USA.
Tel:+1 954 566-2252
Fax:+1 954 566-2044
Em: deerob@bellsouth.net
Specialises in superyacht
interior design and
execution of all phases of
pre-construction and refits.
D.

RMK Marine AS,
Icmeler Mevki,
Ozel Tersaneler Bolgesi,
81700, Tuzla-Istanbul,
Turkey.
Tel:+90 216 395-2865
Fax:+90 216 395-4582
Em: cemt@
rmkmarine.com.tr
B, YS.

RNR Yacht Charters,
809 SW 9th St,
Fort Lauderdale,
Florida 33315, USA.
Tel: +1 954 522-9563
Fax: +1 954 463-4525
Em: info@rnryachts.net
C.

Rogers Yacht Design Ltd,
68 High Street, Lymington,
Hampshire SO41 9AL,
United Kingdom.
Tel:+44 (0)1590 672-000
Fax:+44 (0)1590 670-005
*Em: rogersyachtdesign@
compuserve.com*
Internationally established
yacht design company
specialising in performance
cruising, racing yachts and
power boats. Classical
through to contemporary
design solutions for
custom yachts. Refit
design also undertaken.
NA.

Rolla SP Propellers SA,
Via Silva 5, 6828 Balerna,
Switzerland.
Tel:+41 91.695.2000
Fax:+41 91.695.2001
Em: info@rolla-propellers.ch
Experts in computer assisted
CFD for submerged and
surface propellers. Propulsion
consultants, CFD hull analysis
including sea keeping,
propeller manufacturing in
stainless steel and nibral.
YEM.

Rondal BV,
De Weyert 30, PO Box 52,
8325 ZH Vollenhove,
The Netherlands.
Tel:+31 (0)527-243500
Fax:+31 (0)527-243900
Em: info@rondal.com
Producers of aluminium
rolled plate masts and
extruded masts, carbon-fibre
masts, aluminium and cabon-
fibre booms, hydraulic furling
systems, deck hardware,
aluminium and carbon-fibre
hatches, hydraulic drum
and reel winches.
YEM.

Robin M Rose & Associates,
1500 Cordova Road,
Suite 312, Fort Lauderdale,
Florida 33316, USA.
Tel:+1 954 525-6023
Fax:+1 954 525-0010
*Em: RRoseYacht@
worldnet.att.net*
Specialising in complete
custom interiors and
space planning for
new constructions and
renovations since 1989.
D.

Royal Denship A/S,
Dalgas Avenue 42,
DK 8000 Åarhus C,
Denmark.
Tel:+45 86-117353
Fax:+45 86-117453
Em: info@royaldenship.com
B.
Also:

Royal Denship of America,
1500 Cordova Road,
Suite 308,
Fort Lauderdale,
Florida 33316,
USA.
Tel:+1 954 525-2709
Fax:+1 954 525-2731
BMA.

Royal Huisman Shipyard BV,
PO Box 23,
8325 ZG Vollenhove,
The Netherlands.
Tel:+31 (0)527-243131
Fax:+31 (0)527-243800
*Em: yachts@
royalhuisman.com*
Builders of custom-designed,
luxury aluminium motor and
sailing yachts from 18m to
90m LOA.
B.

Royal Van Lent Shipyard B.V.
Julianalaan 3,
2159 LA Kaag,
The Netherlands.
Tel:+31 (0)252-547123
Fax:+31 (0)252-544341
Em: lentyard@feadship.nl
One of three Feadship Yards
together with De Vries
Scheepsbouw and Feadship
Papendrecht. Feadship is a
joint venture of two
families: De Vries and
Van Lent. De Voogt is the
Feadship Naval architect and
they have one goal to design
and build the most perfect
custom-built luxury yachts
in the world.
B.

Rybovich Spencer,
4200 North Flagler Drive,
West Palm Beach,
Florida 33407,
USA.
Tel:+1 561 844-1800
Fax:+1 561 844-8393
Em: service@rybovich.com
A premier service/repair
facility and world-class
marina. Capable of lifting
300 tons and up to 45m,
undertaking complete
reconstructions, extensions,
interior refits and repairs.
BR, B, YS.

**The Sacks Group,
Yachting Professionals Inc,**
1600 SE 17th Street,
Suite 418,
Fort Lauderdale,
Florida 33316, USA.
Tel:+1 954 764-7742
Fax:+1 954 523-3769
Em: info@sacksyachts.com
Specialising in worldwide
luxury yacht vacations,
charter marketing, yacht
brokerage and new
construction. 'Try before
you buy' programme is
specifically targeted for
the purchase and sale
of yachts for the
charter business.
C, YMA, BR.

Safehaven International Ltd,
PO Box 179,
de Catapan House,
The Grange, St Peter Port,
Guernsey GY1 4HH,
Channel Islands.
Tel:+44 (0)1481 723925
Fax:+44 (0)1481 727778
*Em: marine@
safehaveninternational.com*
International company
and trust formation and
administration. VAT
and legal compliance
consultancy. International
registration, insurance
and finance. Assistance
with contracts for all
aspects of yacht
ownership. Yacht
financial administration.
YS, YMA.

**Jack W Sarin Naval
Architects Inc,**
382 Wyatt Way NE,
Bainbridge Island,
Washington 98110, USA.
Tel:+1 206 842-4651
Fax:+1 206 842-4656
Em: jsarin@jacksarin.com
Full range of design services
for yachts.
NA, D.

Sarnia Yachts Ltd,
PO Box 79, La Plaiderie,
St Peter Port,
Guernsey GY1 3DQ,
Channel Islands.
Tel:+44 (0)1481 709-960
Fax:+44 (0)1481 726-526
Em: info@sarniayachts.co.gg
Specialises in providing
corporate yacht ownership,
yacht registration, estate
planning, marine and
crew insurance, yacht
administration and
accounting, yacht
finance and other
marine related services.
YS.
Also:

Sarnia Yachts Ltd,
PO Box 887 GT,
Grand Cayman,
Cayman Islands.
Tel: +1 345 814-2755
Fax: +1 345 945-8243
*Em: lesley.preston@
ansbacher.com.ky*
YS.

Tim Saunders Design,
Boerenstraat 62,
4201 GB Gorinchem,
The Netherlands.
Tel:+31 (0)183 633005
Fax:+31 (0)183 635031
*Em: info@
timsaundersdesign.com*
TSD is a constantly evolving
enthusiastic and highly
innovative design studio
focusing on a new generation
of luxury sail/motor yachts
(10-100m). Specialising in
conceptualisation, exterior
styling, interior design,
illustration and 3D CAD
modelling. TSD –
Anticipating the future,
daring to evolve.
D.

**Bob Saxon Associates at
Camper & Nicholsons
International,**
1500 Cordova Road,
Suite 314,
Fort Lauderdale,
Florida 33316,
USA.
Tel:+1 954 760-5801
Fax:+1 954 467-8909
*Em: yachts1@
bobsaxon.com*
Management of luxury
yachts, both private and
charter; clearing house
services; charter brokerage;
crew search and placement;
project management.
C, YMA.

Claude Schmitt Organisation,
45 La Croisette,
06400 Cannes,
France.
Tel:+33 (0)4.93.38.22.70
Fax:+33 (0)4.93.99.25.85
*Em: info@
csoyachts.com*
Established in 1959, the
company specialises in
brokerage, charter and
management. Clients are
provided with personal
service and confidentiality.
YMA, BR, C.

**Birgit Schnaase
Interior Design,**
Hochallee 121,
D-20149 Hamburg,
Germany.
Tel:+49 (0)40-4107721
Fax:+49 (0)40-4107725
Em: info@schnaase.de
Interior designers
specialising in the
maritime field. Performance:
Design of interiors for
new builds, refit,
refurbishing of all
sizes of motor and sailing
yachts. Various experience
in major refit projects.
D.

Sea Recovery,
PO Box 2560,
Gardena,
California, 90249
USA.
Tel:+1 310 637-3400
Fax:+1 310 637-3430
*Em: sales@
searecovery.com*
YEM.

Sensation New Zealand,
11 Selwood Road,
Henderson,
PO Box 79-020,
Auckland 8,
New Zealand.
Tel:+64 9-837-2210
Fax:+64 9-836-1775
*Em: sensation@
sensation.co.nz*
New Zealand's largest
superyacht builder
specialising in motor
yacht construction and
design from 30m to 61m
and over. Currently building
in steel, aluminium and
composite materials.
B.

SETE Yachts SA,
PO Box 51304,
14510 Kifissia,
Athens, Greece.
Tel:+30 210 80 18 951
Fax:+30 210 80 18 889
Em: info@sete-yachts.com
With 30 years operational
experience and a
worldwide network of
offices, SETE Yachts is
uniquely placed to
provide specialist design
and construction
management services for
both new construction
and refits as well as
operational management,
chartering and brokerage
for owners of superyachts.
D, YS, YMA, C.

Setzer Design Group,
590 New Waverly Place,
Suite 210, Cary,
North Carolina 27511, USA.
Tel:+1 919 319-0559
Fax:+1 919 319-0557
*Em: setzerdesign@
mindspring.com*
Studio specialising in the
design of luxury yachts and
marine products. Provides
styling, naval architecture,
and interior design. Designs
range from 18m to 75m.
D, NA.

Sikkens Yachtpaints,
(Akzo Nobel Coatings BV),
Kleidijk 88, Postbus 986,
3160 Rhoon,
The Netherlands.
Tel:+31 (0)10-5033543
Fax:+31 (0)10-5033546
*Em: info@
sikkensyachtpaints.com*
Manufacturers of yacht
paints, especially high-
quality varnishes, fillers,
primers and antifoulings.
YEM.

Silver Lining Workshops Ltd,
Aldford, Chester CH3 6HJ,
United Kingdom.
Tel:+44 (0)1244 620-200
Fax:+44 (0)1244 620-277
*Em: all@
silverliningfurniture.com*
Designs and makes
award-winning furniture
from over 100 different
timbers combined with
precious metals, exquisite
glass and rare leathers.
YI.

Silver Yachts,
123-125, rue d'Antibes,
06400 Cannes, France.
Tel: +33 (0)4.92.99.57.57
Fax: +33 (0)4.92.99.57.58
Em: info@silveryachts.com
Also:
Silver Yachts España,
Alfonso XII, 36,
28004 Madrid, Spain.
Tel: +34 (0)913.69.19.93
Fax: +34 (0)913.69.19.84
C,BR.

Simpson Marine Ltd,
Unit 6, G/F Aberdeen
Marina Tower,
8 Shum Wan Road,
Aberdeen, Hong Kong.
Tel:+852 2555-8377
Fax:+852 2873-4014
*Em: simpsonm@
netvigator.com*
Asia's leading yacht sales,
brokerage and charter
company. Established in
1980. Dealer for Azimut,
Beneteau, Searay and other
leading brands. Specialists
in construction and
management of large yachts.
BMA, BR, C, YS.
Also:
Simpson Marine Pty Ltd,
PO Box 28, Main Beach,
Queensland 4217, Australia.
Tel:+61 755-379-463
Fax:+61 755-379-473
*Em: australia@
simpsonmarine.com*
BR, C, YS.
Also:
Simpson Marine Sdn Bhd,
C/o Admiral Marina Club,
5th Mile, Jalan Pant ai,
71050 Port Dickson,
Ngeri Sembilan, Malaysia.
Tel:+60 6 647 6868
Fax:+60 6 647 6617
Em: simpmar@po.jaring.my
BR, C, YMA.

Simrad AS,
PO Box 55, 4379 Egersund,
Norway.
Tel:+47 51462000
Fax:+47 51462001
Em: info@simrad.com
Manufacturer of marine
electronics since 1947,
covering both fishfinding,
steering, navigation and
communication equipment.
Worldwide sales and
service network.
YEM.

**Sinnex Steinheimer
Innenausbau GmbH,**
Bahnhofstrasse 13,
D-71711 Steinheim,
Germany.
Tel: +49 (0)7144-81390
Fax: +49 (0)7144-813925
Em: info@sinnex.com
Luxury yacht interior maker.
YI.

SKG-Yachts,
52 Avenue de la Liberte,
L-1930 Luxemburg.
Tel:+352 26 48 22 55
Fax:+352 26 48 23 60
Em: skgyachts@gmx.net
Marketing agent for Troy
Marine Yachts.
BMA.

Paola D Smith & Associates,
300 Northeast 3rd Avenue,
Suite 150, Fort Lauderdale,
Florida 33301, USA.
Tel:+1 954 761-1997
Fax:+1 954 767-6270
Em: pds@pdsdesign.net
Internationally known for
interior design and exterior
styling of yachts over 25m.
D.

Sam Sorgiovanni Designs P/L,
1/1 Phillimore Street
Freemantle 6160,
Western Australia.
Tel:+61 894-336-355
Fax:+61 894-336-377
Em: ostyle@iinet.net.au
Award-winning yacht
interior and exterior stylists
and project management.
D.

Southampton Yacht Services Ltd,
Saxon Wharf,
Lower York Street,
Northam, Southampton,
Hampshire SO14 5QF,
United Kingdom.
Tel:+44 (0)23 8033-5266
Fax:+44 (0)23 8063- 4275
*Em: sales@southampton
yachtsevices.co.uk*
Builds custom yachts from
15m to 40m. Specialises in
refitting motor and sailing
yachts to 60m. High-quality
yacht joinery and
classic yacht restoration.
Worldwide spares service.
B, YI, YS.

Southern Spars NZ
117 Pakenham Street,
PO Box 90-238,
Auckland, New Zealand.
Tel:+64 9-358-3315
Fax:+64 9-358-3309
*Em: info@
southernspars.com*
Also:
Southern Spars US,
2393 Heybourne Road,
Minden, NV 89423,
USA.
Tel:+1 775 782-6788
Fax:+1 775 782-6799
*Em: us.info@
southernspars.com*
Specialising in the design,
manufacture and servicing
of custom-built carbon rigs
of all sizes.
YS.

St Katherine Haven Ltd,
50 St Katherine's Way,
London E1W 1LA,
United Kingdom.
Tel:+44 (0)20 7481-8350
Fax:+44 (0)20 7702-2252
*Em: mary.pakan@
tayprop.co.uk*
YS.

Sovereign Yachts (Canada) Inc,
23511 Dyke Road,
Richmond, BC V6V 1E3,
Canada.
Tel:+1 604 515-0992
Fax:+1 604 515-0994
*Em: JLloyd@
Sovereign-Yachts.com*
Builds custom GRP
yachts over 30m.
B.

Tommaso Spadolini,
Via Plan del Glullari, 86,
50125 Firenze, Italy.
Tel:+39 0552-23558
Fax:+30 0552-24762
D.

Sparkman & Stephens,
529 Fifth Avenue,
New York,
New York 10017,
USA.
Brokerage Office:
Tel:+1 212 661-6170
Fax:+1 212 661-1235
*Em: brokerage @
sparkmanstephens.com*
Design Office:
Tel:+1 212 661-1240
Fax:+1 212 661-1235
*Em: design@
sparkmanstephens.com*
Complete naval
architecture, engineering
and design services
for motor and sailing
yachts. Consultation
services on refits and
restorations. Brokerage,
charter and insurance
services. Established 1929.
BR, C, D, NA.
Also:
Sparkman & Stephens of Florida,
901 SE 17th Street,
Suite 205,
Fort Lauderdale,
Florida 33316, USA.
Tel:+1 954 524-4616
Fax:+1 954 524-4621
*Em: brokerfl@
sparkmanstephens.com*
BR.

SP Systems,
St Cross Business Park,
Newport,
Isle of Wight PO31 7EU,
United Kingdom.
Tel:+44 (0)1983 828-000
Fax:+44 (0)1983 828-100
Em: info@spsystems.com
Manufacturer of advanced
composite materials for
yacht construction.
Structural engineering
design services in
composites. Technical
support in a variety of
composite manufacturing
processes.
YEM.

SP Technologies,
3 Meridians Cross,
Ocean Way,
Southampton,
Hampshire SO14 3TJ,
United Kingdom.
Tel:+44 (0)23 8023-2601
Fax:+44 (0)23 8023-0954
*Em: info@
sp-technologies.co.uk*
Specialises in the
supply of structural
engineering services for
composite superyachts.
YS.

Donald Starkey Designs,
The Studio,
2 Richmond Road,
Isleworth,
Middlesex TW7 7BL,
United Kingdom.
Tel:+44 (0)20 8569-9921
Fax:+44 (0)20 8569-9862
Em: info@dsdyachts.co.uk
Designer working on the
largest superyachts.
D.

Sterling Lacquer Manufacturing Co,
3150 Brannon Ave,
St. Louis,
Missouri 63139,
USA.
Tel:+1 314 776-4450
Fax:+1 314 771-1858
Yacht painting and coating
system manufacturers.
YEM.

Struik & Hamerslag BV,
Industriestraat 4,
PO Box 5727,
3290 AA Strijen,
The Netherlands.
Tel:+31 (0)78-6742800
Fax:+31 (0)78-6741192
*Em: info@
struikandhamerslag.nl*
Specialises in complete
interior outfitting and
fabrication of fixed and
loose furniture as well as
interior components.
YI.

Studio Scanu,
Largo Risorgimento 6,
55049 Viareggio,
Italy.
Tel:+39 0584-943229
Fax:+39 0584-31879
*Em: studioscanu@
inwind.it*
Guided by Paolo
Scanu since 1983,
this international
design team combines
Italian style with proven
hydrodynamics and
applies this to new
builds and refits of
quality motor and
sailing yachts.
NA, D.

Studiovafiadis,
8, Viale della Astronomia,
00144 Rome,
Italy.
Tel:+39 06- 5920066
Fax:+39 06-5920883
Em: interin@interin.it
An interior design and
exterior styling firm based in
Rome, with branch offices
in Athens and Houston.
D.

Summit Furniture, Inc,
5 Harris Court,
Monterey,
California 93940,
USA.
Tel:+1 831 375-7811
Fax:+1 831 375-0940
Also:
Summit Furniture (Europe) Ltd,
3/24 Chelsea Harbour
Design Centre,
London SW10 0XE
United Kingdom.
Tel:+44 (0)20 7795-3311
Fax:+44 (0)20 7795-3322
*Em: info@
summitfurniture.co.uk*
Designers and
manufacturers of
high quality teak
furniture for decks and
residential terraces.
YEM.

Sundeck SARL,
Résidences du Port Vauban,
19 Avenue du 11 Novembre,
06600 Antibes,
France.
Tel:+33 (0)4.93.34.82.10
Fax:+33 (0)4.93.34.82.57
*Em:info@
sundeckfrance.com*
Specialists in the supply
of top quality furniture
and furnishings for the
marine market.
Representing Summit,
McGuire, The Wicker
Works, Heltzer,
Sunbrella, Marina Mill
and Blenheim Carpets.
YS.

Superyachts International,
2733 NE 21st Court,
Fort Lauderdale,
Florida 33305,
USA.
Tel:+1 954 396-9900
Fax:+1 954 564-4178
Em: superyat@bellsouth.net
BR, C.

Tahiti Ocean,
PO Box 4570,
Papeete,
Tahiti,
French Polynesia.
Tel:+689 455582
Fax:+689 428031
Em: yacht@mail.pf
For all yacht services in
French Polynesia.
YS.

Teignbridge Propellers Ltd,
Great Western Way,
Forde Road,
Brunel Industrial Estate,
Newton Abbot,
Devon TQ12 4AD,
United Kingdom.
Tel:+44 (0)1626 333-377
Fax:+44 (0)1626 360-783
*Em: sales@
teignbridge.co.uk*
Designs and manufactures
propellers and stern gear
for the marine industry
worldwide, specialising
in high-performance
propulsion systems.
YEM.

Thirty Seven South Ltd,
PO Box 1874,
Auckland,
New Zealand.
Tel +64 9-302- 0178
Fax:+64 9-307-0871
Em: service@37south.co.nz
Shore support service
within New Zealand and
South Pacific. Spare part
sourcing and provisioning,
superyacht berthage and
services facilitator.
Charter brokers,
refit and maintenance
co-ordinators.
C, YMA, YS.

Three Quays Marine Services,
12-20 Camomile Street,
London EC3A 7AS,
United Kingdom.
Tel:+44 (0)20 7929-2299
Fax:+44 (0)20 7929-1650
*Em: enquiries@
threequays.com*
Naval Architects and
Marine Engineers
providing technical
consultancy and
project management
for large yacht new
buildings and major
refurbishments. Specialists
in technical design and
safety regulations, including
ISM and MCA code.
NA.

Tiemann Yachts Inc,
4613 University Drive 425,
Coral Springs,
Florida, USA.
Tel:+1 954 255-0706
Fax:+1 954 2550-0805
gtyachts @bellsouth.net
Sales and marketing agent
for Crescent Custom yachts.
BMA.

Tilse Industrie und Schiffstechnik GmbH,
Projecting-Design,
Sottorfallee 12,
22529 Hamburg,
Germany.
Tel:+49 (0)40-561014
Fax:+49 (0)40-563417
Em: tilse@tilse.com
Supply of FORMGLAS,
level gauging systems
with computers,
anti-marine growth
and corrosion systems.
YS.

Titan, Hyde & Torrance,
81 Akti Miaouli,
185 38 Piraeus,
Greece.
Tel:+30 210 42 80 889
Fax:+30 210 41 82 834
Em: tht@hol.gr
Also:
Titan, Hyde & Torrance,
18 Mansell Street,
London E1 8AA,
United Kingdom.
Tel:+44 (0)20 7459-2201
Fax:+44 (0)20 7459-2276
Em: tht@jehyde.co.uk
BR, C, YMA.

Tradewind Cruises AB,
Box 49,
S-471 21 Skarhamn,
Sweden.
Tel:+46 304-671616
Fax:+46 304-674260
*Em: lars-erik.johansson@
tradewind.se*
Specialises in design
and construction of
large, luxurious classic
sailing ships and yachts
with space, comfort
and luxury.
YMA, D, NA.

Trinity Yachts Inc,
4325 France Road,
New Orleans,
Louisiana 70126, USA.
Tel:+1 504 283-4050
Fax:+1 504 284-7318
*Em: wssmith3@
trinityyachts.com*
Build in steel, aluminium or
combinations to classification
society rules with facilities
suitable for yachts up to
140m, with displacement,
semi-displacement and
planing hulls.
B.

Turquoise Yacht Construction Inc,
Mahir iz, Caddesi No 28/3,
Altunizade-Istanbul,
Turkey.
Tel:+90 216 391-6850
Fax:+90 216 391-6853
Em: turkuazyat@turk.net
A well established yard that
built the 50m motor yacht
Turquoise and the 43m
classic motor yacht
Anatolia. Now working on
50m and 53m projects
jointly with Proteksan.
B.

US Paint,
831 S 21st Street,
St. Louis,
Missouri 63103, USA.
Tel:+1 314 621-0525
Fax:+1 314 621-0722
Em: info@uspaint.com
Also:
NOF Europe NV,
Bouwelven 1,
Industriezone Klein-Gent,
B-2280 Grobbendonk,
Belgium.
Tel:+32 14.23.00.01
Fax:+32 14.23.08.80
Specialises in advanced
urethane, epoxy and high-
solids coating systems.
AWLGRIP yacht finishes
including topcoats, acrylic
urethanes, varnishes
and antifouling paints.
ISO 9001 Certified.
YEM.

Vacuum Systems Australia Pty Ltd,
660 Bridge Road,
Richmond 3121,
Australia.
Tel:+61 394-252-222
Fax:+61 396-963-143
*Em: jan.howard@
stockford.net*
Design, manufacture and
supply of lightweight,
custom engineered toilet
systems for smaller luxury
yachts and super yachts.
Also vacuum transport of
liquid wastes (ship to shore)
systems for marinas.
YEM.

JJ Van Nus Yacht BV Holland,
Toevluchtstraat 24,
1171 GG Badhoevedorp,
The Netherlands.
Tel:+31 (0)20-6597073
Fax:+31 (0)20-6597073
Em: vnyinfo@vnyachts.com
More than 40 years
experience in design,
construction and survey
of luxury superyachts,
advisor in megayachts
projects. Recently project
management and survey of
140m yacht projects.
NA, D, BR.

**Van Peteghem Lauriot
Prevost**
11 Boulevard Bourdon
75004 Paris,
France.
Tel:+33 (0)1 42 77 24 00
Fax:+33 (0)1 48 04 98 60
Em: team@MVPVLP.com
NA.

Victory Design Srl,
Via G Melisurgo 15,
80133 Naples,
Italy.
Tel:+39 081-2528243
Fax:+39 081-4206896
Em: victory@victory.it
Also:
Victory Design Srl,
Representative Office,
Via Salaino,
20144 Milan,
Italy.
Em: victory@victory.it
Naval architecture,
marine engineering,
interior design, hull
testing, exterior styling.
Victory Design works
with a full complement
of state-of-the-art hardware
and software including
Silicon Graphics, Unix
Workstations and Alias
software. Renowned as a
high speed specialist.
D, NA.

Vikal International,
5 Rivers Street,
Bibra Lake 6163,
Perth,
Western Australia.
Tel:+61 894-342-480
Fax:+61 894-186-499
Em: info@Vikal.com.au
Builders of motor yachts
in composite up to 35m
and custom Superyacht
Limousine tenders of
the highest quality
in composite.
B.

Vins Sans Frontieres Group,
Espace St. Isidore,
444 Rte. de Grenoble,
06200 Nice,
France.
Tel:+33 (0)4 92 29 88 66
Fax:+33 (0)4 92 29 88 77
Em: vsf@riviera.fr
A service-oriented
supplier of wines
and provisions to
yachts throughout
the Mediterranean.
YS.

Vitters Shipyard bv,
Stouweweg 33,
8064 PD Zwartsluis,
The Netherlands.
Tel:+31 (0)38-3867145
Fax:+31 (0)38-3868433
Em: info@vitters.com
Builder and refitter of power
and sailing yachts up to 70m
including *Thalia*, *Ninemia*,
Timoneer and *African Queen*.
B.

Vosper Thorneycroft,
Victoria Road, Woolston,
Southampton SO19 9RR,
United Kingdom.
Tel:+44 (0)23 8042-6000
Fax:+44 (0)23 8042-6010
*Em:shipsales@
vosperthorneycroft.com*
Vosper Thorneycroft builds
in steel, aluminium or fibre
reinforced plastic. Currently
building at its Southampton
shipyard to a design by Ron
Holland is the *Mirabella V*,
the world's largest sloop
with a LOA of 75m and a
mast of over 90m in height.
B.

**Vosper Thornycroft
Marine Products Limited,**
Hamilton Road,
Cosham, Portsmouth,
Hampshire PO6 4PX,
United Kingdom.
Tel:+44 (0)23 9253-9750
Fax:+44 (0)23 9253-9764
*Em: cpatrick@
vtmc.demon.co.uk*
Manufacturer of Vosper
stabilisers, fitted to over
4,000 vessels. A range of
transverse thrusters and
integrated ride control
systems tailored to meet
vessel requirements.
YEM.

**Vripack Yachting
International Naval
Architects bv,**
Zwolsmanweg 16, Sneek,
The Netherlands.
Tel:+31 (0)515-436600
Fax:+31 (0)515-436634
Em: sales@vripack.com
Renowned firm of naval
architects and marine
engineers famous for its
trawler-style ocean-cruising
and expedition yachts.
Also brokerage.
NA, D, BR.

Waite & Morrow Associates,
515 Seabreeze Blvd,
Suite 226, Fort Lauderdale,
Florida 33316, USA.
Tel:+1 954 764-1789
Fax:+1 954 764-6867
*Em: waitemorrowyacht@
mindspring.com*
A boutique brokerage
specialising in representation
and creative marketing of
luxury sail and power yachts,
new project development,
new build management and
marketing services.
BR.

Wally,
Seaside Plaza,
8 avenue des Ligures,
Monte Carlo,
MC 98000
Monaco.
Tel:+377 93.10.00.93
Fax:+377 93.10.00.94
Em: sales@wally.com
Design and construction of
sail and motor superyachts
that are unmatched reference
points for the unique
combination of high
performance, contemporary
design, simple management,
luxury, comfort and
ease of handling.
B.

Warren Yachts,
Kincumber Pty. Limited,
1 Kerta Road,
Kincumber
NSW 2251, Australia.
Tel:+61 2-4368-1722
Fax:+61 2-4368-1263
Em:info@warrenyachts.com
B

Warwick Yacht Design Ltd,
2B William Pickering Drive,
PO Box 302 156,
North Harbour,
Auckland 1311,
New Zealand.
Tel:+64 9-410-9620
Fax:+64 9-410-8254
Em: wyd@wyd.co.nz
Naval architects, stylists and
interior designers of sail and
power yachts of all sizes.
NA, D.

Webster Associates,
PO Box 030038,
Fort Lauderdale,
Florida 33303, USA.
Tel:+1 954 525-5101
Fax:+1 954 525-5103
Em: jim@jimwebster.com
Yacht sales and charter
broker specialising in
discreet confidential services
for clients worldwide.
BR, C.

Hugh Welbourn Design,
Cuttrye Court, East Allington,
Totnes TQ9 7QN,
Devon, United Kingdom.
Tel:+44 (0)1548 521-356
Fax:+44 (0)1548 521-356
*Em: hughw@
mail.easynet.co.uk*
Designer of high-performance
racing and cruising yachts
of all sizes.
NA.

Westerbeke Corporation,
Myles Standish
Industrial Park,
150 John Hancock Road,
Taunton, MA 02780-7319,
USA.
Tel:+1 508 823-7677
Fax:+1 508 884-9688
Em: help@westerbeke.com
Marine generator
manufacturer.
YEM.

Westport Shipyard,
1807 Nyhus Street,
PO Box 308, Westport,
Washington 98595, USA.
Tel:+1 360 268-1800
Fax:+1 360 268-1900
*Em: info@
westportyachtsales.com*
B.
Also:
Westport Yacht Sales,
888 E Las Olas Blvd. 602,
Fort Lauderdale,
Florida 33301, USA.
Tel:+1 954 727-0005
Fax:+1 954 727-0006
*Em: info@
westportyachtsales.com*
Specialises in fast, luxurious
FRP motor yachts from 30m
to 40m. Marketing agent
for Westport Shipyard.
BMA.
Also:
Westport Yach Sales,
2601 W Marina Place Ste F
Seattle WA 98199, USA.
Tel: +1 206 298-3360
Fax: +1 206 285-0342
BR.

Westship Inc,
1535 SE 17th Street,
Suite 205, Fort Lauderdale,
Florida 33316, USA.
Tel:+1 954 463-0700
Fax:+1 954 764-2675
*Em: inquire@
westshipyachts.com*
Designers and builders of
custom fibreglass yachts,
30m to 45m. Sold under
the Westship name.
BMA.

Westship World Yachts,
5251 West Tyson Avenue,
Tampa, Florida 33611, USA.
Tel:+1 813 839-5151
Fax:+1 813 839-5030
*Em: info@
westshipworldyachts.com*
Composite construction
background encompasses
the latest aerospace and
marine material
technologies. A 7,896m²
manufacturing and service
facility is now constructing
custom yachts from 26m
to 50m. The yard service
and refit division is
equipped with a 500-ton
capacity Syncrolift.
B.

Andrew Winch Designs Ltd,
The Old Fire Station,
123 Mortlake High Street,
London SW14 8SN,
United Kingdom.
Tel:+44 (0)20 8392-8400
Fax:+44 (0)20 8392-8401
*Em: info@
andrew-winch-designs.co.uk*
Specialises in high-quality,
versatile exterior and
interior design of power
and sailing yachts for
both the custom and
production boat markets.
D.

Winston Green Design,
210 Alexandra Parade East,
Clifton Hill,
Victoria 3068,
Australia.
Tel:+61 394-891-114
Fax:+61 394-891-114
*Em: AGWinstongreen@
aol.com*
An innovative design studio
specialising in exterior
styling and interior layouts
of motor yachts.
D.

**Woods Marine
Management Ltd,**
PO Box 38-916, Howick,
Auckland,
New Zealand.
Tel:+64 9-533-6553
Fax:+64 9-533-6554
*Em: info@
woodsmarine.com*
Project management.
Professional owners'
representation for
construction and refit
projects from design to
delivery. Power and sail.
Yacht management and
shore side support.
YS.

**Wolfson Unit for
Marine Technology &
Industrial Aerodynamics,**
University of Southampton,
Southampton,
Hampshire SO17 1BJ,
United Kingdom.
Tel:+44 (0)23 8058-5044
Fax:+44 (0)23 8067-1532
Em: wumtia@soton.ac.uk
Towing tank and wind
tunnel testing for sail
and motor yachts,
seakeeping measurements
at full and model scale,
problem solving and
feasibility studies for design
changes, yacht design
software, and stability
investigations.
YS.

Woods & Oviatt,
Pier 66 Resort and Marina,
2301 SE 17th Street,
Fort Lauderdale,
Florida 33316,
USA.
Tel:+1 954 463-5606
Fax:+1 954 525-8625
Em: pawoods@ix.netcom.com
BR.

Yacht Fuel Services Ltd,
37 St John's Hill,
London SW11 1TT,
United Kingdom.
Tel:+44 (0)20 7738-2124
Fax:+44 (0)20 7738-2127
Em: mail@yachtfuel.com
Along with being the
world's largest supplier
of fuel and lubricants
to superyachts, we also
offer our clients a full
global bunkering
consultancy service.
YS.

**Yachting Partners
International,**
28/29 Richmond Place,
Brighton,
East Sussex BN2 2NA,
United Kingdom.
Tel:+44 (0)1273 571722
Fax:+44 (0)1273 571720
Em: ypi@ypi.co.uk
BR, YMA, C.
Also:
**Yachting Partners
International Ltd,**
Residence de la Mer
6 avenue de la Libération,
06600 Antibes,
France.
Tel:+33 (0)4.93.34.01.00
Fax:+33 (0)4.92.91.70.00
Em: ypifr@ypi.co.uk
Worldwide charter, sale
and purchase of new and
second-hand luxury motor
and sailing yachts from
25m upwards.
BR, YMA, C.

Dick Young Designs,
46 Tournay Road,
London SW6 7UF,
United Kingdom.
Tel:+44 (0) 20 7381-2275
Fax:+44 (0) 20 7385-8793
Em: dydesigns@aol.com
With over 14 years
experience in the industry,
Dick Young Designs offers
a full interior and exterior
design service for sailing
and motor yachts,
production and custom.
The client's brief
remains paramount.
D.

**Zuretti Interior Designers
SARL,**
268 avenue de la Californie,
Nice 06200,
France.
Tel:+33 (0)4.93.72.40.60
Fax:+33 (0)4.93.72.40.66
*Em: Interiordesginers@
zuretti.com*
Interior designer.
D.

Companies trading in the
superyacht arena who wish
to be included in this free
listing should contact:
TheSuperyachts@aol.com

INDEX OF YACHTS FEATURED IN VOLUMES ONE TO SIXTEEN

Yacht	Builder/Naval Architect/Designer	Volume	Page
Endeavour	C&N - Huisman/C&N - Dijkstra/Munford	3	62
Enterprise V	Van Lent/De Voogt/Tanter - Baty	7	96
Esprit	Alloy/Dubois/Dubois	5	84
Europa Sun	Picchiotti/Picchiotti/Picchiotti	1	100
Evergreen	Evergreen/Diana - Van der Baan/Buytendijk	13	106
Evviva	Admiral/Garden/Starkey	8	100

F

Fadlallah	Sensation/Sharp/Sharp	10	100
Fae Lon	Burger/O'Keeffe/Richey - Burger	15	148
Fair Lady	C&N/Nicholson/Newport Marine	1	106
Falco	Lürssen/Lürssen/MPS - Sylvestrin	6	76
Faribana	De Vries/De Voogt/Disdale	3	68
Fiffanella	Van Lent/De Voogt/Puleo	3	200
Fifty-one	Christensen/Glade Johnson/Pagani	7	102
Fortuna	Palmer Johnson/Shead/Maxwell	2	84
Fortuna	FN San Fernando/Blount/dell'Anna	14	102

G

Gallant Lady	De Vries/De Voogt/Smith	8	108
Gallant Lady	Delta Marine/Sharp Design/Las Olas Design	14	108
Gallant Lady	De Vries/De Voogt/Smith	10	106
Gallant Lady VII	De Vries/De Voogt/Smith	6	82
Galu	Benetti/Benetti/Bannenberg - White	1	112
Georgia	Alloy Yachts/Studio Scanu - Dalrymple Smith/Johnson	14	114
Ginny Lou	Picchiotti/Picchiotti/Dilday	4	108
Gitana	Perini Navi/Perini Navi/Perini Navi	3	74
Globana	Abeking & Rasmussen/Ron Holland/A&R - Müller	10	114
Gloria	Jongert/Beeldsnijder/Lowland	2	90
Golden Bay	Benetti/Benetti/Zuretti	11	94
Gonca	Koç/Freivokh/Freivokh	11	100
Gran Finale	Delta/Delta/Espinosa	16	138
Gray Mist	Breaux's Bay Craft/Breaux's Bay Craft - Borland/Marchetti	12	102

H

Hakim	Lloyd's/Curran/Hakim	6	88
Halcyon	De Vries/De Voogt	6	188
Harmony Bay	Cantiere Navale de Pesaro	2	202
Henry Morgan	Bairdmore/Bairdmore/Bairdmore	5	186
Hetairos	Abeking & Rasmussen/King/Winch	9	104
Honey Money	Heesen/Diaship/Diaship	10	120
Hyperion	Huisman/Frers/Beeldsnijder	13	114

I

Idyll	Benetti/Benetti/Longari	6	190
Il Cigno	CNN/CNN/CNN	5	188
Iliki V	Codecasa/Codecasa/Deccarole	8	114
Ilona	Pendennis/Dubois/Redman Whiteley	13	120
Impromptu	Van Lent/De Voogt/Chase	2	96
Independence	Perini Navi/Perini Navi/Perini Navi	12	108
Intuition II	Vosper Thorneycroft/Vosper Thorneycroft/ Southampton Yacht Services	14	122
Invader	Codecasa/Codecasa/Dellarole	14	128
Iroquois	De Vries/De Voogt/Johnson	12	114
Izanami	Lürssen/Gilgenast/Foster	11	106

J

Jefferson Beach	Hakvoort/Beeldsnijder/Beeldsnijder	5	190
Jessica	Astilleros/Holgate/Munford	1	118
Joalmi	Benetti/Benetti/Disdale	6	94
Jonikal	Codecasa/Codecasa/Codecasa	4	114
Juliet	Huisman/Holland/Beeldsnijder	7	108

Yacht	Builder/Naval Architect/Designer	Volume	Page

K

Kalizma	Ramage & Ferguson/Watson/Munford	5	192
Kallista	Broward/Broward/Broward	5	194
Katalina	Blohm & Voss/Ross/Thwaites - Inchbald	1	126
Katamarino	Amels/Hargrave/Garzouzi - Tanter	5	90
Katrion	De Vries/De Voogt/Munford - McQuiston	11	112
Kenora	Wally Yachts/Brenta/Brenta	14	134
Kermit	Amels/Amels/Disdale	15	154
King	Van Lent/De Voogt/Van Lent	6	192
Kiring	Brooke/Three Quays/Disdale	7	114
Kisses	De Vries/De Voogt/Larson	14	140
Kokomo	Alloy/Dubois/Redman Whiteley	15	160
Krisha	Crescent Beach/Sarin/Henderson	9	110

L

La Baronessa	Palmer Johnson/Sparkman & Stephens/Nuvolari-Lenard	13	126
La Corniche	North Coast/Sarin/Henderson	7	120
L'Aprilia	Astilleros de Mallorca/C&N/C&N	3	204
L'Aquasition	Heesen-Diaship/Gilgenast/Smith	4	126
Lady Alice	Hakvoort/Diana/Wade	4	120
Lady Anne	CRN Ancona/CRN Ancona/Franchini	9	116
Lady Ann Magee	Codecasa/Codecasa/Dellarole	16	144
Lady Christine	Oceanco/Oceanco/The 'A' Group - Villate	15	166
Lady Duvera	Hakvoort/Diana/Buytendijk	6	100
Lady Frances	Derecktor/Sparkman & Stephens/Puleo	3	80
Lady Ghislaine	Amels/Diana/Bannenberg	3	202
Ladyhawke	Chantiers de Biot/Holland/Chantiers de Biot	4	222
Lady Halima	Heesen/Diaship/Smith	15	174
Lady in Red	Picchiotti/Fever/Picchiotti	2	204
Lady Janet	Feadship/De Voogt/De Voogt	5	196
Lady Jenn	Palmer Johnson/Fexas	8	120
Lady Lola	Oceanco/Oceanco/Zuretti	16	150
Lady M	Moonen/Brandligt/Moonen	9	122
Lady Marina	Hakvoort/Diana/Starkey	8	126
Lady Marina	De Vries/De Voogt/Starkey	14	148
Lady Suffolk	Brooke/Scanu/Disdale	8	134
Lady Tiffany	DML/Michael Peters/Buytendijk	9	128
Land's End	Ensing/Ensing/De Savary	3	86
La Venetia	Benetti/Benetti/Benetti	6	194
Leander	Peene/Vollers/Nunns - Landon	7	126
Leocrie III	Schweers/Argyriadis/Disdale	1	132
Le Pharaon	Van Lent/De Voogt/Tanter	3	92
Liberty	Perini Navi/Perini Navi/Perini Navi	11	118
Libra Star	Benetti/Benetti/Disdale	8	140
Lionheart	Benetti/Benetti/Natucci	14	156
Luisamar V	Van Mill/Beeldsnijder/Procase	2	102

M

Madinina	Austin & Pickersgill/Parker/A&P	6	196
Maffy Blue	Baglietto/Baglietto/Cichero	5	96
Mamamouchi	Pendennis/Dubois/Whiteley	10	126
Mandalay	Palmer Johnson/Brierly Paine/Plachter	6	106
Maracunda	CRN/CRN/Pinto	5	102
Marala	C&N/C&N/C&N	11	124
Mari Cha III	Sensation/Briand/Munford	12	120
Marcalan IV	Codecasa/Scanu/Dilday	7	134
Margaux Rose	Schweers/MPS - Gilgenast/Munford	2	108
Mariette	Herreshoff/Herreshoff/CN Beconcini	10	132
Marina	Perini Navi/Perini Navi/Perini Navi	1	140
Mariya Uno	CCYD/Holland/Spadolini	4	132
Méduse	De Vries/De Voogt/McMillan	12	128
Mercedes	Oceanfast/Curran/Sorgiovanni	10	138

Yacht	Builder/Naval Architect/Designer	Volume	Page
Midnight Saga	Cammenga/De Vries/Bannenberg	2	114
Mi Gaea	De Vries/De Voogt/Starkey	4	138
Mikado	Zosen/Garden/Parish - Hadley	6	112
Mirabella	Concorde/Farr/Koskenkyla	5	108
Miss Turnberry	Denison/Langlois/Seigall	5	114
MITseaAH	Derecktor/Sparkman & Stephens/Liebowitz	8	146
Moderation	Burger Boat Company/O'Keeffe/Burger Boat Company	12	136
Moecca	Oceanfast/Curran/Bannenberg	6	118
Moonbeam	Fife/Fife/Fife	2	120
Moongoddess	Benetti/Benetti/Benetti	4	144
Moonmaiden II	Beykoz/Beykoz/Beykoz	4	224
Moonraker	Norship/Mulder/Art Line	6	124
Morning Glory	Perini Navi/Perini Navi/Perini Navi	7	140
Mosaique	Proteksan-Turquoise/Dubois/Starkey-Ferrand	15	180
Mylin IV	Van Lent/De Voogt/Starkey	6	130
Mystere	Lloyd's Ships/Lloyd's Ships/Lloyd's Ships	6	198
Mystique	Oceanfast/Curran/Bannenberg	2	128

N

Yacht	Builder/Naval Architect/Designer	Volume	Page
Namoh	Christensen/Christensen/Dee Robinson	10	144
Naos	CCYD/Holland/Winch	6	136
Nazenin III	Palmer Johnson/Alden/Munford	9	134
Nectar of the Gods	Crescent Custom Yachts/Sarin/Scales	14	162
Nena VIII	Denison/Langlois/Puleo	2	134
New Century	Heesen/Diaship/Art-Line	12	142
New Horizon L	Van Lent/De Voogt/Sturchio	1	146
Night Crossing	Benetti/Benetti/Sklarin	1	154
No Escape	Heesen/Diaship/Studio Guilhem	13	134
Northern Light	Feadship-Royal Van Lent/De Voogt/Munford	16	160
Nounou	Cantiere de Pisa/Pisa/Pinto	2	140
Number One	Jongert/Castro/Sijm	13	140
Nvmptia	CRN/Studio Scanu/Zuretti	14	168

O

Yacht	Builder/Naval Architect/Designer	Volume	Page
O'Pari	Intermarine/Intermarine/Vafiadis	11	132
Oceana	Oceanfast/Curran/Bannenberg	8	152
Octopussy	Heesen/Mulder/Art Line	2	146
Oktana	Codecasa/Manfredi & Sforzi/Laws	9	140
Olympia	Feadship-De Vries/De Voogt/Bannenberg - Hampton	16	166
Opal 'C'	Oceanfast/Curran/Bannenberg	3	104
Opus II	Holland/Paszkowski/Marshall	11	138
Orejona	Cammenga/De Vries Lentsch/Belliure	5	198
Orion	C&N - Valdettaro/Nicholson/Nicholson	3	110
Our Blue Dream	C&N/Dubois/Redman Whiteley	14	176

P

Yacht	Builder/Naval Architect/Designer	Volume	Page
Paraffin	Palmer Johnson/Fexas/Disdale	11	144
Parts VI	Oceanfast/Curran/Bannenberg	1	160
Passe Partout	Jongert/Stockman/Sijm	9	146
Patricia	Benetti/Benetti/Righini - Zuretti	16	174
Pegaso	CRN/CRN/Zuretti	10	150
Pegasus	Broward/Broward/Hermanson - Bey	5	120
Perfect Prescription	Oceanfast/Starkey/Starkey	11	150
Perini Navi 37	Perini Navi/Perini Navi/Perini Navi	6	142
Perini Navi 37	Perini Navi/Perini Navi/Perini Navi	10	156
Pestifer	CRN/Scanu/Zuretti	13	146
Philante IX	Brooke/Shead/Twigg	5	126
Phocea	Lürssen/Bigoin/Beiderbeck	14	182
Phryne	Perini Navi/Perini Navi/Private Lives	13	152
Primadonna	Christensen/Christensen/Smith	16	180
Princess Gloria	Delta/Schubert/Harvey - Parker	4	150
Princess Marla	Trinity Yachts/Guarino - Setzer/Robinson	12	148

Yacht	Builder/Naval Architect/Designer	Volume	Page
Princess Tanya	Intermarine/Bannenberg/Stylianou	7	146
Puritan	Electric/Alden/Alden	2	206
P'zazz	Delta/Schubert - Minor/Glade Johnson - Bladt	3	116

Q

Yacht	Builder/Naval Architect/Designer	Volume	Page
Quaeso III	Hakvoort/Beeldsnijder/Beeldsnijder	5	132
Queen M	Benetti/Benetti/Disdale	13	158
Quintessence	Van Lent/De Voogt/Larvor	11	156

R

Yacht	Builder/Naval Architect/Designer	Volume	Page
Rasselas	De Vries/De Voogt/Munford	9	152
Rebecca	Pendennis/Frers/Robbins Black	13	164
Red Sapphire	Heesen/Diaship/Diaship - McFarlane	13	170
Robur IV	Zigler/Zigler/Bannenberg	4	226
Rora V	De Vries/De Voogt/Munford	8	160
Rosenkavalier	Krupp Germaniawerft/Taylor - Williams	6	148
Roxana	Admiral/Codega/Starkey	13	176
Royal Eagle II	C&N - Cornelissen/Holland/Winch	3	122

S

Yacht	Builder/Naval Architect/Designer	Volume	Page
Safe Conduct II	Swiftships/Fryco/Global	4	156
Sahab IV	CRN/Scanu/Disdale	11	162
Ste. Jill	Delta/Delta Design Group/JQB	12	154
Sally Ann	De Vries/De Voogt/Disdale	11	174
Salperton	Alloy Yachts/Dubois/Alloy Yachts	16	186
Sarah	Amels Holland/Amels Holland/Starkey	16	194
Sariyah	Sensation/Sparkman & Stephens/Munford	8	166
Savannah	Alloy/Hood/Linley	12	160
Savarona	Blohm & Voss/Blohm & Voss/Starkey	6	154
Sea Cloud	Krupp/Krupp/Krupp	3	128
Sea Crest	Hall Russell/Russell/Russell	5	200
Sea Sedan	De Vries/De Voogt/Disdale	7	152
Sea Sedan	De Vries/De Voogt/Disdale	11	174
SeaShaw	Cheoy Lee/Mulder/In-Design	10	162
Secret Love	Amels/Amels/Struik & Hamerslag	4	163
Sensation of Auckland	Sensation/Holland/Winch	3	136
Sensei	Admiral/Barnett/Glade Johnson	10	168
Senses	Schweers/Lasse & Pache/ Setton - Miescke & Harder	14	190
September Blue	Van Lent/De Voogt/Disdale	3	142
Shamoun	Dutch Built/Hoek/Hoek	13	182
Shamrock V	Pendennis/Dijkstra/Dijkstra	15	188
Shamwari	Benetti/Benetti/Zuretti	5	138
Shana II	Sovereign/Perla/Johnson	5	144
Shanakee	Palmer Johnson/Holland/Beeldsnijder	7	158
Sheergold	Amels/Diana/Bannenberg	3	206
Shenandoah of Sark	Townsend & Downey/Ferris/Ferris	7	164
Shiralee	CCN/Solé/Natucci	12	166
Silver Lining	Christensen/Starkey/Johnson/CSL - Johnson	11	182
Simson S	Schichau - Unterwasser AG/Setton - Vollers	9	160
Slipstream	Warren/Dubois/Sorgiovanni	15	196
Solaia	Hakvoort/Diana/Buytendijk	15	202
Solemates	Feadship De Vries/De Voogt/Winch	13	188
Sophie Blue	CBI Navi/CLM Engineering/Dini	12	172
Southern Cross III	Oceanfast/Curran/Bannenberg	3	148
Sovereign	Alloy/Dubois/Whiteley	9	168
Stalca	CCYD/Holland/Zamichieli	1	164
Starlight	Southern Ocean/Peterson/Bannenberg	2	152
Stefaren	Brooke/Holland/Bannenberg	3	154
Sulara	C&N/Nicholson/Nicholson	4	228
Surama	Royal Huisman/Hood/Winch	12	178
Sussurro	Feadship De Vries/Shead/De Voogt - Disdale	13	196
Swiftships 150	Swiftships/Robinson/Puleo	6	160

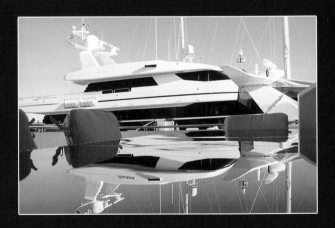

VOLUME SIXTEEN INDEX

ADVERTISERS AND PHOTOGRAPHERS INDEX

ADVERTISERS

PHOTOGRAPHERS

ACKNOWLEDGEMENTS

THE EDITOR WOULD LIKE TO THANK THE UNDERMENTIONED FOR THEIR ADVICE
AND ASSISTANCE DURING THE PRODUCTION OF THIS VOLUME:
J BECKETT, R DUBSKY, C DUNLOP, A GUILLARD, D HAGADONE, B HOUGHTON, M JOHNSON, S JOHNSON,
S LARSEN, C VAN LOON, M VAN LOON, E PREVOST, D RAWLINS, J SECOPOULU, V SHABLIN, DR KP WEISS.